MODERN INSURANCE LAW

AUSTRALIA
LBC Information Services
Sydney

CANADA AND USA
Carswell
Toronto, Ontario

NEW ZEALAND
Brooker's
Auckland

SINGAPORE AND MALAYSIA
Thomson Information (S.E. Asia)
Singapore

MODERN INSURANCE LAW

FOURTH EDITION

by
JOHN BIRDS, LL.M.
Professor of Commercial Law
University of Sheffield

LONDON
SWEET & MAXWELL
1997

First edition 1982
Second edition 1988
Third edition 1993
Fourth edition 1997
Reprinted 1998

Published in 1997 by
Sweet & Maxwell Limited
100 Avenue Road,
Swiss Cottage,
London NW3 3PF
http://www.smlawpub.co.uk

Typeset by LBJ Enterprises Ltd,
Aldermaston and Chilcompton
Printed and bound in Great Britain
by Clays Ltd, St Ives plc.

No natural forests were destroyed to make this product, only farmed timber was
used and re-planted.

ISBN 0421 58700 8

A CIP catalogue record for this book is available from The British Library.

TO MY FAMILY

PREFACE

Insurance law continues to develop at a fair pace, explaining perhaps why only four years have elapsed since the appearance of the last edition of this book. Yet again there has been a reasonable volume of reported case law to incorporate. Of course not all such case law is concerned with the development or application of matters of real principle, but notable developments of that sort since the last edition include *Pan Atlantic v. Pine Top* and subsequent cases on materiality and non-disclosure, the decisions on agency and co-insurance, and a number of cases discussing the question of what, apart from imposing a pre-contractual duty of disclosure, being a contract of the utmost good faith means (not very much it would seem).

On the legislative side, the full implementation of the E.C. directives on insurance services is considered, as are the recent amendments introduced by the Policyholders Protection Act 1997. More significant perhaps for this book, whose emphasis is on insurance contract law, are the Unfair Terms in Consumer Contracts Regulations 1994, which clearly apply to appropriate insurance contracts even if it remains to be seen whether they will have any real effect. We must not forget the continuing "self-regulation" of insurance contract law, led by the Insurance Ombudsman Bureau. It will be interesting to see whether, by the time of the next edition, the calls being made again (especially by the National Consumer Council) for comprehensive reform of aspects of insurance contract law affecting consumers will have borne any fruit.

It is hoped that this edition has managed to capture the essential flavour of the developments in the subject, without the basic format of the book being altered; inevitably perhaps, the length has increased a little. I continue to use *MacGillivray* for many cross-references; in the footnotes it bears the title (*MacGillivray on Insurance Law*) with which it started life and which it will have again in its ninth edition, which should appear later this year; references to it by chapter number alone are references to that forthcoming edition. Where there is a reference to specific paragraphs, those are to the eighth edition (*MacGillivray and Parkington*).

Thanks are due to a number of colleagues, especially Norma Hird, for ideas and suggestions; they are due also to Anne Drakeford without whose valuable research assistance this edition would have been much longer in the preparation, and to the staff at Sweet & Maxwell for seeing the book into production. I hope that I have managed to state the law as of January 1997. It was possible to take account of one or two later developments at proof stage.

John Birds
Sheffield
May 1997

TABLE OF CONTENTS

Chapter 5: Repudiations of Policies and Liability

Chapter 6: Fraud, Non-disclosure and Misrepresentation

Chapter 7: Warranties and Conditions

Chapter 8: Premiums

Chapter 9: Assignment

Chapter 10: Intermediaries

Chapter 11: Construction and Causation: Risks Covered and Risks Excepted

Chapter 12: Claims Under the Policy

Chapter 13: The Measurement of Loss

Chapter 14: Reinstatement

Chapter 15: Subrogation

Chapter 16: Contribution and Double Insurance

Chapter 17: Life Insurance

Chapter 18: Liability Insurance

Chapter 19: Motor Insurance

Chapter 20: Employers' Liability and Other Compulsory Insurance

TABLE OF CASES

TABLE OF STATUTES

TABLE OF STATUTORY INSTRUMENTS

TABLE OF DIRECTIVES

CHAPTER 1

INTRODUCTION: THE NATURE AND DEFINITION OF INSURANCE AND INSURANCE LAW

The contract of insurance is basically governed by the rules which form part of the general law of contract, but equally there is no doubt that over the years it has attracted many principles of its own to such an extent that it is perfectly proper to speak of a law of insurance. Some of these principles owe their existence to the fact that the documents of the standard insurance contract, principally the proposal form and the policy, have long been drafted in a fairly uniform way. The effect of this will be seen throughout this book. In addition, the reasons for many of the principles of insurance can be found by looking at the history of insurance and of the insurance contract. A detailed examination of this history would be inappropriate in a book of this size,[1] but a brief excursus is useful to set the scene.

History

The origins of the modern insurance contract are to be found in the practices adopted by Italian merchants from the fourteenth century onwards, although there is little doubt that the concept of insuring was known long before then. Maritime risks, the risk of losing ships and cargoes at sea, instigated the practice of medieval insurance and dominated insurance for many years. The habit spread to London merchants but not, it appears, until the sixteenth century. At first, there were no separate insurers. A group of merchants would agree to bear each others' risks among themselves. For a long time, the common law played little or no part in the regulation of disputes concerning insurance. For this purpose merchants in 1601 secured the establishment by statute of a chamber of

---

[1] See for more detail, Holdsworth, "The early history of the contract of insurance" (1917) 17 Col. L.R. 85; Clayton, *British Insurance* (1970).

assurance which was outside the normal legal system. However, with the appointment of Lord Mansfield as Lord Chief Justice in the mid-eighteenth century, the common law courts took an interest in insurance contracts. Lord Mansfield applied principles derived from the law merchant as well as more traditional common law concepts to the solution of disputes over insurance, and by the time of his retirement in 1788, the jurisdiction of the courts over insurance matters had been established.

Marine insurance retained its prominent position for some considerable time, and from the late seventeenth century onwards was increasingly transacted at a coffee-house in the City of London owned by a man called Lloyd. There developed the practice that the merchant wishing insurance would pass round to the people willing to provide it, who were gathered there, a slip of paper on which he had written the details of the ship, voyage and cargo etc. The slip was initialed by those willing to accept a proportion of the risk. When the total amount of insurance required was underwritten, the contract was complete.[2] From this practice comes the term "underwriter" which, of course, is still in use today and the name of the owner of the coffee-house attached itself to the institution. Lloyd's of London[3] is now itself a Corporation formed with statutory authority, and it has long since ceased to operate from a coffee-house, but it is notable that the members still conduct their business in much the same way as it was done in the coffee-house.[4] The influence of Lloyd's on insurance and insurance law has been very significant; for example, the standard Lloyd's marine insurance policy was adopted as the statutory form in the Marine Insurance Act 1906.[5] This is not to deny, however, that there have long been numerous other companies and associations transacting the business of insurance.[6]

---

[2] For a more detailed legal analysis of this, see Chap. 4, pp. 79–80.

[3] See further pp. 11–12, below.

[4] Until recently, members of Lloyd's also had unlimited personal liability, but the severe problems of recent years have led to the possibility of limited liability companies being members.

[5] Although this is rarely used today.

[6] See p. 11 for a brief description of those bodies allowed to act as insurers. For a readable description and critique of the British insurance market, although now somewhat dated, see McCrae and Cairncross, *Capital City* (2nd ed., 1985), Chap. 7.

The principles developed in regard to marine insurance have by and large been applied to the other types of insurance subsequently developed.[7] The first of these was fire insurance, its birth stimulated by the Great Fire of London in 1666. This was followed by life and personal accident insurance, the latter growing rapidly as the railways and industrialisation spread rapidly in the nineteenth century. The present century has seen such development that it is now possible to insure almost every conceivable event or thing against the risk of loss or damage. Nevertheless, the law governing all these insurances is basically the same. Marine insurance law was codified in the Marine Insurance Act 1906 and is generally regarded as *sui generis*. This book is not directly concerned with marine insurance,[8] but on occasion reference will be made to sections of the 1906 Act and to marine cases, especially where they establish a principle of general applicability or provide authority for a principle which is also valid for non-marine insurance. In general, the law governing non-marine insurance contracts is still based on case-law, but there have been some statutory inroads,[9] and there is a prospect of further statutory 'reform' in consumer insurance contracts.

Commercial v. consumer insurance law

On a number of occasions, statutory reform of aspects of insurance contract law has been recommended, including by the Law Commission in 1980,[10] and there is considerable protection afforded to some insureds

---

[7] This is perhaps the major reason for the unsatisfactory nature of some of the principles of insurance law, at least as they apply to consumer contracts. There is obviously a vast difference between the circumstances surrounding a marine policy in the early days of insurance and those surrounding the modern mass-produced motor, household, etc., policies. An explanation for the courts' (and indeed the legislature's) failure to intervene and correct these unsatisfactory rules may lie in the fact that Britain has long had a comprehensive social security insurance system, although some might now say that it has in recent years lost much of its comprehensiveness. In contrast, in the United States, where such a system is of a more recent origin and much less extensive, and where therefore private insurance was and is much more important in providing basic protection, the courts have been very active in intervening to protect the position of insureds: see Hasson, "The special nature of the insurance contract: a comparison of the American and English law of insurance" (1984) 47 M.L.R. 505.

[8] For an excellent account, see Bennett, *The Law of Marine Insurance* (1996).

[9] In particular in respect of life insurance (see Chap. 17) and insurances which are compulsory.

[10] Report No. 104, Cmnd. 8064. Brief accounts of the Law Commission's recommendations can be found at pp. 119–200 and 153–154, below. See also, Birds, "The reform of insurance law" [1982] J.B.L. 449.

against an insurer's insolvency, as will be seen in Chapter 2. However, traditionally in Britain there has been no control of policy terms and conditions, in contrast with the position in many other countries, especially those with a civil law system. It may well be that a general freedom from state control has led to benefits for insurance consumers in terms of both the cover provided and its costs.[11]

There are, though, aspects of insurance contract law whose potential unfairness, particularly as far as individual consumers are concerned, has often been recognised and some of these were the subject of the Law Commission Report referred to above. In respect of these aspects, reform by "self-regulation" has become the vogue,[12] and to these must now be added the potential impact of the Unfair Terms in Consumer Contracts Regulations 1994.[13] Indeed, the impact of these various devices is such that it may now be proper to speak of a separate "consumer insurance law" from that which applies to insurance contracts effected by commercial persons or organisations. The 1994 Regulations will be considered further at appropriate parts throughout this book, including the question of whether or not they impose a general requirement of "fairness" on the terms of consumer insurance contracts.[14] For the present, it suffices to note the general requirement applicable to any insurance contract with a consumer[15] — that the insurer must ensure that any written term of a contract is expressed in plain, intelligible language.[16] This has given statutory force to the increasing trend of recent years towards insurance policies drafted in "plain English."

---

[11] For a useful study, comparing the British system with the much more regulatory German system, see the Institute for Fiscal Studies, *Insurance: Competition or Regulation?*, Report Series No. 19 (1985).

[12] For a more detailed account, see Birds, "Self-regulation and insurance contracts," *New Foundations for Insurance Law*, (1987) Chap. 1. For an interesting study of the many agreements, many of them modifying the legal rules, under which the insurance industry operates, see Lewis, "Insurers' agreements not to enforce strict legal rights: bargaining with government and in the shadow of the law" (1985) 48 M.L.R. 275.

[13] S.I. 1994 No. 3159, implementing E.C. Directive 93/13.

[14] See pp. 91–93 and 197–199, below.

[15] Any natural person who is acting for purposes which are outside his business: reg. 2(1).

[16] Reg. 6.

As far as self-regulation is concerned, the first such device was the Statements of Insurance Practice, initially introduced in 1977[17] and later revised in 1986,[18] under which most insurers undertake not to exercise some of their legal rights against their individual policyholders. The Statements of Practice are not legally binding, although no doubt a large majority of insurers generally observes their terms.[19] They are primarily concerned with the consequences of non-disclosure, misrepresentation and breach of warranties and conditions and are referred to in Chapters 6 and 7 below. The second self-regulatory device to be noted is the codes of practice regulating the activities of insurance intermediaries.[20] Thirdly, there are two complaints mechanisms, for individual consumer insureds, outside the traditional court structure. These are the Insurance Ombudsman Bureau (I.O.B.) and Personal Insurances Arbitration Service (P.I.A.S.).[21]

It was the concern that the consumer of insurance was getting a somewhat raw deal that led three of the biggest insurers to set up the I.O.B. in 1981. P.I.A.S. was established as a rival by insurers who feared that the Ombudsman would become a consumer champion. In fact these

---

[17] This was in return for the exemption of insurance contracts from the Unfair Contract Terms Act 1977. See Birds (1977) 40 M.L.R. 677. This exemption survives even though the 1994 Regulations apply to insurance contracts.

[18] The text can be found in Part 7 of the *Encyclopedia of Insurance Law*.

[19] Note, though, that in respect of the original 1977 Statements, it took some considerable time for some insurers to comply; see the report of the Scottish Consumer Council, *Forms without Fuss*, 1981. For a recent survey of compliance with the Statements, see Cadogan and Lewis, (1992) 21 Anglo-American L.R. 123.

[20] See Chap. 10, below, p. 189.

[21] There is a growing literature on the I.O.B. and the other similar private Ombudsmen schemes; for a comprehensive review see James, "The Insurance Ombudsman," Chap. 2 in *Private Ombudsmen and Public Law* (Dartmouth, 1997). See also, for example, Birds, *op. cit.*, n.12, Birds and Graham, "Complaints mechanisms in the financial services industry," (1988) 7 C.J.Q. 313, Birds and Graham, *Complaints against Insurance Companies* (University of Sheffield, 1992, reprinted with amendments in [1993] Consum. L. J 77), and Morris and Hamilton, "The Insurance Ombudsman and PIA Ombudsman: a critical comparison" (1996) 47 N.I.L.Q. 119. The I.O.B. publishes Annual Reports and, a fairly recent innovation, regular case digests, which provide a fascinating picture of the operation of the modern insurance industry. Very little is known about P.I.A.S. as there are no reports on its operation published, mainly because each case will be treated as a private arbitration subject to the ordinary rules about arbitration.

fears proved groundless[22] and P.I.A.S., which operates in essence like an ordinary arbitration with the result binding on both parties, is used by only a very small minority of insurers issuing policies to ordinary consumers. The success of the I.O.B., in contrast, means that it merits further consideration.

The Insurance Ombudsman Bureau

The membership of the I.O.B. now comprises general insurers covering 90 per cent of private policyholders, but it has recently lost jurisdiction over the vast majority of life insurance cases.[23] The Bureau will hear complaints only when all internal mechanisms within a member company, up to chief executive level, have been exhausted. The service is free to complainants and the Ombudsman can make awards of up to £100,000 which are binding on member companies. However, the consumer is not bound by a decision of the Ombudsman. The I.O.B. itself is an unlimited company without a share capital, with a board of directors appointed as representatives of the member insurers. It has an independent Council, the majority of whose members are not insurance industry people, which appoints the Ombudsman. Very rarely does the Ombudsman actually exercise his power to make a formal award; rather, most cases are disposed of by way of conciliation. In the later period of office of the first Ombudsman,[24] a degree of greater formality was introduced in terms of formal hearings with legal representation. The second Ombudsman, establishing a pattern seemingly carried on by his two successors, stressed the importance of informality wherever possible, referring to the issue of "letters of advice" in the vast majority of cases. He emphasised the importance of speed in decision-making, with full, formal and final decisions being made only as a last resort. He was, though, prepared to hold informal hearings where necessary.

The Ombudsman's terms of reference have always expressly required him to make decisions in accordance with "good insurance practice" as well

---

[22] At least initially, under the jurisdiction of the first holder of the post. The later Ombudsmen have been much more prepared to take a "consumerist" stance.

[23] This is because most forms of life insurance are regulated under the Financial Services Act 1986 (see p. 10, below) by the Personal Investment Authority, and complaints are handled by the P.I.A. Ombudsman.

[24] Who was in post until 1989.

insurance involves the third party as much as the insured person. Often in practice, for example, the victim of a car accident may talk in terms of claiming from the negligent driver's insurer rather than from the driver, which in law is the correct way of expressing the position. The law has deemed that in certain cases the third party should be protected from the strict contractual rights and liabilities between insured and insurer.[33] Although this book is not generally concerned with the economics of insurance nor with how efficient it is, it is worth pointing out that in general the third party insurance system is much more expensive and less efficient to operate than first party insurance, a factor, among others, which has led many people to conclude that in certain areas, especially road and work accidents involving personal injury or death, the present system of third party insurance backing up a system of liability in tort should be replaced by first party insurance. The latter could be run by private insurers, but more logically perhaps should be taken over by the state as part of the social security system.[34] It must be admitted, though, that such a development at present appears highly unlikely.

Life and other insurances

A second classification, which is well recognised in law and meaningful in insurance circles, distinguishes between life insurance on the one hand and all other forms of insurance on the other. There is a great variety of forms of life insurance,[35] ranging from pure, whole life insurance, an undertaking to pay a certain sum on the death of the life insured whenever this occurs, to endowment policies whereby the insured receives a sum if he survives beyond a certain age, and to modern devices which combine an element of life insurance with the more substantial element of investment

---

[33] *ibid.*

[34] See generally, *e.g.* Cane, *Atiyah's Accident Compensation and the Law* (5th ed., 1993); Report of the Royal Commission on Civil Liability and Compensation for Personal Injury (The Pearson Report), 1978 Cmnd. 7054. For a interesting study of the impact of liability insurance on the development of the tort of negligence, see Davies, "The end of the affair: duty of care and liability insurance" (1989) 9 L.S. 67.

[35] See Chap. 17.

in securities or property.[36] Whatever the type of life policy, the uncertainty which, as will be seen shortly, is a necessary feature of all insurances is of a different nature from the uncertainty in other insurances. Death is certain; the uncertainty is as to when it will occur. On the other hand, the property insured against loss by fire may never burn down, the motor insured may never be involved in an accident. Accordingly, contracts of life insurance and related ones such as personal accident insurances, are regarded simply as contracts for contingency insurance, in other words, contracts to pay an agreed sum of money when the event insured against occurs. Non-life insurance contracts are, in general, contracts to indemnify the insured only in respect of the loss suffered if it is actually suffered and only to the amount of the loss suffered.[37] We shall return to this distinction at the relevant points throughout this book.

Terminology

There are one or two related points concerning the terminology of insurance. It is sometimes said that the proper description of the contract which insures a life is life *assurance* and this is indeed a common, though not universal, usage. The reason is simply that death is assured of happening, the risks covered by other insurances are not. But because the usage is not universal, we shall in general use the terms "insurance" and "insured" in all cases. It is also not uncommon, both in policies and in statute, to refer to the "policyholder" rather than the insured, but this book will tend to use the latter term.

Types of Insurer

We shall see in the next chapter that the business of providing insurance is closely regulated by government. It is appropriate here to outline the principal types of business which are allowed to engage in insurance.

---

[36] As long as there is a life insurance element, even if that may be no more than the surrender value of the contract at any time, the contract is one of life insurance for the purposes of the regulatory statutes (see Chap. 2) and the Life Assurance Act 1774 (see Chap. 3): *Fuji Finance Inc. v. Aetna Life Insurance Ltd* [1996] 4 All E.R. 608. That in practice many life insurance policies are in reality investments has been recognised by the incorporation of many forms of life insurance within the investor protection framework established by the Financial Services Act 1986. The detailed consideration of this framework is outside the scope of this book, but aspects of it are considered; see especially pp. 327–329, below. See generally, Page and Ferguson, *Investor Protection* (1992).

[37] Valued policies, where the insured is entitled to a stated sum regardless of the exact measure of his loss, are rare but possible in non-marine insurance; see Chap. 13, p. 271.

With the exception of Lloyd's, insurers must be a company registered under the Companies Act,[38] an industrial and provident society or a body corporate established by charter or Act of Parliament. Virtually all large non-life insurers and composite insurers[39] have long adopted the ordinary registered company form. Many of the long-established life insurers are mutual insurers incorporated by charter or statute.[40] A number of industrial and provident societies still operate the form of life insurance known as industrial life assurance, the essential characteristic of which is that premiums are collected at the insureds' homes on a regular basis.

Lloyd's is a unique organisation and operates as such on a world-wide basis.[41] A member of Lloyd's is exempt from the need to obtain authorisation under the Insurance Companies Act 1982.[42] As far as organisation is concerned, there is in fact no insurer called Lloyd's. The Corporation of Lloyd's, which is established under the Lloyd's Acts 1871–1982, does not itself transact insurance business nor does it have any liability on policies issued by Lloyd's underwriters.[43] It is concerned to control the membership of Lloyd's, to provide facilities for the conduct of members' business and to regulate the Lloyd's market under the Lloyd's Acts.[44] Insurance at Lloyd's is effected with individual underwriters, for

---

[38] The Companies Act 1985 or one of its predecessors.

[39] That is, insurers offering both long-term (life) and other insurance business.

[40] Mutual insurance, in the form of clubs owned by shipowners, is also common in the marine insurance market; the clubs themselves will be ordinary registered companies.

[41] It operates overseas through agency arrangements.

[42] S.2(2)(a).

[43] Recent problems at Lloyd's led to considerable litigation regarding the legal relationships involved, in particular as to whether the Corporation of Lloyd's owes any duty of care to its "names"; see *Ashmore v. Corporation of Lloyd's* [1992] 2 Lloyd's Rep. 1; *ibid.*, (No. 2) [1992] 2 Lloyd's Rep. 620.

[44] This regulation, which serves to protect the investing members of Lloyd's, *i.e.* the names, rather than to protect policyholders, has been the subject of much discussion in recent years. There have been cases of fraud by working members and managing agents causing loss to investing names, conflicts of interest arising from the same people having interests in both managing agencies and in firms of Lloyd's brokers (through whose hands all insurance placed at Lloyd's must go) and, more recently, allegations of negligent underwriting. It is likely that the litigation referred to in the previous footnote will continue, as will further modifications to the regulatory structure of Lloyd's. Indeed it seems likely that Lloyd's, as an investment mechanism rather than as an insurer, will be brought within the ambit of the Financial Services Act 1986 or some similar regulatory

many years grouped into syndicates. Working members run the day-to-day business of the syndicates, the "names" (who constitute the vast majority of the underwriters) being passive investors.[45] Unless advantage is taken of the recent introduction of limited liability,[46] each underwriter is potentially liable without limit on the insurance contracts entered into on his/her behalf, and that liability is several not joint.[47]

The Legal Definition of Insurance

An essential task at this stage is to attempt to formulate a legal definition or at least an explanation of the meaning of the contract of insurance. As has been pointed out judicially,[48] this is not an easy matter. The statutes dealing with the regulation of insurance business, of which the Insurance Companies Act 1982 is the current one, have never contained a definition, no doubt because of the risk of inadvertently excluding contracts which should be within their scope.[49] One effect of this, though, must be that it gives the regulatory authority, the Department of Trade and Industry, a considerable discretion. This discretion can be challenged effectively only by a body going to court in order to seek a declaration that it is not carrying on insurance business or having to defend an application by the Department for a declaration that it is or a petition by the Department to wind up the company. Apart from the desirability of defining the scope of what the law of insurance applies to, clearly the

---

structure, as was recommended by a House of Commons Select Committee in 1996. When the Lloyd's Act was first introduced, it was thought that self-regulation would be sufficient, but this has proved to be false optimism. See further, Ellis and Wiltshire, *Regulation of Insurance*, Part B7, Ferguson, "Self-regulation at Lloyd's: The Lloyd's Act 1982" (1983) 46 M.L.R. 56 and Page and Ferguson, *Investor Protection*, pp. 243–244.

[45] There are approximately 30,000 underwriting members of Lloyd's.

[46] See p. 2, above.

[47] Lloyd's Act 1982, s. 8(1), relied upon by the House of Lords in *Touche Ross & Co. v. Baker* [1992] 2 Lloyd's Rep. 207 holding that, in the absence of anything to the contrary in the policy, a "discovery extension" clause in a professional indemnity policy issued by a group of insurers could be exercised against one Lloyd's syndicate notwithstanding that it was not exercised against the other insurers involved.

[48] *Department of Trade and Industry v. St Christopher Motorists' Association Ltd.* [1974] 1 All E.R. 395; *Medical Defence Union v. Department of Trade* [1979] 2 All E.R. 421 at 429.

[49] See the *St Christopher* case, at 396–7.

fundamental reason for any attempt to define the meaning of insurance contract is because the business of providing insurance under contracts of insurance is closely regulated. We shall briefly consider the nature of this regulation in the next chapter.

However, there are other reasons. Insurance law has its peculiar principles, for example the doctrine of *uberrima fides,*[50] and it may be necessary to know whether a contract is one of insurance in order to know whether this doctrine applies. Furthermore, a statute may include within or exempt from its operation "contracts of insurance" without defining these. The obvious case is the exemption of such contracts from the Unfair Contract Terms Act 1977.[51]

As it happens, almost all the decided cases which have considered this problem have been concerned to discover whether or not a business was subject to regulation as insurance. Others have been concerned with tax statutes and one or two only with principles peculiar to the insurance contract.[52] It will be assumed for the present that a definition can be found which works for all purposes; we shall then briefly consider whether, in fact, it might not be useful to have different definitions for different purposes.

A definition for regulatory purposes

It is suggested that a contract of insurance is any contract whereby one party assumes the risk of an uncertain event,[53] which is not within his control, happening at a future time, in which event the other party has an interest, and under which contract the first party is bound to pay money or provide its equivalent if the uncertain event occurs. It would follow that anyone who regularly[54] enters into such contracts as the party bearing the

---

[50] See Chap. 6.

[51] Sched. 1, para. 1(a): see the text above at n.17.

[52] One area which has given rise to litigation and to difficulties is that of distinguishing contracts of insurance from contracts of guarantee. It is clear that what the contract is called does not matter. The leading case is *Seaton v. Heath* [1899] 1 Q.B. 782, and see Blair, "The conversion of guarantee contracts" (1966) 39 M.L.R. 522.

[53] It is clear that the uncertain event need not be adverse to the other party, though in cases other than certain endowment and annuity policies, it will be. See *Gould v. Curtis* [1913] 3 K.B. 84, qualifying the definition given in the leading case of *Prudential Insurance Co. v. I.R.C.* [1904] 2 K.B. 658, and the discussion by Megarry V.-C. in the *Medical Defence Union* case, above at 427–428.

[54] Although regularity may not be necessary: see Chap. 2, p. 26.

risks is carrying on insurance business for the purposes of the statute regulating insurance business. Several aspects of this definition merit closer attention.

Legal entitlement

First, there must clearly be a binding contract, and the insurer must be legally bound to compensate the other party. A right to be considered for a benefit which is truly only discretionary is not enough. In *Medical Defence Union v. Department of Trade*,[55] the plaintiff was a company whose members were practising doctors and dentists. Its business consisted primarily of conducting legal proceedings on behalf of members and indemnifying them against claims made against them in respect of damages and costs. However, under its constitution, its members had no right to such benefits, merely the right to request that they be given assistance or an indemnity. It was held that the company was not carrying on insurance business. The contracts between it and its members were not contracts of insurance because to be that a contract must provide for the right of the insured to money or money's worth on the happening of the uncertain event. The right to request assistance was not such a right.

Uncertainty

Secondly, the uncertainty which is a necessary feature of insurance, as we have already seen, is in most cases as to whether or not the event insured against will occur. In life insurance, it is as to the time when it will occur.[56]

Insurable interest

Thirdly, the other party, the insured, must have an insurable interest in the property or life or liability which is the subject of the insurance. This requirement will be examined in detail in Chapter 3.

Control

Fourthly, it seems essential that the event insured against be outside the control of the party assuming the risk. No English case has directly

---

[55] [1979] 2 All E.R. 421.
[56] See *Gould v. Curtis*, above.

considered this point, but it has been raised in two cases when it was not necessary for decision.[57] The potential problem can be illustrated by considering the case of a manufacturer who contractually guarantees his products to his consumers. The example may be taken of a washing machine manufacturer who undertakes to repair any fault arising from defective manufacture within a year of purchase. He has clearly undertaken to provide a service in money's worth in assuming the risk of an uncertain event in which the consumer clearly has an interest. Yet surely he has not entered into a contract of insurance as most people would understand it. It is suggested that the answer is to introduce the element of control.[58] In the example, all that the manufacturer has done is to guarantee to put things right which he has put wrong in the first place, *i.e.* defects in manufacture. Therefore, his guarantee is not a contract of insurance.[59] On the other hand, however, someone who in return for a consideration guarantees a product against certain risks which are not within his control because they are not his products, nor has he sold them, is, it is thought, entering into contracts of insurance.[60] The same would be true if a manufacturer did more than simply guarantee his products against manufacturing defects, for example, if he undertook to replace them if they were damaged from specified causes.[61] Associations which provide a repair or recovery service

---

[57] The *St Christopher* case, above, at 401; the *Medical Defence Union* case, above at 424.

[58] Perhaps "control" is a misleading term, as in practice a manufacturer may have very little actual control over his warranted products. An alternative formulation might be whether the alleged insurer is in fact responsible for producing the event giving rise to the claim for indemnity.

[59] See the American cases cited in Hellner, "The scope of insurance regulation: what is insurance for the purposes of regulation?" (1963) 12 Am. J. Comp. L. 494 at 505.

[60] See *Re Sentinel Securities plc* [1996] 1 W.L.R. 316, where a "guarantee" to repair double glazing and other home improvement products if the original supplier went out of business was held to constitute insurance.

[61] *ibid.* at 505-506. The leading U.S. case is perhaps *State ex rel. Duffy v. Western Auto Supply Co.* 134 Ohio St. 163 (1938). The New York Insurance Law, s. 41, among others, incorporates the control test into its definition of insurance contracts. However, the use of this test has been criticised; see, *e.g.* Hellner *op. cit.*, especially at 500–502. If such a manufacturer were held to be entering into contracts of insurance, that does not necessarily imply that he is carrying on the business of insurance for the purposes of the 1982 Act; see Megarry V.-C. in the *Medical Defence Union* case at 431–432. It should be noted that were this the result, the manufacturer is not strictly entitled to carry on any other commercial business (Insurance Companies Act 1982, s.16) which would obviously be ridiculous. See also Parkash, [1985] *Law Society's Gazette* 3547.

for car owners upon breakdown might also be regarded as providing insurance, assuming that their members have a right to their services and not just a right to be considered.[62]

Provision of money's worth

Fifthly, there seems no reason in principle why it should be necessary for the insurer to have to undertake to pay money on the occurrence of the uncertain event, and there is clear authority that the provision of something other than money is enough, provided that it is of money's worth. In *Department of Trade and Industry v. St Christopher's Motorists' Association Ltd*,[63] the defendant undertook to provide its members with chauffeur services should they be disqualified from driving due to being convicted of having more than the permitted level of alcohol in the blood. It was held that this constituted insurance. The fact that the benefits were not in money was irrelevant.[64] As was pointed out in the subsequent case of *Medical Defence Union v. Department of Trade*, which has already been examined, it is not sufficient nor accurate to say that the provision of services is enough.[65] It is better to say that it must be the provision of something that is clearly worth money, whether that be a right to valuable services, a right to advice[66] or a right to have an item of property repaired or replaced.

---

[62] This is implicitly recognised by the fact that the activities of such associations are exempt from the control of the Insurance Companies Act 1982; see reg. 3 of the Insurance Companies Regulations 1994 (S.I. 1994 No. 1516), made under s.2(5) of the 1982 Act.

[63] [1974] 1 All E.R. 395. It should be noted that by the time the case was heard, the defendant had in fact made arrangements for insurance which were satisfactory to the Department of Trade, so that they did not appear in court. Such insurance was in fact probably contrary to public policy (see p. 242, below), and is no longer sold in this country.

[64] This decision was followed in *Re Sentinel Securities plc* [1996] 1 W.L.R. 316 (the benefit provided by the insurer was the repair of defects in double-glazing and other home improvements).

[65] [1979] 2 All E.R. at 428.

[66] It was also said in the *Medical Defence Union* case, above, at 430, that a right to advice and assistance conferred on members of a club should involve the "insurer" in additional expenses, rather than being merely part of the general costs of running the club for the benefit of members generally. Megarry V.-C. would therefore add "or the provision of services to be paid for by the insurer" to "money or money's worth."

Other requirements?

Certain authorities suggest, however, that the above definition may not be sufficiently comprehensive. *Hampton v. Toxteth Co-operative Society*[67] and *Hall D'Ath v. British Provident Association*[68] both appear to suggest that there can be no insurance business carried on in the absence of a clearly stipulated premium and policy. In the *Hampton* case, membership of a local co-operative society was expressed to confer the right to a sum of money on the death of a member's spouse, the sum to be calculated by reference to the member's purchases from the society over a certain period. This was held not to constitute the provision of life insurance, so that the society was not required to deposit the sum of £20,000 under the relevant regulating statute, the Assurance Companies Act 1909. It is clear that the majority of the Court of Appeal[69] did regard the absence of a policy as crucial; the decision may also have turned upon the fact that under the rules of the society as the court read them, there was no enforceable contractual right to the sums concerned. It has already been seen how this is essential.

The absence of a policy was probably crucial because the 1909 Act, in sections 1 and 30, expressly referred to the carrying on of insurance business under policies of insurance. The *Hampton* case[70] can therefore be read as turning on a point of statutory construction.[71] The present definition in Schedules 1 and 2 of the Insurance Companies Act 1982 refers merely to contracts of insurance, and it is suggested therefore, that these older cases are of no relevance to the construction of the modern statute and to a modern definition of insurance at least for regulation purposes.[72] It would indeed be most strange if a business could escape from regulation as insurance merely by introducing less formality, even if in all

---

[67] [1915] 1 Ch. 721.

[68] (1932) 48 L.T.R. 240.

[69] Phillimore L.J. dissented strongly.

[70] The same must be true of the *Hall D'Ath* case.

[71] This also distinguishes the earlier case of *Nelson v. Board of Trade* (1901) 84 L.T. 565, where tea merchants who offered married women who bought their tea over a certain period annuities on the deaths of their husbands were held to be subject to the Life Assurance Companies Act 1870. Although "policies" appeared in that Act, this was only part of the relevant definition; the other part referred simply to the granting of annuities upon human life, with no reference to the necessity for a policy.

[72] Whether or not the *Hampton* case might be used as the basis for a definition for other purposes is discussed briefly below.

respects the contracts it entered into fell within a definition of the sort that has been given here. The legislature has deemed that insurers should be more closely scrutinised as regards their financial situation than most other businesses, because of the importance of insurance, the risks involved, and the need to ensure that insureds do not suffer at the hands of reckless or fraudulent insurers.

A wider view

It may indeed be arguable that there should be no great concern to find a formal definition of insurance for regulation purposes. It could be enough to say that any transaction that looks like insurance by displaying the necessary characteristics of assumption and distribution of risk, and which is transacted on a reasonable scale, should be the subject of regulation.[73] On this view, technical questions as to the enforceability of the right by the insured, and whether or not the benefit he has promised is worth money, may be irrelevant. If, in fact, the "insurer" regularly dispenses real benefit, he should be regarded as an insurer. As has been pointed out with respect to the *Medical Defence Union* case,[74] it is extremely rare for that company to refuse assistance to its members, and it is unlikely that any member faced with an allegation of negligence would deny that he was getting his money's worth from the company. There are strong arguments that such a body is in the business of insuring to such an extent that the protection of its members requires that it be subject to the regulatory provisions of the Insurance Companies Act.

Definition for other purposes

If, in order to qualify as insurance for the purposes of regulation, it is sufficient that a transaction displays the necessary characteristics, the question arises whether a similar description will suffice for other purposes. Take, for example, the sort of deal that involves the assumption of risk outside the control of the party assuming the risk, but which is not referred to, nor perhaps would most people think of it, as insurance. As well as the examples given earlier, an actual instance involved a manufacturer of engine lubricants who, when he sold these, also guaranteed that

---

[73] See especially, for a full and persuasive argument on these lines, to which the text does no justice at all, the article by Hellner cited in n.59.

[74] Roberts (1980) 43 M.L.R. 85; Merkin (1979) 1 *Liverpool Law Review* 125.

the purchaser's car would not break down from any cause for a certain period. Clearly this went beyond risks which were within his control. Could such a manufacturer claim, for example, that his contracts are exempt from the statutory control of exclusion clauses in the Unfair Contract Terms Act 1977, because they are contracts of insurance? It is suggested that he should not be able to do so.[75] For regulation purposes, for the reasons mentioned, a wide definition of insurance should be used which would indeed catch this sort of case. However, the Unfair Contract Terms Act exemption was clearly intended to apply to contracts of insurance as normally understood and described.[76] The policy of the Act dictates that anything which does not choose to identify itself as insurance cannot claim the advantage of the exemption. It is suggested therefore, that for this purpose, and perhaps for the purposes of applying the special rules of insurance law such as the doctrine of *uberrima fides,* there is merit in the views expressed in the *Hampton* case and others — that the transactions are accompanied by the usual incidents of insurance, namely some sort of policy[77] and an identifiable premium.

[75] In any event, now, such a manufacturer will be subject to the Unfair Terms in Consumer Contracts Regulations 1994 because, as we have seen, these apply to contracts of insurance, although the scope of their application is unclear.

[76] Because the insurance industry promulgated *Statements of Practice* in return; see p. 5 above.

[77] Although it is not suggested that it is necessarily called a "policy."

CHAPTER 2

THE REGULATION OF INSURANCE

Of the two parties to the contract of insurance,[1] the law requires of the insured only that he has an insurable interest in what he insures[2] and that he has the usual capacity to contract.[3] In contrast, a body can act as an insurer only if it satisfies the regulatory requirements established by detailed and complex legislation. This chapter is concerned to give a fairly brief description of these requirements[4] and then to examine the law which exists to protect insured persons should the system of state control fail.[5] As we shall see, this is an area where the influence of European Community Law has been significant and the development of this merits some special consideration.

The development of State control

State control of insurers began in 1870.[6] It followed the failure some two years previously of two sizeable life insurance companies. The pattern

---

[1] Although there are only two parties to the contract, much insurance business, both in terms of entering into contracts and subsequent dealings thereon, is effected through the agency of an intermediary. The law relating thereto is considered in Chap. 10.

[2] This is considered in detail in Chap. 3.

[3] The detailed law on capacity may be found in any standard text on the law of contract.

[4] What is not considered is the system for regulating most types of life insurance under the Financial Services Act 1986. This is beyond the scope of this book. An excellent account can be found in Page and Ferguson, *Investor Protection*.

[5] The account here is inevitably only an outline. For a detailed description, see Ellis and Wiltshire, *The Regulation of Insurance Business*. An annotated version of the legislation may be found in the *Encyclopedia of Insurance Law* (Sweet & Maxwell) and the *Compendium of Insurance Law* (Lloyd's of London Press).

[6] Life Assurance Companies Act 1870. This and amending statues until the 1930s required only that insurers deposit a sum of money with the court as security.

has been repeated until relatively recently in the sense that the subsequent revisions and extensions of control have generally followed some major insurance collapse which drew attention to the defects in the existing law or the way that it was applied. For example, the circumstances surrounding the liquidation of the Fire, Auto and Marine Insurance Company in the mid-1960s led to a substantial amendment (by Part II of the Companies Act 1967) of the system then established under the Insurance Companies Act 1958. Even more disastrous was the failure of the "cut-price" motor insurer, the Vehicle and General, in 1971, when overnight approximately one million motorists found themselves without cover.[7] As a result, the 1958 Act was further amended by the Insurance Companies Amendment Act 1973. The legislation was then consolidated in the Insurance Companies Act 1974. However, this Act was premature because it almost immediately had to be amended in order to take account of requirements emanating from the first E.C. Directive.[8] Since then, the story has been one of changes due to further E.C. measures; these are briefly described below. The primary source of the law is now the Insurance Companies Act 1982, although this has been considerably supplemented and amended by regulations, principally now the Insurance Companies Regulations 1994.[9]

Added to the fact that the Department of Trade and Industry, the Government Department charged with insurance supervision, now has more expertise and manpower in the insurance field than it once possessed, the 1982 Act and the regulations ought to provide a fairly watertight system for the financial regulation of insurers. Should this perchance fail, the Policyholders Protection Act 1975, which will be described later, will operate in the last resort to ensure that some insureds are very little, if at all, out of pocket as the result of an insurance insolvency.

The impact of E.C. Law

As already indicated, E.C. law has had a significant effect on the regulation of insurance business. The first directives were concerned to

---

[7] The Department of Trade was severely criticised over this by a Tribunal of Inquiry: 1972 H.C. Papers 133. See Chapman, "The Vehicle & General affair: some reflections for public administration in Britain" (1973) Public Administration 273.

[8] The Directive regarding Freedom of Establishment in Non-Life Insurance, No. 73/239 (July 23, 1973), concerning the right of insurers from one E.C. Member State to establish branches or agencies in other E.C. States. This was followed by the Establishment Directive on Life Business, No. 79/267 (March 5, 1979).

[9] S.I. 1994 No. 1516.

establish freedom of establishment within the Community, initially with regard to non-life insurance business and then with regard to life insurance.

Freedom of establishment

As far as non-life insurance was concerned, the directive[10] introduced a uniform system of solvency margins[11] calculated as a percentage of annual premiums or claims (whichever gave the higher result)[12] and prescribed a procedure to be followed in the event that an insurer failed to show possession of the necessary margin.[13] It gave insurers from one E.C. State the right to establish branches or agencies in other E.C. States and prescribed, in broad outline, the authorisation procedure to be followed in such cases.[14] There were also provisions[15] as to the regime to be applied to branches and agencies of insurers with their head offices outside the E.C. (the authorisation of such insurers remaining discretionary). The provisions of the life directive[16] were in many ways similar to those of the non-life directive. The principle of a solvency margin was again introduced, though in this case based on the insurer's mathematical reserves.[17] The most difficult problem which had to be resolved in the negotiations leading to this directive was the existence of "composite" life and non-life insurers in the United Kingdom, whereas the majority of E.C. States require life assurance to be carried on by "specialist" life companies not involved in any other class of business. The outcome was that no new "composites" may be authorised in the United Kingdom. Existing "composites" may continue and may set up branches or agencies in other E.C. states for the conduct of non-life business. If, however, they wish to do life business elsewhere in the Community, they must set up subsidiaries.[18]

Freedom of services

Substantial changes were made to the 1982 Act in order to implement freedom of services within the E.C. and the EEA. The Non-life Insurance

---

[10] No. 73/239.
[11] The U.K. had adopted this system some years ago.
[12] Art. 16.
[13] Arts. 20, 22.
[14] Arts. 10–12.
[15] Arts. 23–29.
[16] No. 79/267.
[17] See art. 18.
[18] Art. 13.

Services Directive[19] gave non-life insurers licensed to write insurance business in any E.C. member State the right to offer "large risks"[20] across national frontiers without the need for authorisation. This was followed by the Second Life Directive.[21] These were quickly superseded when in July 1992, the Council of Ministers adopted the Third Non-Life Directive[22] and the Third Life Directive.[23] These took freedom of services to its logical conclusion by introducing the single European licence. An insurer authorised in any member State is automatically allowed to sell most types of non-life insurance anywhere else in the Community, either through a branch or agency in the host State or via direct selling in the host State. The home State controls all its activities and its solvency.[24]

The United Kingdom implemented the Third Directives, with effect from July 1, 1994, by the Insurance Companies (Third Insurance Directives) Regulations 1994.[25] Schedule 2F deals first with E.C. insurance companies carrying on or providing business in the U.K. and secondly with EFTA companies providing insurance in the United Kingdom.[26] As regards E.C. insurers, there is thus a distinction between the insurer who carries on business, which requires the company to have a United Kingdom branch, and the insurer who merely offers insurance in the United Kingdom, but who carries out the relevant paperwork elsewhere; the latter is merely a provider of insurance and not carrying on insurance business in the United Kingdom.

[19] 88/357.

[20] There were three type of large risks, namely (1) broadly, marine, aviation and transit business, (2) credit and suretyship insurance where the policy holder carried on business and (3) property, pecuniary and liability insurances relating to a business carried on by the insured where the business met two out of three criteria: (a) 250 employees, (b) an annual turnover of 12 million ECU, (c) a balance sheet total of 6.2 million ECU.

[21] 90/619.

[22] 92/49.

[23] 92/96.

[24] Although there is provision for the host State to take action where the home State defaults in so doing. The Directive also requires that no new system of what is called "material control," that is any system for the prior approval of policy terms and premium rates, can be introduced. States which previously had such a system can retain it, but insurers authorised in a member State which does not exercise such control will not be required to submit policy terms and premium rates to the authorities of any host State that does exercise such control.

[25] S.I. 1994 No 1696, inserting ss.81A and 81B and Schedules 2F and 2G into the 1982 Act. Schedule 2G is concerned with the recognition of U.K. insurers in other EEA States.

[26] As to the latter, see paras. 18 to 24 of Schedule 2F.

An E.C. insurance company wishing to carry on direct insurance business in the United Kingdom[27] must be authorised in its home State in accordance with the relevant provisions of the first Insurance Directives, and its supervisory authority must provide the Secretary of State with a notice containing details of it and a certificate attesting to its margin of solvency and indicating the classes of business for which it is authorised. The details required are the name of the company and its authorised agent, the address of its United Kingdom branch, a scheme of operations prepared in accordance with any requirements of its supervisory authority and, in the case of a motor insurer, confirmation that it has become a member of the Motor Insurers' Bureau.[28] In addition, either the Secretary of State must have informed the supervisory authority of the conditions which, in the general good, must be complied with by the company in carrying on insurance business through the branch or two months must have lapsed from the date of receipt of the notice and certificate.

E.C. insurers wishing to provide insurance in the United Kingdom must similarly be authorised to provide the relevant class or classes of business in their home State and are subject to generally similar conditions. So, their supervisory authority must provide a notice and a certificate, the only material difference being that in this case there will be no branch details or authorised agent.

In respect of any E.C. insurer operating in the United Kingdom market, the Secretary of State has many of the general powers which he has in relation to United Kingdom companies.[29] Specifically, he has the power to prevent the disposal of assets by the insurer, powers to obtain information, the general power to protect policyholders under section 45 if requested to do so by the home State supervisor, a general power to intervene for the breach of any relevant legal provision and the power to withdraw recognition.

Authorisation under the Insurance Companies Act 1982

Under section 2, only the following are permitted to carry on insurance business:

> (a) bodies authorised under section 3 or, under section 4, which existed prior to the 1982 Act by virtue of having been authorised under earlier legislation;

---

[27] The requirements for insurers wishing to effect reinsurance business are similar.
[28] As to the M.I.B., see Chap. 19.
[29] Schedule 2F, paras 12 to 17. As to these powers, see p. 31 below.

(b) members of Lloyd's[30];

(c) an E.C. insurance company[31] carrying on business via a United Kingdom branch[32];

(d) registered friendly societies[33]; and

(e) for the purposes of the provision of provident or strike benefits only, trade unions or employers' associations.

In addition, it is permissible for a bank to carry on credit and similar types of insurance without authorisation if this is solely in the course of carrying on, and for the purposes of, banking business,[34] and the Secretary of State can exempt insurers who provide exclusively or primarily benefits in kind.[35]

Authorisation is required if either the entry into insurance contracts or the payment of claims is effected within the United Kingdom,[36] although "in the vast majority of circumstances, the same insurance company will both effect the contract and carry it out (*i.e.* perform the obligations under

---

[30] Authorisation is not required of members of Lloyd's, although it is required that they, taken together, must satisfy the solvency margin requirements described below.

[31] Defined in s.2(6) as an insurance company which is incorporated in or formed under the law of a member State other than the U.K., whose head office is in that member State and which is authorised in accordance with art. 6 of the first general insurance Directive or art. 6 of the first long term insurance Directive.

[32] 1982 Act, s.2(1A), provided the requirements of Part I of Schedule 2F have been complied with and the company is duly authorised in its home State. This implements the E.C. Directives described earlier.

[33] These are governed by the Friendly Societies Act 1992, consolidating earlier legislation, and are principally concerned to sell industrial life assurance, that is life insurance sold door-to-door with regular collections of premiums. There is a Registrar of Friendly Societies who exercises tight control over these bodies.

[34] s.2(4).

[35] The classic example is vehicle recovery services offered by motoring organisations in the event of breakdown, exempted by the Insurance Companies Regulations 1994 (S.I. 1994 No. 1516), reg. 3.

[36] *The Bedford Insurance Co. Ltd v. Instituto de Ressaguros do Brasil* [1984] 1 Lloyd's Rep. 210; *Stewart v. Oriental Fire and Marine Insurance Co.* [1984] 2 Lloyd's Rep. 109. In both cases the reasoning turned on the words in Sched. 1 to the 1982 Act, defining the various classes of insurance business (see below), which use the phrases "effecting" and "carrying out" contracts of insurance. These were construed disjunctively so that either activity required authorisation.

it, in particular the obligation to pay claims)."[37] However, an insurance company is not to be taken to be carrying on insurance business "by reason only of the fact that it provides insurance in the United Kingdom"[38]; this provision is concerned with freedom of services within the E.C., as already considered, and seems to mean that an insurer who merely offers insurance in the United Kingdom, but who carries out the relevant paperwork elsewhere in the E.C. is merely a provider of insurance and not carrying on insurance business in the United Kingdom.[39] More generally, in order to determine whether or not an insurer is carrying on business in the United Kingdom, it is necessary to look at the business as a whole; a crucial factor will be where the underwriting decisions are taken.[40] It is clear that the words of section 2 — "carrying on insurance business" — connote some element of continuity as opposed to mere isolated transactions, but it is thought that a single transaction of some magnitude could nonetheless amount to the carrying on of business,[41] and section 2 is contravened by the negotiation of a prospective insurance contract without authorisation.[42]

An insured who enters into a contract with an unauthorised insurer has the right to elect whether or not to treat the contract as enforceable and if he elects not to enforce it, he can recover his premium and compensation for any loss.[43] The insurer can only enforce such a contract if it persuades

---

[37] *per* Lord Goff of Chieveley in *Scher v. Policyholders Protection Board* [1993] 3 All E.R. 384 at p. 412; see also Lord Donaldson M.R. in the Court of Appeal at 393. The exceptional circumstances envisaged by Lord Goff which would require the phrase to be read disjunctively were — where it might be necessary because of transitional provisions in insurance companies legislation (as was the case in the decisions cited in the previous footnote), or where there was an assignment of a contract of insurance by an overseas insurer to one carrying on insurance business in the U.K.

[38] s.81A(5).

[39] The distinction may not always be easy to apply in practice.

[40] See *Re Companies Nos. 007816 and 007818-007822 of 1994*, unreported, 1995; see (1995) 7 Insurance Law Monthly (7) 5.

[41] *Cornelius v. Phillips* [1918] A.C. 199.

[42] *R. v. Wilson* [1997] 1 All E.R. 119.

[43] s.132, Financial Services Act 1986. Life insurance contracts which constitute investments under the 1986 Act are governed in this respect by the substantially similar s.5. As to the temporal effect of s.132, see *Group Josi Re v. Walbrook Insurance Co. Ltd* [1995] C.L.C. 1532.

the court to exercise its discretion to allow enforcement.[44]

An applicant for authorisation must submit its business proposals and financial forecasts[45] to the Secretary of State for Trade and Industry,[46] and a decision must be made within six months, with written reasons being given for any refusal.[47] The Secretary of State must not authorise an applicant which is a United Kingdom or non-E.C. company[48] if it appears to him that the criteria of sound and prudent management are not or will not be fulfilled.[49] These criteria[50] refer to integrity, care and skill in the running of the business, the fitness and propriety of directors, controllers,[51]

[44] Under s.132(3). S.136(6) provides that a contravention of s.2 of the 1982 Act does not make a contract of insurance illegal or invalid to any greater extent than is provided in the section. It seems therefore that if an insured elects to enforce a contract with an unauthorised insurer, the latter can rely on any defence, e.g. of non-disclosure or breach of warranty or condition, and pursue subrogation rights against a third party; cf. *McCall v. Brookes* [1984] R.T.R. 99.

[45] The detail is prescribed in the Insurance Companies Regulations 1994 (S.I. 1994 No. 1516), reg. 4 and scheds. 1 (long-term business) and 2 (general business).

[46] An application may not cover both long-term and general business unless the applicant is already lawfully carrying on business of both kinds in the U.K. or the long-term business which he proposes to carry on is restricted to reinsurance or, in the case of a U.K. company, the general business is restricted to accident and health insurance: s.6.

[47] s.5. The D.T.I. has issued detailed guidance notes for applicants, which are reproduced in Part 6 of the *Encyclopedia of Insurance Law*.

[48] A U.K. company is an insurance company incorporated and with its head office in the U.K. and authorised under s.3 or s.4; a non-E.C. company is an insurance company who head office is not in a member State, which is authorised under s.3 or s.4 and whose business in the U.K. is not restricted to reinsurance: s.5(4).

[49] s.5(1A).

[50] They are set out in detail in sched. 2A.

[51] The term "controller" is defined in s.96C as the following categories of person in relation to the company itself and, in most cases, to any parent company of the company. The categories are (1) a managing director, (2) a chief executive, (3) a person in accordance with whose directions or instructions the directors are accustomed to act (4) in the case of a U.K. company, a "shareholder controller", meaning a person who, alone or with associates (defined by s.96(4)), controls 10 per cent of shares or shareholders' votes or is able to exercise a significant influence over the management of the company through the holding of shares or the exercise of voting power at any general meeting, and (5) except in the case of a U.K. company, a person who, alone or with associates (defined by s.96(4)), controls 15 per cent of shareholders' votes.

managers[52] and main agents,[53] proper direction and management of the company and the conduct of business in a sound and prudent manner.[54]

An applicant whose head office is in the United Kingdom must be a company within the Companies Act, a registered society or (but only in the case of an existing insurer applying for an extended or amended authorisation) a body corporate established by royal charter or Act of Parliament.[55] An applicant whose head office is in a member State other than the United Kingdom and which is not an E.C. company or whose head office is in an EFTA State or Switzerland[56] must have a general representative in the United Kingdom.[57] Applicants whose head offices are outside the EEA must possess assets of a prescribed value in the United Kingdom and must lodge a deposit of a prescribed amount.[58]

The Secretary of State is directed by s.7(3) not to authorise an applicant whose head office is in the United Kingdom, if it appears to him that any director, controller, manager or main agent of the applicant is not a fit and proper person to hold the position held by him. The equivalent power in relation to applicants with head offices in other Member States is confined to the fitness of main agents and "relevant executives."[59] As regards applicants with head offices outside the EEA, it applies to the applicant's United Kingdom general representative, main agents and any director, controller and manager. There is no definition of "fit and proper person" and no criteria are laid down to guide the Secretary of State in the exercise of this power, nor does the legislation expressly provide any remedy for a

---

[52] Defined by s.96D as an employee other than a chief executive who exercises managerial functions or keeps accounts or records, not being one whose functions relate exclusively to business carried on outside the U.K.

[53] Defined by s.96E as a person having authority, in respect of general business in the U.K., to enter into contracts either without limit or with a limit in excess of 10 per cent of the premium limit as determined by subs. (3) to (6).

[54] This is primarily concerned with financial management, but also includes paying due regard to the interests of policy holders and potential policyholders, the need to comply with obligations under the Act and the proper supervision of any subsidiary undertaking.

[55] s.7(1).

[56] An EFTA State is an EEA state which is not a member of the E.C.: s.5(4). In the case of a Swiss company, the authorisation sought must be to carry on general business not restricted to reinsurance.

[57] ss.8(1). See also s.10 for provisions as to the powers of the general representative.

[58] s.9.

[59] s.8(2). See s.8(4) for the definition of "relevant executive" (broadly speaking, these are executives having control of the applicant's U.K. business).

complaint against a decision of the Secretary of State, although it is clear that the public law remedy of judicial review would be available.

As far as financial matters are concerned, the Department has to be satisfied that adequate financial resources exist to support the business described in the application and provide the requisite margin or margins of solvency, or the minimum guarantee fund if greater, needed at the beginning of the fourth year following authorisation. These aspects are considered below. It also has to be satisfied that adequate reinsurance arrangements exist if a class of business requires reinsurance and that the investments forming the insurance funds will be suitable.

Authorisation is given in respect of specified classes of insurance business,[60] as detailed in Schedules 1 and 2 of the 1982 Act. Broadly speaking, these classes divide into nine types of long-term (*i.e.* life and related insurances) and 18 types of general business.[61] Since 1981 it has not been possible for new insurers to combine long-term and general business,[62] but this remains possible in respect of insurers previously authorised.

An authorisation can be revoked, wholly or partly, at the insurer's request or

(1) if it appears to have failed to satisfy its obligations,
(2) if there are grounds on which it would be refused authorisation if that were being sought,[63]
(3) if, in the case of an insurer from another E.C. State, its home state has withdrawn its authorisation or
(4) if it has ceased to carry on insurance business or failed to commence business within a year of authorisation.[64]

Continuing duties of insurers

As already mentioned, the insurance companies legislation imposes a number of duties on insurers, the most important of which are as follows.

---

[60] s.3.
[61] Part II of Sched. 2 groups together a number of the general business classes.
[62] s.6.
[63] *e.g.* on the basis that a key person is not fit and proper.
[64] ss.11 and 12. In all but the fourth case, written notice must be served on the insurer stating the ground for the proposed action and one month allowed for representations to be made.

Maintaining solvency margins

The concept of the solvency margin has been central to insurance company supervision for many years. Simply, insurers are required to maintain a minimum amount whereby their assets exceed their liabilities.[65] By this means, it is hoped, insurers will never approach actual insolvency. The actual calculation of the margin required is a complex business, involving, in addition, the application of statutory requirements as to the valuation of assets and liabilities.[66]

Non-insurance activities

Under section 16, insurers cannot carry on activities other than in connection with or for the purposes of their insurance business. However, the section does not indicate the effect of a breach on a contract entered into by an insurance company. In *Fuji Finance Inc. v. Aetna Life Insurance Co. Ltd,*[67] it was held at first instance that a contract entered into in breach of section 16 is not unlawful and unenforceable on public policy grounds, the sanction against an insurance company which breaches it being the powers of intervention conferred on the Secretary of State.[68] The views of the Court of Appeal[69] on this point are clearly *obiter,*[70] but the court was divided, Morritt L.J. following the views of the trial judge,[71] Sir Ralph Gibson preferring the contrary view and Hobhouse L.J. declining to express a conclusive view except that the arguments were nicely balanced. It is thought that the view of Morritt L.J. should be preferred because of the potential impact which could occur if a breach of section affected the validity of contracts.[72]

Localisation and matching of assets

Section 35 contains power for the Secretary of State to take regulations to introduce into the law the provisions of the E.C. Directive requiring that

---

[65] s.32.
[66] As already indicated, the solvency margin requirements apply to the members of Lloyd's taken together: s.84.
[67] [1994] 4 All E.R. 1025.
[68] See below.
[69] [1996] 4 All E.R. 608.
[70] The case was decided on another ground; see pp. 40 and 48.
[71] Although for slightly different reasons.
[72] As the Court of Appeal stated, it would be preferable for Parliament to make the matter clear for the sake of the Directives affecting insurance and other investment directives.

the reserves of an insurer required to meet known and estimated liabilities must be covered by assets situated in the country where the business is carried on.

Accounts, actuarial investigations and statements

More detailed accounts are required[73] of insurance companies than of registered companies generally, and, *inter alia*, these must be deposited with the Secretary of State. Companies which carry on long-term business are subject to actuarial investigation every year, and must appoint their own qualified actuary. All companies are required to prepare periodical statements of business in respect of each class of insurance business they underwrite.

Separation of assets

Companies which combine long-term and general insurance business must maintain separate funds in respect of the different kinds of business and the assets representing the long-term fund are available only for that business and, on a winding up, are available only to meet liabilities attributable to that business.[74] In addition, a company is prohibited from declaring a dividend when its long-term liabilities exceed its long-term assets. These are important provisions aimed obviously at protecting the policyholders with life insurance.

Changes in management and control

In accordance with the fact that the Secretary of State exercises wide powers over who manages and who controls an authorised insurer, insurers are obliged to notify him whenever there is a proposed change in this respect.[75]

The powers of intervention vested in the Secretary of State

Sections 37 to 48 of the Act give extremely wide powers to the Secretary of State. He is empowered to intervene in the affairs of an insurer

[73] ss.17–24.
[74] ss.27–29.
[75] s.62.

for a number of reasons or grounds, among the most important of which are:

(1) that he considers it necessary in order to protect a company's policyholders against the risk that the company may be unable to meet its liabilities;

(2) in the case of a United Kingdom or non-E.C. company, that it appears to him that any of the criteria of sound and prudent management is not or has not been or may not be or may not have been fulfilled with respect to the company;

(3) that a company has failed to fulfil an obligation under the Act, which refers especially to the maintenance of the solvency margin;

(4) that a company has furnished misleading or inaccurate information; and

(5) that it appears to him that a director, manager or controller of the company is not a fit and proper person.

Once a ground to intervene exists, the Secretary of State has power to require a company to do or not to do a number of things. These include the maintaining of assets in the United Kingdom, limiting premium income, producing information and the making or realising of specified investments. In the last resort, where the specific powers are not considered sufficient, he "may require a company to take such action as appears to him to be appropriate for the purpose of protecting policyholders or potential policyholders against the risk that the company may be unable to meet its liabilities or, in the case of long-term business, to fulfil the reasonable expectations of policyholders or potential policyholders".[76] The breadth of these powers is obvious.

In general, no formality surrounds the exercise of a power to intervene except that, when exercising it, the Secretary of State is required to state the ground upon which he is exercising it. Only in one case does the legislation require that notice of possible action be given to the company, which then has a chance to make representations. This is when the Secretary of State intends to take action on the ground of unfitness.[77] However, the principles of administrative law and judicial review should ensure that the powers are exercised fairly and in one notable instance of

[76] s.45.
[77] s.46.

an allegation of unfitness, the Department of Trade was severely criticised by the Ombudsman for not allowing the person concerned to present his view fully, and for not presenting to him all the evidence against him.[78]

Despite these wide ranging powers, it is clear that the Department of Trade and Industry much prefers to operate informally.[79] That, of course, is easy to do when there are strong legal powers behind informal suggestion.

Finally, in the context of the Secretary of State's powers, it should be noted that he has special powers to petition for the winding up of an insurance company.[80]

Remaining provisions of the Act

The Insurance Companies Act contains a number of other provisions concerned with the financial regulation of insurers. Notable in this connection are the provisions applicable to linked long-term policies, that is life insurance combined with a substantial investment in securities and/or property, and the provisions which apply specially to Lloyd's. The former regulate in particular the types of property which can be used for investment.[81] The latter require, inter alia, that premiums received be kept in trust funds, with separate ones in respect of life and general business, that each underwriter's accounts be audited, and that the Committee of Lloyd's deposit every year with the Secretary of State a statement summarising the extent and character of the insurance business done by the members of Lloyd's in the year.[82]

The protection of policyholders

In the event that the regulatory structure established to ensure the solvency of insurance companies fails, the law has a mechanism to ensure

---

[78] See the Second Report of the Parliamentary Commissioner for Administration, Session 1976–1977, H.C. Papers 116.

[79] A most useful account of the way the Department viewed its powers was given in the *British Insurance Law Association Bulletin*, No. 37, March 1976, by M.S. Morris, then Under-Secretary in the Insurance Division of the Department of Trade. It is unlikely that the views have changed much in the intervening years.

[80] ss.53–59.

[81] See s.78 and the Regulations made thereunder (S.I. 1994 No. 1516, reg. 43). These resulted from the recommendations of the Scott Committee on Linked Life Assurance, 1973, Cmnd. 5281.

[82] ss.83 and 86.

that policyholders are largely protected financially, by virtue of the provisions of the Policyholders Protection Acts 1975 and 1997.[83] The 1975 Act established the Policyholders Protection Board,[84] which is empowered to act for the benefit of persons holding policies of insurance issued by insurance companies which were authorised under section 3 or 4 of the 1982 Act.[85] The term "policyholder" is defined[86] as "the legal holder of the policy" and has been interpreted to mean primarily the person or persons (other than the insurer) who is or are parties to the contract contained in or evidenced by the policy.[87]

The 1997 Act significantly alters the scope of the 1975 Act but only to policies taken out after its commencement. The original scheme will continue to apply in some cases for some years. Under this, a crucial point is that protection is given to holders of "United Kingdom policies".

A "United Kingdom policy" exists where the performance by the insurer of any of his obligations under the contract evidenced by the policy would constitute the carrying on by the insurer of insurance business of any class in the United Kingdom.[88] A wide construction has been given to these words so that the performance of obligations under an insurance policy effected in the United Kingdom, notably the paying of claims, will always constitute the carrying on of insurance business within the United Kingdom wherever the claims are paid, because payment under such a policy is part and parcel of carrying on insurance business in the United Kingdom.[89] However, the restriction of the original Act to authorised insurance companies, which includes both United Kingdom insurers and foreign insurers authorised to set up branches, means that it does not apply to insurers from other E.C. member States providing services under the

---

[83] The original Act was introduced following the spectacular and very public failure of a large life insurance company.

[84] s.1 of the 1975 Act.

[85] ss.3 and 4 of the 1975 Act.

[86] s.32 of the 1975 Act by reference to s.96 of the 1982 Act.

[87] *Scher v. Policyholders Protection Board* [1993] 3 All E.R. 384, [1993] 4 All E.R. 840, [1994] 2 All E.R. 37. It can also mean a person to whom a sum is due under the policy before the beginning of the liquidation, if all the preconditions to the liability of the insurer have been satisfied (this could include someone with statutory rights under the Third Parties (Rights against Insurers) Act 1930 — see Chap. 18 — or the Road Traffic Act 1988 — see Chap. 19). It does not include someone who becomes a policyholder in this sense subsequently to the commencement of the liquidation.

[88] s.4(2).

[89] *Scher v. Policyholders Protection Board* [1993] 3 All E.R. 384.

Third Directives,[90] nor to Lloyd's underwriters, nor to companies which act without authorisation. The 1997 Act amends the scope of the 1975 Act by, in particular, including policies issued by E.C. insurers and defining the risks protected by reference to their location within the United Kingdom or within the E.C. if the policy is issued by an authorised insurance company.

The Board has two principal functions. First, it is under a duty to ensure that certain measures are taken when an insurance company goes into liquidation.[91] In respect of the liabilities of a liquidated company concerning compulsory insurances,[92] it must ensure that these are fully met.[93] In respect of non-compulsory insurances, it must ensure that private policyholders[94] receive 90 per cent of the benefits which are due to them.[95] In the case of long-term policies which have not matured, this must be done by securing the continuity of the policies, for example by transfer to another insurer.[96]

The second function of the Board is to assist an insurance company which is in financial difficulties by giving direct financial assistance or by arranging for the transfer of business under the provisions of the 1982 Act.[97]

The Board is financed, when necessary, by a levy on all authorised insurance companies which must not exceed one per cent of a company's net premium income in the relevant year. In appropriate cases, the Board can also demand a levy from certain intermediaries.[98]

---

[90] For this reason, such insurers must disclose that they are not U.K.-authorised: Insurance Companies Regulations S.I. 1994 No. 1516, reg. 33.

[91] ss.5 to 12 of the 1975 Act.

[92] That is, motor insurance required by the Road Traffic Act 1988, employers' liability insurance required by the Employers' Liability (Compulsory Insurance) Act 1969, insurance effected under s.1 of the Riding Establishments Act 1964 and insurance effected under s.19 of the Nuclear Installations Act 1965.

[93] Under s.7 of the 1975 Act, the Board has a direct duty to satisfy the claims of a third party victim of a motor accident who would be entitled to sue the insurer under s.151 of the Road Traffic Act 1988; see pp. 375–378, below.

[94] "Private" here means an individual or partnership or other unincorporated body, all of the members of which are individuals, but it is not confined to non-commercial policyholders: *Scher v. Policyholders Protection Board* [1993] 4 All E.R. 840, [1994] 2 All E.R. 37.

[95] As to the meaning of this, see n.87, above.

[96] s.11.

[97] ss.16 and 17.

[98] ss.18 to 22.

CHAPTER 3

INSURABLE INTEREST

Insurable interest is a basic requirement of any contract of insurance unless it can be, and is, lawfully waived. At a general level, this means that the party to the insurance contract who is the insured or policyholder must have a particular relationship with the subject-matter of the insurance, whether that be a life or property or a liability to which he might be exposed. The absence of the required relationship will render the contract illegal, void or simply unenforceable, depending on the type of insurance. We have already stressed the essential differences between life and other insurances in many respects,[1] and the law regarding insurable interest is one situation where the differences can be crucial. A brief examination of the history of the insurable interest requirement[2] reveals this.

History of the requirement

Simply, a contract of life insurance was enforceable at common law despite the absence of any relationship between the insured and the life insured, and even in the face of judicial reluctance. The reason for this was that wagers in general were legally enforceable[3] and thus the courts had no option but to enforce wagers in the form of life insurance contracts. An increase in these practices, which were clearly distasteful[4] and which indeed could serve as an inducement to murder, led to growing concern and, ultimately, legislative action in the form of the Life Assurance Act 1774.

As far as other types of insurance were concerned, namely indemnity contracts, there was abundant authority recognising as valid marine

---

[1] See Chap. 1.

[2] For more detail, see *MacGillivray*, Chap. 1.

[3] See, *e.g. March v. Piggott* (1771) 2 Burr. 2862, a bet as to which father of the parties would live longer. In certain instances wagers were not enforceable, particularly where public policy intervened or where the matter was regarded as a waste of the court's time.

[4] See the preamble to the Life Assurance Act 1774.

policies without interest,[5] which, as has been seen earlier, were the other common form of insurance at the time. However, statute, in the form of the Marine Insurance Act 1745, put a stop to this practice. The exact position with regard to non-marine indemnity policies is not clear. By analogy with life and marine policies, the mere fact of there being no interest, at least at the date of the contract, should not have affected the validity of such policies. However, as such contracts were and are, in most cases,[6] contracts only to indemnify the insured against a loss he actually suffers, the insured could only recover if he showed that he had suffered a loss, in other words that he had an interest at the time of loss.[7] Further, there is authority concerning a fire policy on buildings,[8] which precedes any statutory requirement, that interest was required by the common law both at the date of the contract and at the date of the loss.

In any event, the legislature intervened with a series of statutes, finally rendering all contracts by way of gaming or wagering void under section 18 of the Gaming Act 1845. The details of the relevant provisions will be examined shortly, but it is useful at this stage briefly to summarise how the various statutory provisions apply to the various types of insurance:

    (i) marine policies are now governed by the Marine Insurance Act 1906, by section 4 of which such policies without interest are void[9];

    (ii) life policies are governed by the 1774 Act and a failure to show interest renders a policy illegal[10];

    (iii) all other policies except those on "goods and merchandises"[11] may also be covered by the Life Assurance Act, despite the misleading short title[12];

    (iv) in respect of policies on goods, there is no statutory requirement of insurable interest *per se*. However, the Gaming Act 1845 will strike down any goods policy which is really a wager, and, it seems, the Marine Insurance Act 1788 still

---

[5] See *MacGillivray*, (8th ed.) para. 15.

[6] See Chap. 13.

[7] *Lynch v. Dalzell* (1729) 4 Bro.P.C. 431.

[8] *Sadler's Co. v. Badcock* (1743) 2 Atk. 554.

[9] But not illegal: *Edwards (John) & Co. v. Motor Union Insurance Co.* [1922] 2 K.B. 249.

[10] *Harse v. Pearl Life Assurance Co.* [1904] 1 K.B. 558; see further below, p. 47.

[11] s.4 of the 1774 Act expressly exempts these.

[12] This is a controversial question which is discussed below at pp. 48–52.

technically requires that every goods policy contain the name
of a person interested therein.[13]

We shall now examine quite separately the requirement of insurable
interest in life insurance on the one hand and in property insurances on the
other. One general point should, however, be stressed at this stage, which
is that the strict legal requirements may in some instances be honoured
more in the breach than the observance, particularly in the field of life
insurance. Illustrations of this are certain policies insuring the lives of
children and some group insurances of employees. There is no justification
for this state of affairs and detailed examples and suggestions for reform
will be made at the appropriate stages.

Insurable Interest in Life Insurance[14]

Section 1 of the Life Assurance Act 1774 requires the insured to have an
insurable interest in the life insured. The other relevant provisions of the
Act require the names of persons interested to be inserted in the policy
(s.2) and declare that when the insured has an interest, he can recover no
more than the amount of the value of his interest (s.3). These provisions
raise four basic questions: the time at which interest is required; the very
nature of insurable interest; attempted evasions and the meaning of section
2; and the effect of a policy without interest.

The time when interest is required

It is convenient to consider this first, simply because it is the most
straightforward question. There can be little doubt that section 1 of the
Act on its own can be read as requiring interest at the time a policy is
effected, but no more. However, section 3 of the Act, talking as it does in

---

[13] This Act applied to land policies on goods as well as marine policies. It was
repealed by the 1906 Act but only in so far as it related to marine risks (see
Sched. 2). It is a matter for doubt how far the requirement is ever consciously
heeded. Certainly purely oral insurance policies on goods are recognised as valid
despite it (see Chap. 4).

[14] Life insurance for these purposes includes any insurance where there is some
cover provided in the event of the death of the life insured, even if the cover is no
greater than the surrender value of the policy at any time: *Fuji Finance Inc. v.
Aetna Life Insurance Ltd* [1996] 4 All E.R. 608. For a general critique, see Merkin,
(1980) 9 Anglo- American L.R. 331.

terms of the insured recovering only the value of his interest, might be thought to require interest at the time of loss, *i.e.* at the date of the death of the life insured. This was the decision in the old case of *Godsall v. Boldero*,[15] which held, in effect, that a policy by a creditor on the life of his debtor was an indemnity policy because section 3 permitted recovery in language appropriate to the concept of indemnity against a loss.

However, *Godsall v. Boldero* was overruled in the landmark case of *Dalby v. India and London Life Assurance Co.*,[16] a decision which has stood unchallenged for well over a century and which established beyond doubt that it is necessary for the insured to have an interest only at the time the policy is effected. The *Dalby* case was not strictly a case of life insurance, but rather the reinsurance of a life policy.[17] The plaintiff was the director of a company which had insured the life of the Duke of Cambridge, and which reinsured the risk with the defendant. The original policies were cancelled, but the plaintiff kept paying the premiums on the reinsurance policy until the Duke died. The defendant then denied liability on the ground that the plaintiff had no interest in the Duke's life at the date of his death, having himself nothing to pay out on it. The Exchequer Chamber found for the plaintiff, holding that section 3 of the 1774 Act applied only to require the insured to value his interest at the date of effecting the policy. As section 1 was satisfied, because the plaintiff did have interest at the time he reinsured, and as there was no common law requirement that the plaintiff prove interest at the date of loss, he was entitled to recover.

While there are difficulties with regard to the construction of section 3, which looks as though it refers to the time of loss, and while the *Dalby* case could lead to certain mischiefs to which we shall refer, there is no doubt that the decision is totally justifiable. To hold the contrary would be against justice and fair dealing, as the premiums paid on a life policy are calculated on actuarial principles according to the probable duration of the life. They are fixed just as the sum payable on death is fixed. There is no comparison with the assessment of a risk under an indemnity policy, even though it can hardly be denied that certain life policies are intended to

---

[15] (1807) 9 East 72, followed in *Henson v. Blackwell* (1845) 4 Hare 434.

[16] (1854) 15 C.B. 365. In fact the insurers in *Godsall v. Boldero* repented and paid out, following the outcry against them after the decision: see Lord Blackburn in *Burnand v. Rodocanachi* (1882) 1 App.Cas. 333, at 340–341.

[17] See also on this, following *Dalby, Southern Cross Assurance Co. Ltd v. Australian Provincial Assurance Association Ltd* (1935) 53 C.L.R. 618 (High Court of Australia).

indemnify against a possible loss, a point we shall return to again. To allow an insurer who has assessed the risk under a life policy in the usual way to resile from his bargain for these reasons would be quite absurd.[18]

Consequences of Dalby

However, the *Dalby* case has consequences which may be regarded as mischievous. These will arise only where the insured is not also himself the life insured or where an insured assigns[19] a policy on his own life to a party with no interest. An example will illustrate the point. As will be seen, a creditor may insure his debtor's life for the amount of his debt. Indeed it is not uncommon for financiers to effect group policies on their debtors. The debt may be repaid shortly thereafter, yet the creditor may keep up the policy until the debtor dies, which may be many years later. Is there not an element of wagering here? One of the reasons for requiring insurable interest has been said[20] to be the removal of an inducement to murder the life insured, yet the creditor has a strong motive for murder.[21] In essence, this sort of policy is surely intended to indemnify the creditor against the loss he may suffer by the debtor not repaying his debt before he dies, and the same can be said of other common types of policy, for example, by employers on the lives of their employees. It could be suggested that once the insured ceases to have an interest in the life insured, the latter should have the option of taking over the policy for his own benefit, subject to some compensation to the insured in respect of the premiums he has paid.[22] Thus, in effect, the consent of the life insured would be necessary

---

[18] Further, many forms of life insurance today are in reality investments where the actual insurance element is a relatively minor part of the benefits provided, and there is very little expectation that death will occur during the currency of the policy. For an example of the latter point, see *Fuji Finance Inc. v. Aetna Life Insurance Ltd* [1996] 4 All E.R. 608, where the sum insured on death was the same as the surrender value of the policy at any time, and the potential return if the switching of investments had continued as successfully as it had been effected up to the date the policy was surrendered, was the gross national product of the U.K. for 460,000 years! The policy was surrendered for a mere £1,100,000!

[19] As to assignment of a life policy, see Chap. 17.

[20] See *Worthington v. Curtis* [1875] 1 Ch.D. 419; McGovern, "Homicide and succession to property," (1969) 68 Mich.L.Rev. 65 at 78.

[21] Of course one would hope that he would be deterred by the criminal consequences, but not all murders are solved. Should the civil law permit the survival of an inducement to murder?

[22] An alternative would be to confine recovery by the insured to the surrender value of the policy at the time interest ceases.

for the continuation of a policy where interest had ceased. This is an area which deserves careful consideration at least in the context of the general examination of the insurable interest requirement which, it will be argued, is desirable.

The nature of insurable interest

Despite stipulating that an interest is required, the 1774 Act does not say, in so many words, exactly what is an insurable interest in a life. However, the provisions of section 3, to which we have already adverted, indicate that it means a pecuniary or financial interest, because the section talks of "the amount of the value of the interest of the insured." In general this has been the approach adopted by the courts.

There are two cases, though, where insurable interest is presumed and where section 3 is regarded as inapplicable, the reason being that they are outside the mischief of wagering which the 1774 Act was passed to prevent.[23] Insurances on the insured's own life[24] or on the life of a spouse[25] are automatically valid regardless of the amount insured. This presumption probably extends to the fiancé(e) insuring the life of his or her fiancé(e).[26] However, it does not extend to other family relationships.

Apart from in these cases, the requirement of pecuniary interest means that the law is very strict, and, indeed, is no doubt stricter than common practice would indicate. Essentially, the insured must show that he would suffer financially by the loss of a legal right on the death of the life insured and it is only the amount of likely loss that can be covered. The law is perhaps best illustrated by examining separately family relationships, other than that of husband and wife, from other relationships.

Family relationships

So far as family relationships are concerned, it is clear that a child who is a minor would have an insurable interest in the lives of his or her parents,

---

[23] *Griffiths v. Fleming* [1909] 1 K.B. 805, esp. at 821. Because of the lack of, or the lack of the need for, a pecuniary interest in one's own life, it has been held that there is no loss recoverable in a negligence claim against a person who fails, in breach of duty, to effect a policy: *Lynne v. Gordon Doctors & Walton, The Times*, June 17, 1991.

[24] *Wainewright v. Bland* (1835) 1 Moo. & R. 481.

[25] *Griffiths v. Fleming*, above. Cf. Married Women's Property Act 1882, s.11, (see Chap. 17) which allows a married woman to insure her own and her husband's life.

[26] This is certainly the view of one Insurance Ombudsman; see the Annual Report for 1989, paras 2.31–2.35. It is suggested that the presumption should also apply to an unmarried couple living together.

if they are legally obliged to support the child, as the child would clearly therefore suffer financially, by the loss of a legal right on their death. Whether or not there is such a legal obligation is unclear. There is no such obligation under English common law,[27] but statutory procedures may lead to such an obligation. For example, if a maintenance order has been made, compelling a parent to provide for a child, the child must have an insurable interest in the parent's life. In all cases, though, there is the problem of valuing the interest as required under section 3 of the 1774 Act. It may be that an unlimited interest could be presumed as in the case of spouses. Insurance by an minor child on the life of a parent is surely outside the mischief of the Act. However, on principle and authority,[28] an adult child can have no such insurable interest unless he can prove some legal obligation arising on the death of his parent. In *Harse v. Pearl Life Assurance Co. Ltd*,[29] a son insured the life of his mother who lived with him and kept house for him. The insurance was expressly declared to be "for funeral expenses." It was held by the Court of Appeal that the policy was illegal for lack of interest, there being no legal obligation on the son to bury his mother when she died, and she not being legally bound to keep house for him. The existence of a legal obligation of any sort must in practice be extremely unlikely. In all these cases, of course, there is no objection to a parent insuring his or her own life and even naming a child as beneficiary, provided that the insurance is genuinely own-life, a point to which we shall return.

The converse situation of a parent insuring the life of a child raises interesting problems, for there is no doubt that such insurances are effected in practice. *Halford v. Kymer*[30] is authority for the fact a parent would not usually have the necessary interest, except possibly to cover funeral expenses,[31] because there is no other financial loss arising. There can be no other legal obligation on a parent to incur expenditure on the death of a

---

[27] *Bazeley v. Forder* (1868) L.R. 3 Q.B. 559. In Scots Law, there is such an obligation which extends quite widely throughout the family; see *MacGillivray*, (8th ed.) paras. 101–105.

[28] *Shilling v. Accidental Death Insurance Co.* (1857) 2 H. & N. 42; *Harse v. Pearl Life Assurance Co. Ltd* [1904] 1 K.B. 558.

[29] [1904] 1 K.B. 558.

[30] (1830) 10 B. & C. 724.

[31] While there used to be an obligation to bury one's children, this may now in fact be obsolete, as local authorities are now obliged to bury any person who dies in their area; see *MacGillivray*, (8th ed.) para. 92. Insurance of funeral expenses used to be permissible in the area of industrial life assurance.

child. Even if a parent is being supported by his adult child, there is no obligation and hence no interest,[32] and it goes without saying that the parent who is not being supported has no interest. It appears that in practice parents do insure the lives of their children. One example[33] is a personal accident policy taken out when the family is travelling. Clearly such insurance is justified on the ground that extra expense would be incurred if the child died away from home. But as there is no obligation to incur such expense, it is difficult to see strictly how there is insurable interest in this sort of case, and even if there is, under section 3 of the 1774 Act, the amount recoverable is only the actual costs likely to be incurred which should be valued when the policy is effected. Some statutory authorisation of these insurances, to a carefully defined extent, seems essential.

Outside the context of parent and child, there is one curious case[34] holding that a *de facto* guardian had an insurable interest in the life of her infant step-sister, on the ground that she had promised the child's dying mother that she would take care of her and thus incurred expenditure. This decision simply cannot be supported in the absence of an obligation on the child to repay the guardian, so that the latter would suffer financial loss in the event of the child's prior demise; such an obligation is surely most unlikely in practice. This case has never been overruled but there is a Privy Council decision to the opposite effect on similar facts.[35]

Business relationships

In respect of relationships of a business character, insurance may be effected by, for example, a creditor on the life of his debtor, an employer on the life of his employee, or vice versa, and a partner on the life of his partner. In all these cases, however, the amount of interest is limited again to the pecuniary interest of the insured. The point is nicely illustrated by the old case of *Hebdon v. West*.[36] A bank clerk insured his employer's life

---

[32] See *Halford v. Kymer*, above.

[33] Another might be school fees insurance, depending upon how it is effected. The problems here have their parallels in cases involving trusts or alleged trusts of life policies. These cases are considered in Chap. 17.

[34] *Barnes v. London, Edinburgh & Glasgow Life Assurance Co. Ltd* [1892] 1 Q.B. 864.

[35] *Anctil v. Manufacturer's Life Insurance Co.* [1899] A.C. 604; see also the comments of the Court of Appeal in *Griffiths v. Fleming*, above, at 819 and of Lord Alvestone C.J. in *Harse v. Pearl Life Assurance Co.* [1903] 2 K.B. 92 at 96, doubting the decision in *Barnes*.

[36] (1863) 3 B. & S. 579.

with two insurers, one policy being for £5,000, the other for £2,500. The clerk had a contract of employment for seven years at a salary of £600 *per* annum, and he owed his employer £4,700, the latter having promised that he would not call in the debt during his lifetime. When his employer died, the clerk received the £5,000 from the first insurer. The refusal of the second insurer to honour its contract was upheld by the court. It was accepted that the insured had an insurable interest in his employer's life to the extent of what he was contractually entitled to under his contract of employment, *i.e.* a maximum of £4,200, because he stood to suffer this loss by the loss of a legal right. However, he had no interest by virtue of the promise not to call in the debt as he had provided no consideration and hence the promise was not legally enforceable.[37] As his interest was more than satisfied by the payment of the first insurer,[38] the second was not liable.

Perhaps more than the decisions involving family relationships, *Hebdon v. West* illustrates that, in substance and despite what has often been said, the effect of section 3 of the 1774 Act is to render this sort of life insurance in law a contract of indemnity, the difference from the normal indemnity principle being that the measure of the insured's loss is judged at the time the policy is effected rather than at the time of loss. The result is hardly just, particularly when compared with that in the *Dalby* case. *Hebdon* was not a case of gaming or wagering and the insurer had received premiums based, one assumes, on usual actuarial considerations.

It seems most unlikely that in practice the decision is applied. Provided that the insured has an interest in the life insured, a valuation of that interest within the strict confines of section 3 is unlikely. Take, for example, the case of an employer insuring the life of an employee, a common practice particularly under group insurance policies. As a matter of strict law, the employer's interest will be only the value of the services which he will lose if the employee dies.[39] While, in the case of a most valuable employee with a lengthy service contract, that may be a substantial sum, in the case of a less exalted employee, it can be at most the equivalent of the period of notice that the employee must lawfully give

---

[37] *Quaere* whether the promise might not now be binding under the doctrine of promissory estoppel.

[38] Presumably the first insurer could not recover back the "excess" he had paid, as it was money paid under a mistake of law, which is generally irrecoverable: see Chap. 12 at p. 258.

[39] *Simcock v. Scottish Imperial Insurance Co.* (1902) 10 S.L.T. 286.

to determine his employment. In fact employees are insured for sums which may bear no relation to the strict legal value. Two relatively recent cases illustrate this, although in neither was the point the subject of any dispute between the parties.[40] In *Green v. Russell*,[41] an employee architect was one of a group insured by the employer. The sum insured was £1,000. In law the employer received the money when the employee was killed and the latter's representatives had no claim.[42] It is difficult to believe that that figure was strictly the pecuniary interest of the employer. Similarly, in *Marcel Beller Ltd v. Hayden*,[43] the relevant facts involved a group policy. Here the insurable interest point was adverted to, and the learned judge commented[44] that it was not in question that the insured employers had an insurable interest in their deceased employee's life. While this is perfectly correct, the amount of that interest may not strictly have been the £15,000 for which the employee was insured, but the point was simply not considered. It cannot be said that a section of a statute which is so obviously ignored serves any useful purpose.

Attempted evasions and section 2

Section 1 of the Life Assurance Act 1774 does not require simply that the insured has an interest in the life insured. It also stipulates that any person "for whose use, benefit, or on whose account" a policy is made must have an interest, and by section 2,[45] the names of the insured and any beneficiaries must be inserted in the policy, on pain of the policy being illegal. The purpose behind these provisions is clearly to prevent evasions of the basic requirement so that if, for example, A appears to insure his own life, but in fact B is insuring A's life, or the insurance is for B's benefit, B must have an interest and B's name must appear in the policy.

[40] See also the sums involved in the *Fuji Finance* case, referred to in n.18, above, and at p. 48, below, where the insured was the company which insured the life of its controller.

[41] [1959] 2 Q.B. 226.

[42] See below at p. 337. The case is cited by the Law Commission (Law Com. 242, 1996, paras 12.23 and 12.24) as an example of where their suggested reforms of the law of privity of contract (see p. 65, below) might still not entitle the employee's representatives to claim directly on the policy.

[43] [1978] Q.B. 694. See further below at p. 212.

[44] *ibid.* at p. 697.

[45] Subject to the Insurance Companies Amendment Act 1973, s.50, discussed below.

The word "benefit" in this context must not be read too widely. The fact that a man in insuring his own life intends ultimately to benefit his wife and children, as must be common, does not mean that the wife and children must have an interest under section 1 and be named under section 2. Only if the direct purpose of effecting the policy is to confer an immediate benefit on another[46] can the requirement be applicable.

A strict application of section 2 can lead to unjust results. In *Evans v. Bignold*,[47] a wife appeared to insure her own life. In fact the insurance was effected because her husband borrowed money from the trustees of a will under which the wife was entitled to money when she became 21. The trustees insisted on the husband providing security, and the surety insisted that he insure his wife's life. The husband was not named in the policy. It was held that he should have been, as a person interested, under section 2, and the failure to do so meant that the policy was illegal. In fact, of course, he had an insurable interest in his wife's life, so section 1 was satisfied, and the result is unnecessary.

It is suggested that section 2 is in fact superfluous. If A insures his own life for the benefit of B, but B has an insurable interest, whether or not B is named in the policy should not affect its validity, as there is no element of gaming or wagering. If B has no interest in A's life, the policy is illegal under section 1, even if B is expressly named in the policy. If B is not named, and on the face of it the policy appears to be effected by A on his own life, the court can nonetheless enquire into the realities of the situation and find such a policy illegal under section 1 if it was really intended for B who has no interest. In *Shilling v. Accidental Death Insurance Co.*,[48] a father effected a policy on his own life, but the evidence showed that it was his son who was entirely instrumental in the transaction and who paid the premiums, and that the policy was for the benefit of the son, as the father immediately afterwards executed a will in his favour. It was held that in reality the policy was made by the son on the life of his father in which he had no insurable interest. It was, therefore, illegal under section 1.[49]

However, as will be seen in detail later,[50] there is no bar to an insured's assigning a policy of life insurance to someone without interest. This would appear to be the easiest legal solution to the problem of cases without

---

[46] As in *Evans v. Bignold* (1869) L.R. 4 Q.B. 622, discussed below.
[47] (1869) L.R. 4 Q.B. 622.
[48] (1857) 2 H. & N. 42.
[49] It would also have failed s.2.
[50] See Chap. 17.

interest. Provided that A who effects a policy on his own life does so genuinely, when he has done so, he can assign the policy to whomsoever he pleases (to B) and there is no need at all for B to have an interest in A's life nor to have his name inserted under section 2. The line appears to be a very fine one between A taking out a policy in order to benefit B, and A *bona fide* effecting a policy with an intention of assigning the benefit but with no particular assignee in mind. The first case would fall foul of section 2 if B's name were not inserted and of section 1 if it was really a case of B insuring A's life in which he had no interest. The second is perfectly valid.[51]

It has already been pointed out that section 2 of the 1774 Act appears superfluous. In certain instances it was clearly also a most inconvenient nuisance, particularly in respect of group policies, for example, a policy taken out by an employer to cover the whole of, or the whole of a class of, his employees. If the policy was solely for the employer's benefit, then of course section 2 would not apply. But if the policy were effected for the benefit of the employees, they would all have had to be named in it. Because of the inconvenience, section 50 of the Insurance Companies Amendment Act 1973 now provides that, in such a case, section 2 of the 1774 Act does not invalidate a policy for the benefit of unnamed individuals within a class or description if the class or description is stated in the policy and every member is identifiable at any time.

The effect of a policy without interest

There is a difference between the wording of sections 1 and 2 of the 1774 Act. Failure to comply with section 2 expressly renders the policy unlawful, but section 1 says merely that policies without interest "shall be null and void to all intents and purposes whatsoever." Despite this, there is clear authority[52] that a breach of section 1 does render a policy illegal. The usual practical consequence of this concerns the recovery of premiums paid on an illegal policy if the insurer in fact takes the point.[53] Except in such cases, of which in any event there is no modern reported example,[54]

---

[51] *M'Farlane v. Royal London Friendly Society* (1886) 2 T.L.R. 755.
[52] *Harse v. Pearl Life Assurance Co. Ltd* [1904] 1 K.B. 558.
[53] This is dealt with in Chap. 8.
[54] Note, though, the case that went to the Ombudsman (n.26, p. 41, above) where the insured argued for the return of his premiums on the ground that the policy he had effected was illegal for lack of interest.

insurers do not often raise the point for the obviously sensible reason that
to do so in respect of a policy on which premiums had been duly paid
could rightly attract unfavourable publicity. It is noteworthy, though, that
the insurers did successfully plead that a contract of life insurance was void
for lack of insurable interest[55] in the recent decision in *Fuji Finance Ltd Inc.
v. Aetna Life Insurance Ltd*,[56] in order that they could resist a claim for
damages for breach of contract.[57]

If insurers have paid out under an illegal policy and there is a dispute
between rival claimants to the money, the illegality is ignored.[58] If an
insurer did not pay, not because of illegality but relying upon some other
defence, the Court should raise the illegality point and refuse to enforce the
contract on this ground.[59]

Reform of the law

The law on insurable interest in life insurances is clearly out of touch
with reality in many respects, as has been pointed out in the preceding
account. It is suggested that a general reform is necessary which might
well follow the useful precedent set by the Australian Insurance Contracts
Act 1984.[60] This assumes that a requirement of interest is still desirable,
but sets out a list of relationships in respect of which it is permissible for
one person to insure the life of another.[61]

Insurable Interest in Property Insurance

Statutory or contractual requirement

Turning to the law regarding insurable interest in property insurances,
the first consideration must be an attempt to clarify the extent to which

---

[55] Or at least that the interest was substantially more than permitted by s.3.
Strictly, the whole policy must have been void and illegal, but the insurers had
paid the surrender value at the time they terminated it.
[56] [1996] 4 All E.R. 608; see n.18, above.
[57] The insurers had terminated the contract because of the phenomenal success of
the life insured in "switching" the linked investments (see n.18). The insured
claimed that this was in breach of contract.
[58] *Worthington v. Curtis* (1875) 1 Ch.D. 419, *Carter v. Renouf* (1962) 36 A.L.J.R. 67.
[59] *e.g. Gedge v. Royal Exchange Assurance Corp.* [1900] 2 Q.B. 214.
[60] ss.18 and 19. See also the article by Merkin referred to in n.14 above and Tarr
(1986) 60 A.L.J. 613.
[61] For discussion of other possibilities, namely abandoning the requirement of
interest altogether and relying on the general prohibition on wagering and on
public policy or imposing a requirement of consent by the life insured, see the
Australian Law Reform Commission's Discussion Paper No. 7, paras. 26 and 27
and their Report No. 20, paras. 134-138.

the statutory requirements apply. There is no doubt that section 18 of the Gaming Act 1845 applies to all such insurances,[62] so that any insurance on property with which the insured has no connection at all nor any prospect of a connection is void. This requirement cannot, however, be too difficult to satisfy and is certainly much easier to satisfy than the strict requirement of insurable interest which will be discussed shortly.

Application of the 1774 Act

The Life Assurance Act 1774 clearly does not apply to insurances of goods, for these are expressly exempted by section 4. Whether or not it applies to insurances of real property is a question of some difficulty which has occasioned opposing views. In one Court of Appeal case, *Re King*,[63] it was stated, *obiter,* that the Act did apply, while a more recent dictum of the same court in *Mark Rowlands Ltd v. Berni Inns Ltd*[64] is to the contrary effect. In the latter case, where the insurer of a landlord was arguing that the landlord's unnamed tenant could not benefit from the insurance because the tenant was not named in the policy as required by section 2, Kerr L.J. stated that "this ancient statute was not intended to apply, and does not apply to indemnity insurances, but only to insurances which provide for the payment of a specified sum upon the happening of an insured event."[65] More recently, in *Siu Yin Kwan v. Eastern Insurance Co. Ltd*,[66] the Privy Council followed the opinion of Kerr L.J. in holding that section 2 did not apply to a policy of liability insurance. It was said that the words "event or events" were not apt to describe an insured's potential liability and that section 2 must take colour from the short title and preamble to section 1. "By no stretch of imagination could indemnity insurance be described as 'a mischievous kind of gaming'. Their Lordships

---

[62] *Macaura v. Northern Assurance Co. Ltd* [1925] 2 A.C. 619.
[63] [1963] Chap. 459 at 485 (per Lord Denning M.R.). This dictum was relied upon by *MacGillivray and Parkington*, 8th ed., para. 153, in support of the application of the Act to real property insurance, but was ignored in Ivamy's *Fire and Motor Insurance*, pp. 175–181, putting the opposite view. Clarke, *The Law of Insurance Contracts*, para. 4–4A, points out that, whatever the strict legal position, insurance practice has largely ignored the Act. See also the Australian High Court decision in *British Traders' Insurance Co. v. Monson* (1964) 111 C.L.R. 86.
[64] [1986] Q.B. 211. The ratio of this case concerns an insurer's subrogation rights and this aspect of it is discussed below at pp. 303–305.
[65] [1986] Q.B. at 227.
[66] [1994] 1 All E.R. 213. The case is considered further at p. 66, below.

are entitled to give section 2 a meaning which corresponds with the obvious legislative intent."[67]

While it must be recognised that the decision in *Siu Yin Kwan* can be interpreted as having resolved the issue, it is respectfully submitted that the reasoning and the authorities, especially those relied upon by Kerr L.J. in *Mark Rowlands Ltd* are not wholly convincing,[68] and it is thought that the matter still merits some discussion. The strongest support for the modern view comes perhaps from the decision in *Mumford Hotels Ltd v. Wheler*,[69] a case where a tenant unnamed in a landlord's insurance policy was held entitled to compel the landlord to use insurance moneys for reinstatement, this right being implied from the terms of the lease.[70] On the other hand, a literal reading of sections 1 and 2 seems clearly to suggest, with the reference to "other event or events", that they comprehend real property insurance, even if, as was clearly only the strict ratio of *Siu Yin Kwan*, they may not be apt to refer to liability insurance. Although it may be admitted that indemnity insurances of real property were not within the primary mischief the Act was designed to prevent, since the principal reason was to prohibit wagering on lives and, well before the Act was passed, there was authority that the common law required an insurable interest in insurances on buildings at the time of the policy,[71] it seems unlikely that there were in existence in 1774 non-indemnity, *i.e.* valued, insurances on buildings which could be caught by the Act. Given that section 4 expressly exempted marine and goods policies and that it is unlikely that in 1774 forms of insurance other than life, marine, goods and buildings insurance existed, the words "other event or events" must surely literally incorporate ordinary insurances of real property. It is also notable that when passing later legislation, Parliament seems to have assumed that the 1774 Act had a wider application than Kerr L.J.'s dictum would allow.[72] Further, reliance on the short title of the

---

[67] *ibid.* at 224, per Lord Lloyd of Berwick.
[68] Although Kerr L.J. made no reference to the dictum in *Re King*, the Privy Council did, dismissing Lord Denning's view on the ground that his observation was *obiter* and the point was not argued.
[69] [1964] Chap. 117.
[70] This case is discussed further below at p. 283.
[71] *Sadler's Co. v. Badcock* (1743) 2 Atk. 554.
[72] See especially s.148(7) of the Road Traffic Act 1988, discussed further at p. 365, below, where the words "Notwithstanding anything in any enactment" seem apt to refer to the 1774 Act by allowing enforcement of a motor policy by anyone

1774 Act seems somewhat misplaced as that was only "added" a century after the Act was passed.

The application of section 1 to real property insurances would cause no problems, and there is an attractive construction of section 2 which would remove the difficulties posed in the recent decisions. This was propounded in the Australian case of *Davjoyda Estates Ltd v. National Insurance Co. of New Zealand*,[73] and is to the effect that section 2 applies only when the insured himself has no interest to satisfy section 1 but is insuring on behalf of another with an interest who must therefore be named. This construction is consistent with the mischief which the 1774 Act was designed to prevent and does remove the inconvenience of having to list all the persons interested in an insurance. It is perhaps a pity that it was not considered in *Mark Rowlands Ltd* or *Siu Yin Kwan*.[74]

However, there is a problem in applying section 3 to real property insurances. This provides that where the insured has an interest, no greater sum can be recovered from the insurer than the amount of the value of his interest. It thus appears to imply that even where another person would be named in the policy, in accordance with section 2, and that other person's interest is insured, only the value of the insured's interest can strictly be recovered. If, for example, a tenant insures the house and names his landlord as interested, recovery is limited to the value ·of the tenant's interest, which may be much less than the value of the property or the sum insured.[75] Furthermore, section 3 is unnecessary in the case of property insurances for these are usually contracts of indemnity and the insured can recover only the value of his interest at the date of loss. This

named in the policy, notwithstanding that the actual insured has no insurable interest in a named person's liability. The fact that case-law reached the same result (see p. 60, below) does not destroy the force of this point. In fact in many of the cases on "waiver" of insurable interest (see pp. 58–60, below), it seems to have been assumed that the 1774 Act applied to all insurances except those on goods, as the argument has often turned on the meaning of "on goods" rather than on any wider point such as that propounded in *Mark Rowlands Ltd* and *Siu Yin Kwan*. See especially *Williams v. Baltic Insurance Association of London* [1924] 2 K.B. 282.

[73] (1967) 65 S.R. (N.S.W.) 381 at 428, *per* Manning J. This construction was cited with approval by the Australian Law Reform Commission, Report No. 20, para. 112, although, as noted elsewhere (p. 54), Australia has solved any problems in this area by a wide-ranging reform.

[74] It is also inconsistent with the dictum in *Re King*!

[75] The point was not considered in *Re King*, above, but there the tenant insured had an interest to the full value of the property, because he had covenanted to repair.

principle clearly existed before the 1774 Act was passed. A possible solution to this problem would be to read section 3 as not applying to property insurances, as not being within the mischief intended to be prevented,[76] or as no more than confirmation of the principle of indemnity in property insurance.

It is respectfully suggested, therefore, that there are strong arguments, not wholly convincingly rebutted by *Mark Rowlands Ltd* and *Siu Yin Kwan*, that sections 1 and 2 do, as a matter of strict law, apply to real property insurance. This does seem unnecessary. As with life insurance, any dangers that the Act was intended to cover are amply guarded against by the prohibition on wagering; in addition, the principle of indemnity will ensure that no one profits from a loss in respect of which they have no interest. To make the point absolutely clear, the 1774 Act needs to be repealed in this respect.

Even if the Act does not apply to real property insurance, there is, as already mentioned above, a common law requirement of interest at the date of contract[77] and this seems to mean insurable interest in the strict sense which will be described below. In the case of goods, however, all that is required at the date of contract is sufficient not to fall foul of the Gaming Act and here a genuine expectation of acquiring an interest will suffice. But in all cases of insurances of property, insurable interest is prima facie required at the date of loss, simply because such insurances are only contracts to indemnify the insured against a loss actually suffered.[78] This is merely a necessary incident of the contract and as such can be, and sometimes is, dispensed with.[79]

The meaning of insurable interest

We can now turn to consider exactly what constitutes an insurable interest in property, regardless of whether or when it is statutorily or

---

[76] This would perhaps be consistent with balancing literal and mischief constructions of the Act. To read "the insured" in s.3 as comprehending the insured and any interested person whose name is inserted in the policy would be misleading, because there is one clear case where, by statutory authority (Fires Prevention (Metropolis) Act 1774 s.83, see Chap. 14, pp. 279–282) a person interested in real property may compel the insurer to expend the insurance moneys on reinstatement, regardless of whether or not he was named in the policy and regardless of the insured's strict entitlement.

[77] *Sadler's Co. v. Badcock* (1743) 2 Atk. 554.

[78] *Macaura v. Northern Assurance Co. Ltd* [1925] A.C. 619.

[79] See pp. 58–60, below.

contractually required. As with life insurance, the law in this country is stricter than is probably necessary.[80] The starting-point must be the classic decision in the marine insurance case of *Lucena v. Craufurd*.[81] Here the Crown Commissioners insured a number of enemy ships which had been captured by British vessels but were still on the high seas. The statute giving them authority empowered them to take charge of such ships only when they reached British ports. A number of the ships were lost at sea before reaching port. Whether or not the Commissioners had an insurable interest in them caused a great division of opinion, and the matter was debated by the judges before the House of Lords whose decision was that there was no interest, at the time of loss the Commissioners having no present proprietary right to the ships. In the classic words of Lord Eldon,[82] insurable interest is "a right in the property, or a right derivable out of some contract about the property, which in either case may be lost upon some contingency affecting the possession or enjoyment of the party." A complete modern definition would add interest created by the existence of a legal obligation to bear any loss arising from destruction of, or damage to, the insured property.[83]

Factual expectation of loss?

A wider "factual expectation" test had been propounded by some of the judges, although it was clearly not accepted by the House of Lords. This wider test was expressed by Lawrence J. as follows[84]: "A man is interested in a thing to whom advantage may arise or prejudice happen from the circumstances which may attend it and whom it importeth, that its condition as to safety or other quality should continue . . . To be interested in the preservation of a thing is to be so circumstanced with respect to it as to have benefit from its existence, prejudice from its destruction." Curiously, this dictum was cited by Kerr L.J. in *Mark Rowlands Ltd v. Berni Inns Ltd*,[85] even though that it does not represent prevailing English law is obvious from many decisions, particularly that of the House of Lords in

---

[80] For a useful critique, see Harnett and Thornton, "Insurable interest in property; a socio-economic re-evaluation of a legal concept" (1948) 48 Col.L.R. 1162.

[81] (1806) 2 B. & P.N.R. 269.

[82] *ibid.* at 321.

[83] *Glengate-KG Properties Ltd v. Norwich Union Fire Insurance Society* [1996] 1 Lloyd's Rep. 613, 624.

[84] (1806) 2 B. & P.N.R. at 302.

[85] [1986] Q.B. at 228.

Macaura v. *Northern Assurance Co. Ltd*,[86] which is discussed below.[87] That it should perhaps represent the law is another question.[88]

Proprietary or contractual right

As the law stands, therefore, a mere expectation or even a moral certainty of loss should particular property be destroyed is not enough. There must be a present right to a legal or equitable interest or a right under contract. A remainderman whose interest is vested has an insurable interest,[89] but the person with a contingent interest does not, nor does the beneficiary of property under the will of a dying testator.[90] The contingency may not happen; the testator may, in theory, revoke his will. In a famous American case,[91] a turnpike company insured a bridge spanning a stream which connected two parts of the company's road, but the company had no legal or equitable interest in the bridge, and it was held that they had no insurable interest in it.

In *Macaura v. Northern Assurance Co. Ltd*,[92] the sole shareholder of a limited company, who was also a substantial creditor of the company, insured in his own name timber owned by the company. The House of Lords held that he had no insurable interest in the timber which had been subsequently destroyed by fire. As a shareholder he had no right to the property owned by the company, the latter being a separate legal person, even though his shares would fall in value in the event of the destruction of the company's property. This was merely a moral certainty of loss. Similarly, as creditor, as Macaura had no right to the company's property

---

[86] [1925] A.C. 619.

[87] See also *Glengate-KG Properties Ltd v. Norwich Union Fire Insurance Society* [1996] 1 Lloyd's Rep. 613, also discussed below.

[88] The wider test has been adopted judicially by the Canadian Supreme Court in *Constitution Insurance Co. of Canada v. Kosmopoulos* (1987) 34 D.L.R. (4th) 208, which decided that the time had come to refuse to follow any more the *Macaura* case (see below). It has also been adopted legislatively in the Australian Insurance Contracts Act 1984, s.17. For discussion, see Birds [1987] J.B.L. 309, Wolfe [1989] S.L.T. 103, Clarke, *The Law of Insurance Contracts*, para. 4.3, Birds, "Insurable Interests" in *Interests in Goods*, eds. Palmer and McKendrick, 1993, Hasson (1995) 33 Osgoode Hall L.J. 680 at 681–683.

[89] *per* Lord Eldon in *Lucena v. Craufurd*, above, at 314.

[90] *ibid.* at 325.

[91] *Farmers' Mutual Insurance. Co. v. New Holland Turnpike Road Co.*, 122 Pa. 37 (1888).

[92] [1925] A.C. 619 See also *Arif v. Excess Insurance Group Ltd* 1987 S.L.T. 473.

in the sense of a mortgage or charge over it, or some other proprietary security interest,[93] he had no interest in it. One may wonder whether this is not too narrow a view. In both the above capacities, the insured did have a real economic interest in the company's property, and of course he could so easily have put matters right by arranging for the company to insure the timber.[94] It should be noted, though, that a shareholder can insure his shares against loss of value due to the failure of an adventure that his company is embarked upon,[95] and a creditor may insure against his debtor's insolvency,[96] so that the practical results of the decision in *Macaura* can be substantially mitigated.

The recent decision of the Court of Appeal in *Glengate-KG Properties Ltd v. Norwich Union Fire Insurance Society*[97] was concerned with the interpretation of the phrase "the interest of the insured" in a policy covering the insured owner of a building against consequential loss following a fire or other insured peril. The issue was whether or not the insured could recover for the loss of architects' plans which were owned by the architects although they might one day have been acquired by the insured. All the members of the Court of Appeal held that the insured had an interest in the plans, notwithstanding the lack of a proprietary interest in them, but it is clear that the majority regarded that interest as being to insure in respect of consequential loss and not to insure the plans themselves.[98]

Possession of property

One other point of general interest which arises out of the *Macaura* case is that possession of property by itself is not enough to found insurable

---

[93] e.g. the statutory right in *Moran Galloway & Co. v. Uzielli* [1905] 2 K.B. 555.

[94] Note that the insurer initially resisted Macaura's claim on the ground of fraud which, although the allegation failed, may have influenced their resistance. In the USA a shareholder does have an insurable interest in his company's property - see Vance, *Handbook on the Law of Insurance*, p. 175. In Canada, the *Kosmopoulos* case (n.88 above) concerned a "one-man" company and as already noted the Supreme Court decided that the time had come to depart from the narrow English law exemplified by *Macaura*. *Macaura* was distinguished in a recent marine case (*The Moonacre* [1992] 2 Lloyd's Rep. 501), where the bailee of a boat had full control of it and hence a insurable interest, although it was owned by "his" company.

[95] *Wilson v. Jones* (1867) L.R. 2 Ex. 139.

[96] *Waterkeyn v. Eagle Star Insurance Co.* (1920) 5 Ll.L.R. 12.

[97] [1996] 1 Lloyd's Rep. 614.

[98] See especially the judgment of Auld L.J. at 623–4. Sir Iain Glidewell (at 625–6) took the view that the owners of the property could have insured the plans, applying the broad test of Lawrence J. literally.

interest. The timber in question was standing on Macaura's land. There must be some right of enjoyment of the property or some legal liability in respect of it. However, it would only be on facts as unusual as *Macaura*,[99] where the insured had no right to enjoy the timber, that possession would not give interest. There is authority that a finder can insure the property he has found,[1] on the ground that possession in English law is a good root of title generally defeasible only by the true owner. What is clear beyond doubt is that possession with legal liability, such as that of a bailee, gives the possessor an insurable interest.

Sales of goods

The party to a contract for the sale of goods who either has property in the goods or bears the risk of their loss has an insurable interest.[2] So far as hire purchase agreements are concerned, the owner of the goods will retain an insurable interest so long as the property or the right to repossess the goods remain vested in him.[3] The hirer will also have an interest as bailee, in addition to a likely obligation to insure the goods.[4]

People living together

Whether or not spouses, or other people living together, have an insurable interest in what is solely the property of the other has never been

---

[99] Compare *Boehm v. Bell* (1799) 8 T.R. 154: the captors of a ship had an interest because of the rights and duties attaching.

[1] *Stirling v. Vaughan* (1809 11 East 619.

[2] *Inglis v. Stock* (1885) 10 App. Cas. 263. It seems unlikely that an innocent purchaser of stolen goods, without good title to them, has an insurable interest: *Chadwick v. Gibraltar General Insurance Co.* (1981) 34 O.R. (2d) 488; *Thompson* v. *Madill* (1986) 13 C.C.L.I. 242; see Hasson, (1983-84) 8 Canadian Business Law Journal 114. The Insurance Ombudsman, however, appears to take a different view; see his Annual Report for 1991, para. 2.25.

[3] Even if his right is liable to be defeated because of failure to comply with the statutory requirements of the Consumer Credit Act 1974.

[4] The Insurance Ombudsman decided (Annual Report for 1991, para. 2.25) that a buyer under a conditional sale agreement has an insurable interest in the full value of the goods. Clearly such a buyer has an insurable interest, although the extent of his interest should depend on his liability under the agreement. If, for example, he is relieved of liability in the event of a theft, his recovery should be limited (see pp. 57–58, below), unless he can recover for the benefit of the owner under the principles described at pp. 60–69, below.

decided. In principle the answer should be in the negative unless the non-owner has possession sufficient to insure, in other words use of the property is shared.[5] But, for example, a husband without a claim to ownership or possession can hardly have an insurable interest in his wife's jewellery, though there may be other ways in which the law permits him in effect to insure it, as we shall see later.

Limited interests in property

The categories of legal or equitable interest which will support insurable interest otherwise include the interests of mortgagor and mortgagee, vendor and purchaser, landlord and tenant and trustee and beneficiary. But once the insured is not the sole, unencumbered owner of property, whether real or personal, the question of the extent of his interest becomes of importance. This does not turn upon any statutory requirement of insurable interest, but stems from the fact that such insurances are contracts of indemnity. Anyone who has a proprietary interest in property may insure it up to its full value; any statutory requirement is thereby satisfied. However, contractually the insured must have an interest at the time of loss and the value of his interest is crucial. He can prima facie recover only sufficient to indemnify himself.[6]

For example, any tenant of property has an insurable interest in it and can therefore insure it for up to its full value. If he is merely a weekly tenant with no obligation to insure or repair, his recovery is limited to the value of his insurable interest, which can at most be the equivalent of four week's rent, assuming the premises to be a dwelling house.[7] If he has a fixed term lease under which he is liable to pay the full rent regardless of the destruction of the property, he will have an interest at the time of loss to that extent. If he is under an obligation to insure or to repair, his interest will be the full value of the property. Conversely, in all cases, it seems that the landlord's interest as reversioner extends to the full value of the property, even where the tenant is liable to repair, because of the risk of the tenant failing to comply with his obligation.[8]

---

[5] *Goulstone v. Royal Insurance Co.* (1858) 1 F. & F. 276.

[6] The modern case which, it is suggested, most clearly explains the distinction between the existence of an insurable interest and the value of it is the Australian case of *Davjoyda Estates v. National Insurance Co. of New Zealand* (1967) 65 S.R. (N.S.W.) 381.

[7] Because of the statutory requirement of four weeks' notice to terminate such a lease (Protection from Eviction Act 1977, s.5).

[8] Important subrogation issues may arise; see Chap. 15.

The same points can be made in respect of all the other categories of limited owners which have been mentioned. Each has sufficient legal or equitable interest to insure, but they will prima facie recover only what they have lost. A mortgagee will recover only the value of his outstanding debt,[9] the vendor of land may recover nothing if he can still enforce the contract of sale against his purchaser.[10] Insurance by someone with a limited interest in property raises the further question whether there are any circumstances when such a person can recover more than the value of his interest in the property, in order to account for the balance to another. This will be considered shortly.

The insured is not necessarily confined to recovering the value of his proprietary interest in the property. He has an insurable interest in an expectancy based upon his proprietary interest, for example, in the profits he would expect to make from his ownership or occupation of the property.[11] This, however, has to be insured quite separately; the usual indemnity policy on property will not indemnify against consequential losses.[12]

Waiver of insurable interest

If the Life Assurance Act 1774 applies to insurances of real property, it is clear that the statutory requirement imposed thereby cannot be dispensed with. In respect of goods insurance, however, the only statutory requirement is the prohibition on gaming or wagering. Otherwise the requirement of insurable interest is merely implied into the contract as a consequence of the principle of indemnity and applies only at the time of loss. *Macaura v. Northern Assurance Co.*, discussed above, illustrates this quite neatly. The insurers had initially referred the dispute to arbitration pursuant to a term in the policy. The insured argued that having done so they were precluded from alleging that the contract was void for want of insurable interest. It was held that the insurers were not alleging that the contract was void for failure to comply with any statutory obligation. They

[9] *Westminster Fire Office v. Glasgow Provident Investment Society* (1888) 13 App. Cas. 699.

[10] See this question discussed later, pp. 164–167 and 288.

[11] *City Tailors Ltd v. Evans* (1922) 91 L.J.K.B. 379. In this situation, it may not be necessary to have an insurable interest in the property itself: see *Glengate-KG Properties Ltd v. Norwich Union Fire Insurance Society* [1996] 1 Lloyd's Rep. 613, discussed above.

[12] See p. 225, below.

recognised the contract as valid, but denied (successfully) that the insured had at the time of loss the interest necessarily required in such a contract of indemnity.

On principle, there is no reason why, in an appropriate case, this contractual requirement should not be waived or dispensed with,[13] and there are clear authorities to this effect. In *Prudential Staff Union* v. *Hall*,[14] the plaintiff association of employees insured with Lloyd's against any loss suffered by any of its members of money held by them as agents or collectors of their employer. Clearly the association had no insurable interest in its members' liabilities, yet this was held to be no bar to its enforcing the insurance contract, the 1774 Act being inapplicable[15] and the contractual undertaking of the insurer to pay the association waiving any requirement of insurable interest.[16] Similarly, in *Thomas v. National Farmers' Union Mutual Insurance Society*,[17] the tenant of a farm insured the hay and straw thereon which was destroyed by fire, but after his lease had ended. The policy provided that it ceased to cover all property insured which passed from the insured "otherwise than by operation of law." The hay and straw had become the landlord's property on the expiration of the lease but only by operation of law owing to a provision in the Agricultural Holdings Act 1948. Thus, although the tenant no longer had any property in the goods, and thus no insurable interest, this was "by operation of law" and the insurer was contractually liable to pay him. What exactly is the obligation of the insured in cases like these with respect to the insurance moneys he receives will be considered shortly.

If the insurable interest requirement in respect of goods insurance can be waived, the question arises as to what are "goods" for the purpose of the exemption in section 4 of the 1774 Act. Obviously covered are the straightforward insurances of personal property.[18] However, there is also authority that the exemption extends to any policy of liability with respect to goods. So in *Williams v. Baltic Insurance Association of London*,[19] it was

[13] But see Clarke, *The Law of Insurance Contracts*, para. 4.1.D.
[14] [1947] K.B. 685.
[15] Money is goods for these purposes, although it would not be for the purposes of the Sale of Goods Act. The modern trend noted above (see p. 49) would seemingly dispense with the need to enquire as to the applicability of the 1774 Act.
[16] In fact the action failed as it was held that the plaintiff suffered no loss.
[17] [1961] 1 W.L.R. 386.
[18] *Cf.* the definition of "goods" in the Sale of Goods Act 1979, s.61(1).
[19] [1924] 2 K.B. 282.

held that a liability policy on a car, or the liability section of a general motor policy, was exempted from the 1774 Act. While this may have been a rather benevolent construction,[20] it is well established and obviously sensible as will be seen.[21]

Insurance of Third Parties' Interests

We must now return to the question of when a limited owner, or indeed someone without insurable interest in particular property, can recover on an insurance policy for the benefit of a third party not named therein. Because, as has just been seen, the requirement of insurable interest can be waived in respect of goods insurance, this situation clearly admits of the possibility. In respect of real property, the law is less developed, and that question is left to be considered quite separately.

Insurance on goods

If the insured has a limited interest in the goods insured, but has insured them for their full value, which is perfectly permissible, as has been seen, he may, in certain cases, be entitled to recover the full value upon a loss, holding the balance on trust for the third party or parties entitled to the other interest or interests in the goods. Indeed if he himself has suffered no loss, he may recover the full value for the third party. The essential requirements are that the insured does have an interest in the goods and that as a matter of construction of the insurance contract, the policy does cover more than that limited interest. It is a question primarily of what the parties intend as derived from the construction of the contract, rather than from extrinsic evidence of actual intention.[22]

The insured with an interest

In *Waters v. Monarch Fire and Life Assurance Co.*,[23] the plaintiffs were flour and corn factors who effected a floating policy over the goods in their

---

[20] But s.4 does refer to insurance *on* goods, not of goods.

[21] Although in the context of motor insurance it is not generally necessary: see the Road Traffic Act 1988, s.148(7); see Chap. 19, p. 365. In the light of the decision in *Siu Yin Kwan v. Eastern Insurance Co. Ltd* [1994] 1 All E.R. 213 that the 1774 Act does not apply to liability insurance (see p. 49, above), this aspect of the decision was in fact unnecessary.

[22] *Hepburn v. A. Tomlinson (Hauliers) Ltd* [1966] A.C. 451; *contra, British Traders' Insurance Co. Ltd v. Monson* (1964) 111 C.L.R. 86.

[23] (1856) 5 E. & B. 870. See also *London & N.W. Railway Co. v. Glyn* (1859) 1 E. & E. 652.

warehouse, whether their own or those held "in trust or on commission." A fire destroyed all the goods in the warehouse at a particular time. It was held that the plaintiffs were entitled to recover the full value of the goods; they would retain sufficient to cover their own interest and were trustees[24] for the owners of the goods as to the rest. It was clear from the words of the policy cited above that it covered the interests of the owners. The fact that the latter were unaware of the policy was irrelevant. By contrast, in *North British & Mercantile Insurance Co. v. Moffat*,[25] tea merchants insured chests of tea in their warehouses which were their own or "in trust or on commission for which they are responsible." Fire destroyed certain chests which had been resold by the insured. It was held that, because property in those chests had passed to the purchasers, the insured had no interest in them. They could not recover for the purchasers because the words "for which they are responsible" qualified both the phrases "in trust" and "on commission". They could thus recover only for those third parties to whom they were in some way liable, which was not the situation.

The leading case is *Hepburn v. A. Tomlinson (Hauliers) Ltd.*[26] Carriers effected insurance on a quantity of tobacco which was stolen in circumstances attaching no legal liability to them. The policy was clearly expressed as a goods in transit policy, that is, insurance of the goods as such while they were being transported from one place to another, and not one simply insuring the carriers' potential legal liability. The owners of the goods were expressly named and the terms of the policy were those appropriate to a first party and not a liability policy. In these circumstances the House of Lords held that the carriers were entitled to recover the full value of the tobacco for the benefit of the owners.[27] There was no gaming involved, the carriers did have an interest in the goods, because of their potential legal liability in respect of them if they were negligent, and the only question for decision was whether they intended to insure as it appeared from the construction of the contract.

The principle of *Waters* and *Hepburn* is most easily applicable to the situation where a bailee or carrier, for reasons of commercial convenience,

---

[24] As to whether or not they were trustees in the strict sense, see below.
[25] (1871) L.R. 7 C.P. 25.
[26] [1966] A.C. 451.
[27] As to whether or not there was double insurance if the owners had also insured, see p. 317, below.

insures goods on behalf of their owner as well as on his own behalf.[28] It has, though, been applied, expressly for reasons of "commercial convenience," to an insurance of contract works under a contractor's all risks policy and to the insurances of a ship and an oilwell under construction. In *Petrofina Ltd v. Magnaload Ltd*,[29] it was held that an insurance effected by the owners and main contractors covering the construction of an extension to an oil refinery, under which all the sub-contractors working on the site were included within the definition of "the insured," enured to the benefit of each and every sub-contractor in respect of all the property insured. Arguably this point was unnecessary for the decision as the real issue was not whether the principal insured could recover for the benefit of a third party, but whether or not the insurer could exercise subrogation rights in the name of the principal insured against the negligent sub-contractors responsible for the loss;[30] it was surely not necessary to find that the sub-contractors had an interest in the whole works in order to disallow subrogation.[31] *Petrofina* was followed in the more recent cases of *Stone Vickers Ltd* v. *Appledore Ferguson Shipbuilders Ltd*[32] and *National Oilwell (U.K) Ltd v. Davy Offshore Ltd*[33] In *Stone Vickers*, the suppliers of the propeller for a new ship claimed the protection of a policy effected by the principal contractors and in *National Oilwell*, the suppliers of a component for a floating oil production facility claimed to be insured under the contractors' policy. In both cases, the judge at first instance engaged in a lengthy analysis of the insurable interest of the suppliers, although again it is

---

[28] The reference to commercial convenience should not be read as implying that the principle is applicable only to commercial insurances. There is no reason why it should not apply, on appropriate facts, to *e.g.* a private hire of goods; see *Guardian Royal Exchange Assurance of New Zealand Ltd v. Roberts* [1991] N.Z.L.R. 106.

[29] [1984] 1 Q.B. 127.

[30] As to this aspect of the case, see p. 305, below.

[31] Further it is arguable that on the construction of the policy, the sub-contractors did not have an interest in the whole contract works because the words "for which they are responsible" were expressed to limit the property insured; cf. the *Moffat* case (text at n.25, above). See further, [1983] J.B.L. 497.

[32] [1991] 2 Lloyd's Rep. 288. The decision was reversed by the Court of Appeal, [1992] 2 Lloyd's Rep. 578, on the question of the construction of the policy in question. The relevance of insurable interest issues was therefore not considered in their judgment.

[33] [1993] 2 Lloyd's Rep. 582. See further on this case below.

thought that this should be unnecessary for real point in issue, namely whether the insurers have subrogation rights.[34]

The insured without an interest

Turning to the case of insurance of goods where the insured himself has no interest in them, as we have already seen, there is clear authority that the insured can recover if the contract admits of the construction that the requirement of insurable interest was waived.[35] In *Williams v. Baltic Insurance Association of London*,[36] the plaintiff effected a motor policy on his car including cover against liability to third persons injured by use of the car. The policy was also expressed to cover any friend or relative of the insured driving with his consent. The plaintiff's sister, driving the car with consent, negligently injured some people who recovered damages from her. The question was whether or not the insured could recover an indemnity in respect of these damages on his sister's behalf. Plainly, he had no insurable interest in his sister's legal liability, but, equally, the wording of the policy was expressed to cover that liability, so that the principal question was whether or not it was necessary for the plaintiff to have an insurable interest. Roche J. held that the policy was one on goods[37] so that it was exempted from any statutory requirement other than the prohibition on gaming and wagering, of which it clearly did not fall foul. As the common law did not require insurable interest in such a case, except as a consequence of the principle of indemnity, the very application of which was in issue, he was able to construe the contract as waiving any requirement of interest (and hence the principle of indemnity) because the policy expressly extended to the sister's liability.

Third party's right to the money

It is clear that the insured who is entitled to and does recover for the benefit of a third party is obliged to account to the latter, although until

---

[34] As already indicated, subrogation in these co-insurance situations is more fully considered later. There seems little doubt that the law finds it difficult in a number of respects properly to get to grips with the situation where there is more than one person insured under one insurance policy. See, further, below.

[35] *Prudential Staff Union v. Hall* [1947] K.B. 685; *Thomas v. National Farmers' Union Mutual* [1961] 1 W.L.R. 386; see p. 59, above.

[36] [1924] 2 K.B. 282.

[37] See p. 59, above.

recently it had not been finally decided exactly what the basis for this, whether trusteeship or quasi-contractual liability, was.[38] The matter arose directly in *Re E. Dibbens & Sons Ltd.*[39] Here, Harman J. rejected trusteeship, arguing, correctly it is suggested, that references to "trust" in the earlier cases,[40] which were made by common law judges, were not to be read literally.[41] He held that bailees who had contracted for insurance of the goods with their owners were to be regarded as under a fiduciary duty to insure and hold any proceeds for the bailors.[42] Such bailors could thus claim insurance moneys as against the insured's insolvent estate. However, if there was no contractual agreement to insure, the bailors had no proprietary claim to the proceeds and in an insolvency were left to their claims as general creditors.[43]

Third party's right to claim directly

What is not so clear is whether the third party has a direct claim against the insurers in the event of the insured being unwilling or unable to claim himself. Conventional analysis, based on the doctrine of privity of contract, would suggest that he will be able to do so only if he can show specific statutory authority[44] or that the insured contracted as trustee or agent for him, unless in some situations[45] the law is willing to develop a theory of co-insurance which says that there are separate sub-contracts between the insurer and each insured.[46] Outside trust and agency, the third party is

---

[38] The matter was left open in *Hepburn v. Tomlinson*, above.

[39] [1990] B.C.L.C. 577.

[40] Including *Waters v. Monarch*, above.

[41] See also *D.G. Finance Ltd v. Scott*, unreported, Court of Appeal, June 15, 1995, referring to Lord Diplock in *The Albazero* [1977] A.C. 774 at 845.

[42] The compatibility of a fiduciary relationship with a contract had been confirmed in *Barclays Bank Ltd* v. *Quistclose Investments Ltd* [1970] A.C. 567.

[43] See further, Adams, "The insured insolvent hire-purchaser" [1991] J.B.L. 291.

[44] As is the case in respect of compulsory motor insurance: s.148(7) of the Road Traffic Act 1988; see p. 365, below.

[45] This may not work in the relatively simple bailee cases, but it could do so in the sort of cases exemplified by *Petrofina Ltd v. Magnaload Ltd*, above.

[46] For an attempt to discuss some of the issues, see Birds, "Insurable Interests" in *Interests in Goods*, eds. Palmer and McKendrick, 1993, which in this respect draws heavily on some Australian literature, especially Nicholson, "Conundrums for co-insureds", (1990) 3 Insurance. L.J. 218 and (1991) 4 Insurance. L.J. 126, Brownie, "Composite insurance", (1991) 4 Ins. L.J. 250, Derrington and Ashton, *Law of Liability Insurance*, pp. 69–91.

faced with the doctrine of privity of contract.[47] Whether an English court would be as bold as the Australian High Court[48] in dispensing with privity in this sort of context seems doubtful,[49] although the Law Commission has recently recommended some statutory abrogation of the privity rule which would clearly work to the benefit of third parties in the sort of situations we are concerned with.[50]

As far as trust is concerned, although there are dicta referred to above which could have been read as supporting this, the decision in *Re Dibbens* would seem to preclude this in many cases.[51] More hopeful is the

---

[47] *Vandepitte v. Preferred Accident Insurance Corporation of New York* [1933] A.C. 70, where the doctrine was applied to a situation on all fours with *Williams v. Baltic Insurance Association*, above, except that the writ was issued by the third party not the insured; *D.G. Finance Ltd v. Scott*, above. The latter case involved a hirer insuring goods, as obliged to do under the contract of hire, but declining to claim for their loss (being bankrupt and disinterested by the relevant time). The owner, a finance company which had leased the goods, sought to make a direct claim against the insurers on the basis of trust, but this was rejected for reasons briefly considered below; agency was not pleaded. It is clear that the parties, and the Court of Appeal, accepted the prima facie application of the privity rule. See Price, (1996) 59 M.L.R. 738.

[48] *Trident General Insurance Co. v. McNiece Bros Pty Ltd* (1988) 165 C.L.R. 107. See now the Australian Insurance Contracts Act 1984, s.48.

[49] It may perhaps be so in the context of construction insurance: in *Petrofina Ltd v. Magnaload Ltd* [1984] Q.B. 127, which has been considered above, the tenor of Lloyd J.'s judgment could be read as supporting the view that he would have permitted a direct action by the third party sub-contractor. Curiously this was not cited in *Trident*, above, although both cases arose from the same sort of background. A dictum of Kerr L.J. in *Mark Rowlands Ltd v. Berni Inns Ltd* [1986] Q.B. 211 at 226 could be read as dispensing with the strict requirements of privity. He said: "Provided that a person with a limited interest has an insurable interest in the subject matter of the insurance . . . there is no principle of law which precludes him from asserting that an insurance effected by another person was intended to enure for his benefit to the extent of his interest in the subject matter." However, this can equally be read as merely giving the third party rights against the insured, not the insurer, and this was not a co-insurance case. It might also be read as support for the use of agency doctrines to escape the privity problem and as such is supported by more recent authorities, as explained further below.

[50] *Privity of Contract: Contracts for the Benefit of Third Parties*, Law Com. No. 242, 1996. Note also the fairly recent comments adverse to the privity rule of Steyn L.J., as he then was, in *Darlington B.C. v. Wiltshier Northern Ltd* [1995] 3 All E.R. 895 at 903–905 (a building contract case).

[51] If an insured does insure as trustee, the third party, as beneficiary, could sue the insurer, joining the insured as defendant: *Vandepitte v. Preferred Accident Insurance Corporation of New York* [1933] A.C. 70.

application of agency principles. If the insured was given actual authority to insure, then he can clearly claim if the agency was disclosed, and this may not be too difficult to show in a case where the insured himself has a limited interest.[52] According to recent authority,[53] it may even be possible to use the doctrine of the undisclosed principal. If the insured did not have actual authority to insure, the conventional view was that the third party could ratify and claim on the contract only if he did so before loss,[54] but this view may now be wrong in the light of a second recent decision.[55] Both these recent decisions merit detailed consideration as in part they are not free from difficulty.[56]

In *Siu Yin Kwan v. Eastern Insurance Co. Ltd*,[57] Hong Kong shipping agents (R) purportedly effected employers' liability insurance on behalf of shipowners (A). Some members of a vessel owned by the latter were killed in circumstances entitling them to claim compensation from A, but A was wound up and the representatives of the deceased sought to recover from the insurers, E.[58] E resisted the claim on the basis that R had acted as undisclosed agents for A and that the doctrine of the undisclosed principal was inapplicable to insurance contracts.[59] Based on the finding that R had clearly had actual authority to effect the insurance on behalf of A, the

---

[52] *e.g.* if the insured is known to be a bailee, an insurance of goods by him must be at least partly for the benefit of the owner. In the *Waters* case (1856) 5 E. & B. 870 at 881, Lord Campbell C.J. seemed to treat the question as one of agency, as well as referring to "trust".

[53] *Siu Yin Kwan v. Eastern Insurance Co. Ltd* [1994] 1 All E.R. 213.

[54] *Grover & Grover Ltd v. Mathews* [1910] 2 K.B. 401. The absence of express authority and hence the need for ratification is likely in practice to be much more of a problem where the insured himself has no interest, *e.g.* a householder's policy may cover the property of the insured and members of her family permanently living with her. It is by no means certain that, for example, a spouse or child would be aware of this until a loss was suffered. Note that the third party in *Williams v. Baltic Insurance Association of London* [1924] 2 K.B. 282 did ratify before the loss (see the finding of the arbitrators reported at p. 284), but curiously did not herself sue the insurers.

[55] *National Oilwell (U.K.) Ltd v. Davy Offshore Ltd* [1993] 2 Lloyd's Rep. 213. An appeal in this case was settled after it had been argued but, unfortunately, before judgment was given by the Court of Appeal.

[56] See further [1994] J.B.L. 386.

[57] [1994] 1 All E.R. 213.

[58] Under the Hong Kong equivalent of the Third Parties (Rights against Insurers) Act 1930 (See Chap. 18).

[59] A point was also raised on the applicability of the Life Assurance Act 1774; see p. 49, above.

Privy Council held that the doctrine of the undisclosed principal was applicable to insurance contracts, they being not sufficiently personal to preclude the operation of the doctrine.[60] "Since the contract in the present case is an ordinary commercial contract, [A] were entitled to sue as undisclosed principal unless [R] should have realised that [E] were unwilling to contract with anyone other than themselves."[61] As the proposal form questions were answered as if they referred to A, and fully answered, there was nothing expressly or impliedly to exclude A's rights to sue as undisclosed principal. The Privy Council then dismissed the separate argument for the insurers[62] to the effect that the contract of insurance is such a personal one as to preclude the operation of the doctrine of the undisclosed principal. It was clear that the actual identity of A was a matter of indifference to E as they received full information on the proposal form. However, the judgment went further, holding that insurance contracts can never be so personal as to deny the operation of the undisclosed principal doctrine.

The result of what looks more a case of an unnamed than an undisclosed principal seems entirely justified since it is clear that the insurers were sufficiently aware of all material circumstances concerning the risk. However, it is respectfully submitted that the rejection of the broader arguments for the insurers concerning the personal nature of the insurance contract is open to challenge. Rather curiously, there seems to have been no reference to the special nature of insurance contracts as contracts of the utmost good faith.[63] As a general rule, full completion of the proposal form does not of itself satisfy the requirement of full disclosure. Of course, if the agent in fact knows of material facts which he fails to disclose, the contract would be voidable, as the undisclosed principal doctrine requires that any defence which the third party may have against the agent is available

---

[60] The facts of the case are hardly typical of undisclosed agency, because E knew that R were shipping agents and not the owners of the vessel, but the Privy Council was obliged to treat the case in this way because the trial judge had specifically ruled against inferring knowledge to E that A was the true insured.

[61] [1994] 1 All E.R. at 221, *per* Lord Lloyd of Berwick, applying a dictum of Diplock L.J. in *Teheran-Europe Co. Ltd v. S.T. Bolton (Tractors) Ltd.* [1968] 2 Q.B. 545 at 555.

[62] Based on *Peters v General Accident Fire and Life Assurance Corp. Ltd* [1937] 4 All E.R. 628; see p. 171, below.

[63] This is surely implicit in the rule that non-marine indemnity insurance contracts cannot be assigned; see p. 171, below. As to utmost good faith and the duty of disclosure, see Chap. 6.

against his principal.[64] However, what if the agent does not know of highly material facts and does not disclose them for that reason? It surely cannot be the case that the "true" insured would be allowed to step in and enforce the contract, and to that extent the reasoning in the *Siu Yin Kwan* case must, it is respectfully thought, be qualified.

As indicated earlier, *National Oilwell (U.K.) Ltd v. Davy Offshore Ltd* was another construction case. Here Colman J. used both the doctrine of the undisclosed principal and the doctrine of ratification as support for a co-insured being able to make a direct claim on the insurance contract. The use of undisclosed agency seems open to the objections already noted, but the clarification of the application of ratification is, it is thought, most welcome. Colman J. summarised the position as follows:

> "Where at the time when the contract of insurance was made the principal assured or other contracting party had no actual authority to bind the other party to the contract of insurance, but the policy is expressed to insure not only the principal assured but also a class of others who are not identified in that policy, a party who at the time when the policy was effected could have been ascertained to qualify as a member of that class can ratify and sue on the policy as co-assured if at that time it was intended by the principal assured or other contracting party to create privity of contract with the insurers on behalf of that particular party."[65]

Perhaps more important are the views of Colman J. on the question of the timing of ratification. The earlier leading authority is the decision in *Grover & Grover Ltd v. Mathews*,[66] where the plaintiffs insured their piano factory through an agent at Lloyd's. Without consulting them, the agent wrote seeking renewal of the policy when it expired. A fire happened after this expiry and after the agent wrote, but before the plaintiffs knew what the agent had done. When they did find out, they purported to ratify his acts. It was held that the insurers were not liable. While ratification after loss has long been regarded as permissible in marine insurance,[67] Hamilton

---

[64] As confirmed by Lord Lloyd, [1994] 1 All E.R. at 220.

[65] [1993] 2 Lloyd's Rep. at 596–7. Evidence as to intention may be provided by the terms of the policy itself, by the terms of any contract between the principal assured or other contracting party and the alleged co-assured or by any other admissible material showing what was subjectively intended by the principal assured.

[66] [1910] 2 K.B. 401.

[67] *Williams v. North China Insurance Co.* (1876) 1 C.P.D. 757.

J. regarded this rule as anomalous and not to be extended to non-marine insurance.[68] It is arguable that this case is wrong in principle and that it conflicts with other authority.[69] Recognising the force of criticisms like this, in *National Oilwell*, Colman J. would have been prepared[70] to allow ratification after loss in such a situation. It is to be hoped that a case arises soon when there is the opportunity actually to overrule the *Grover & Grover* case.

Insurance on real property

In respect of insurances on real property, the first crucial question is whether the Life Assurance Act 1774 applies.[71] If it does, then the insured without an interest in the property insured cannot recover for the benefit of another simply because the policy will be illegal under section 1, and even if it does not, it seems that the common law reaches the same result.[72] Even if the insured has an interest, it may be that section 2 requires any third party to be named, but it seems highly unlikely that a court will now hold section 2 applicable,[73] and, in any event, the construction of the section propounded in *Davjoyda Estates Ltd v. National Insurance Co. of New Zealand*[74] provides an alternative and sensible solution to this problem.

However, whether or not the 1774 Act applies, it seems less likely in respect of real property insurances, as compared with insurances on goods, that a policy will be open to a construction that allows the insured to recover for the benefit of a third party or allows the third party himself to sue on the policy. It must be stressed that we are here concerned with this limited question, the answer to which is not necessarily the same as the answer as to whether or not the third party has an interest in any insurance moneys actually recovered or as to whether he can use the

---

[68] He regarded himself as bound by the *Williams* case in which, he said, the court had recognised the anomaly of the rule. With respect, this is a curious reading of the *Williams* case.

[69] *e.g.* a dictum in *Waters v. Monarch Fire & Life Assurance Co.*, above.

[70] Strictly this comment was clearly *obiter* as the third party failed to show that they were actually insured in the circumstances of the case.

[71] This question is discussed earlier at pp. 48–52.

[72] *Sadler's Co. v. Badcock* (1743) 2 Atk. 554; see p. 37, above.

[73] See p. 49, above.

[74] (1967) 65 S.R. (N.S.W.) 381; see p. 51, above. In Canada, where the 1774 Act clearly does not apply, there are a number of authorities applying the *Waters* principle to insurances of real property on appropriate facts; see *e.g. Commonwealth Construction Co. v. Imperial Oil* (1976) 69 D.L.R. (3d) 558.

compulsory reinstatement provisions of the Fires Prevention (Metropolis) Act 1774.[75] Just because, for example, the terms of a lease can be construed to entitle the tenant to the benefit of money received by his insured landlord[76] does not necessarily mean that the landlord was entitled under the insurance contract to recover for the benefit of the tenant nor that the tenant could sue on the insurance contract if the landlord chose not to.

Bearing this in mind, the same basic principle of construction as applies to insurances of goods for the benefit of third parties will apply to insurances of real property. Thus the contract as properly construed must reveal an intention to cover the third party's interest,[77] and the insurance will have to be of the full value of the property rather than merely of the interest of the insured as limited owner.[78] This seems to be fairly likely where the relationship between the insured and the third party is that of trustee and beneficiary[79] or mortgagor and mortgagee[80]; in the first case,

---

[75] As to this, see Chap. 14 and especially the decision in *Lonsdale & Thompson Ltd v. Black Arrow Group plc* [1993] 3 All E.R. 648, discussed at p. 281.

[76] As in, for example, *Mumford Hotels Ltd v. Wheler* [1964] Ch. 117 (see p. 283) and, it seems, *Mark Rowlands Ltd v. Berni Inns Ltd*, [1986] Q.B. 211; see p. 49, above. See also *Beacon Carpets Ltd v. Kirby* [1985] Q.B. 755, n.83 below. Compare *Re King*, [1963] Ch. 459.

[77] *Hepburn v. Tomlinson* [1966] A.C. 451; see p. 61, above. Compare the decision of the High Court of Australia in *British Traders Insurance Co. v. Monson* (1964) 111 C.L.R. 86, where, wrongly, the matter was said to turn upon whether or not the insured could show that he intended to insure for the benefit of the third party. Clearly though the decision in that case was correct. A tenant proposing to purchase the freehold of the property insured it for its full value and as freehold owner, making no mention of the landlord's interest. However, the purchase fell through before the fire which damaged the property. It was held that the tenant could recover only sufficient to indemnify him for his loss and nothing for the benefit of his landlord.

[78] Note that there is no rule of law requiring an insured to specify his interest in the insured property, although normally this would be required by the terms of the proposal form or stated in the policy.

[79] See *Davjoyda Estates Ltd v. National Insurance Co. of New Zealand*, above, where the plaintiff company entered into a contract to purchase land as agent for another company and insured the land; the insurers were aware of the true principal, but the latter was not named in the policy. Before completion, fire damaged the property. Applying the analogy of the "bailee cases" (pp. 60–61, above) and getting round the problem posed by s.2 of the 1774 Act in the way described at p. 51, above, it was held that the plaintiff insured as trustee for the other company and could recover the full value of the property. On the construction of

the interests of the parties are similar, whereas in the second there is most likely to be a noting of both interests on the insurance policy. It seems less likely to be the case where the interests of the parties are quite distinct, as where they are vendor and purchaser[81] or landlord and tenant. In *Re King*,[82] the Court of Appeal refused to apply the analogy of the "bailee cases" to an insurance by a tenant under a covenant to repair and reinstate. The case involved a dispute between landlord and tenant, the insurer not being involved. The tenant had a full insurable interest and could not be said to be insuring for the benefit of the landlord; the latter in fact was also named in the policy, but this was held to be merely to ensure that the landlord was able to control the receipt of the moneys and insist on reinstatement.[83]

the policy, what was insured was the property itself and not merely the limited interest of the insured; there was no presumption of law, merely of fact, that an insured insures only his own interest and in the case of insurance by a trustee, he must also be insuring the interest of the beneficiary since their interests are essentially the same and of necessity the proceeds are held on the same trusts as the property is held.

[80] See *e.g. Hepburn v. Tomlinson*, above, at 481–482, per Lord Pearce.

[81] *Rayner v. Preston* (1881) 18 Ch. D. 1; see Chap. 9 at p. 164.

[82] [1963] Ch. 459.

[83] Compare *Beacon Carpets Ltd v. Kirby* [1985] Q.B. 755, where the relevant provisions in both the lease and the insurance policy were quite different. Again the dispute was between landlord and tenant, the insurer being quite unconcerned having paid out the insurance moneys. See also an interesting unreported Irish case, *Church and General Insurance Co. v. Connolly*, noted (1983) 5 D.U.L.J. (N.S.) 291, where a tenant at will recovered under a fire policy for the benefit of its landlord. The arrangement was a very informal letting of premises used as a youth centre and quite unlike the usual formal lease. The 1774 Act was held not to apply to Ireland.

CHAPTER 4

FORMALITIES AND FORMATION OF THE INSURANCE CONTRACT

This chapter is concerned with a number of matters, some of which at least involve merely the application of general requirements of the law of contract to the particular context of the insurance contract. While we are first concerned with questions as to formation and formalities required, it is convenient to consider also a number of related matters, namely temporary cover and cover notes, and the law concerning the duration, renewal, cancellation and surrender of insurance contracts.

Formation of The Insurance Contract

The insurance contract is no exception to the general rule requiring offer, acceptance, consideration and an intention to create legal relations in order to find a binding legal contract.[1] The last two requirements, however, will invariably be satisfied automatically and need not be considered further.

Offer and acceptance

An offer to enter into an insurance contract may be made by a prospective insured or by an insurer. At the initial stage,[2] it will in practice be made by the proposed insured,[3] usually, but by no means necessarily, by means of completing a proposal form.[4] Proposal forms are of course

---

[1] See generally Treitel, *Law of Contract*, Chaps. 2 to 5. As to the information which statute requires insurers to supply to all prospective insureds, see below pp. 77–78.

[2] Compare the position on renewal, discussed later pp. 89–90.

[3] For an illustration, see *Rust v. Abbey Life Assurance Co.* [1979] 2 Lloyd's Rep. 334.

[4] Proposal forms are not used in all classes of business nor often in respect of temporary cover (see later). In *Adie v. The Insurance Corp.* (1898) 14 T.L.R. 544, the offer by the insured took the form of a letter attaching his old policy from a different insurer.

standard mass-produced documents prepared by insurers.[5] The insurer may simply accept the offer made or may "accept" it with qualifications, in which case the "acceptance" may in law amount to a counter-offer. Assuming for the present that there appears to have been an offer and an unqualified acceptance of that offer, the question arises as to what must be comprised in this agreement for there to be a binding insurance contract.

Agreement on material terms

It was once suggested in the House of Lords[6] that all the terms and conditions of the contract must be agreed by both parties. Clearly there are certain essential matters on which there must be accord, namely, the amount of the premium[7]; the nature of the risk, including the subject-matter of the insurance[8]; and the duration of the risk.[9] But otherwise it is suggested that the better view, despite the authoritative dictum already referred to, is that these matters are the only ones upon which agreement is required, for the reason that the proposer for insurance is deemed to have applied for the usual form of policy issued by the insurer in respect of the particular type of insurance in question. He is thus deemed to have agreed to the usual terms and conditions to be found in the insurer's policy.[10] In *General Accident Insurance Corporation v. Cronk*,[11] the proposal form which the applicant completed did not contain some terms which were in the policy he subsequently received. He declined to pay the

---

[5] Under the Statements of Insurance Practice (see p. 5, above), proposal forms issued to individual proposers must contain a statement that a copy of the completed form is automatically provided for retention at the time of completion, will be supplied as part of the insurer's normal practice or will be supplied on request within three months after completion. *Quaere* whether automatic supply should not be the rule, given the importance of the proposal form; see Chaps. 6 and 7, below. However, the insurer must not raise an issue under a proposal form without supplying a copy; this relates to issues of non-disclosure and misrepresentation, as do other aspects of the Statements which are considered in those later chapters.

[6] *Alliss-Chalmers Co. v. Fidelity & Deposit Co. of Maryland* (1916) 114 L.T. 433 at 434.

[7] *ibid.* In the case of an ordinary risk, however, the amount may be deemed to be in accordance with the insurer's usual tariff. The premium need not actually be paid.

[8] *Beach v. Pearl Assurance Co. Ltd* [1938] I.A.C. Rep. 3.

[9] See generally *Murfitt v. Royal Insurance Co.* (1922) 38 T.L.R. 334 at 336.

[10] *General Accident Insurance Corp. v. Cronk* (1901) 17 T.L.R. 233; *Rust v. Abbey Life* [1979] 2 Lloyd's Rep. 334.

[11] Above.

premium, arguing that the sending of the policy with different terms was merely a counter-offer which he chose not to accept. It was held that he was liable for the premium for the reasons already outlined. In practice nowadays, apart from the situation when an application is made orally, for example for a cover-note,[12] no difficulty is likely to arise on this point, as invariably proposal forms stipulate that the proposer's offer is subject to the insurer's usual terms and conditions.

Counter-offer

It may well be that the insurer does not simply accept the proposer's offer, but states that acceptance is subject to payment of the first premium. It is clear that in law this generally amounts to a counter-offer,[13] so that there is no binding contract until the premium is in fact paid.[14] On general principle, until this act of acceptance, either party should be free to withdraw. However, the law appears to be that the insurer's act constitutes a counter-offer which the proposer may decline to accept but which the insurer cannot revoke, unless there is a change in the risk involved between the time of the original offer and the insured's acceptance by payment of the premium. In other words, the insurer is bound by its counter-offer so long as the risk remains the same. If the risk changes, the tender of the premium by the insured constitutes a new offer which the insurer is at liberty to reject. In *Canning v. Farquhar*,[15] a proposal for life insurance was "accepted" on December 14, on the terms that no insurance was to take effect until the first premium was paid. The premium was tendered on January 9, but four days previously the proposer had fallen and suffered serious injuries from which he subsequently died. The Court of Appeal ruled that the insurer was not bound, the majority[16] reasoning along the

---

[12] See pp. 80–86, below.

[13] It may even be merely an invitation to treat, whereupon the proposer must make a new offer on this basis: *Locker v. Law Union and Rock Insurance Co. Ltd* [1928] 1 K.B. 554.

[14] *Canning v. Farquhar* (1886) 16 Q.B.D. 727, 733.

[15] (1886) 16 Q.B.D. 727. See also *Harrington v. Pearl Life Assurance Co.* (1914) 30 T.L.R. 613.

[16] Lindley and Lopes L.JJ.

lines already discussed.[17] However, it may be that the insurer is estopped from denying that there is a binding contract. This will be the case if, for example, the policy contains a statement that the premium has been paid, as in *Roberts v. Security Co. Ltd*,[18] where this overrode a condition that the insurance was not effective until the premium was paid.

Changes in risk

If there are any material changes in the risk between the date of proposal and the date of the conclusion of the contract, then these must be disclosed to the insurer in accordance with the general duty of disclosure.[19] Failure to do so renders the contract voidable at the option of the insurer. If, in *Canning v. Farquhar*, the insurer had accepted the premium tendered, not knowing of the insured's fall, they would have been able to avoid liability for this reason. However, this principle applies only so long as there is no contract in existence. If, for example, the insurer accepts the insured's offer unconditionally, he is thereupon bound, even if the contract provides that the risk will not run until the premium is paid.[20] Non-disclosure of a change in the risk before the premium is paid will not entitle the insurer to avoid the contract, although it would not be liable for any loss occurring before the premium was paid.

Communication of acceptance

It is a general rule of the law of contract that acceptance of an offer is not effective until communicated to the offeror; this rule obviously applies

---

[17] Lord Esher M.R. decided the case primarily upon the ground that tender of the premium could never be acceptance of an offer by the insurers, even if there had been no change in risk. The tender would be an offer by the proposer requiring to be accepted by the insurers. With respect, this must be incorrect. The insurer's letter of December 14, was more than a mere statement of intent or invitation to treat. This is not to deny, of course, that such a reply by insurers to a proposal could not in an appropriate case be construed as merely an invitation to treat if matters other than the mere payment of the premium were left open; see *e.g. Locker v. Law Union*, above.

[18] [1897] 1 Q.B. 111; see p. 76 below.

[19] See Chap. 6.

[20] See *MacGillivray*, (8th ed.) paras. 319–323. This position is unlikely in practice. A provision that the risk does not run is perhaps most likely to be construed as meaning that no contract is in force. It has indeed been held that there is a strong presumption, in the case of life insurance, that no contract comes into existence until the premium is paid and the policy issued: *Southern Cross Assurance Co. Ltd v. Australian Provincial Assurance* (1939) 39 S.R. (N.S.W.) 174.

to the insurance contract. There are some well-established exceptions to this rule, however, three of which appear of particular relevance in the context of insurance. First, where an offer is unilateral, acceptance is constituted simply by performance in accordance with the terms of the offer. There are one or two examples of this in the insurance field. It used not to be uncommon for newspapers and diaries to offer accident insurance to people who having bought the article, filled in the relevant coupon. A modern example of such coupon insurance is cover against death or injury during aeroplane fights which can be purchased at airport counters. There can be no doubt that in law the provision of such insurance is a unilateral offer by the insurer which the proposer accepts simply by filling in the relevant details requested on the form.

The second exception to the communication of acceptance rule, which can be of some importance, is where a policy is issued under seal. Assuming that the insurer's acceptance is unconditional, or that any condition as to prepayment of the premium is waived, if the acceptance takes the form of the signing and sealing of a policy,[21] there is no requirement of communication to the insured. In *Roberts v. Security Co. Ltd*,[22] the plaintiff filled in a proposal form for burglary insurance on December 14. On December 27, the directors of the insurer fixed the company's seal to the policy accepting the proposal, which provided that it was effective from December 14. On the night of December 26, obviously before he knew of the insurer's acceptance, since it had not then taken place, the insured suffered a loss. It was held that the insurer was liable.

Thirdly, the rule requiring communication of acceptance obviously implies that silence or delay does not constitute acceptance. While this is certainly prima facie the case, an insured who acts in reliance on an offer from an insurer will be regarded as having accepted it even in the absence of express communication.[23] In *Rust v. Abbey Life Assurance Co. Ltd*,[24] the proposer for a form of linked life policy retained the policy for seven months before disputing that she was bound by it. She alleged that she had never intended to enter into that sort of contract and had been misled by the insurer's agent. It was found that the nature of the contract had

---

[21] See generally *MacGillivray*, Chap. 5.
[22] [1897] 1 Q.B. 111; a condition that the policy was not effective until the premium was paid was waived by a recital that the premium had been paid. See above.
[23] See, *e.g. Taylor v. Allon* [1966] 1 Q.B. 304, discussed below, p. 82.
[24] [1979] 2 Lloyd's Rep. 334.

been fully explained to her and that she was bound by it. Even if she had not made an offer to the insurer which the latter had accepted by issuing the policy, which the court considered was the case,[25] the insurer's issue of a policy was an offer which she had accepted by doing and saying nothing for seven months.

Statutory requirements

Finally, in connection with the formation of insurance contracts, there are a number of statutory provisions which should be noted. First there are some requirements introduced as a result of the Third E.C. Insurance Directives discussed in Chapter 2. These impose requirements on insurers to give specified information to prospective insureds and, in the case of life insurance, to provide some continuing information.[26] The requirements in respect of life insurance are described in Chapter 17. The first requirements for pre-contractual disclosure in general insurance apply to contracts entered into by a U.K. or E.C. company[27] or a member of Lloyd's which constitute the carrying on in the United Kingdom of general business which is not reinsurance business or the provision in the United Kingdom of general insurance,[28] provided that the risk covered by the contract is situated in the United Kingdom. Before entering into such a contract the insurer must provide the prospective insured with the following information in writing[29]:

    (a) any arrangements for handling complaints concerning the contract[30];

    (b) that the existence of a complaints body does not affect any right of action which the insured may have against the insurer;

    (c) whether the parties are entitled to choose the law applicable to the contract and if so, the law which the insurer proposes to choose, or the law which will be applicable.

[25] Following *Adie v. The Insurance Corp.*, n.4, above, and *General Accident v. Cronk*, n.10, above.

[26] The requirements are contained in Sched. 2E to the Insurance Companies Act 1982, as inserted by S.I. 1994 No. 1696. Where a contract involves two or more insureds, the information must be provided to each of them: para. 5(1).

[27] As to these terms, see p. 27, above.

[28] They thus catch insurance sold from an establishment in the U.K. and insurance sold directly from another E.C. State.

[29] para. 3.

[30] Including the name and address of any appropriate body.

The other requirements apply as before except that they do not apply to a United Kingdom company or a member of Lloyd's unless the effecting of the contract constitutes the provision of general insurance in the United Kingdom. First, there is a requirement to inform the prospective insured of the member State in which is situated the establishment which will cover the risks.[31] Secondly, any proposal form, policy or other document which, or statements contained in which, will or may bind the prospective insured must state (a) the address of the establishment through which the risk is to be covered and (b) where the contract provides compulsory motor insurance in the United Kingdom, the name and address of the claims representative.[32]

Under section 72 of the Insurance Companies Act 1982,[33] which merely provides criminal sanctions for a failure to comply and has no civil consequences, regulations can be made as to the form and contents of insurance advertisements, defined as advertisements[34] inviting persons to enter into or offer to enter into insurance contracts, or containing information calculated to lead to such entry or offers.[35] The regulations[36] apply primarily to advertisements for life insurance by overseas insurers not authorised to carry on business in the United Kingdom and require that these facts be disclosed. The only regulation of relevance to authorised domestic insurers specifies that if any advertisement by them refers to their authorised capital, it must also state the amount of subscribed and paid up capital.[37]

Section 133 of the Financial Services Act 1986 provides that it is an offence for any person to induce or attempt to induce another to enter into a contract of insurance with an insurer by making dishonest or reckless statements or promises or forecasts or by dishonestly concealing material

---

[31] Any document issued by the insurer to the insured(s) must also contain that information. If this information is not given in writing before the contract is entered into, the requirement is complied with if it is also furnished in writing as soon as practicable thereafter.

[32] para. 4.

[33] See also s.72B regarding information for policy holders of EFTA companies.

[34] "Advertisement" itself is widely defined in subs. (6) as every form of advertising. It may well include any document sent out by an insurer, even to private addresses; cf. R. v. Delmayne [1970] 2 Q.B. 170.

[35] s.72(5).

[36] Insurance Companies Regulations 1994 (S.I. 1994 No. 1516), regs. 36 and 37.

[37] Note also the restriction on promoting insurance contracts which are investment contracts (as to this, see p. 325, below) in s.130 of the Financial Services Act 1986.

facts.[38] This is obviously aimed at misleading statements, promotional material and the like issued by insurers or their agents. An individual who was so induced to enter into an insurance contract could have a civil remedy, in addition to the criminal sanction in the section, if the representation was one of fact.

Formalities

Subject to one or two exceptions,[39] there is no general requirement of English law that an insurance contract be in any particular form. Indeed, an oral agreement, provided that it can be proved, is binding, provided that there is the necessary agreement on the material terms.[40] In practice, of course, apart from cases of temporary cover, insurance contracts are invariably recorded in a policy, but there is no legal need for this,[41] unless it is a term of the insurer's acceptance that they are not liable until a policy has been issued. The areas where there are particular formalities are those of life insurance and compulsory motor insurance. Consideration of these can be found in Chapters 17 and 19, respectively.

Forming The Contract At Lloyd's

Where the insurer is a member of Lloyd's, there are sufficient peculiarities concerning the procedure adopted in the formation of a contract to justify brief[42] separate consideration. We adverted in Chapters 1 and 2 to the special position of Lloyd's underwriters, whose procedure for the consideration of an offer for insurance involves the submission of a slip with details of the risk etc. to each relevant underwriter in turn. It should be noted that the proposer himself cannot do this; he must act through a Lloyd's broker.[43] The legal conundrum is simply when the contract is

---

[38] This section only applies to non-investment insurance contracts, but investment contracts (most forms of life insurance) are covered by the substantially similar s.47.

[39] Especially marine policies (Marine Insurance Act 1906, s.22) and guarantee policies (Statute of Frauds 1677, s.4).

[40] *Murfitt v. Royal Insurance Co.* (1922) 38 T.L.R. 334.

[41] See *Scher v. Policyholders Protection Board* [1993] 3 All E.R. 384 at 396 per Lord Donaldson M.R.

[42] For a fuller account, see *MacGillivray*, Chap. 35.

[43] See Chap. 10. Brokers may have authority to grant temporary cover: *Praet v. Poland* [1960] 1 Lloyd's Rep. 416; see further below.

concluded. Is each underwriter bound when he has accepted the offer by initialing the slip, even though later underwriters might decline the offer or amend its terms, or is there a contract only once the whole of the offer, the full amount of insurance requested, has been accepted?

It has been authoritatively decided by the Court of Appeal[44] that the underwriter is bound from the moment he initials the slip, despite the fact that in theory this could lead to odd legal results, for example if a later underwriter accepts on different terms. Strictly therefore the insured may have separate contracts with different underwriters rather than the one whole insurance contract. In reaching this conclusion, the Court of Appeal applied the well-established customs of the London insurance market.[45]

It also seems from the Court of Appeal's judgment[46] that the insured has no right to cancel a contract with an underwriter who has accepted his offer if a later underwriter refuses to accept the offer, so that the insured is only partially covered, or "accepts" it on terms unacceptable to the insured. Again in theory this could lead to odd results, though no doubt in practice disputes would rarely arise.

Temporary Cover and Cover-Notes

It is, of course, common practice in many different types of insurance, but most commonly in motor insurance, for insurers to agree to temporary cover upon first receipt of a proposal, pending full consideration and possible acceptance of the offer, and issue of a policy. Such "cover-notes," as they are usually called, are undoubtedly fully effective contracts of insurance.[47] There is a comparative dearth of legal authority concerning them, but a number of important legal questions arise which are examined in the following paragraphs.

Authority to issue cover-notes

Whereas the acceptance of an offer for a full contract of insurance can invariably be made only by the insurer, authority to conclude a binding

---

[44] *General Reinsurance Corporation v. Forsakringsaktiebolaget Fennia Patria* [1983] Q.B. 856; *contra Jaglom v. Excess Insurance Co. Ltd* [1972] Q.B. 250. See also *Eagle Star Insurance Co. Ltd v. Spratt* [1971] 2 Lloyd's Rep. 116.

[45] If the contract is subsequently incorporated into a policy, as will normally be the case, the letter constitutes the contract and the slip is not admissible as an aid to construction of it: *Yowell v. Bland Welch & Co. Ltd* [1992] 2 Lloyd's Rep. 127.

[46] Compare the views of Staughton J. at first instance in the *General Reinsurance* case: [1982] Q.B. 1022.

[47] *Mackie v. European Assurance Society* (1869) 21 L.T. 102.

cover-note will often be vested in an agent. Some of the relevant agency principles are examined in detail in Chapter 10. In this context, it is necessary merely to say that, regardless of whether or not an insurer has expressly conferred authority on an agent to issue cover-notes, the fact that an agent is entrusted with blank cover-notes or their equivalent appears sufficient to confer upon him either implied actual authority or ostensible authority.

In *Mackie v. European Assurance Society*,[48] the plaintiff insured his mill and warehouse through W, at the time an agent for the Commercial Union. Subsequently W became an agent of the defendant. The plaintiff's policy with the Commercial Union expired and he asked W for a new one. W gave him a cover-note, in the form of a receipt, for a month in the name of the defendant. Despite the fact that at the time the plaintiff did not realise that the insurer was different,[49] and despite the fact that the defendant no longer transacted fire business, Mallins V.-C., in a judgment notable for its criticism of the defendant's attitude, held that there was a binding temporary contract of insurance between the parties. Having provided W with cover-notes, the defendant had conferred authority on him to bind them. The principle must apply to any agents entrusted with cover-notes, even if they are brokers and normally agents of the insured.[50]

An agent not entrusted with blank cover-notes will not usually be regarded as having authority to bind the insurer.[51] The decision in *Murfitt v. Royal Insurance Co.*,[52] where an agent was held to have implied actual authority to enter into temporary oral contracts of fire insurance, must be regarded as exceptional. The judge stressed that the facts were special, because the agent in question had been giving such cover orally for two years with the knowledge and consent of his superiors. However, it would appear that the position of brokers may be different. There is a clear dictum[53] that they have implied authority to issue interim contracts of insurance in a case where the only acknowledgement by the broker was oral. This appears to be a clear recognition of a common practice whereby insurers do confer such authority on brokers. It must be stressed, however, that this can apply only where there is a pre-existing arrangement between insurer and broker.

---

[48] (1869) 21 L.T. 102.

[49] Though this should be irrelevant; the plaintiff merely wanted to be insured.

[50] See *Stockton v. Mason* [1978] 2 Lloyd's Rep. 430, discussed below and in Chap. 10.

[51] *Dicks v. S.A. Mutual Fire & General Insurance Co.* [1963] (4) S.A. 501.

[52] (1922) 38 T.L.R. 334.

[53] *Stockton v. Mason*, above at 431, per Lord Diplock.

Conclusion of the temporary contract

In the ordinary case, this should be a simple matter, the contract being concluded by the insurer or its agent's temporary acceptance of the proposer's offer, provided that the material terms are agreed, as discussed earlier. It will then last for the stated period or until earlier termination by the insurer if, as is usual, this is permitted, or upon being superseded by a formal policy. There can be no objection, sufficient terms being agreed, to the conclusion of a temporary contract by telephone.[54] It should be noted, however, that as a cover-note is a proper contract of insurance, the proposer is under a duty to disclose all material facts to the insurer prior to its conclusion, on pain of the contract being voidable at the latter's option.[55]

There is one contrasting situation where, it seems, this analysis of an offer by the proposer being accepted by the insurer will not apply. This is where temporary cover is offered by the insurer upon the termination of a formal contract. In practice this appears to be confined to motor insurance in order to enable the insured to satisfy the compulsory insurance requirements of the Road Traffic Act 1988.[56] What happens is that the insurer, sometimes by way of a slip attached to the motor insurance certificate, alternatively by the notice sent out inviting renewal of the policy, offers to cover the insured for a short period, usually 15 days, upon expiry of the old policy.[57] Any legal problem surrounding this is likely to arise only when the insured does not renew his old policy or effect a new one with a different insurer in time. This was the case in *Taylor v. Allon*[58] where the insured's policy with insurer A expired on April 5, but he possessed the sort of temporary slip described. He had decided to change his insurer to B, and from B he obtained new cover from April 16. However, he drove his car on April 15, and was charged with driving without insurance.[59] The Divisional Court held that he had been rightly

---

[54] Which is good news for the increasing number of people who initially insure in this way with "direct" insurers.

[55] *Mayne Nickless Ltd v. Pegler* (1974) 1 N.S.W.L.R. 228, criticised in (1977) 40 M.L.R. 79 (Birds); *Marene Knitting Mills v. Greater Pacific General Insurance Ltd* [1976] 2 Lloyd's Rep. 631. As to the duty of disclosure, see Chap. 6.

[56] See Chap. 19.

[57] This temporary extension is normally only in respect of the compulsory requirements.

[58] [1966] 1 Q.B. 304.

[59] Under what is now Road Traffic Act 1988, s.143.

convicted of that offence. Obviously he was not insured by B on April 15. A's cover-note was, it was held, merely an offer by A to insure him from the expiry of the policy, which was binding only if he accepted it.[60] On the facts there was no evidence that the insured accepted that offer. Clearly the insured had not expressly communicated his acceptance to A, though the Court was prepared to assume that this was the sort of situation where the usual rule as to communication of acceptance did not apply. However, even on this assumption, acceptance by conduct was necessary and there was no evidence of this, which would usually be by the insured's driving his car in reliance upon the offer.

Terms incorporated into the cover-note

The question next arises as to what are the terms of the contract constituted by a cover-note. Here the question of when the contract is concluded may be crucial. Obviously, the material terms[61] must be agreed, but it may be important to know whether conditions regarding the claims process, for example, contained in the insurer's standard policy are incorporated.

The careful insurer will ensure that its acceptance of the insured's offer is expressly made subject to its usual terms and conditions for the class of insurance in question.[62] Alternatively, the cover-note may be issued following completion of a proposal form which incorporates the relevant terms.[63] However, it might be thought that this is unnecessary, by virtue of the rule examined earlier that a proposer's offer for insurance is deemed to be for the usual form of policy issued by the insurer. It would appear, though, that this rule does not apply to cover notes.

No implied incorporation

In *Re Coleman's Depositories Ltd and Life & Health Assurance Association*,[64] a company applied for a policy of employer's liability insurance. They completed a proposal form on December 28 and on that day received a

---

[60] Even though A stated in evidence that they regarded themselves as bound to the insured.

[61] See above.

[62] See, *e.g. Dawson v. Monarch Insurance Co. of New Zealand* [1977] 1 N.Z.L.R. 372.

[63] See, *e.g. Houghton v. Trafalgar Insurance Co. Ltd* [1953] 2 Lloyd's Rep. 18.

[64] [1907] 2 K.B. 798. See also *Insurance Corporation International Ltd v. American Home Assurance Co.* (1974) 42 D.L.R. (3d) 46.

cover-note with no reference to any conditions. The insurers accepted the offer by the sealing of a policy on January 3, which was expressed to run from January 1, and which was delivered to the company on January 9. On January 2, one of the insured's employees was injured. At the time his condition was not considered dangerous, but he subsequently developed dangerous symptoms and died on March 15. On March 14, the insured gave notice of a possible claim against them to the insurers. The latter denied liability on the ground that the insured had failed to give immediate notice of the claim as required by a condition in the policy. By a majority, the Court of Appeal held that the insured was not bound by this condition, reasoning that it could not apply until communicated to the insured, which was not until January 9, and after the injury to the employee.[65] Although there is an obvious element of justice in the decision, the reasoning is not easy to follow. If the insured was simply relying upon the cover-note, and indeed the policy was not executed until after the accident, although it was stated to apply retrospectively, there is a case for saying that as it did not contain any reference to conditions, and in particular the condition requiring notice, the insured was not bound by any. Even this, however, runs contrary to the decisions in cases like *General Accident v. Cronk*[66] and there are contrary authorities.[67] However, the insured had relied upon the terms of the policy in agreeing initially to go to arbitration and there was no suggestion that they were not suing on the policy. In these circumstances, it is difficult to see how they could deny that they were bound by other terms in the policy, it being irrelevant that they may not have had actual knowledge of them at the relevant time.

While *Re Coleman* must stand as clear authority for the proposition that conditions imposing obligations on the insured apply to cover-notes only when expressly incorporated, it is perhaps safe to assume that it has survived largely unchallenged only because since then insurers have always stipulated expressly that their cover-notes incorporate their policy terms. In any event, it must be the case that terms of the usual policy defining the scope of the cover are impliedly incorporated into the cover-note.

---

[65] The Court was also of opinion that in any event the condition was not a condition precedent to liability. On this distinction, see Chap. 7.

[66] (1901) 17 T.L.R. 233; see p. 73 above.

[67] e.g. *Wyndham Rather Ltd v. Eagle Star & British Dominions Insurance Co. Ltd* (1925) 21 Ll.L. Rep 214.

An oral contract?

It may be that the insured is able to argue that a contract was concluded before the written cover-note or any incorporation by reference on a proposal form was made available to him. The facts of the Australian case of *Mayne Nickless Ltd v. Pegler*[68] illustrate this quite neatly. The insured purchased a car and the vendor immediately arranged for insurance, seemingly by telephone. The insured later received a cover-note bearing the date of purchase of the car and incorporating the insurer's usual terms. The case was decided upon other grounds, but it must be at least arguable that a binding insurance contract was concluded orally by telephone before the insured was aware of any express terms. The point was not argued, but if this is the correct legal analysis, and the situation may arise commonly in motor insurance, it is difficult to see, consistently with the decision in *Re Coleman* how an insurer can rely upon express incorporation of policy conditions, unless of course there is mention of this when the oral contract is being concluded.

The cover-note in the *Pegler* case also stated that it was "subject to . . . a satisfactory proposal for your insurance." It was held that the effect of this was to enable the insurer to avoid liability under the cover-note because of a misstatement in the proposal form subsequently completed by the insured. The proposal was not "satisfactory." With respect, it might be argued that the phrase simply warned the insured as to the need to complete a proposal form before a formal policy could be issued, or simply that "satisfactory" meant proper in the formal sense rather than in the sense of everything being absolutely correct. There was at least some ambiguity which was surely sufficient to invoke the *contra proferentem rule.*[69] Further, the effect of the decision is that if a proposal form is never completed, which may be for quite innocent reasons, for example, a subsequent accident[70] or the insured's decision to approach another insurer, the cover-note is technically worthless. It is suggested that in a case where such a qualification is attached to a cover-note, the court should disregard it on the grounds that it may render the protection allegedly provided useless.

[68] (1974) 1 N.S.W.L.R. 228.
[69] See Chap. 11 at pp. 206–208.
[70] See (1977) 40 M.L.R. 79 at 82.

Termination of the cover-note and its relationship with a subsequent policy

Finally, it is necessary to consider when the contract contained in a cover-note comes to an end, otherwise than by the expiry of its stated period. In practice, it may well provide that it can be terminated by the insurer, and there can be no objection to an insurer's acting in reliance upon such an express right, although the insured must receive notice of cancellation. In the absence of such a right, a cover-note would clearly not be terminable until it duly expired.[71]

It must frequently be the case, however, that a formal policy is issued before the cover-note's expressed duration has run. Here it would appear that the policy takes over from the date it is issued but not before. Even if the policy is expressed to be retrospective, it must be arguable that a claim arising before its issue falls under the cover-note only.[72] This can only be of any real consequence, however, if there is a relevant difference between the terms of the cover-note and the policy, which, as has been seen, is not very likely nowadays.

Duration and Renewal of Insurance Policies

The question of the length of an insurance contract is a matter for the policy itself to provide. There are no rules of law. However, it is safe to state as a general rule that the life contract is quite different from other insurance policies. There must be at least a presumption that a life contract is entire, is one contract, existing until the death of the life assured, or a specified fixed date in the case of an endowment or term policy.[73] So, provided that the premiums due are properly paid,[74] the insurer cannot refuse to renew a life policy, nor can he allege non-disclosure of material facts which happen after the contract is first concluded. We shall advert to this question later when considering "days of grace."

In contrast, most other policies are of limited duration, normally of one year, though, of course, there is no bar to the agreement of a policy for a

---

[71] *Smith v. National Mutual Fire Insurance Co. Ltd* [1974] 1 N.Z.L.R. 278.

[72] *Re Coleman*, above. Rather oddly in that case, as we have seen, the insured appeared to be suing on the policy rather than the cover-note.

[73] *Stuart v. Freeman* [1903] 1 K.B. 47 at 53–54 and 55; compare *Pritchard v. Merchants' and Tradesmen's Mutual Life Assurance Co.* (1858) 3 C.B. (n.s.) 622 at 643.

[74] *Pritchard v. Merchants' and Tradesmen's Mutual Life Assurance Co.*, above.

shorter or longer term. But upon expiry of such a policy, if the parties choose to renew the contract, the renewal is clearly in law a fresh contract[75] and thus, for example, the duty of disclosure arises again.[76]

Cancellation

Many non-life policies contain a condition entitling either party to cancel them upon giving notice to the other party, usually of seven or 14 days, but a clause permitting immediate cancellation would no doubt be valid. Some such conditions may require the insurer who seeks to cancel to show cause, but this is not essential and an absolute right to cancel is enforceable.[77] That such a right is capable of being abused, though it is an open question how often it may be abused, is evident from the cases.

In *Sun Fire Office v. Hart*,[78] the Privy Council upheld the cancellation of a fire policy under a clause providing for termination by the insurers "from any . . . cause whatever" after the insured had suffered several fires and had received an anonymous letter threatening arson.[79] More extreme perhaps are the facts in the Indian case of *General Assurance Society v. Chandermull Jain*.[80] There the insured's property was covered against loss or damage by flood. The River Ganges, which ran near the insured's property, had already started to flood further up its course when the insurers served notice of cancellation. The Supreme Court of India held that the insurers were perfectly justified in taking this action, there being nothing unreasonable about unrestricted cancellation rights,[81] provided

---

[75] *Stokell v. Heywood* [1897] 1 Ch. 459.

[76] *Lambert v. Co-operative Insurance Society* [1975] 1 Lloyd's Rep. 465; see Chap. 6.

[77] *Sun Fire Office v. Hart* (1889) 14 App. Cas. 98.

[78] (1889) 14 App. Cas. 98.

[79] The Court of Appeal of Grenada had refused to uphold the clause, saying that it would permit cancellation for any reason, which would be absurd. The Privy Council justified their decision partly on the ground that the insured could go elsewhere. This must be somewhat unrealistic. What insurer would insure at anything like the same premium an insured who has been threatened with arson, and the fact of cancellation must be a material fact which should be disclosed to any subsequent insurer, which again is hardly likely to dispose it to look kindly on the insured.

[80] A.I.R. (1966) S.C. 1644.

[81] The insured had a similar right of cancellation which, it was said, complimented the insurer's. This is ridiculous. The insured who cancels does not jeopardise the position of the insurer who can retain at least the premium appropriate for the risk he has borne. As the facts of the case show, the insured may very easily be substantially harmed by the insurer's cancellation.

that cancellation is effected before the risk insured against has run. This is a question of fact; presumably there has to be some danger to the property insured before a cancellation would be illegitimate.

It should be noted that usually, upon cancellation, the insured is entitled under the standard condition to a pro rata return of premium. In the absence of such an express right, he would not be entitled to anything, the risk having run.[82]

One would imagine that nowadays insurers only rarely exercise their cancellation power arbitrarily,[83] but, even if this is so, there would appear to be an unanswerable case for the restriction of such rights, particularly in the field of motor insurance, where insurance is compulsory.[84] What is needed is a guaranteed minimum period of notice before cancellation can take effect, in order to enable the insured to seek fresh cover, and, particularly, a requirement that the insurer have good reason to cancel.

Life policies

Life policies do not, of course, contain cancellation clauses of the same kind but commonly, at least apart from term assurance, they do contain provisions enabling the insured to terminate the policy. They may permit the insured to surrender the policy after a certain number of years, so that the insured then receives a lump sum, the surrender value, or they may provide for the policy to become paid-up, so that no more premiums are due, but the benefits payable on death are reduced to the appropriate sum according to the amount of premium actually paid. At the early stages of a life policy, these values are inevitably low and may be much less than the value of the premiums paid, the insurer having to take account of his administrative costs. What these entitlements are must be provided in writing to the insured,[85] but the law does not prescribe any minimum entitlements.[86]

---

[82] See Chap. 8.
[83] A modern reported example of what appears to have been a fairly arbitrary cancellation is *J. H. Moore v. Crowe* [1972] 2 Lloyd's Rep. 563. The dispute concerned the consequences of a cancellation.
[84] Compare the position in the USA: see (1969) Duke Law Journal 327.
[85] Insurance Companies Act 1982, Sched. 2E; see p. 326, below.
[86] Compare the Australian Life Insurance Act 1945–1973, ss.95-99 and Sched. 6, prescribing such minima.

Renewal and days of grace

Apart from life policies, there is no right to renew an insurance contract in the absence of a term of the contract to that effect.[87] Nor is an insurer under any general obligation to send out a renewal notice,[88] or any form of warning that a policy is about to expire, though this is common practice. Neither does an insurer need any reason for not renewing.[89] As we have seen, the renewal of a non-life policy constitutes the effecting of an entirely new contract.

In practice of course insurers do generally renew, and they may allow "days of grace" after the expiry of the old contract, for the renewal premium to be paid. The precise effect of such a period depends upon the wording of the policy in question, but as a general rule, as this is a concession, it is unlikely that the insured is protected while the premium remains unpaid, so that a loss before payment would not be covered. It must also be doubtful whether an insured could, after a loss, insist upon renewal by tendering the premium within the days of grace and thus purporting to accept the insurer's offer.[90] However, there does appear to be a clear exception in the case of life policies which permit days of grace. As these are continuing policies, subject to lapse only upon non-compliance

---

[87] For an example, see the policy in *Kirby v. Cosindit Spa* [1969] 1 Lloyd's Rep. 75; compare *Jones Construction v. Alliance Assurance Co. Ltd* [1961] 1 Lloyd's Rep. 121 and *Webb v. Bracey* [1964] 1 Lloyd's Rep. 465.

[88] *Simpson v. Accidental Death Insurance Co.* (1857) 2 C.B. (N.S.) 257.

[89] Query whether an insurer should have, for the reasons suggested in connection with cancellation. In theory problems could arise when, as is common in motor insurance, an insured has the right to a "no claims" or "loyalty" bonus entitling him to a discount on the normal premium. For example, an insurer may promise that the bonus will adhere if the insured makes no more than a limited number of claims over a period of some years, that is spanning several legally separate contracts. The question may arise as to how such a promise is legally enforceable. A possible solution is that the insurer makes a standing offer to continue to insure, subject no doubt to there being no unacceptable or undisclosed material changes in risk; this would of course be contrary to the usual legal position governing non-life contracts, as explained earlier (p. 86). Another possibility might be an enforceable collateral contract, so that the insured would be entitled to damages, namely the extra cost of other insurance, if the insurer unjustifiably failed to renew, but not actually to any right to a new contract of insurance. It is conceivable perhaps that the insurer failing to renew in these circumstances would be in a breach of a general duty to act with the utmost good faith (see p. 123 below), but this would not give the insured an effective remedy.

[90] cf. *Canning v. Farquhar* (1886) 16 Q.B.D. 727, discussed earlier.

with conditions as to payment of premium, payment within the days of grace, but not of course afterwards,[91] is effective, even if the loss, *i.e.* the death of the life assured, has already occurred.[92] The only situation where this would not be the position is where the insurer has the right not to accept payment of the premium after the renewal date,[93] but in this case it is hardly correct in any event to speak of there being days of grace.

[91] *Pritchard v. Merchants' and Tradesmen's Mutual Life Assurance Society* (1858) 3 C.B. (N.S.) 622.

[92] *Stuart v. Freeman* [1903] 1 K.B. 47.

[93] *Simpson v. Accidental Death Insurance Co.* (1857) 2 C.B. (N.S.) 257.

CHAPTER 5

REPUDIATIONS OF POLICIES AND LIABILITY

Lying at the heart of insurance contract law are those situations where an insurer can lawfully refuse to pay a claim. This may arise because what has happened is simply not within the scope of the policy in question, a matter of construing the provisions which describe the cover and any exceptions to it which is dealt with in Chapter 11. Alternatively, the insurer may successfully allege lack of insurable interest or public policy in support of his refusal to pay; the former has already been dealt within Chapter 3 and the latter is considered separately, later, in Chapter 12.

More importantly for present purposes, there is a range of situations when an insurer's refusal to pay is by reason of his claim that the policy is void or voidable or properly repudiated or that he is discharged from liability or can repudiate liability without denying the validity of the actual contract. The substantive detail of the most important grounds upon which such claims can be made is considered in the next two chapters, but, because this is an area where general principles are easier to state than always to apply, this chapter gives an overview of the grounds upon which an insurer can claim such a refusal. Some of these grounds arise from circumstances surrounding the initial application for or renewal of, a policy, which in itself justifies their consideration at an early stage in this book; these are principally claims arising out of non-disclosure or misrepresentation of material facts or some breaches of warranty. Others arise from allegations of breaches of warranty or condition contained in the body of the insurance policy.

Unfair Terms in Consumer Insurance Contracts

Where any of the above grounds arises as a result of a term of the contract,[1] their operation may be affected by the operation of the Unfair

---

[1] This will not be the case where a policy is void or voidable by reason of some general legal principle, such as non-disclosure or misrepresentation, but will be where an insurer may not be liable because of the operation of a warranty or condition in the policy.

Terms in Consumer Contracts Regulations 1994,[2] where the insured is a "consumer."[3] As indicated earlier,[4] these regulations apply to insurance contracts, but a crucial question in determining their impact on the issues we are concerned with here is the meaning and applicability of the phrase "any term which . . . defines the main subject matter of the contract."[5] Such a term, provided that it is worded in "plain intelligible language"[6] is not subject to assessment on the ground of unfairness.[7] It is clear that a condition in an insurance contract which is concerned solely with some obligation on the insured following the occurrence of a loss cannot be such a term and is therefore liable to be set aside on the ground that it is unfair. On the other hand, the true insurance warranty, as explained below, imposes an obligation on the insured to control the risk run by the insurer. Therefore, it could possibly be regarded as defining the main subject matter of the contract and outside the scope of the Regulations.[8]

Whatever the true scope of the Regulations, a matter which ultimately will have to be decided by the court, a term is unfair if "contrary to the requirement of good faith [it] causes a significant imbalance in the parties' rights and obligations under the contract to the detriment of the consumer."[9] Assessment must take account of the nature of the services and refer, as at the time of the conclusion of the contract, to all circumstances attending the conclusion of the contract and to all the other terms of the contract.[10] In determining whether a term satisfies the requirement of good faith, regard must be had in particular to the matters in Schedule 2,[11] and Schedule 3 contains an indicative and illustrative list

---

[2] S.I. 1994 No. 3159.

[3] A natural person not acting for business purposes.

[4] See p. 4.

[5] reg. 3(2)(a).

[6] It will not always be easy to determine whether or not a term is worded plainly and intelligibly, presumably from the perspective of a reasonable consumer of insurance.

[7] This seems a narrower exclusion than that permitted by the E.C. Directive 93/13 which the Regulations implement. The Directive in its preamble excludes insurance terms "which clearly define or circumscribe the insured risk."

[8] Certainly most of the obligations imposed by warranties could be rewritten as exclusions of the insurer's liability, and plain, intelligible exclusions must be outside the control of the Regulations; see p. 198, below.

[9] reg. 4(1).

[10] reg. 4(2).

[11] reg. 4(3). These are (i) the strength of the bargaining positions of the parties; (ii) whether the consumer had an inducement to agree to any term; (iii) whether the insurance was supplied to the special order of the consumer; and (iv) the extent to which the insurer has dealt fairly and equitably with the consumer.

of terms which may be regarded as unfair. Even if the Regulations apply to insurance warranties or conditions affecting the risk, it does not follow that they can be struck down as unfair. For example, a common requirement on an insured to take reasonable care of insured property[12] may well be quite fair in the circumstances of the contract. What would clearly not survive the Regulations, in so far as any such terms still exist in consumer insurance contracts, are conditions which impose unreasonable deadlines on the insured, for example in giving notice of a loss,[13] and, possibly, terms which given the insurer complete control over the actions of an insured following an insured loss, for example some of the standard terms in liability insurance policies.[14]

It should be noted that there are no overriding rules of law as to how a particular term in an insurance contract is to be classified. Insurers have complete freedom as to the terms they use and what any term is in any particular policy will depend on how the particular insurer concerned has chosen to draft his policy. Further, it has to be said that the legal distinctions between warranties, conditions precedent and mere conditions, which are adverted to below, are sometimes confusing, and the questions involved are perhaps the most difficult to resolve in insurance law.

Void contracts

In certain, although rather rare, situations an insurance contract may be void.[15] The most obvious example is a contract which is void by reason of illegality.[16] It is also conceivable, although perhaps unlikely in practice, that an insurance contract could be void for mistake.[17] For present purposes,[18] an insurance contract may be illegal and void for one of the following two reasons:

---

[12] See p. 201, below.

[13] See p. 244, below.

[14] See pp. 348–353, below.

[15] Insurers sometimes claim that a policy is "void", *e.g.* for non-disclosure, even using the word as a verb as in "The policy is voided", in situations where strictly this is an incorrect usage. They mean that a policy is voidable or that they have the right to treat it as repudiated.

[16] This is different from the situation where performance of an insurance contract may be illegal on public policy grounds; as already indicated, this is dealt with later in Chap. 12.

[17] As to mistake, see, *e.g.* Treitel, *Law of Contract*, Chap. 8.

[18] Illegality may also arise by reason of lack of insurable interest; as already indicated, this has been considered in Chap. 3.

(1) the contract may have been entered into to achieve a purpose which is illegal or contrary to public policy;

(2) the contract may be vitiated by the unlawful use of property.

There are few examples of these situations. One example of (1) would be a contract of insurance on the property of an enemy agent.[19] Another at common law is a contract entered into by an unauthorised insurer.[20] The most likely example of (2) comes from marine insurance law, where there is a principle that an unlawful voyage renders the marine insurance contract unlawful. The same principle presumably applies in theory to non-marine insurance contracts, so that if the property insured is always used unlawfully,[21] the insurance contract would be void, but it is clear that occasional or temporary illegal use does not have this effect. In *Leggate v. Brown*,[22] for example, the use of a tractor in circumstances prohibited by the Road Traffic Act, but covered by the insured's motor policy, was held not to render that policy illegal.

Voidable or discharged contracts

Of particular importance in insurance law are those areas of law which have the effect of giving the insurer (or, sometimes, the insured) the option to avoid the contract in its entirety or which achieve a similar result by reason of either an automatic discharge of the insurer from liability or the insurer having the right to treat the contract as repudiated.[23] Strictly, the only circumstances in which an insurance contract is voidable are where one party can avoid by reason of the other's fraud or non-disclosure or misrepresentation of material facts or some other breach of the duty of utmost good faith. These circumstances are examined in detail in the next

---

[19] At a time of war, the legislature often makes express provision as to the illegality of insurance contracts effected in this country on enemy property etc.

[20] *Phoenix General Insurance Co. of Greece S.A. v. Administratia Asiguraliror de Stat* [1986] 2 Lloyd's Rep. 552. Statute now makes express provision for this situation; see p. 26 above.

[21] It may not be possible to recover in respect of property obtained unlawfully, but this is a consequence of public policy (see Chap. 12) and does not affect the validity of the insurance contract.

[22] (1950) 66(2) T.L.R. 281.

[23] For a more detailed attempt to explore these and other issues regarding the termination of an insurance contract, see Birds, Chap. 4 in *Termination of Contracts*, eds. Birds, Bradgate and Villiers, 1995.

chapter. As already noted, it is strictly incorrect to talk about a policy being void in these circumstances.

A distinct situation is where the liability of the insurer is automatically discharged.[24] This will arise where the insured is guilty of a breach of warranty.[25] A warranty in insurance is essentially a term involving a promise by the insured which controls the risk run by the insurer.[26] In this respect, insurance law usage regarding the warranty as a fundamental term in an insurance contract differs from the position in general contract law, where a warranty is normally regarded as a relatively minor term, the breach of which only ever entitles the innocent party to damages.[27] Full consideration of warranties is given in Chapter 7.

Repudiating the contract or claim

In addition to warranties, insurance contracts invariably contain what they describe as "conditions." Indeed, what in one policy may be covered by a warranty may in another fall under the heading or description of condition. Having said that, it is probably safe to say that if something is described as a warranty, it will normally[28] be held to be such, and the same result will follow in respect of terms where a breach is expressly described as giving rise to avoidance of the policy. as a whole[29] or discharging the insurer from all liability.

What is clear is that an insurance contract can provide for a condition to have the same effect as a condition in general contract law, namely that on

[24] Unless he chooses to waive this possibility; see p. 132, below.

[25] *Bank of Nova Scotia v. Hellenic Mutual War Risks Association (Bermuda) Ltd, The Good Luck* [1991] 2 W.L.R. 1279; see pp. 129–133, below.

[26] Not all such terms, though, will necessarily be warranties; see below.

[27] As in the Sale of Goods Act 1979. Of course the term "warranty" may be used in other senses, *e.g.* as meaning guarantee (manufacturers' warranties etc). The fact that modern case-law in contract generally (see, *e.g. Schuler v. Wickman* [1974] A.C. 235) has reconsidered the whole question of the relationship between and description of the terms of a contract seems irrelevant to insurance contract law. Cases in the latter area proceed along their own lines and, while the courts could review the classification of terms in insurance contracts without regard to their actual description, it seems most unlikely that they will do so. See *The Good Luck*, above, discussed at pp. 129–133, below and the relatively recent decision in *Cox v. Orion Insurance Co. Ltd* [1982] R.T.R. 1 (p. 137, below), where the Court of Appeal considered the effect of conditions precedent in an insurance contract without reference to general contract principles.

[28] Though by no means always; see pp. 141–145, below.

[29] This is of course strictly an incorrect usage, as already explained.

breach, the insurer can treat the whole contract as repudiated. This will normally be done by making performance of the condition precedent to any liability of the insurer. However, it does seem clear that repudiation is allowed only if there is a causal connection between the breach and the loss for which the insured has made a claim.[30] In this respect there is a clear distinction from the warranty, where a breach is in law actionable regardless of any such causal connection.[31] A term with a slightly less significant effect is the condition which is merely precedent to the insurer's liability to pay for a particular claim.[32] Even less significant, although likely to be found rarely these days, is a "mere" condition, that is a condition which is not declared to be precedent to anything, on breach of which the insurer is entitled only to claim damages for such loss as he has suffered.[33] Full discussion of the relevant distinctions is left to Chapter 7. Apart from those matters which may also be the subject of warranties, namely those matters which affect the risk run by the insurer, the usual matters covered by conditions precedent are duties to be performed by the insured, often upon the making of a claim. It is this sort of term which is clearly potentially subject to the controls of the Unfair Terms in Consumer Contracts Regulations, as already discussed.

Another term which has a similar consequence to a condition precedent, but which is conceptually different, is the suspensive condition, often known as the condition or clause descriptive of, or delimiting, the risk. This normally, but not always,[34] arises from the contents of a completed proposal form. Its effect is that the insurer is not on risk, and therefore not liable for any loss, while the term is not being complied with, but the risk attaches or reattaches, as the case may be, when the term is being complied with. It thus operates in the same way as an exception contained in the body of a policy. It differs from a warranty in that it cannot lead to a complete discharge of the insurer and from a condition precedent in that a breach does not entitle the insurer to repudiate the contract.

---

[30] See p. 138.
[31] See p. 128.
[32] The insurer can repudiate liability for a claim for breach of this sort of condition while affirming the contract generally; see *e.g. Mint Security Ltd v. Blair* [1982] 1 Lloyd's Rep. 188; compare the ruling in *West v. Motor Accident Insurance Union* [1954] 1 Lloyd's Rep. 461, [1955] 1 All E.R. 800, discussed at p. 133, below, although, as suggested there, this decision may not be supportable in the light of the decision in *The Good Luck*, above.
[33] Although if the amount of the insurer's damages equals the amount of the insured's claim, the result will be the same as if it were a condition precedent.
[34] See pp. 141–145.

Loss of the right to avoid or repudiate

Finally, there are a number of circumstances in which an insurer may lose the right to rely upon a non-disclosure or misrepresentation, or a breach of warranty or condition. This can arise first by application of the doctrines of waiver or estoppel. The essence of the matter is that the insurer, by what it says or does, leads the insured to believe that it will not insist upon its strict legal rights. The law then precludes the insurer from doing so. Waiver and estoppel may be conceptually different. This is a question more fully discussed later,[35] as indeed are the principles surrounding the application of these doctrines. Other illustrations of cases of waiver and estoppel will be found in the next two chapters.

Indisputable policies

Sometimes insurers provide that their policies are to become indisputable after they have been in force for a particular time. In practice this is only likely to apply to life policies. The effect of an indisputability clause is that the insurer cannot rely upon defences which would entitle it to avoid the policy, or liability under it, from its inception.[36] Thus it will apply to non-disclosure, misrepresentation and certain breaches of warranty, but not, for example, to conditions or the coverage or definition of risk in the policy.[37] Furthermore, it cannot be relied upon to cure the lack of an insurable interest whose absence renders the policy illegal and void.[38] In addition, an indisputability clause never precludes the insurer from alleging that a policy was obtained by fraud.

---

[35] See Chap. 12 at pp. 251–254.

[36] *Anstey v. British Natural Premium Life Assurance Ltd* (1909) 99 L.T. 765.

[37] See, *e.g.* Cardozo J. in *Metropolitan Life Insurance Co. v. Conway* 252 N.Y. 449, 169 N.E. 642 (1930). In some American states, indisputability clauses are compulsory. Compare the Australian Life Insurance Act 1954, s.84 which is to the same effect.

[38] *Anctil v. Manufacturers' Life Insurance Co.* [1899] A.C. 604.

CHAPTER 6

FRAUD, NON-DISCLOSURE AND MISREPRESENTATION

As described in the last chapter, an insurer has the right to avoid the contract of insurance in its entirety if the insured was guilty of fraud, non-disclosure or misrepresentation before the contract was entered into. The questions of fraud and misrepresentation are common to all contracts. Non-disclosure is peculiar to a class of contracts — contracts of the utmost good faith — of which the insurance contract is the prime example. The principle of utmost good faith does not have consequences just for the proposer or insured. Insurers are also subject, at least in theory, to a resulting duty. This question is given separate consideration at the end of this chapter.

It should be noted that in practice, in many instances where the insured is an individual consumer, the law as to non-disclosure and misrepresentation is not applied strictly, partly because of the *Statements of Insurance Practice* and partly because the impact of rulings of the Insurance Ombudsman.[1] While this point should always be borne in mind, it is first necessary to describe the strict legal position and leave the question of practice and indeed of reform of the law to later in the chapter.

Fraud

This topic can be disposed of quickly; more detailed discussion can be found elsewhere.[2] A proposer is guilty of fraudulent misrepresentation if he knowingly makes a statement which is false, without belief in its truth or recklessly as to whether it is true or false.[3] In addition to the right to avoid a contract entered into by an insured who has been fraudulent, the insurer

---

[1] See p. 6.
[2] See *e.g. MacGillivray*, Chap. 16.
[3] *Derry v. Peek* (1889) 14 App. Cas. 337.

may also have the right to claim damages in the tort of deceit, and can in addition retain any premium paid.

Misrepresentation

An insurer can avoid an insurance contract if he was induced to enter into it by a misrepresentation of fact made by the proposer which was false in a material particular, whether the proposer acted negligently or quite innocently. This right differs little from that attaching generally in the law of contract.[4] Historically, misrepresentation in the strict sense has not been of particular importance in the insurance context. This is partly because the extreme width of the duty to disclose material facts, as described below, has meant that often non-disclosure has subsumed questions of misrepresentation. Cases have frequently failed to distinguish between the two defences taken by an insurer and indeed it appears to be standard practice for an insurer, where possible, to plead both defences. While this may be conceptually unsatisfactory,[5] it is well established, the rationalisation being that it is said to be part of the insured's duty of good faith to answer correctly questions on a proposal form.[6] On the other hand, there is clearly a distinction between an innocent misrepresentation, where the proposer does not know the truth, and an innocent non-disclosure, where the proposer knows the truth but does not appreciate that he should disclose the fact in question. It seems, however, that this distinction does not matter.[7]

Another reason for the relative unimportance, historically, of misrepresentation is that it applies only to those statements made before a contract is concluded which are properly mere representations and not terms of the contract. The usual, although not the only, source of such representations by the insured will be the statements he makes on the proposal form. Traditionally, by the device known as the "basis of the contract" clause,

---

[4] See *e.g.* Treitel, *Law of Contract*, Chap. 9. Until the decision of the House of Lords in *Pan Atlantic Insurance Co. v. Pine Top Insurance Co.* [1994] 3 All E.R. 581, it was unclear whether or not "inducement" was an element of misrepresentation in insurance contracts, especially because s.20 of the Marine Insurance Act 1906, codifying marine insurance law, does not contain it. Now it clearly is a requirement; see further below p. 109.

[5] See Hasson (1975) 38 M.L.R. 89.

[6] *Everett v. Desborough* (1829) 5 Bing. 503.

[7] *Pan Atlantic Insurance Co. v. Pine Top Insurance Co.* [1994] 3 All E.R. 581, discussed further below. See Birds and Hird, (1996) 59 M.L.R. 285.

which is examined in the next chapter, such statements have been made terms of the contract and the law of misrepresentation is therefore irrelevant to them. However, basis clauses are less common in modern practice, and indeed should not be used at all for proposals by individual insureds.[8] Misrepresentation therefore may be more relevant now than formerly.[9]

In any event, most of the legal questions that arise in the context of misrepresentation, in particular the need for the misrepresented fact to be material and how materiality is judged, are the same as apply to non-disclosure and these will be fully discussed shortly.

Finally, it should be noted that, in theory at least, section 2(2) of the Misrepresentation Act 1967 could operate as a restriction on the insurer's right to avoid for misrepresentation. That subsection gives the court discretion to award damages in lieu of rescission or avoidance. It has been held, *obiter,* that the discretion would never be used in respect of commercial contracts of insurance,[10] a dictum which clearly leaves open the possibility of it being available to individual insureds, and indeed the Insurance Ombudsman has stated that he may use it in cases coming before him.[11] On the other hand, since the insurer would, as noted above, probably be able in the alternative to rely upon a non-disclosure, the point seems academic, since it seems clear that the wording of section 2(2) cannot be applied to non-disclosures.[12]

Utmost good faith and non-disclosure

The contract of insurance is the primary illustration[13] of a class of contracts described as *uberrimae fidei,* that is, of the utmost good faith. As a result, the potential parties to it are bound to volunteer to each other before the contract is concluded information which is material. A matter

---

[8] The Statement of General Insurance Practice, para. 1(b). See p. 154, below.

[9] However, by para. (a) of the Statement of Practice, the declaration at the foot of a proposal form should make it clear that the form is completed only to the best of the proposer's knowledge and belief. Where this is complied with, any statements on the form will be statements of opinion and not of fact and thus outside the realm of misrepresentation.

[10] *Highlands Insurance Co. v. Continental Insurance Co.* [1987] 1 Lloyd's Rep. 109.

[11] See the Annual Report for 1990, para. 2.3; see p. 122, below.

[12] See Hudson (1969) 85 L.Q.R. 524.

[13] Others are family arrangements and contracts to take shares in public companies, the disclosure obligations in the latter case being imposed largely by statute.

that has been raised in recent caselaw is whether the requirement of utmost good faith also applies throughout the contract.[14] This point is discussed later.[15]

As indicated earlier, the principle of utmost good faith applies to insurers as well as insureds, but for the present we concentrate on the duty of disclosure it imposes on the proposer or insured. The basic effect of the duty can be stated quite simply. An applicant for insurance is under a duty to disclose to the insurer, prior to the conclusion of the contract,[16] but only up to this date, all material facts within his knowledge which the latter does not or is not deemed to know. A failure to disclose, however innocent, entitles the insurer to avoid the contract *ab initio,* and upon avoidance it is deemed never to have existed.[17] The insurer must avoid within a reasonable time of becoming aware of the non-disclosure. The duty arises whenever a fresh contract is concluded and, most importantly, this includes upon a renewal of any contract except that of life insurance; this point has already been considered in an earlier chapter.[18] A number of important questions arise from this description and these are examined under the following headings.

The rationale for the rule

In the leading case which established the duty of disclosure in insurance contracts, *Carter* v. *Boehm,*[19] Lord Mansfield said:[20]

---

[14] The founding case is *Black King Shipping Corporation v. Massie (The Litsion Pride)* [1985] 1 Lloyd's Rep. 437, but the authority of this case has been doubted, especially in *New Hampshire Insurance Co. v. MGN Ltd* [1996] C.L.C. 1692.

[15] See p. 117 in the context of a duty to notify increases in risk and p. 254 in the contexts of fraudulent claims. The duty of disclosure does not depend on an implied term in this insurance contract: see p. 126, below.

[16] The exact date when this occurs (see Chap. 4) may therefore be of the greatest importance.

[17] *Mackender v. Feldia A.G.* [1967] 2 Q.B. 590 appears to have decided to the contrary, but is distinguishable: see *MacGillivray*, (8th ed.) para. 656.

[18] See Chap. 4, p. 87.

[19] (1766) 3 Burr. 1905. Rather curiously in *Banque Financière de la Cité v. Westgate Insurance Co. Ltd* [1990] 1 Q.B. 665, affirmed [1991] 2 A.C. 249, it was held that the duty of disclosure is equitable in origin, and this view was repeated in *Pan Atlantic Insurance Co. v. Pine Top Insurance Co.* [1994] 3 All E.R. 581. See further p. 126, below.

[20] (1766) 3 Burr. 1905 at 1909.

"Insurance is a contract upon speculation. The special facts, upon which the contingent chance is to be computed, lie most commonly in the knowledge of the insured only: the under-writer trusts to his representation, and proceeds upon the confidence that he does not keep back any circumstance in his knowledge, to mislead the under-writer into a belief that the circumstance does not exist, and to induce him to estimate the risque as if it did not exist."

There can be no doubt that the contract of insurance is a special one in the terms that Lord Mansfield expressed, but two comments can at this stage be made about his formulation of the doctrine of non-disclosure. First, it is by no means certain that he was intending to lay down as broad a doctrine as subsequent cases have established,[21] although this is a purely academic question today. Certainly the U.S. courts developed a much narrower duty of disclosure from the same source.[22] It is also noteworthy that Lord Mansfield regarded his principle of good faith as he called it as applying to all contracts.[23] He could hardly have been referring to the broad duty of disclosure as it is known today. Secondly, it is important to remember that *Carter v. Boehm* involved a contract entered into at a time when communications were poor and insurers were not equipped with means easily to discover all the information they needed to know by the asking of questions of the proposer. It must be concluded that the justification for an all-ranging duty of disclosure is not so apparent today and indeed this has been accepted by insurers themselves in respect of insurances effected by individuals.[24] This is a question to which we shall return later.

Statements of fact

The duty of disclosure and the duty not to misrepresent require that statements made by the proposer be of facts not opinion. A misstated

---

[21] See Hasson, "The doctrine of uberrima fides in insurance law: a critical evaluation" (1969) 32 M.L.R. 615.

[22] Vance on *Insurance* (3rd ed.) pp. 370 et seq; *Sebring v. Fidelity Phoenix Insurance Co.* 225 N.Y. 382 (1931).

[23] See (1766) 3 Burr. at 1910.

[24] It was also accepted by the House of Lords when they restated the test of materiality in *Pan Atlantic Insurance Co. v. Pine Top Insurance Co.* [1994] 3 All E.R. 581 (see p. 109, below), although whether that restatement is of great benefit to insureds is open to question.

opinion is actionable only if not given in good faith.[25] However, the distinction between questions of fact and questions of opinion is not always an easy one and may not matter greatly in practice. This point can be illustrated particularly by the example of proposals for life insurance, where a proposer may very well not know highly material facts regarding his health, because he is not an expert, or if he does know something, may very well fail to appreciate its significance. In *Joel v. Law Union & Crown Insurance Co.*,[26] a statement as to the health of the proposer, made by her, was regarded as a statement of opinion. This accords with common sense, as the proposer who is not a medical expert or told specifically by such an expert of facts as to his health, cannot be expected to give more than an opinion. However, in a later case[27] concerning a similar issue, a proposer who failed to disclose a visit to a specialist was held to be guilty of non-disclosure of a material fact, even though he did not know that there was anything seriously wrong with him. Thus, although a mere statement as to health without more is a statement of opinion, at least where the proposer does not know any relevant facts, if a proposer for life insurance has consulted a doctor in more than an ordinary way, the fact of consultation will almost certainly be a material fact requiring to be disclosed.

Knowledge and opinion of the proposer

The question of the knowledge or the opinion of the proposer for insurance raises three further questions; first, his knowledge of the duty to disclose, secondly, whether his opinion as to materiality is relevant, and thirdly, what knowledge of the material facts on his part is required. As to the first point, it is clear that whether or not the proposer knows that he is under a duty to disclose is totally irrelevant. Innocent non-disclosure is as actionable as negligent non-disclosure or concealment, as all the cases assume. Similarly, the insured's opinion as to the materiality of non-disclosed facts is irrelevant even though he may well have acted in good faith. As has been pointed out, it is the law that a man may act in perfect good faith within the ordinary meaning of the phrase, yet still be held not to have acted in the utmost good faith in the legal sense.[28]

---

[25] *Anderson v. Pacific Fire & Marine Insurance Co.* (1872) L.R. 7 C.P. 65.

[26] [1908] 2 K.B. 863. See also *Life Association of Scotland v. Forster* 1873 11 Macph. 351.

[27] *Godfrey v. Britannic Assurance Co. Ltd* [1963] 2 Lloyd's Rep. 515.

[28] See, *e.g.* McNair J. in *Roselodge Ltd v. Castle* [1966] 2 Lloyd's Rep. 113 at 129.

Constructive knowledge

More problematic is the question as to whether or not the insured is bound to disclose only those material facts which he actually knows or whether his "knowledge" includes facts which he ought to know. Clearly he is not bound to disclose what he does not know, and some cases, particularly in the life insurance field, have assumed that only actual knowledge imposes a duty. In *Joel v. Law Union & Crown Insurance Co.*,[29] one of the issues was whether the proposer was bound to disclose the fact that she had suffered from acute depression, it being accepted that she was unaware of the fact. It was held not and the judges were at pains to point out that there is no duty to disclose what the proposer does not know.[30] However, it has later been said that the question as to disclosure of constructive knowledge is an open one so far as non-marine insurance is concerned.[31] It is arguable that a proposer is under a duty to disclose what he constructively knows, because that is the law in respect of marine insurance, and section 18 of the 1906 Act, which so provides, is merely a codification of the duty of disclosure in respect of marine insurance which reflected the common law rules in respect of all classes of insurance.[32]

Knowledge of proposer's agent

What cannot be disputed is that the knowledge of his agent, acquired in the course of his duties, is the knowledge of the proposer. If therefore, for example, the managing director of a company knows a material fact, but it is not known to the officer of the company who actually makes the proposal for insurance on the company's behalf, the company is deemed to know and the non-disclosure of the fact to the insurer will entitle the latter

---

[29] [1908] 2 K.B. 863.
[30] See especially Fletcher Moulton L.J., [1908] 2 K.B. at 884.
[31] McNair J. in *Australia and New Zealand Bank v. Colonial and Eagle Wharves Ltd* [1960] 2 Lloyd's Rep. 241 at 252.
[32] But even this was left open by McNair J., *ibid*. More recent cases, especially *Pan Atlantic Insurance Co. v. Pine Top Insurance Co.* [1994] 3 All E.R. 581, assume in respect of other aspects of the duty of disclosure that s.18 merely codified the common law applying to all insurances. It is in cases of life policies that actual knowledge only has been required. This is not altogether surprising given the difficulties faced by the average proposer with regard to knowledge of his state of health (see p. 103, above). Perhaps the simplest and most logical solution would be to treat life cases as *sui generis*. See also *Simner v. New India Assurance Co. The Times*, July 21, 1994.

to avoid the contract. The same principle will apply if the agent is a broker, although in this case the proposer would almost certainly have an action in negligence against the broker who failed to disclose the fact to the insurer.[33]

What need not be disclosed

Facts which are material need not nonetheless be disclosed to the insurer if (i) they diminish the risk; (ii) they are facts which the insurer knows or is presumed to know or are matters of common knowledge; or (iii) they are facts of which the insurer waives disclosure. Many of the points under heads (i) and (ii) are self-explanatory. *Carter v. Boehm* itself was a case where the insurers could not rely upon the non-disclosure because, it was held, the material facts were a matter of common knowledge. The insurance was of a fort in Sumatra by the Governor of the then colony. The material fact was that the fort was likely to be attacked by the French. It was held that the underwriters in London should have known that as well as the insured; indeed it was said that they were more likely to know. Another good example is the dangers of asbestos, of which insurers have been held deemed to know.[34]

Knowledge of insurer's agent

An insurer will be deemed to have the knowledge that his agent has if that knowledge was acquired by the agent acting in the scope of his authority, actual or ostensible.[35] It is essential that the agent is in law the agent of the insurer, a question discussed more fully in Chapter 10. The device of imputing an agent's knowledge to his principal may be of great importance in the context of the duty of disclosure. For example, in *Ayrey v. British Legal & United Provident Assurance Co.*,[36] the district manager of the insurer knew the fact that the insured, who effected a life policy and was by occupation and on the proposal form described as a fisherman, was also a member of the Royal Navy Reserve. It was held that this knowledge

---

[33] See further, Chap. 10, pp. 185–188.
[34] *Canadian Indemnity Co. v. Canadian Johns-Manville Co.* (1990) 72 D.L.R. (4th) 478, Canadian Supreme Court.
[35] A more detailed description of basic principles of agency law is given in Chap. 10.
[36] [1918] 1 K.B. 136.

was imputed to the insurer who could not therefore rely upon its non-disclosure by the insured. In *Blackley v. National Mutual Life Association of Australasia*,[37] the agent knew before the contract was concluded that the life insured had a brain tumour which had just been operated upon. Again this knowledge was imputed to the insurer.[38] It should be noted, though, that the fact that the agent could have known of the material fact, for example, by a proper medical examination, is not enough. Similarly, the fact that the insurers have the means of knowledge, for example, the name of the doctor of a proposer for life insurance, does not relieve the insured of his duty of disclosure.

It should also be noted that the position regarding imputation of an agent's knowledge will probably be different where the proposer warrants the accuracy of an incorrect statement even when the agent knows the true position. This question is discussed in the next chapter.

Waiver

Waiver of disclosure raises a number of points. First are those that arise from the fact that in the majority of cases insurance is effected following the completion by the proposer of a proposal form on which a great deal of information is in practice solicited. It is clear that the fact that many questions are expressly asked does not relieve the proposer of his duty to disclose facts outside the scope of the questions,[39] but in some cases the form of questions asked may reduce the scope of the duty of disclosure. Similarly, if the proposer leaves a blank to a question which is accepted without inquiry by the insurer, this will normally be taken as a waiver by the insurer of any duty of disclosure in respect of the matters covered by the question.[40] This would not be the case, however, if in the circumstances, the blank space implies a negative answer to the question. If this is so, and a negative answer is incorrect, the insurers will be entitled to avoid the contract.[41]

---

[37] [1972] N.Z.L.R. 1038. The judgments in the New Zealand Court of Appeal contain a very comprehensive review of the principles governing the imputation of an agent's knowledge to his principal.

[38] See also *Woolcott v. Excess Insurance Co.* [1978] 1 Lloyd's Rep. 533, which is discussed at p. 181, below.

[39] *Glicksman v. Lancashire & General Assurance Co.* [1927] A.C. 139; *Schoolman v. Hall* [1951] 1 Lloyd's Rep. 139.

[40] *Roberts v. Avon Insurance Co.* [1956] 2 Lloyd's Rep. 240.

[41] *ibid.* Properly, though, the grounds for avoidance will be misrepresentation or breach of warranty.

Waiver as a result of the form of questions asked will usually arise where an express question asks for some details of certain facts or types of facts.[42] Disclosure of other details will be waived if it is felt that a reasonable man reading the proposal form would consider that the insurer did not seek the other details. For example, a question asking the proposer for details of previous losses he has suffered within a five-year period would waive disclosure of losses outside that period even though such losses might well be material facts according to the usual test. Similarly, a question asking about the claims history of the proposer in relation to the type of insurance for which he is applying might well be regarded as waiving any duty of disclosure of losses or claims in respect of other types of insurance which in some circumstances might be regarded as material facts.[43]

Where a question asked on a proposal form is ambiguous, a fair and reasonable construction must be placed upon it and it will be construed *contra proferentem* when the proposal form is incorporated into the contract. If, for example, the answer of the proposer is true according to a construction which a reasonable man might have put on the question, the insurers cannot rely upon its inaccuracy.

The test of materiality

Much of the criticism of the wide-ranging nature of the duty of disclosure has been directed at the central question of the test for determining materiality. A fact is material for the purposes of both non-disclosure and misrepresentation if it is one which would influence the judgment of a reasonable or prudent insurer in deciding whether or not to accept the risk or what premium to charge.[44] This test was conclusively adopted for non-marine insurance purposes in *Lambert v. Co-operative*

---

[42] *McCormick v. National Motor Accident Insurance Union Ltd* (1934) 49 Ll.L.R. 361, 363, *per* Scrutton L.J.; *Schoolman v. Hall*, above, at 143, *per* Asquith L.J.

[43] In *Hair v. Prudential Assurance Co. Ltd* [1983] 2 Lloyd's Rep. 667, it was held that the effect of a general warning on a proposal form of the need for disclosure, of the sort required by the Statements of Insurance Practice, was to waive the proposer's need to do any more than answer the questions put to him. However, this seems to be going too far (see [1984] J.B.L. 163).

[44] Or, possibly, whether to impose particular terms in the contract such as an exclusion or an excess. This may well be within the ambit of the present test; the Law Commission (Report No. 104, para. 4.48) thought so and that, in any event, it should expressly be brought within it.

Insurance Society,[45] the Court of Appeal holding that its statutory formulation in these terms in section 18 of the Marine Insurance Act 1906[46] was a codification of the common law applicable to all insurance contracts.

However, the words of section 18 — "influence the judgment" — are capable of at least two interpretations. One view is that the non-disclosed fact must have had a decisive influence on the judgment of the prudent or reasonable insurer. Another is that all that is required is that the prudent insurer would have wished to know about the fact when reaching his decision. Surprisingly, perhaps, until fairly recently no case had adopted a definitive view on this matter. The first occasion when it was properly raised and decided was in *Container Transport International Inc. v. Oceanus Mutual Underwriting Association (Bermuda) Ltd.*[47] Here it was held that, for the purposes of section 18, the requirement that a fact must be one which "would influence the judgment" of a prudent insurer did not mean that an insurer must have acted differently if he had known the fact, but merely that he would have wanted to know of the fact when making his decision; "judgment" was construed as meaning "the formation of an opinion," not "the final decision."[48] It was arguable, however, that the decision was based on a misreading of earlier authorities,[49] and it certainly imposes a particularly heavy burden on the insured.

---

[45] [1975] 2 Lloyd's Rep. 485. See Merkin (1976) 39 M.L.R. 478. Some earlier non-marine cases, *e.g. Joel v. Law Union* [1908] 2 K.B. 863, suggested a test depending on the opinion of the reasonable insured. The Court of Appeal in *Lambert* did not like having to reach their decision and thought that the law should be changed. See also *Kelsall v. Allstate Insurance Co. Ltd, The Times*, March 20, 1987, where the test was accepted, but was modified by an express provision in the contract, "no known adverse facts," which had the effect of requiring the insured to disclose only those facts known by him, as a reasonable man, to be adverse.

[46] See also s.151(9) of the Road Traffic Act 1988 which lays down the same test for certain motor insurance purposes; see p. 377 below.

[47] [1984] 1 Lloyd's Rep. 467.

[48] This case was followed in *Highlands Insurance Co. v. Continental Insurance Co.* [1987] 1 Lloyd's Rep. 109, where the judge felt bound to accept it in a non-marine misrepresentation case, though clearly with some misgivings.

[49] See the excellent article by Brooke, "Materiality in Insurance Contracts" [1985] L.M.C.L.Q. 437 analysing all the earlier cases, especially the Privy Council case of *Mutual Life Insurance Co. of New York v. Ontario Metal Products Co. Ltd* [1925] A.C. 344. This case concerned the construction of a Canadian statute which required, in respect of life insurance, not just that a misrepresentation be material but also that it induced the actual insurer to enter into the contract (*cf.* s.151(9) of the Road Traffic Act 1988, n.46 above, which contains the same requirement).

More recently, in *Pan Atlantic Insurance Co. v. Pine Top Insurance Co. Ltd*, the House of Lords had the opportunity to rule authoritatively on the question, and, by a bare majority of 3 to 2, they decided to follow the *C.T.I.* ruling.[50] Although this may be regarded as unfortunate, and the dissenting opinion of Lord Lloyd in favour of the decisive influence test seems to read as persuasively as the leading majority judgment of Lord Mustill, the question is clearly now settled.[51]

However, *Pan Atlantic* introduced a novel additional requirement into the law of non-disclosure, the majority clearly being influenced by the need to temper the harshness of the general test. This additional requirement is that the non-disclosed fact, material in the opinion of the prudent insurer, must also have induced the actual insurer to enter into the contract.[52] This was effected by reasoning first that the inducement requirement for misrepresentation in general contract law must also be held apply to misrepresentations in insurance law.[53] Then, it was held simply that the same requirement should also apply to non-disclosure, even though, as we have seen earlier,[54] conceptually, misrepresentation and non-disclosure are

As Brooke points out, the Privy Council was careful to distinguish these two points and was clearly of opinion as regards the first that a non-disclosed or misrepresentation fact must actually have influenced a reasonable insurer to decline the risk or to have stipulated for a higher premium in order to be material; see Lord Salveson at 351. See also the judgment of Lloyd J. at first instance in the *C.T.I.* case [1982] 2 Lloyd's Rep. 178. The *C.T.I.* case was not followed in some common law jurisdictions; see *e.g. Barclay Holdings (Australia) Pty Ltd v. British National Insurance Co. Ltd* (1987) 8 N.S.W.L.R. 514; see Ying [1990] J.B.L. 97. For a general review, see Clarke "Failure to disclose and failure to legislate: is it material?" [1988] J.B.L. 206, 298.

[50] Note that the Court of Appeal in *Pan Atlantic* ([1993] 1 Lloyd's Rep. 443) had adopted a "middle way", requiring proof that a prudent insurer would have treated the fact as increasing the risk, even though ultimately he might not have rejected the risk or charged a higher premium

[51] It is thought, though, that the adoption of the decisive influence test would have produced a fairer result; for a detailed critique, see Birds and Hird (1996) 59 M.L.R. 285.

[52] In effect this is a causation requirement which had been hinted at earlier in *Berger v. Pollock* [1973] 2 Lloyd's Rep. 442. For certain motor insurance purposes (n.49 above), statute imports a requirement of inducement, and it has always been possible for a policy to provide for it.

[53] Notwithstanding the fact that s.20 of the Marine Insurance Act 1906, which codified misrepresentation in marine insurance, does not contain the requirement. It was held that inducement comes from the development of the equitable jurisdiction to permit rescission of a contract, and that this was impliedly included in the codification.

[54] p. 99, above.

quite different creatures, certainly when they are "innocent",[55] and it is somewhat difficult to see how anyone can be induced by something of which they were unaware![56]

What still remains somewhat unclear, though, is the force of the inducement requirement. In *Pan Atlantic*, there are clear dicta that there is a presumption of inducement,[57] and this was followed by the subsequent Court of Appeal decision in *St Paul Fire & Marine Insurance Co. (U.K.) Ltd v. McDonnell Dowell Constructors Ltd.*[58] Here it was also held that it is sufficient if the non-disclosed fact was *an* inducement and not necessarily *the* inducement. This clearly lessens the impact of this judicial "reform" of the law on non-disclosure, although there is at least one first instance decision where a more robust attitude was taken,[59] and it may be that this aspect of *Pan Atlantic* is not yet finally settled.

Evidence of materiality

Because the test of materiality depends initially on the opinion of a reasonable insurer, the courts have long been prepared to accept the opinion of other insurers as evidence of whether or not particular facts are

---

[55] Again, the fact that the 1906 Act (s. 18 in this instance) does not require inducement was regarded as no obstacle. In the words of Lord Mustill, "If this requires the making of new law, so be it" ([1994] 3 All E.R. at 617).

[56] Perhaps a more fundamental objection is that the "equitable" notion of inducement (see n.53, above) should have no place in a common law based doctrine, which, with respect, is what the duty of disclosure is, based as it clearly is upon the common law jurisdiction of Lord Mansfield. See also, p. 101, above and p. 126, below.

[57] See especially Lord Mustill [1994] 3 All E.R. at 610 and 617. Even though this is clearly a presumption of fact, rather than of law, it could still obviously be very difficult for an insured to prove that the actual insurer was not induced by the non-disclosure.

[58] [1995] 2 Lloyd's Rep. 116; see Hird [1995] J.B.L. 608.

[59] *Marc Rich & Co. A.G. v. Portman* [1996] 1 Lloyd's Rep. 430. Here Longmore J. held, albeit before the Court of Appeal decision in *St Paul*, that the presumption can only operate where the actual underwriter cannot, for good reason, give evidence and there is no reason to suppose that he acted other than prudently. "[W]here he is called and the court cannot make up its mind, the defence of non-disclosure should fail because he will not have been able to show that he had been induced . . . At the end of the day it is for the insurer to prove that the non-disclosure did induce the writing of the risk . . ." (at 442). This decision has been upheld by the Court of Appeal (December 1996), without full consideration of this point.

material.[60] In some cases, such opinions appear to have been accepted very readily, but some of the modern decisions emphasise that they are in no way binding on the court which must decide the issue as a question of fact. For example, in *Roselodge Ltd v. Castle*,[61] an insurer's evidence to the effect that it would be material to an application for insurance many years later that the proposer was caught stealing apples at the age of 12 was ridiculed by McNair J. Similarly, the judgment of Forbes J. in *Reynolds v. Phoenix Assurance Co.*[62] is instructive. He rejected the arguments that if an insurer is telling the truth and he is held to be a reasonable insurer, the court must accept his evidence as conclusive. The evidence is expert evidence which assists the court but never binds it. This is particularly so, of course, where there is conflicting evidence from different insurers.

Examples of material facts

While the test to be applied to determine whether or not a non-disclosed fact is material is a question of law, the actual determination of the issue in any particular case involves the resolution of a question of fact.[63] As such, it is generally a question solely for the trial judge or arbitrator and not subject to appeal, and, furthermore, strictly no decision is actually binding in a later case under the doctrine of precedent. However, there are some categories of facts which are obviously material and others which have arisen so often in decided cases that they would normally be so regarded. It is appropriate, therefore, to describe and illustrate some of these categories. It must be remembered that in any given case the actual insurer must also have been induced by the non-disclosure of such a fact, although as regards most of these "traditional" material facts, this is unlikely to be a difficult requirement to satisfy, regardless of where the burden of proof lies.

Material facts relate in general either to the physical hazard, that is the property, life or liability insured, or to the moral hazard. Facts relating to the physical hazard are those which are generally obviously material. In property insurance, they would include, for example, the nature, construction or use of an insured building, or whether it is particularly exposed

---

[60] See, *e.g. Babatsikos v. Car Owners' Mutual Insurance Co.* [1970] 2 Lloyd's Rep. 314, for a general survey, but compare the comment of Lord Mansfield in *Carter v. Boehm* (1766) 3 Burr. 1905 at 1918. For a general criticism, see Hasson (1969) 32 M.L.R. 615. See also Evans (1984) 12 Australian Bus. L. Rev. 4.

[61] [1966] 2 Lloyd's Rep. 113 at 132.

[62] [1978] 2 Lloyd's Rep. 440 at 457–459.

[63] *e.g. Glicksman v. Lancashire & General Assurance Co.* [1927] A.C. 139.

to risk; in life insurance, they would include health or a high risk occupation or hobby or the results of any health tests known to the insured;[64] in liability insurance, they would include a bad accident record. The modern cases rarely concern such issues, not least because they are invariably the subject of questions on a proposal form when the answers may be warranted and materiality is irrelevant.

Moral hazard

Facts as to the moral hazard of the proposer are, it seems, less likely to be the subject of express questions, although they should be in non-commercial insurances according to the terms of the Statements of Insurance Practice.[65] Moral hazard cases can perhaps be regarded as falling into three categories: (i) those relating to the insurance history of the applicant; (ii) those relating to his nationality or origins; and (iii) those relating to criminal convictions.

The insurance history of the proposer includes both previous refusals to insure by other insurers as well as his claims history. In *Glicksman v. Lancashire & General Assurance Co.*,[66] G and his partner applied for burglary insurance. It was held that the fact that G had when trading on his own previously been refused insurance was material, regardless of the reasons for the previous refusal and of the fact that there was on the proposal form a question which elicited such information in a way which could have been interpreted as applying to a previous proposal made by the applicants together. The House of Lords, in deciding the case, was full of regrets, but really there was nothing their Lordships could do. The materiality of the fact was a question of fact which had been conclusively decided by the arbitrator. It should be noted that, in vivid contrast, in marine insurance a previous refusal to insure is not material.[67]

---

[64] For example, for HIV, or even genetic tests. While there can be no doubt that such facts are material as a matter of strict law, whether or not the insurance industry should always be entitled morally to know of them is another matter and one which has been much discussed in recent years.

[65] Statement of General Insurance Practice, para. 1(d); Statement of Long-Term Insurance Practice, para. 1(c). This requirement seems to conflict with the trend in the insurance industry towards shorter proposal forms. There certainly do seem to be proposal forms in existence which do not solicit all material facts other than by general question.

[66] [1927] A.C. 139. See also *London Assurance v. Mansel* (1879) 11 Ch.D. 363 for an example in life assurance.

[67] *Glicksman* in the Court of Appeal, [1925] 2 K.B. 593 at 608.

Whether or not a previous refusal to insure in respect of a type of insurance other than that for which the proposer is applying is material is not so clear. In *Ewer v. National Employers' Mutual & General Insurance Association*,[68] Mackinnon J. clearly rejected such a wide proposition, but in *Locker & Wolf Ltd v. Western Australian Insurance Co.*,[69] a previous refusal of motor insurance was held material to a proposal for fire insurance, quite apart from the fact that there was a general question on the proposal form. It would appear that such a previous refusal may be material when it relates in a general way to the integrity of the proposer.[70] A mere refusal would therefore not be material, but a refusal based on the insurance history of the proposer, for example, as to his claims experience, might well be.[71]

Previous losses of the sort which the proposer is seeking insurance against are clearly material,[72] although in practice these will be solicited by express questions and the answers warranted, and, quite possibly, any duty to disclose outside the scope of the question waived. Many of the other facts relating to the moral hazard of the proposer are affected by legislation. Although the nationality of the proposer was held to be material in *Horne v. Poland*,[73] the decision cannot stand now in the light of the Race Relations Act 1976 which prohibits discrimination by insurers, among others, on "racial grounds."[74] Similarly, discrimination against an applicant on the grounds of sex is prohibited by the Sex Discrimination Act 1975, except in relation to certain matters in life and related policies.[75]

Criminal history

Perhaps the most important fact affecting the moral hazard of the proposer, apart from insurance history, is any criminal history. Certainly most of the modern cases have been concerned with this question. This too may be affected by legislation, in this insurance the Rehabilitation of

---

[68] [1937] 2 All E.R. 193 at 202–203.

[69] [1936] 1 K.B. 408.

[70] *ibid.* at 414, per Slesser L.J.

[71] But what if the insurers were told of the claims experience, but not of the refusal based on it?

[72] *e.g. Arterial Caravans Ltd v. Yorkshire Insurance Co.* [1973] 1 Lloyd's Rep. 169.

[73] [1922] 2 K.B. 364. But see the comment of McNair J. in *Roselodge Ltd v. Castle* [1966] 2 Lloyd's Rep. 113 at 130.

[74] s.20; see ss.1 and 3 for the definitions.

[75] s.45.

Offenders Act 1974. A number of cases involving mostly the insurance of valuables establish that criminal convictions for offences of dishonesty are normally material, including those which relate to "a dim and distant past," 12 years[76] and, possibly, 20 years[77] prior to the insurance application. In *Roselodge Ltd v. Castle*,[78] though, a conviction for bribery was held not material to the insurance of diamonds, though a smuggling conviction was material. It appears also, logically enough, that the mere commission of an offence may be material, even if the proposer is acquitted by a jury, provided, of course, that the insurer can prove to the satisfaction of the civil court that the proposer did commit the offence.[79] A wrongful conviction should also be disclosed,[80] but judicial opinion has been divided as to whether a proposer must disclose the fact of arrest where he was innocent.[81] In *Lambert v. Co-operative Insurance Society*,[82] it was the convictions of the proposer's husband that were material facts. Although the result of this case has been criticised,[83] the offences were of dishonesty, and the insurance was an all risks one on jewellery, including some which was owned by the proposer's husband.

Woolcott v. Sun Alliance & London Insurance[84] appears to be a more extreme example because here there was no obvious connection between the non-disclosed conviction and the sort of insurance applied for. The plaintiff proposed for fire insurance on his house through the building society to which at the same time he was making a mortgage application.[85] He failed to disclose the fact that he had been convicted of robbery some 12 years previously. It was held that the insurers could avoid the policy.[86]

---

[76] *Schoolman v. Hall* [1951] 1 Lloyd's Rep. 139.
[77] *Regina Fur v. Bossom* [1957] 2 Lloyd's Rep. 466.
[78] [1966] 2 Lloyd's Rep. 113.
[79] *March Cabaret Club & Casino Ltd v. London Assurance* [1975] 1 Lloyd's Rep. 169.
[80] *ibid.*
[81] *ibid.* at 177; *contra, Reynolds v. Phoenix Assurance Co. Ltd* [1978] 2 Lloyd's Rep. 440 at 460.
[82] [1975] 2 Lloyd's Rep. 465.
[83] Merkin (1976) 39 M.L.R. 478.
[84] [1978] 1 All E.R. 1253.
[85] There was no proposal form; the insurance application was simply the answer to one question on the mortgage application form.
[86] But the building society which was also insured was able to recover as the policy was not a joint one. This result has been criticised; see Nicholson (1990) 3 Ins. L.J. 218 esp. at 229 and the comments of Samuels J.A. in *Advance (N.S.W.) Insurance Agencies Pty Ltd v. Matthews* (1988) 12 N.S.W.L.R. 250 at 261. As to joint policies, see pp. 256 and 305 below.

The learned judge appears to have accepted, without demur, the evidence called for the insurers that the fact related to Woolcott's moral hazard. With respect, it is not at all obvious why a convicted robber should be more risky in relation to the insurance of a building than anyone else, even though it must be accepted that Woolcott's conviction was serious. In contrast, in *Reynolds v. Phoenix Assurance Co.*,[87] after perhaps a more thorough review of the law, Forbes J. held that a conviction for receiving was not a material fact in relation to fire insurance. Admittedly the matter was comparatively trivial and the insured was merely fined. It was held that the matter depended basically on the extent of the dishonesty and the age of the conviction. As the learned judge admitted, hard and fast rules cannot be laid down about this sort of case. This must be correct, even though it makes the application of the law somewhat uncertain, and the insured in the unenviable position of having to find evidence to challenge that of the insurers. One interesting comment in the judgment in *Reynolds* relates to the lack of experience among the experts called of actual disclosures by proposers of their previous convictions. Forbes J.[88] understandably found this surprising in view of the large numbers of crimes dishonestly committed every year and the almost universal adoption of some form of insurance for buildings. Clearly he did not believe some of the more extreme evidence as to materiality put forward in that case.[89]

It seems, in summary, that any conviction relevant to the insurance sought will be regarded as material unless it is both trivial and old. An irrelevant conviction, that is one not directly germane to the risk, will affect the moral hazard of the proposer certainly when it is serious, presumably meaning punished by imprisonment or a substantial fine. An ancient trivial offence would not be material. It is less certain whether a recent unconnected trivial offence would be material. In the decided cases of relevance, the offences were all quite old.

Spent convictions

However, regardless of the above, an applicant for insurance is never bound to disclose a conviction which has become spent under the terms of

---

[87] [1978] 2 Lloyd's Rep. 440. As to the other important issues in this case, see pp. 269–270, below.
[88] *ibid.* at 460.
[89] See also p. 111, above. Today, this would surely also affect the question of inducement.

the Rehabilitation of Offenders Act 1974.[90] There are different periods laid down for rehabilitation depending on the seriousness of the sentence imposed. Most importantly, a conviction resulting in a sentence of two and a half years' imprisonment or more can never become spent. Otherwise, convictions with custodial sentences of between six months and two and a half years become spent after 10 years and those of less than six months after seven years. In respect of other sentences, the period is five years, except in relation to absolute discharges (six months) and conditional discharges and probation (one year).

There is one provision, though, in section 7(3) of the 1974 Act, which gives the court a discretion to admit evidence as to spent convictions if the court is satisfied that "justice cannot be done in the case except by admitting it." The issue arose in earlier proceedings in *Reynolds v. Phoenix Assurance Co.*[91] because the offence already referred to came to light only after the case commenced and the insurers sought to amend their pleadings to allege its non-disclosure. The Act did not apply when the plaintiff applied for the insurance in 1972, but it did when the matter came to trial. The Court of Appeal held that the pleadings should be amended on the ground that no prejudice would be caused to the plaintiff. Whether or not the evidence of the conviction should be admitted was then a matter for the trial judge. Forbes J. subsequently held that the evidence should be admitted, although this did not matter in the result as he held that the conviction was not material, as we have already seen.

It is unfortunate that in the *Reynolds* litigation the courts did not really decide the effect of section 7(3) on the duty of disclosure. They may have been influenced by the fact that the alleged non-disclosure took place before the 1974 Act existed. It can hardly be said to be just to admit evidence of spent convictions in relation to insurance effected after 1974 when, since that time, the proposer has been under no duty to disclose them.

Disclosure During The Contract

The duty to disclose material facts is cast upon the proposer or insured only before the contract or a renewal is concluded. At common law, there is no general duty to disclose material facts which occur when they occur during the period of insurance. The authority for this is the old case of *Pim*

[90] s.4(3)(a).
[91] [1978] 2 Lloyd's Rep. 22.

v. Reid,[92] where the insured changed his trade and caused a large amount of highly inflammable material to be brought on to the insured premises. It was held that his non-disclosure of this fact to the insurer was not actionable. This basic common law position has recently been confirmed by the Court of Appeal,[93] although it will not apply where there is such a fundamental change that the subject matter of the insurance becomes different.[94]

Certain contracts of insurance, though, most notably those of fire insurance, do, in practice, impose a duty on the insured to disclose facts occurring during the insurance which materially increase the risk.[95] The term which imposes such a duty is usually, though not necessarily, a promissory warranty, since it provides that upon a failure to disclose, the insurer can avoid the policy.[96] Although we shall be examining promissory warranties in general in the next chapter, it is appropriate here to consider this common type, since it clearly imposes a duty of disclosure analogous to that imposed by virtue of the principle of *uberrima fides*.

---

[92] (1843) 6 M. & G. 1.

[93] *Kausar v. Eagle Star Insurance Co. Ltd,* [1997] C.L.C. 129. This is line with what appears to be the better view that there is no duty of continuing utmost good faith and disclosure on an insured, except in so far as there is a duty at the claims stage, especially not to make a fraudulent claim (see pp. 254–256, below). See in particular the Court of Appeal's view in *New Hampshire Insurance Co. v. MGN Ltd* [1996] C.L.C. 1692, discussed in (1997) 9(1) *Insurance Law Monthly*, rejecting the argument that an insurer's contractual right to cancel the policy entitled it to any information which might be relevant to a prudent insurer in deciding whether or not to exercise the right of cancellation. Compare *Hussain v. Brown (No. 2)*, unreported, November 1996, discussed *ibid.*, where at first instance it was held that an increase of risk clause attracted a duty of utmost good faith, except that on the facts the wording of the express provision excluded any wider duty. The latter view is clearly inconsistent with *Kausar*. See also *Manifest Shipping Co. Ltd v. Uni-Polaris Shipping Co. Ltd (The Star Sea), The Times,* January 23, 1997.

[94] *ibid.* The position may be different if the insured has warranted the description of the property and the change is such as to amount to a breach of that warranty.

[95] There is evidence that such a duty is being imposed more widely by insurers, *e.g.* in household policies, and the need for clear wording to impose such a duty is illustrated by the decision in *Kausar*, above; see further below.

[96] Strictly it should say that the insurer is discharged from liability (see pp. 129–133 below), although the practical effect is the same.

Increase of risk clauses

A simple increase of risk clause, as it may be called, only operates when the increase is permanent and habitual. In *Shaw v. Robberds*,[97] a fire policy was effected upon a granary which contained a kiln for drying corn. On one occasion, the insured allowed a third party to dry some bark in the kiln and this, in fact, occasioned the fire which brought about the dispute. It was held that the insurers were liable, despite the presence of an increase of risk clause. The change was merely temporary. It mattered not of itself that drying bark was a much more hazardous business than drying corn.

If, therefore, an insurer wishes to be notified of merely temporary increases in risk, it must insert express clauses to that effect.[98] It is also notable that the standard clause in fire policies on buildings only relates to alterations to the building itself and not to any alteration of its contents which may increase the risk.[99] Insurers must also be careful when replacing the traditional clause by one worded in "plain English." A provision which stated: "You must tell us of any change of circumstances which increases the risk of injury or damage. You will not be insured under the policy until we have agreed in writing to accept the increased risk" has been held ineffective when, in an insurance of a shop, the insured failed to tell the insurers that threats to damage the shop had been made by the tenants and (unlawful) sub-tenants.[1]

An analogous specific disclosure requirement often imposed in fire policies relates to the property being unoccupied for a specified period and requiring that fact to be reported to the insurer. Unoccupancy relates, it has been held, to the absence of a physical presence in the building insured.[2] If, in fact, no-one is regularly and daily present therein, the building is unoccupied, unless the absence is merely temporary, for example, by reason of the insured being on holiday.[3]

---

[97] (1837) 6 A. & E. 75. Compare *Farnham v. Royal Insurance Co.* [1976] 2 Lloyd's Rep. 437.

[98] See, *e.g. Glen v. Lewis* (1853) 8 Ex. 607.

[99] *Exchange Theatre Ltd v. Iron Trades Mutual Insurance Co. Ltd* [1984] 1 Lloyd's Rep. 149; see [1984] J.B.L. 363.

[1] *Kausar v. Eagle Star Insurance Co. Ltd*, [1997] C.L.C. 129. The result may be justifiable on the ground that this was not in any event a permanent increase in risk: see above.

[2] *Marzouca v. Atlantic and British Commercial Insurance Co. Ltd* [1971] 1 Lloyd's Rep. 449.

[3] *Winicofsky v. Army and Navy General Insurance Co.* (1919) 88 L.J.K.B. 111.

Practice In And Reform Of Non-Disclosure And Misrepresentation

The point that the law is capable of operating harshly regarding the disclosure of material facts in particular has already been made earlier in this chapter. Indeed it has often been said that a proposer for insurance may act with perfect good faith and yet not satisfy the duty of disclosure which the law requires because he did not realise that particular facts were in law material, or did not realise that he had to do any more than truthfully complete the answers to questions on a proposal form. It could be argued that there is no real need for a duty of disclosure in modern conditions other than one requiring the insured to answer honestly questions expressly put to him.[4]

Until fairly recently it seemed as though the law would be reformed in this respect. This was because recommendations for reform have been made by both the Law Reform Committee in 1957[5] and by the Law Commission in 1980.[6] The important and carefully considered recommendations of the Law Commission, which in practice would probably have meant the withering away of a pure duty of disclosure,[7] were accepted

---

[4] It must be doubtful whether the lack of a pure duty of disclosure would have any real effect on premiums, at least in typical "consumer" insurances. Certainly insurers in many countries, including the U.S.A., manage without the law imposing any such duty.

[5] Fifth Report, Cmnd. 62.

[6] Report No. 104, *Insurance Law: Non-Disclosure and Breach of Warranty*, Cmnd. 8064. Note that the impetus for this report was the existence of a proposed E.C. Directive on certain aspects of insurance contract law, linked to the then proposed Directive on Freedom of Services. The likelihood of this Directive being implemented seems to have virtually disappeared for the foreseeable future and no detail is given here. Freedom of Services has been effected (see pp. 22–24) without the need to harmonise any aspects of insurance contract law. The relevant aspects of the Contract Law Directive are fully examined in the Law Commission's Report.

[7] Because the duty to disclose would have been limited to what a reasonable man would think should be disclosed and this would surely have meant that, except in rare cases, a reasonable man would not have expected to do more than answer express questions. It may be that the Commission did not go far enough in terms of limiting the insurer's right of avoidance for non-disclosures or misrepresentations. Although they were no doubt right to reject the overly mathematical and unworkable proportionality approach to the proposed Directive, based on French law, it still does not seem right in non-fraud cases that the insured should forfeit all rights and the Insurance Ombudsman has been persuaded of the fairness of this point of view; see p. 122 below.

by the government, but were strongly opposed by the insurance industry particularly in respect of their application to business insurance.[8] The unfortunate result of this[9] has been that actual legal reform seems unlikely at present.[10] Instead, the government has accepted "reform" by way of self-regulation by the insurers themselves. For this reason, it is felt that detailed description of the Law Commission's proposals would be inappropriate in a book of this size.[11]

Statements of insurance practice

As has been noted earlier,[12] this self-regulation takes the form of declaratory Statements of Insurance Practice. In so far as they do, in practice, provide a measure of protection for the individual insured,[13] they are obviously to be welcomed. In addition, we must note the influence of the Insurance Ombudsman in this area, as discussed below. Unfortunately one cannot be certain that the statements are universally complied with because those insurers who are not members of the Association of British Insurers or of Lloyd's are not party to them, although they are "expected" to comply.[14] A brief review of their terms is necessary.[15]

The revised Statements issued in 1986 reflect the Law Commission's recommendations. As far as non-disclosure and misrepresentation are concerned, their effect is that insurers undertake not to rely on an innocent

---

[8] One of the strongest arguments raised by insurers against legal reform is that they always apply the law fairly and use a technical defence like non-disclosure only when they suspect fraud. While this may be true of many reputable insurers, it is certainly not universally true and it is hardly acceptable that insurers should be such judges in their own cause.

[9] See North, "Law Reform; processes and problems" (1985) 101 L.Q.R. 338 at 349–350.

[10] Although the National Consumer Council has recently (May 1997) published a report arguing for this again, and it may be that there will be some governmental response to this.

[11] For more detail, see the first edition of this book (1982) at pp. 99–104 and Birds, "The reform of insurance law" [1982] J.B.L. 449.

[12] See p. 5.

[13] Though not for the business insured however "small" he may be. The lack of protection for such as the one-man business seems an unnecessary omission.

[14] It is difficult to see how an E.C. insurer selling directly in the U.K. under the Insurance Directives can be "controlled" in this respect.

[15] For a more detailed examination, see Forte, "The revised Statements of Insurance Practice," (1986) 49 M.L.R. 754 and Birds, "Self-regulation and insurance contracts," *New Foundations for Insurance Law*, Chap. 1.

breach by the insured. By paragraph 2(b) of the Statement of General Insurance Practice,

> "An insurer will not repudiate liability to indemnify a policy-holder:
> (i) on grounds of non-disclosure of a material fact which a policy-holder could not reasonably be expected to have disclosed;
> (ii) on grounds of misrepresentation unless it is a deliberate or negligent misrepresentation of material fact."

Paragraph 3(a) of the Long-Term Statement provides rather more clumsily and ambiguously,

> "An insurer will not unreasonably reject a claim. In particular, an insurer will not reject a claim or invalidate a policy on grounds of non-disclosure or misrepresentation of a fact unless: (i) it is a material fact; and (ii) it is a fact within the knowledge of the proposer; and (iii) it is a fact which the proposer could reasonably be expected to disclose. (It should be noted that fraud or deception will, and reckless or negligent non-disclosure or misrepresentation of a material fact may, constitute grounds for rejection of a claim.)"

These paragraphs must be read in conjunction with the requirements that proposers must be warned on proposal forms and on renewal notices of the need for disclosure.[16] What is not certain is what effect warnings would be regarded as having on the reasonableness of a proposer's actions; could a plea of ignorance of the need for disclosure possibly be regarded as reasonable? How does a conscientious proposer read the warning in the light of the other requirement that insurers are expected to ask clear questions about facts which have generally been found to be material?[17]

Disclosure and the Insurance Ombudsman[18]

As we have just seen, under the Statements of Practice, if an insured negligently fails to disclose or misrepresents a material fact, the insurer is

---

[16] Warnings on proposal forms must be "prominent" (para. 1(c) and (a) of the General and Long-Term Statements, respectively). However, those on renewal notices need not be; quaere whether they ought not to be, as many people probably do not realise the importance of disclosure at the time of renewal. As to the possible legal consequences of a warning, see n.43 on p. 107.

[17] See also the comment at n.65 on p. 112.

[18] As to the Insurance Ombudsman generally, see pp. 6–8 above.

entitled to avoid the policy (and avoid paying a claim) in its entirety. The first holder of the position of Insurance Ombudsman tended to follow the line of the Statements and modify the application of the law accordingly, but his successor went further than this in two ways. In the 1989 Annual Report,[19] it was stated that he would apply a principle of proportionality in such cases. By this, the insurer cannot avoid liability for a claim entirely, but has to pay the proportion of a claim that the premium actually paid bears to the premium that would have been charged if the insurer had known the truth. This principle (derived from French Law), incidentally, was rejected as unworkable by the Law Commission in its 1980 Report.[20] In the 1990 Annual Report,[21] the Ombudsman went further than this and stated that, in some cases, he would not allow the insurer to avoid the policy at all, but would allow them to avoid, wholly or partially, a claim. In doing so, he relied on the jurisdiction of the court to refuse rescission of a contract and award damages in lieu in respect of a negligent misrepresentation,[22] pointing out that in personal insurances, most non-disclosures are in reality misrepresentations since they arise from the incorrect answers on proposal forms.[23]

There can be no doubt that the impact of the Statements of Practice and of the practices of the Insurance Ombudsman[24] have a substantial effect on the way in which the law as to non-disclosure and misrepresentation works in practice, at least as concerns the vast majority of private insureds. Indeed, in effect we may now be said to have a consumer insurance law different in this area from commercial insurance law.[25] Having said that,

---

[19] Para. 2.17.

[20] See above. The Ombudsman was criticised for adopting this proportionality principle; see Parkington, British Insurance Law Association Journal, No. 77 (September 1991), p. 36.

[21] Para. 2.3.

[22] Misrepresentation Act 1967, s.2(2).

[23] He relied on the requirement of the Statements of Practice that insurers are required to ask specific questions about material facts. This is clearly a correct approach, although there may still be a minority of pure non-disclosure cases arising out of original applications for personal insurance and in practice all cases arising out of a non-disclosure on renewal will be non-disclosure in the strict sense.

[24] There seems no doubt that the current Insurance Ombudsman will continue to adopt the approach described in the 1989 and 1990 Reports.

[25] There are other differences of course, notably as a result of the application of the Unfair Terms in Consumer Contracts Regulations to consumer insurance contracts; see p. 91, above.

however, there still appears to be a need for "proper" law reform, first to protect those who insure with insurers who are not members of the A.B.I. and/or of the I.O.B. and secondly to protect at least those commercial insureds who seem as deserving of protection as individual insureds.

The Insurer's Duty of Utmost Good Faith and Disclosure

It has long been said[26] that the requirement of utmost good faith applies to both parties to the insurance contract, in other words that it imposes a duty of disclosure on the insurer as much as on the insured. Until the recent case of *Banque Financière de la Cité S.A. v. Westgate Insurance Co. Ltd*,[27] this did not, however, seem to have any real significance. In this fascinating piece of litigation, there was a bold attempt by the judge at first instance, having applied such a duty on an insurer, to give it some real teeth by awarding damages for breach of the duty. However, while the Court of Appeal and House of Lords accepted that there was a duty, they held that the only remedy for breach was the traditional one of avoidance of the contract.[28]

A number of banks agreed to make some very substantial loans on condition that, *inter alia*, binding contracts of credit insurance had been issued before the money would be advanced. The manager of the firm of brokers responsible for arranging the insurance fraudulently issued cover notes to the banks in respect of the first loan representing that insurance

---

[26] See the founding judgment of Lord Mansfield in *Carter v. Boehm* (1766) 3 Burr. 1905; see also the judgment of Farwell L.J. in *Re Bradley and Essex and Suffolk Accident Indemnity Society* [1912] 1 K.B. 415, 430.

[27] [1991] 2 A.C. 249, affirming the Court of Appeal, [1990] 1 Q.B. 665, reversing the judgment at first instance, sub nom. *Banque Keyser Ullman S.A. v. Skandia Insurance Co.* [1987] 1 Lloyd's Rep. 69.

[28] Part of the problem with the case was that, wound up with the pure insurance aspects, in terms of utmost good faith and disclosure, was a claim in tort for, in effect, pure economic loss. It arose at the time when the higher courts were cutting back on the availability of tortious remedies for pure economic loss and may have suffered accordingly, with the special insurance attributes being in effect overlooked. The only other English case where the question of the remedy for a non-disclosure had been expressly considered was *Glasgow Assurance Corp. v. Symondson* (1911) 16 Com. Cas. 109, 121, where Scrutton J. stated that the only remedy was avoidance. However, this dictum was clearly *obiter*, although it was relied upon by the Court of Appeal in the *Banque Financière* case in support of their decision.

cover was complete when in fact there was a shortfall. Some months later, the senior underwriter discovered what had happened and realised that there had been a substantial gap in the insurance coverage during those months, although by that time the gap had largely been filled. He failed to inform the banks of this and the banks made further loans. The whole scheme proved to have been a massive fraud by the borrower who defaulted in repaying any of the money. In addition to making a claim against the brokers, which was settled, the banks claimed on the insurance contracts. However, their claim was rejected[29] on the ground that the contracts contained a clause excluding the insurers' liability for "any claim or claims arising directly or indirectly out of or caused directly or indirectly by fraud attempted fraud misdescription or deception by any person firm organisation or company". They then sued the insurers for damages for the latter's failure to disclose to them the broker's fraud. At first instance, their claim was largely successful. The Court of Appeal allowed an appeal by one of the insurers involved, holding that, although there had been a breach by the insurers of the duty of disclosure, the only remedy for breach of the duty was avoidance of the contract and return of the premiums, not damages.

When one of the banks appealed to the House of Lords, the arguments proceeded along rather different lines. Their lordships held the losses suffered by the banks were not the consequence of any breach of a duty of disclosure by the insurers. The brokers' fraud was not within the fraud exclusion clause since that fraud did not cause a claim under the policy to arise. The insurers could therefore not have repudiated liability on the ground of the brokers' fraud, nor could they have been under any duty to disclose it to the insureds since no negotiating party could be under a duty to disclose to the opposite party information that the agent of the opposite party had committed a breach of the duty he owed to his principal in an earlier transaction. So any failure to disclose that fraud did not cause the banks' loss. The sole cause of that was the fraud of the borrower which was excluded under the policies. However, the House of Lords did approve of the reasoning of the Court of Appeal to the effect that an insurer is under a

---

[29] In the litigation, the banks conceded that they could not claim on the contracts. This was perhaps unfortunate. Otherwise they might, for example, have argued that the effect of the insurers' non-disclosure was to preclude their relying on the exclusion clause by analogy with cases like *Curtis v. Chemical Cleaning and Dyeing Co.* [1951] 1 K.B. 805. However, they would still have had to overcome the causation problem, as resolved in the House of Lords; see below.

pre-contractual duty of disclosure to his insured but only in respect of matters which are material to the risk or to the recoverability of a claim. Breach of such a duty could not sound in damages, whether in contract or tort.

Even if the conclusion on causation was correct,[30] it has to be disappointing that the case establishes a rather narrow duty of disclosure on an insurer and a fairly ineffective remedy limited to avoidance and return of the premium. As far as the insurer's duty of disclosure is concerned, it seems to extend to disclosure of all facts known to the insurer which are material either to the nature of the risk sought to be covered or the recoverability of a claim under the policy which a prudent insured would take into account in deciding whether or not to place the risk for which he sought cover with that insurer.[31] The reasoning of the Court of Appeal, approved by the House of Lords,[32] as to why a breach of a duty of disclosure could not result in damages is unsatisfactory. That court, in

[30] This is, perhaps doubtful; see Trindade (1991) 107 L.Q.R. 24 and compare, in a different context, *Swingcastle v. Alistair Gibson* [1991] 2 A.C. 223.

[31] This was how the Court of Appeal described it and this was expressly approved by Lord Bridge, with whom Lords Brandon and Ackner agreed. Lord Templeman did not consider it necessary to consider whether there was a duty of disclosure by reason of the obligation of an insurer to deal with the proposer of insurance with the utmost good faith. Lord Jauncey referred to the insurer's duty of disclosure in fairly narrow terms, as relating to facts which would reduce the risk such as the insurer's knowledge that the house which was the subject of a proposal had already been demolished, referring to the well-known example of Lord Mansfield in *Carter v. Boehm*, above, p. 101, of the insurer insuring a ship for a voyage knowing that the ship had already arrived. It could not, in his view, extend to a situation of a broker's fraud which neither increased not decreased the risk to the insured. Nor was there any duty to disclose supervening facts which come to the knowledge of either party after conclusion of the contract, subject always to such exceptional cases as a ship entering a war zone or an insured failing to disclose all facts relevant to a claim. Presumably here he was thinking of *The Litsion Pride* [1985] 1 Lloyd's Rep. 437 (see p. 255, below), although the case was not cited by him. At first instance, Steyn J. had referred to a much broader duty: "in a proper case, it will cover matters peculiarly within the knowledge of the insurers, which the insurers know that the insured is ignorant of and unable to discover, but which are material in the sense of being calculated to influence the decision of the insured to conclude the contract of insurance. In considering whether the duty of disclosure is activated in a given case a Court ought in my judgment to test any provisional conclusion by asking the simple question: Did good faith and fair dealing require a disclosure?" [1987] 1 Lloyd's Rep. at 97.

[32] Especially at [1990] 1 Q.B. 773–781.

rejecting Steyn J.'s adoption of the principle *ubi jus ubi remedium*, stated that it was necessary to found a claim in damages that there was a breach of contract, a tort, a breach of statute or a breach of a fiduciary relationship. Neither of the last two were applicable.[33] The duty of disclosure did not result from an implied term of the contract of insurance, so that there was no breach of contract. This seems acceptable.[34] The only final argument was that a breach of the obligation was itself a tort.[35] The Court of Appeal, and by adoption, the House of Lords, were disinclined to create such a novel tort. There was no authority in support, although it is unclear why this should be decisive,[36] and there were at least four further reasons. The first related to the supposed equitable origin of the relief for non-disclosure of material facts. This, with respect, seems quite simply fallacious reasoning. The duty of disclosure stems from the common law courts of Lord Mansfield.[37] The second referred to the fact that in relation to avoidance, the effect on the actual insurer (of non-disclosure by the insured) or the actual insured (of non-disclosure by the insurer) is irrelevant.[38] So there would be difficulties in translating this approach to a case where the insured is seeking damages. At the time this may have been

---

[33] *Quaere* perhaps whether more could have been made of the quasi-fiduciary nature of the insurance relationship, although this sort of argument would clearly have got nowhere in the House of Lords.

[34] It seems fairly clear, historically, that the principle of *uberrima fides* and the consequential duty of disclosure is inherent in the nature of the insurance contract and that it is not proper to talk of it as being based on an implied term in the usual contractual sense; *cf.,* however, Matthews, "*Uberrima fides* in modern insurance law", in *New Foundations for Insurance Law*, ed. Rose (1987), p. 39.

[35] This was quite separate from the argument based on negligence, which of course failed also and, as indicated earlier, got very little mention in the House of Lords. In the light of recent caselaw, it seems impossible that an argument based on a negligence claim for pure economic loss would have got anywhere anyway.

[36] There are modern cases where the judges have in effect created new torts to give a damages remedy where one was not available before; see *e.g. Seager v. Copydex* [1967] 2 All E.R. 415, [1969] 2 All E.R. 718 and *Fraser v. Thames Television* [1983] 2 All E.R. 101, awarding damages for breach of confidence. Further, in its most recent pronouncement on insurance law, the House of Lords was quite content to create new law by introducing the requirement of inducement into the duty of disclosure: *Pan Atlantic Insurance Co. v. Pine Top Insurance Co.* [1994] 3 All E.R. 581; see p. 109, above.

[37] See p. 101, above, but it is an error which the House repeated in *Pan Atlantic*, above.

[38] Citing *Container Transport International v. Oceanus Mutual Underwriting Association (Bermuda) Ltd* [1984] 1 Lloyd's Rep. 476; see p. 108, above.

correct, although it hardly seems an insuperable difficulty if the actual insured (or for that matter insurer) can prove an actual loss arising from the non-disclosure. In the light of *Pan Atlantic Insurance Co. Ltd v. Pine Top Insurance Co.*,[39] holding that the effect of an insured's non-disclosure on the actual insurer is relevant, this point clearly does not stand.

The Court of Appeal's third reason was based on the fact that the Marine Insurance Act 1906 did not refer to damages being available for a breach of the requirement of utmost good faith (section 17) or a non-disclosure by the insured (section 18). With respect, this is very poor reasoning and it is surprising that the House of Lords was content to adopt it. The 1906 Act was merely a codification of the law as it had developed as at a particular date. In those circumstances, the statement that if Parliament had contemplated damages as a remedy, "it would surely have said so"[40] is, with respect, nonsense. This view is also reinforced by the decision in *Pan Atlantic Insurance Co. Ltd v. Pine Top Insurance Co.*,[41] where the House of Lords did read words into the 1906 Act.[42] Finally, the court referred to the fact that the damages remedy would have to be reciprocal and would cause hardship because of the draconian nature of the duty of disclosure, not being dependent on fault at all. This is somewhat more convincing but not wholly so. After all, a party in breach of contract can be liable in damages to the other party without any fault or other blameworthiness at all.

In conclusion this case was, at least in part, very badly reasoned and leaves the distinct impression of a timid judiciary. It might have been the start of the exciting development of a broad duty of good faith in insurance law, but, sadly, that seems unlikely now to happen.[43]

---

[39] [1994] 3 All E.R. 581; p. 109, above.

[40] [1990] Q.B. at p. 781.

[41] Above.

[42] In holding that inducement was an implied requirement of s.20.

[43] For useful general comments, in addition to those already cited, see Kelly, "The insured's rights in relation to the provision of information by the insurer" (1989) 2 Ins. L.J. 45; Yeo, "Of reciprocity and remedies: duty of disclosure in insurance contracts" (1991) 11 L.S. 131; Fleming, (1992) 108 L.Q.R. 357.

CHAPTER 7

WARRANTIES AND CONDITIONS

This chapter is concerned with the terms of the contract of insurance other than those which describe the risk covered and exceptions to it. The nature of these terms was described in a general way in Chapter 5. The contract of insurance will invariably in practice consist of not just the policy document itself, but also the completed proposal form where relevant, and often, in addition, other documents including in some cases renewal notices. This contract may contain three sorts of relevant terms, namely warranties, conditions and clauses descriptive of the risk. There is, however, no necessity for this, and it may be, for example, that a particular contract contains only conditions in the sense that they have been described earlier.[1]

The warranty is the most fundamental term and will therefore be considered first before we distinguish and describe clauses descriptive of the risk and conditions. Because, moreover, warranties are often created by means of declarations on a proposal form, and in practice it seems that proposal forms may be completed by agents rather than the proposer himself, the body of law relating to this particular situation will also be considered in this chapter. In addition, we must note that in practice the strict law is not always applied, by virtue of the Statements of Insurance Practice. This point is considered at the end of this chapter.

Warranties

It has already been pointed out[2] that a warranty is a term of the insurance contract upon breach of which the insurer is discharged from all liability as from the date of the breach. This date will vary depending on what type the warranty is.[3] Warranties must be strictly complied with. It

---

[1] See p. 95, above.
[2] See p. 95, above.
[3] See below, p. 133.

is quite irrelevant that the breach is unconnected with a loss that occurs. One of the oldest cases illustrates this point very neatly. *De Hahn v. Hartley*[4] involved a marine policy covering a ship and its cargo from Africa to its port of discharge in the West Indies. The insured warranted that the ship sailed from Liverpool with 50 hands on board. In fact it sailed with only 46 hands but it took on an extra six hands in Anglesey, very shortly out of Liverpool, and it thus had and continued to have 52 hands. It was held that the insurer could avoid all liability for breach of warranty, even though it was obvious that the breach could have had no connection with the loss which subsequently occurred.

The effect of a breach of warranty

Until recently, it was conventional, at least in respect of non-marine insurance contracts, to treat a warranty as a fundamental term of the contract, breach of which entitled the insurer to repudiate the contract in its entirety.[5] However, this view, which had some support from caselaw,[6] must now be regarded as at the very least highly suspect in view of the decision of the House of Lords in *Bank of Nova Scotia v. Hellenic Mutual War Risks Association (Bermuda) Ltd, The Good Luck*.[7] Here it was held that a breach of warranty in a marine policy automatically discharged the insurer from liability, in accordance with the literal meaning of the words in section 33(3) of the Marine Insurance Act 1906.[8]

---

[4] (1786) 1 T.R. 343. See also the earlier case of *Pawson v. Watson* (1778) 2 Cowp. 785. Both cases were decided by Lord Mansfield, clarifying and establishing the distinction between warranties and representations.

[5] See *e.g.* the Law Commission's treatment of warranties in its Report No 104, *Insurance Law: Non-Disclosure and Breach of Warranty*, 1980 Cmnd. 8064 and the draft Bill appended to that Report, which used the language of repudiation in this way, equivalent to the way in which a breach of condition is viewed in general contract law.

[6] See the cases cited at n.21, below. In the Court of Appeal in *The Good Luck* [1990] 1 Q.B. 818 (see below), the judges took the diametrically opposite view to that taken subsequently by the House of Lords and were concerned to bring insurance contracts into line with contracts in general. On first thoughts (see *e.g.* [1989] J.B.L. 348) this seemed sensible, but on reflection the reasoning of the House of Lords is perhaps more convincing. See further below.

[7] [1991] 2 W.L.R. 1279. For comments, see Birds (1991) 107 L.Q.R. 540; Bennett [1991] J.B.L. 598; Clarke [1991] L.M.C.L.Q. 437.

[8] "If [a warranty] be not [exactly] complied with, then, subject to any express provision in the policy, the insurer is discharged from liability as from the date of the breach of warranty, but without prejudice to any liability incurred by him before that date."

An insured shipowner had clearly acted in breach of warranty by taking the ship into a prohibited area.[9] The benefit of the insurance had been assigned to a bank which had lent money to the insured and was a mortgagee of the ship; the insurers, who had been notified of the assignment, gave an undertaking to advise the bank promptly "if the ship ceases to be insured". Notwithstanding this, the insurers failed to advise the bank until some weeks after it had discovered the breach of warranty and the loss of the ship. At this time the bank decided to make a further advance to the insured, which, it was held, it would not have done had the insurers complied with the undertaking to advise it promptly. Restoring the judgment at first instance[10] and reversing the Court of Appeal, the House of Lords upheld the bank's claim for damages on the basis that the club had acted in breach of the undertaking. The insurance automatically ceased, pursuant to section 33(3) of the 1906 Act, when the warranty was broken.

In the Court of Appeal the issue had been approached from a general contract law perspective[11] by regarding the warranty as equivalent to a condition in contract law generally, with the provisions of the 1906 Act relegated to secondary consideration. Lord Goff of Chievely, giving the only reasoned speech in the House of Lords, was totally dismissive of this approach to construing a codifying statute whose language was, in his opinion, clear. In his view, the Court of Appeal had confused the distinction between conditions as fundamental terms of a contract and conditions precedent:

> "Section 33(3) of the 1906 Act reflects what has been described, in successive editions of Chalmers' *The Marine Insurance Act 1906*, as the inveterate practice in marine insurance of using the term 'warranty' as signifying a condition precedent . . . Once this is appreciated, it becomes readily understandable that, if a promissory warranty is not complied with, the insurer is discharged from

---

[9] The warranty was contained in the rules of the shipowners' mutual insurance club of which the insured was a member. The prohibited area was the Persian Gulf at the time of the Iran-Iraqi conflict.

[10] Where alternative claims had been advanced, unsuccessfully, based on general tort and a breach of the duty of utmost good faith; as to the latter, see p. 123, above.

[11] In addition, the court cited non-marine insurance law sources, including reports of the Law Reform Committee (*Conditions and Exceptions in Insurance Policies*, 1957, Cmnd. 62) and the Law Commission, *op cit*.

liability as from the date of the breach of warranty, for the simple reason that fulfilment of the warranty is a condition precedent to the liability or further liability of the insurer. This moreover reflects the fact that the rationale of warranties in insurance law is that the insurer only accepts the risk provided that the warranty is fulfilled. This is entirely understandable; and it follows that the immediate effect of a breach of a promissory warranty is to discharge the insurer from liability as from the date of the breach. In the case of conditions precedent, the word 'condition' is being used in its classical sense in English law, under which the coming into existence of (for example) an obligation, or the duty or further duty to perform an obligation, is dependent upon the fulfilment of the specified condition. Here, where we are concerned with a promissory warranty, *i.e.* a promissory condition precedent, contained in an existing contract of insurance, non-fulfilment of the condition does not prevent the contract from coming into existence. What it does (as section 33(3) makes plain) is to discharge the insurer from liability as from the date of the breach."[12]

There is a logic to this reasoning. It makes the warranty more like an exception to the risk than a condition in the usual contractual sense, since the operation of an exception is in no way dependent upon a decision of the insurer.[13] The contract may survive a breach of warranty in the sense of there being obligations of the insured which may survive the breach (for example, to pay a premium), although this is likely to be a rare occurrence. In practice the contract will come to an end.[14] The language of repudiation is inappropriate, as Lord Goff points out, at least in terms of repudiating or avoiding the policy. "[I]t is only in the sense of repudiating liability . . .

---

[12] [1992] 2 W. L. R. at 1294–5.

[13] Although it could be argued that the effect of a breach of condition in a contract of sale of goods is similar: see Bradgate and White, Chap. 3 in *Termination of Contracts*, eds. Birds, Bradgate and Villiers (1995).

[14] Although, rights of the insurer may survive, *e.g.* to rely on a term in the contract notwithstanding a breach of warranty (see, for example, cases upholding a forfeiture of premium clause — *Duckett v. Williams* (1834) 2 Cromp. & M. 348, *Thomson v. Weems* (1884) 9 App. Cas. 671, *Sparenborg v. Edinburgh Life Assurance Co.* [1912] 1 K.B. 195, *Kumar v. Life Insurance Corporation of India* [1974] 1 Lloyd's Rep. 147 (see p. 159, below) — and *Stebbing v. Liverpool & London & Globe Insurance Co.* [1917] 2 K.B. 433 upholding an arbitration clause — see p. 250).

that it would be right to describe [the insurer] as being entitled to repudiate." However, the decision is not wholly free from difficulties,[15] particularly because a breach of warranty can be waived.[16]

There seems no reason not to apply *The Good Luck* to non-marine insurance contracts.[17] Indeed, while Lord Goff was primarily concerned to construe the marine insurance provisions, much of what he said, including in the passage cited above, was not so confined.[18] The Court of Appeal has recently referred to the breach of a non-marine warranty as leading to "automatic cancellation of the cover."[19] Thus, authorities which have assumed that, in a non-marine context, the effect of a breach of warranty is to give the insurer the right to repudiate the policy[20] must be regarded as wrong.[21] The most difficult to reconcile with *The Good Luck* is the decision

---

[15] One arises out of s.34(2) of the 1906 Act providing that where a warranty has been broken, the assured cannot avail himself of the defence that the breach has been remedied, and the warranty complied with, before loss; this now appears redundant.

[16] s. 34(3). This is obviously essential in the sense that there will be many occasions where an insurer is content to overlook a breach of warranty, but the concept of waiver is difficult to understand in the face of an automatic termination of a contract. Should it be read as referring to some sort of reinstatement? Further, does the insurer have the right to insist on waiver or "reinstatement", in a case where the insured might be quite content for the insurer to be discharged from liability? For a more detailed discussion, see Birds, Chap. 4 in *Termination of Contracts*, eds. Birds, Bradgate and Villiers (1995).

[17] Where, as we shall see shortly, warranties are not just promissory or continuing, but may arise at the inception of a policy.

[18] The consequence would be a more logical structure to insurance law, and, it may be hoped, more sensible policy wordings. See the comment made on p. 93 about the confused use of language in insurance situations. It should also be noted that the Statements of Insurance Practice, which use the language of repudiation, should be redrafted; see below, p. 155.

[19] *Hussain v. Brown* [1996] 1 Lloyd's Rep. 627 at 630.

[20] Sometimes, it has been said that the insurer has the right to avoid or that the contract is rendered voidable. Strictly, the use of this language should perhaps have been reserved for non-disclosure and misrepresentation, namely those situations where a contract can be avoided by reason of general principles rather than as a result of the provisions of the contract. The reason for its use in the context of insurance warranties is that, as will be seen below, these often arise from the contents of completed proposal forms and are thus very similar to representations.

[21] There are few unequivocal judicial statements to this end, but see the dicta of Lord Goddard C.J. in *West v. National Motor and Accident Insurance Union Ltd* [1954] 1 Lloyd's Rep. 461 at p 463 and of Donaldson J. in *de Maurier (Jewels)*

in *West v. National Motor and Accident Insurance Union*.[22] Here, the insured was alleged to be in breach of a warranty as to the value of property insured. The insurers purported to reject his claim while relying upon a term of the policy to enforce arbitration. It was held that, by relying on the term, the insurers had waived their right to avoid the policy which was the only right they had.[23] The decision has been criticised as inconsistent with general contractual principle,[24] but in fact, following *The Good Luck*, it must be wrong as inconsistent with insurance principles. If the insured's breach simply discharged the insurers from liability, but did not necessarily affect the contract as a whole, the reliance on an arbitration clause by itself could not have been a waiver.[25]

Warranties as promises

Warranties are essentially promises made by the insured relating to facts or to things which he undertakes to do or not to do, as the case may be. They will invariably affect the risk to which the insurer is subject. There are three sorts of warranties: warranties as to present or past facts as at the date they are made; warranties as to the future; and warranties of opinion.

Warranties of past or present fact

Warranties as to past or present facts will usually, but not necessarily, arise as a result of a completed proposal form. The exact legal mechanism for this will be examined shortly. It is probably correct to say that the

---

Ltd v. Bastion Insurance Co. Ltd {1967} 2 Lloyd's Rep. 550 at 558. The clearest statements to this effect are in the reports of the Law Reform Committee and the Law Commission referred to in n.11 above. If *The Good Luck* does apply to non-marine policies, it may render largely redundant, outside proposal form warranties, the device of the clause descriptive of the risk which is considered below at pp. 141–145.

[22] Above, affirmed [1955] 1 All E.R. 800.

[23] This holding can be criticised in any event. Unless the warranty of value was incorrect at the time it was made, that is when the proposal form was completed, there seems, with respect, to have been no ground for allowing the insurers to repudiate. The warranty does not seem to have been a continuing warranty (see below), and warranties on a proposal form are not implied indefinitely into renewals of the contract: Winn L.J. in *Magee v. Pennine Insurance Co.* [1969] 2 Q.B. 507 at 517.

[24] See the Law Commission's Report No. 104 (n.5, above), 6.6 and 6.23.

[25] See also the cases referred to in n.14, above.

statements and questions and answers thereon, if they are warranted, will be presumed to be as to existing or past facts.

Promissory warranties

Warranties as to the future are known as promissory or continuing. They are continuing promises by the insured that facts will or will not exist in the future or will or will not continue to exist for the future. Common examples are warranties to maintain alarms or sprinkler systems in commercial fire policies and a warranty to maintain property in a reasonable condition, which may be found in all sorts of policies. Whereas a breach of warranty as to past or present facts will discharge the insurer from liability *ab initio*, since inevitably the breach occurred at the commencement of the contract, breach of a promissory warranty discharges the insurer from liability from the date of breach, but it is valid up to that date. The insurer would thus, for example, be liable for a loss which occurred before the breach.[26]

Promissory warranties may arise from completed proposal forms or from the body of the policy. Whether a warranty is promissory or simply present depends on the language used. There appears to be no bar to its being both,[27] but in order to be promissory, it must contain in its wording a clear reference to the future. In *Woolfall & Rimmer v. Moyle*,[28] the insured warranted when it completed a proposal form for employers' liability insurance that its machinery, plant and ways "are . . . properly fenced and guarded, and otherwise in good order and condition." The Court of Appeal had no difficulty in rejecting the argument of the insurers that the warranty was promissory. The use of the present tense rather than the future tense was decisive. Lord Greene M.R. said:[29] "If the underwriters intended to refer to the future, it is most unfortunate that a printed document of this kind . . . should not be so expressed. Had they intended that . . ., nothing would have been easier than to say so. If they did not mean it, I am at a loss to understand how the point comes to be taken." Similarly, in *Kennedy v. Smith*[30] a warranty in a proposal form for motor

---

[26] cf. s.33(3) of the Marine Insurance Act 1906.

[27] This is implied in *Dawsons Ltd v. Bonnin* [1922] 2 A.C. 413, as to which see below.

[28] [1942] 1 K.B. 66.

[29] [1942] 1 K.B. at 71.

[30] 1976 S.L.T. 110. See also *Sweeney v. Kennedy* [1950] Ir.R. 85; *Kirkbride v. Donner* [1974] 1 Lloyd's Rep. 549.

insurance which read: "I am a total abstainer from alcoholic drinks . . ." was held to relate simply to the past and the time it was made. In *Hair v. Prudential Assurance Co. Ltd*,[31] a warranty in a fire policy that the property was occupied, worded clearly in the present tense, was held not to have continuing effect.[32]

Recently, in *Hussain v. Brown*,[33] the Court of Appeal has reaffirmed the principle of *Woolfall & Rimmer v. Moyle* in a case where a warranty as to intruder alarms was clearly worded in the present tense. Doubt was cast[34] on the earlier decision in *Hales v. Reliance Fire and Accident Insurance Co.*,[35] where a present tense warranty regarding the nature of goods kept in a shop was read as a promissory warranty by reference to a supposed principle that in fire and other policies on property, warranties as to the nature of the premises and precautions taken against loss will prima facie be read as to the future, on the ground that otherwise they would be of little or no value to the insurer.

> "In my judgment . . . there is no special principle of insurance law requiring answers in proposal forms to be read, prima facie or otherwise, as importing promises to the future. Whether or not they do depends on ordinary rules of construction, namely consideration of the words the parties have used in the light of the context in which they have used them and (where the words admit of more than one meaning) selection of that meaning which seems most closely to correspond with the presumed intentions of the parties."[36]

There was another exception to the requirement of futurity in the language used which might survive the decision in *Hussain v. Brown*. This states that if a provision can only be read as to the future, it will be promissory. In *Beauchamp v. National Mutual Indemnity Insurance Co.*,[37] the plaintiff, a builder, effected a policy to cover the demolition of a mill. He had never previously done demolition work. He warranted that he did not

---

[31] [1983] 2 Lloyd's Rep. 667.
[32] According to Woolf J. (*ibid.* at 672–673), any other construction would have been unreasonable.
[33] [1996] 1 Lloyd's Rep. 627; see Hird, [1996] J.B.L. 627.
[34] See also Birds, "Warranties in insurance proposal forms" [1977] J.B.L. 231 at 237.
[35] [1960] 2 Lloyd's Rep. 391.
[36] [1996] 1 Lloyd's Rep. at 629 per Saville L.J.
[37] [1937] 3 All E.R. 19.

use explosives in his business in words which were clearly in the present tense. This was true at the time it was made, but the insured did later use explosives and this was held to be a breach of warranty. In the circumstances, because he had not used explosives before, the question addressed to him and his answer could only be read as referring to the future.

Warranties of opinion

Warranties of opinion are less severe than warranties of facts because if the insured merely warrants that facts are or will be true to the best of his knowledge and belief, there will be a breach of warranty only if he dishonestly or recklessly supplies an incorrect answer. The insured must exercise due care when making his warranty, but that is sufficient.[38] This is of particular importance in the context of consumer insurance proposal forms which, following the Statement of Insurance Practice,[39] should be worded so as to require only warranties of opinion rather than warranties of fact.

Creation of warranties

There are a number of ways in which warranties may be created. Some of these may be found in the body of the policy whereas one in particular is found in proposal forms, namely the "basis of the contract clause." We shall consider this device separately.

The policy may create warranties by the use of the word "warranty" itself, such as in the phrase "the insured warrants . . .," but even this may not be conclusive if the court concludes that as a matter of construction the parties could not have intended a warranty.[40] A provision whereby the contract is declared to be void or voidable in certain circumstances probably has the same effect.[41] A classic illustration here is the standard

---

[38] *Huddleston v. R.A.C.V. Insurance Pty. Ltd* [1975] V.R. 683; cf. *Mammone v. R.A.C.V. Insurance Pty. Ltd* [1976] V.R. 617. See also *Macphee v. Royal Insurance Co.* 1979 S.L.T. 54.

[39] See p. 154 below, for other relevant parts of the Statement.

[40] See *e.g. De Maurier (Jewels) Ltd v. Bastion Insurance Co.* [1967] 2 Lloyd's Rep. 550 and *C.T.N. Cash and Carry Ltd v. General Accident Fire & Life Assurance Group plc* [1989] 1 Lloyd's Rep. 229, discussed below.

[41] The use of "void" or "voidable" is misleading because, as we have seen (pp. 129–133, above), a breach of warranty discharges the insurers from liability and does not render the contract void or avoidable. Despite this, it is thought that it is still proper to regard such provisions as warranties.

increase of risk clause in fire policies which was discussed in the previous chapter.[42] In addition, it must be open to the court to conclude that on the construction of the policy, the wording of a particular term gives rise to a warranty.[43]

Warranty or condition?

The use of the words "condition precedent" can give rise to difficulties. As has been seen,[44] there is a legal distinction between warranties and conditions precedent to a particular liability, but in fact, a warranty may equally be referred to as a condition precedent, provided it is clear that performance of the condition is precedent to the validity of the policy.[45] Modern policies do not appear always to make the distinction clear. It seems clear that a general declaration making the terms of the policy conditions precedent to the validity of the policy is not sufficient to create warranties or fundamental terms of all of these terms, because by their nature some of them will be of the sort that cannot conceivably be regarded as precedent to the liability of the insurer, for example terms which after indemnity confer rights on the insurer such as subrogation rights. It does seem, however, that even matters which cannot objectively be regarded as fundamental to the validity of the contract, such as conditions relating to the claims process, can be made so fundamental by appropriate wording and in some ways equivalent to warranties in the sense we have described them.[46]

Insurers, though, cannot be blamed entirely for this confusion by reason of the wordings they adopt. Some of the decided cases are equally unclear. For example, judges have sometimes used the description "condition" in referring to what here are meant by warranties. Even a similar term has attracted different appellations and different legal consequences in decided cases. Two contrasting examples will suffice. In *Conn v. Westminster Motor*

---

[42] See p. 118.

[43] Law Com. No. 104, 6.3.

[44] Chapter 5, pp. 95–96.

[45] See the extract from the judgment of Lord Goff in *The Good Luck* [1991] 2 W.L.R. 1279 cited at p. 130, above.

[46] See *e.g.*, *Cox v. Orion Insurance Co.* [1982] R.T.R. 1, where the Court of Appeal held that a breach of a condition relating to the furnishing of particulars of loss entitled the insurer to treat the whole contract as repudiated because the policy contained a provision making its conditions "conditions precedent to any liability of the company to make any payment under this policy."

Insurance Association,[47] a term in a motor policy requiring the insured to maintain his vehicle in an efficient condition appears to have been regarded as a warranty in the proper sense. While the Court of Appeal did talk in terms of its being a condition precedent, they appear to have regarded the term as precedent to the validity of the policy because they held that upon any breach the insurers would be discharged from liability. In *W. J. Lane v. Spratt*,[48] on the other hand, a term in a goods in transit policy requiring the insured to take all reasonable precautions for the protection and safeguarding of the goods was regarded as a term, breach of which could be relied upon only if there was a causal connection between the breach and a particular loss.[49] The ground for the distinction between what on the face of them appear to be the same sort of term is not obvious. It is suggested that this sort of conceptual confusion is not satisfactory. Even though it may not matter in all cases to an insured or an insurer whether the latter is completely discharged from all liability or can merely repudiate a particular claim, there are some situations where the distinction is vital[50] and it would become of the utmost importance if ever the recommendations of the Law Commission were implemented,[51] for the latter are concerned solely with warranties in the sense that they have here been defined.

The basis of the contract clause

Historically, perhaps the most common and easiest way of creating warranties in non-marine policies was the basis of the contract clause contained at the foot of the proposal form. While this device may not be so wide-ranging in its effects as it has been, because of the provisions of the Statement of Insurance Practice mentioned earlier, it is still of importance in areas where the Statement does not apply and still appears to be used in "consumer-type" insurances to create warranties of opinion.[52]

---

[47] [1966] 1 Lloyd's Rep. 407. See further p. 372, below.

[48] [1970] 2 Q.B. 480.

[49] In fact Roskill J. referred to the term as a warranty, but it is clear that he was using the terms condition and warranty in the opposite sense to what is the usual practice and the practice adopted here (and by the Law Commission). See also *Port-Rose v. Phoenix Assurance plc* (1986) 136 N.L.J. 33 (see p. 202), where a "condition" requiring the taking of reasonable care was held not to be actionable unless the breach caused the loss.

[50] See, *e.g.* p. 150, below.

[51] As to these, see p. 154, below.

[52] Further, it still appears to be acceptable to use a basis clause to create promissory warranties: see the rather ambiguous para. 1(b) of the Statement of General Insurance Practice, discussed at p. 154, n.25, below.

By making the questions and answers and declarations on a proposal form the basis of the contract, and providing that in the event of any untruth the contract could be voidable, insurers succeeded in equipping themselves with a potential defence to an action on the policy much wider than that arising by virtue of the duty of disclosure.[53] The device was first adopted in proposal forms for life insurance in the last century. In *Thomson v. Weems*,[54] a question on a proposal form asked: (a) "Are you temperate in your habits and (b) have you always been strictly so?" The proposer answered "(a) temperate; (b) yes." The form contained a basis clause which expressly said that in the event of an untruth, the policy would be void. As the proposer was in fact a heavy drinker, the House of Lords had no difficulty in upholding the insurers' repudiation of liability. Materiality, they said, was irrelevant, even though, in fact, the matter must have been material on the facts of the case.[55]

In contrast, in *Dawsons Ltd v. Bonnin*,[56] it was accepted that the incorrect answer was immaterial.[57] A motor proposal concerning a lorry asked where it was garaged. The proposer wrongly answered that it was garaged at an address in central Glasgow, whereas, in fact, it was garaged at an address on the outskirts of the city. The proposal form merely declared that it was to constitute the basis of the contract; there was no reference to the policy being void or voidable in the event of an untrue answer, something which in the dissenting judgments was regarded as of great significance.[58] Despite this, by a bare majority, at least one of whose members[59] was not happy

---

[53] For a persuasive attack on the device, see Hasson, "The basis of the contract clause in insurance law" (1971) 34 M.L.R. 29. Hasson points out that the warranties held to be created by basis clauses in the early cases were material to the risk and these cases could therefore have been distinguished in later cases where the warranties were not material, of which *Dawsons Ltd v. Bonnin*, below, is a classic example. This, however, would have been most unlikely at a time when the prevailing doctrine was freedom of contract.

[54] (1884) 9 App. Cas. 671. Earlier cases are *Duckett v. Williams* (1834) 2 C. & M. 348; *Anderson v. Fitzgerald* (1853) 4 H.L.C. 483.

[55] But was not the question really asking for the proposer's opinion rather than a statement of fact? See Hasson, *op. cit.* at pp. 34–35. It is difficult to justify the view taken in most of the cases that questions asked of the health of a proposer for life insurance can be answered factually by a non-expert: see the trenchant comment of Fletcher Moulton L.J. in *Joel v. Law Union and Crown Insurance Co.* [1903] 2 K.B. 863 at 885, cited in Hasson, *loc. cit.* See also the related problem in the area of non-disclosure, discussed in Chap. 6 at p. 103.

[57] But see *MacGillivray*, (8th ed.) paras. 607–608.

[58] See Viscount Finlay at 430–431, and Lord Wrenbury at 436–437.

[59] Lord Dunedin at 434–435.

with the result, the House of Lords held that the insurer could repudiate all liability. "Basis" was sufficient to render the contents of the proposal form into fundamental terms of the contract. With respect, "basis of the contract" by itself could simply have been interpreted as the starting point on which negotiations were to be based, so that incorrect answers on the proposal form justified repudiation only if they amounted to material misstatements.[60] However, whatever criticisms may be made, the decision has long stood as authority for the simple proposition that a basis of the contract clause converts all statements on a proposal form into warranties.[61]

It follows that in addition to materiality being irrelevant, unless there is a term in the contract which requires this, it is also irrelevant that the proposer has answered the questions in good faith and to the best of his knowledge and belief if, in fact, answers are inaccurate. An even more harsh example of this is the decision in *McKay v. London General Insurance Co.*[62] The proposer for motor insurance stated on the proposal form that he had never been convicted of a motoring offence. In fact he had been fined ten shillings many months previously for driving without efficient brakes because a nut had become loose on his motor cycle. Even though this was held not to be a material fact for the purposes of the duty of disclosure, the insurers were entitled to repudiate liability for breach of warranty.[63]

Needless to say, this strict legal position has attracted considerable criticism, and it is noteworthy that judges have been as critical as other commentators.[64] Proposals for reform will be considered later.

---

[60] This point is strengthened by the fact that the policy contained a condition expressly providing that material misrepresentation or non-disclosure would render it void; see Hasson, *op. cit.,* at p. 36.

[61] See, *e.g.* the later decision of the House of Lords in *Provincial Insurance Co. v. Morgan* [1933] A.C. 240, discussed below. In the recent unreported Scottish case of *Unipac (Scotland) Ltd v. Aegon Insurance Co. (U.K.) Ltd*, it was held that the effect of a basis clause was not affected by a following declaration "and that no material fact has been withheld or suppressed." The latter was to be read quite distinctly. See Hird, [1996] J.B.L. 404.

[62] (1935) 51 Ll.L.R. 201.

[63] Swift J. did not like the result, though; see his comments at 202.

[64] The leading criticisms are referred to by the Law Commission, Report No. 104, at 7.2 and 7.3. Even if it is the case that insurers have not generally relied on their strict legal rights, it is suggested that this fact is no answer to the necessity for reform of the law.

Interpretation of warranties

Some mitigation of the strictness of the law of warranties, and in particular of the effects of a basis clause, has been effected by the courts adopting strict rules of interpretation. In particular, as it is usually the insurer who formulates the wording, in the event of any ambiguity, the warranty will be construed *contra proferentem*. The leading example is the decision of the House of Lords in *Provincial Insurance Co. v. Morgan*.[65] A firm of coal merchants insured a lorry under a standard motor policy. Part of the completed proposal form, which was the basis of the contract, read as follows: "State (a) the purposes in full for which the vehicle will be used; and (b) the nature of the goods to be carried. (a) Delivery of coal; (b) coal." One day the lorry was carrying some timber, as it did occasionally, as well as five hundredweight of coal. After the timber and three fifths of the coal had been delivered, and while the lorry was being driven to deliver the remaining coal, it was damaged in an accident. It was held that the insurers could not repudiate liability for breach of promissory warranty. The insured warranted only that the lorry would in general be used for carrying coal, which was complied with; he did not, on the wording of the question and answer, warrant that the vehicle would be used to carry only coal. "In insurance a warranty . . ., though it must be strictly complied with, must be strictly though reasonably construed."[66]

Another example of the reasonable interpretation of warranties is afforded by the cases concerning obligations imposed on a liability insured to take reasonable precautions. These are considered in Chapter 18.[67]

Clauses Descriptive of the Risk

Sometimes a term in an insurance policy which at first sight looks like a warranty, may be construed not as a warranty (or as a condition), but as a statement or clause descriptive of or delimiting the risk.[68] This sort of term, relating to the use of insured property, has a similar effect to an exception to the risk properly so-called.[69] The insurer is not on risk while

[65] [1933] A.C. 240.
[66] Lord Wright at 253–254; and see his comments at 254–256. The other point which arises from the case is considered below.
[67] p. 353.
[68] Sometimes the description "warranty describing the risk" has been used (see *e.g. De Maurier (Jewels) Ltd v. Bastion Insurance Co.* [1967] 2 Lloyd's Rep. 550), but this seems a rather confusing appellation.
[69] See Chap. 11.

the term is not being complied with, but non-compliance does not discharge the insurer from all liability and the risk reattaches when the term is being complied with. There is no need for the insurers to prove a causal connection between the "breach" of such a term and a loss, so in this respect the term is similar to a warranty and different from an exception and a condition.[70] Originally, this device was used in respect of appropriate statements on proposal forms with basis clauses and used, it seems, to protect an insured from the harsher consequences which would follow from the construction of the term as a warranty.[71] More recently, a term in the body of an insurance policy has been held to have similar effect, as will be seen below.

For example, in *Farr v. Motor Traders' Mutual Insurance Society*,[72] the plaintiff insured his two taxi-cabs. In answer to the question on the proposal form — "State whether the vehicles are driven in one or more shifts per 24 hours," he answered — "Just one." For a short period, because one of the taxis was being repaired, the other was driven in two shifts in the course of one day. The relevant accident occurred much later when both cabs were on the road and neither was being used in more than one shift per day. It was held that the insurers were liable in respect of this accident. The statement was not a promissory warranty, for breach of which they could repudiate, that each cab would only ever be driven in one shift per day. It was merely descriptive of the risk. Had the accident occurred at the time when only one cab was in use, the insurers would not have been liable. Presumably also, if the statement had been untrue at the time it was made, it could have been relied upon as a warranty of present facts.

In *De Maurier (Jewels) Ltd v. Bastion Insurance Co.*,[73] an all risks insurance effected by jewellers contained the following term:[74] "Warranted road vehicles fitted with locks and alarm systems approved by underwriters and in operation." The insured suffered two losses. At the time of the first, the locks on the car in question were not of the required sort; at the time of the second, there were no faults. At first the insurers repudiated the policy, and hence liability for both losses, seemingly on the ground that a

---

[70] See *e.g. C.T.N. Cash & Carry Ltd v. General Accident Fire and Life Assurance Corporation plc* [1989] 1 Lloyd's Rep. 259, which is discussed below.

[71] See Baer (1978) 2 Can. Bus. L.J. 485.

[72] [1920] 3 K.B. 669. See also *Roberts v. Anglo-Saxon Insurance Co.* [1927] K.B. 590.

[73] [1967] 2 Lloyd's Rep. 550.

[74] This was contained in a slip, not on a proposal form as such, though the effect is the same.

promissory warranty had been broken before the first loss. Subsequently, however, they admitted liability for the second loss.[75] It was held that the insurers were not liable for the first loss, as the risk was suspended because the locks were not approved. The term cited, despite the presence of "warranted," was not a warranty in the full sense, but merely a warranty descriptive of the risk.

The basis for the reasoning in these cases seems to be that in neither could the terms in question be clearly construed as promissory warranties, presumably because the language did not sufficiently refer to the future, and they thus attracted the lesser categorisation of statements descriptive of the risk, because they related to the use of property insured. There has been no suggestion that this categorisation would attach to statements on a proposal form not of this sort. The holding in the *De Maurier* case is a little curious because the term was drafted not by the insurers but by brokers acting for the insured. It seems that the insurers could have been discharged from all liability on the ground of breach of warranty of present facts because the car which was involved in the first loss did not have the required locks at the time the warranty was made, but on the facts it was held that the insurers had waived this right.

If a statement on a proposal form can be both a warranty as to past or present facts, and descriptive of use for the future, as these decisions suggest, the question remains whether it can be both a promissory warranty and a statement descriptive of the risk. The point arose in *Provincial Insurance Co. v. Morgan*,[76] the facts of which have already been given, where the decision of the Court of Appeal[77] was firmly based on the ground that the relevant question and answer were descriptive of the risk. On this analysis, the insurers were liable because the lorry was carrying only coal at the time of the accident. In the House of Lords, this view was taken by Lord Russell, for whom it was the only reason for the decision, and by Lord Wright as subsidiary to his main reason which rested, as we have seen, on the interpretation of the question and answer as a promissory warranty. The question arises as to what would have been the result of the case if the lorry had been carrying timber as well as coal at the time of the accident. On a strict view of Lord Buckmaster's reasoning, with which Lord Blanesburgh agreed,[78] the insurers would still have been liable

---

[75] They were criticised by Donaldson J. for not having done so earlier.
[76] [1933] A.C. 240.
[77] [1932] 2 K.B. 70.
[78] Lord Warrington agreed with both Lords Wright and Buckmaster.

because there was no breach of promissory warranty as he interpreted it. Against that are the views of Lords Russell and Wright and those of the members of the Court of Appeal which point to the opposite result. The latter is presumably the correct view, although it can be criticised as not designed to let the insured clearly know where he stands.

As already indicated, recently the categorisation of a clause descriptive of the risk has been applied to a term in the body of an insurance contract, rather than to a statement on a proposal form. In *C.T.N. Cash & Carry Ltd v. General Accident Fire & Life Assurance Corporation plc*,[79] on renewal of a general commercial policy insuring the plaintiff's cash and carry business, the insurers inserted a term under which the insured "warranted" that certain anti-theft security measures would be complied with. It was held that this was a clause descriptive of the risk and not a warranty in the strict sense. A warranty in the strict sense is only a clause which goes "to the root of the transaction between the parties which ought to avoid or relieve the [insurers] from their liability under the policy."[80] Here, the "warranty" could relate only to two sections of a policy[81] which was a general commercial policy with 12 sections in total.

While the result of the case seems sensible, it does appear somewhat out of line with some of the leading cases on warranties, particularly on proposal form warranties, where insignificant or immaterial breaches did entitle the insurers to be completely discharged.[82] Furthermore, the device here was used for the benefit of the insurers, who had drafted the term using the word "warranted",[83] not to protect the insured as in the earlier leading cases. The reason for the insurers' successful argument was that they did not wish their liability under the whole contract to be discharged, because they wanted simply to repudiate a claim. It was thought that they could not do this by alleging a breach of warranty in the strict sense, because of the decision in *West v. National Motor and Accident Insurance Union Ltd*.[84] However, as already indicated, it seems clear that the decision in *West* is wrong. The insurers in the *Cash & Carry* case could perhaps have

[79] [1989] 1 Lloyd's Rep. 299. See [1989] J.B.L. 355.
[80] Bankes L.J. in *Roberts v. Anglo-Saxon Insurance Co.* [1927] K.B. 590 at 591, cited by Macpherson J. in the *Cash & Carry* case, above at 302.
[81] *i.e.* only those protecting the insured against the risk of theft of cash from the warehouse.
[82] See, especially, *Dawsons Ltd v. Bonnin* [1922] 2 A.C. 413; above p. 139.
[83] As we have seen earlier, the quality of drafting in this area and the whole issue of categorisation of terms in insurance contracts leaves a lot to be desired.
[84] [1955] 1 All E.R. 800. See p. 133, above.

argued that they were discharged from liability by reason of the breach of warranty and repudiated the claim accordingly, but could have accepted that otherwise the contract still stood.[85]

Agents and the Proposal Form

As we have seen, a common source of warranties is the proposal form which contains a basis clause. It is not uncommon for an insurance transaction to be negotiated through an agent of one sort or another and frequently it would seem, in this case, the agent actually fills in the proposal form. Normally this would of course be done in consultation with the proposer, but there are reported cases which show that occasionally this is not the case. If an answer is incorrect due to the fault or with the knowledge of the proposer, then obviously the policy can be repudiated according to the law that has been considered. If, however, the proposer tells the agent the truth, but the latter chooses to falsify an answer, and the proposer does not become aware of what has happened, because he does not check what the agent has done, the question arises whether the proposer is bound by what the agent has done. Certainly he is if the agent is in law his agent at all times, and it has even been held that in this case he has no right to sue the agent in damages.[86] If, however, the agent is a full-time agent of the insurer, for example, a canvassing agent or another full-time employee, it might be argued that his knowledge of the truth should be imputed to the insurer.

It has already been seen[87] that in the context of the disclosure of material facts, this is the legal position. In the context of the answering of questions on a proposal form, however, the law has in general taken the opposite view. This is an area which has given rise to a comparatively large

---

[85] There are still difficulties with this sort of analysis. In *The Good Luck*, the House of Lords appears to have assumed that the whole contract would, in practice, come to an end so far as the insurers' liabilities were concerned, even if it might survive in terms of the insured's obligation to pay an outstanding premium or to enable the insurers to rely upon an arbitration clause. See p. 132, above. What is clearly needed, outside some well-thought out statutory guidelines, is an appeal court case which properly considers the effect of *The Good Luck* and the variety of insurance terms in a non-marine context.

[86] *O'Connor v. Kirby* [1972] 1 Q.B. 90, discussed in Chap. 10 at p. 187. Compare, however, *Dunbar v. A. & B. Painters Ltd* [1986] 2 Lloyd's Rep. 38, which is also discussed later. See that chapter also for a fuller discussion of whose agent in law a particular agent is, and the question as to imputation of knowledge.

[87] Chap. 6, p. 105.

number of reported cases in all common law jurisdictions. We shall here concentrate on the English decisions, but make reference to some particularly apposite Commonwealth cases.

Knowledge imputed

The first authority which must be examined is perhaps the earliest in time, a Court of Appeal decision which appears at first sight to be out of line with subsequent cases. *Bawden v. London, Edinburgh & Glasgow Assurance Co.*[88] concerned a proposal for accident insurance by a proposer who was illiterate and had only one eye. This fact was known to the agent of the insurers who completed the form for him. That form, however, warranted that the proposer had no physical deformity, which was obviously incorrect. Subsequently the insured suffered an accident in which he lost the sight of the other eye. It was held that he could recover under the policy for total loss of sight. The agent's knowledge of the truth at the time of the proposal was imputed to the insurer.

Knowledge not imputed

Bawden was, however, distinguished in a number of subsequent cases[89] and in particular in the leading case of *Newsholme Bros v. Road Transport & General Insurance Co.*[90] Here the proposal was for motor insurance and the incorrect answers, which related to previous losses, were warranted to be true. It was found as a fact that the agent who filled in the form knew of the true facts. He was an agent employed by the insurers to canvass for proposals, but he was not authorised to effect insurance whether temporary or permanent. The arbitrator held that the agent's knowledge of the truth was imputed to the insurers who could not therefore repudiate liability, but his decision was overruled by the trial judge and the Court of Appeal.

The leading judgment was delivered by Scrutton L.J. who gave two principal reasons for the decision. First, he said,[91] if the agent filled in the form at the request of the proposer, for that purpose he must have been acting as the agent of the proposer and not of the insurers. Secondly,[92] "I

---

[88] [1892] 2 Q.B. 534.
[89] See, *e.g., Biggar v. Rock Life Assurance Co.* [1902] 1 K.B. 516; *Keeling v. Pearl Assurance Co.* (1923) 129 L.T. 573.
[90] [1929] 2 K.B. 356.
[91] *ibid.* at 369 and 375.
[92] *ibid.* at 376.

have great difficulty in understanding how a man who has signed, without reading it, a document which he knows to be a proposal for insurance, and which contains statements in fact untrue, and a promise that they are true and the basis of the contract, can escape from the consequences of his negligence by saying that the person he asked to fill it up for him is the agent of the person to whom the proposal is addressed."

Greer L.J. also relied upon the agency point,[93] but he laid greater stress upon another reason, namely, that to allow evidence of what the agent actually knew to be introduced would be a violation of the parol evidence rule whereby oral evidence is generally inadmissible to vary the terms of a written contract.[94] Here the proposal form was part of the contract because, as usual, it formed the basis of it and its terms were warranties. Greer L.J. was thus able to distinguish the *Bawden* case on the grounds that in the latter, because of the special circumstances of the proposer's illiteracy, the court could rightly ignore the parol evidence rule or put a special meaning on the words used in the contract.[95] In contrast, Scrutton L.J. came very close to saying that the *Bawden* case was wrong.[96]

Agency

As to the agency point, the judges seemed particularly impressed by the fact that the agent did not have actual authority to fill in proposal forms. With respect, this should not be conclusive. The fact that agents are armed with such forms and frequently complete them, probably to the knowledge of insurers, must arguably give them ostensible authority to do so, unless any such authority is negatived, for example, by a notice on the proposal form,[97] yet the principles of ostensible authority were ignored in the *Newsholme* case. Further, even if an agent does become the agent of the proposer, or at least his amanuensis, for the purpose of filling in the form, at that stage the form is merely an offer to enter into an insurance contract and it is not easy to see why the correct knowledge of the agent should not

[93] *ibid.* at 382.
[94] *ibid.* at 379–380.
[95] See *ibid.* at 381.
[96] The *Bawden* case had previously also been subjected to considerable criticism in a number of cases in different jurisdictions. These are cited in the judgment of Scrutton L.J.
[97] See *Facer v. Vehicle & General Insurance Co.* [1965] 1 Lloyd's Rep. 113. Such a provision might not, though, survive the Unfair Terms in Consumer Contracts Regulations; see pp. 91–93, above.

be imputed to the insurer if the facts warrant it.[98] On this basis the strict parol evidence rule could be ignored, as the court has already admitted extrinsic evidence for the insurer that the answer on the form was incorrect.

Signing of form

However, the second reason of Scrutton L.J. as described above seems valid and strictly in accordance with the law governing the signature of documents, which holds a person bound by what he has signed, except in the limited circumstances when he can plead *non est factum*.[99] Therefore, it is suggested that the decision in *Newsholme* is correct, and cases to the contrary must either be wrong or regarded as exceptions, a point to which we shall return.

Whether the result is a fair one is an entirely separate question. The Law Reform Committee[1] certainly thought not and recommended statutory reversal of the rule. However, their recommendation, framed in terms that the agent should be regarded as at all times the agent of the insurer may not go far enough. If the analysis of the true ratio for the rule given here is the correct one, the parol evidence rule and the rule relating to the signature of documents would still present problems if the contents of the proposal form are part of the written contract. The need for some reform was also pointed out in a Government White Paper in 1977,[2] but hitherto, there have been no more concrete proposals.

---

[98] See Tedeschi, "Assured's misrepresentation and the insurance agent's knowledge of the truth" (1972) 7 Israel L.R. 475.

[99] See Treitel, *Law of Contract*, Chap. 8. The *Bawden* case might thus be regarded as a case where the insured could plead *non est factum* because of his illiteracy and consequent inability to check the form.

[1] Fifth Report, 1957 Cmnd. 62.

[2] Insurance Intermediaries, Cmnd. 6715, para. 16. The comment here was rather ambivalent. Having supported the Law Reform Committee's recommendation, the White Paper then says; "But it is not the Government's intention that the proposer should be relieved of responsibility for the accuracy of statements made by him in response to questions expressly put to him in the proposal form." The Insurance Ombudsman has been prepared to depart from the rule in *Newsholme* when he thinks it fair to do so.

Newsholme overruled?

It has, however, been decided in Canada[3] that the decision in *Newsholme* has been effectively overruled by the most recent English case, namely the Court of Appeal decision in *Stone v. Reliance Mutual Insurance Society.*[4] Here the plaintiff's fire policy with the defendants had lapsed. An inspector employed by the defendants called on the plaintiff's wife and persuaded her to effect a new policy. On the proposal form, the answer "none" was put to a question asking for details of lapsed policies and previous claims. This was incorrect. The plaintiff had made a claim on the defendants and had previously, obviously therefore, insured with them. The inspector had filled in the proposal form as indeed he was instructed to do by the insurers. It was held that the policy subsequently issued was not voidable. Megaw and Stamp L.JJ. regarded the case as turning on its special facts, namely that the inspector was actually authorised to fill in proposal forms. Lord Denning's judgment could be more widely interpreted, but equally it is suggested that his decision really turned on the authority of the agent, not simply as regards the imputation of knowledge of the agent, but also because he had authority to represent that the form had been correctly filled in, particularly because it was accepted that the plaintiff's wife with whom he dealt was a person of little education. This is sensible. If an agent is fairly senior within an insurer's hierarchy, the circumstances should be such as to allow the admittance of what he did and said and to regard him as having authority to vary the terms of a written contract.

Another reason for regarding *Stone* as merely an exception to the general rule is that the insurers themselves must have known that the answers were false and what the truth was, because they were the insurers with whom the previous lapsed policy had been held and against whom the previous claim had been made.[5] To have allowed them to repudiate the policy in such circumstances would have been ridiculous. This point was not actually taken in the case itself, but it must be correct.

It is suggested therefore, that there is no mandate for regarding the decision in *Stone* as overruling that in *Newsholme Bros.* The latter remains

---

[3] *Blanchette v. C.I.S. Ltd* (1973) 36 D.L.R. (3d) 561. This Supreme Court case, in fact, involved the slightly different situation referred to below, namely the agent filling in a blank form after signature by the proposer.

[4] [1972] 1 Lloyd's Rep. 469. See also Timmins, "Misrepresentation in insurance proposal forms completed by agents" (1974) Vict.Univ. of Wellington L.R. 217, who is also, it is suggested, over-optimistic.

[5] See Ritchie J., dissenting, in *Blanchette v. C.I.S. Ltd* (1973) 36 D.L.R. (3d) at 572.

the governing decision, but there are exceptions in the case of illiterate and possibly poorly educated proposers and, possibly, where the agent in question is more than a mere canvassing agent but can be regarded as having some authority to vary the terms of the contract.

Form signed in blank

There is some Commonwealth authority which supports a further exception, namely where the agent fills in the proposal form after it has been signed in blank by the proposer, the latter relying upon the agent's representation that he has the necessary information.[6] This is perhaps tenable, assuming that the proposer acts quite innocently and in the circumstances the agent can be regarded as having the authority to represent that the insurer would be estopped from relying upon a breach of warranty. On the other hand, it is clear that if the proposer signs the form after the agent has filled it in himself without asking any information of the proposer, the latter is bound by what he signs.[7]

Conditions

It has already been pointed out that insurance policies almost universally list a number of terms of the contract under the heading "Conditions." While it is difficult to generalise, it is probably accurate to say that at least some of these terms do not relate directly to the risk covered or to statements of fact, but are in the nature of collateral promises or stipulations. Some "conditions" may, of course, be warranties in the sense described earlier in this chapter, as has been seen. One further important reason for distinguishing warranties from conditions other than those already considered, even when both terms might appear in the same part of a policy, is that it has been held that compliance by an insured with a condition may be dispensed with if it is unnecessary, for example, by reason of information which the insurer possesses from another source. The actual decision which seems to establish this[8] will be considered in a later chapter.[9] It can hardly apply to warranties properly so called which, as we

---

[6] *Blanchette v. C.I.S. Ltd*, above. See also *Western Australian Insurance Co. v. Dayton* (1924) 35 C.L.R. 355.
[7] *Biggar v. Rock Life Assurance Co.* [1902] 1 K.B. 516.
[8] *Lickiss v. Milestone Motor Policies at Lloyd's* [1966] 2 All E.R. 972.
[9] See Chapter 12 at p. 247.

have seen, must always be strictly complied with. In addition, a breach of condition is said to be actionable only if it causes the loss,[10] whereas, as we have seen, there is no such requirement as regards warranties.

Nature of conditions

Conditions which are in the nature of collateral terms are of two kinds. First, there are promises or obligations imposed on the insured, primarily with regard to the claims procedure, which are not made fundamental to the validity of the contract.[11] Second are conditions conferring rights on the insurer, often repeating or enlarging rights given by the general law. Examples here include conditions governing subrogation rights and the rights of insurers to control proceedings by or against their insureds, and conditions concerning double insurance. Detailed consideration of the usual obligations and rights conferred by this sort of condition will be given in subsequent chapters. The questions to be considered here are first the effect of conditions imposing obligations on the insured, namely whether they are precedent to the insurer's liability for a particular loss or whether upon breach the insurer has merely the right to claim damages for such loss as it has suffered, and secondly the onus of proof where it is alleged that there has been a breach of such conditions.

Conditions precedent or mere conditions

If there is no reference to the sorts of condition in question being precedent to the insurer's liability, then it is clear that a breach does not entitle the insurer to repudiate liability.[12] This, however, seems unlikely to be the case nowadays. Policies will usually contain some general reference to their conditions being conditions precedent, if not a specific reference in a particular condition. The only legal problem which then appears likely to arise is where there is a general declaration, but within a particular condition there are parts which cannot conceivably be precedent to the insurer's liability, perhaps because the obligation thereunder can only be performed after the insurer has paid or because a relevant part does not actually impose an obligation on the insured.

---

[10] See p. 138, above.
[11] As we have seen earlier (p. 137), even these sorts of obligations can be made the subject of fundamental terms.
[12] *e.g. Stoneham v. Ocean, Railway and General Accident Insurance Co.* (1887) 19 Q.B.D. 237.

In *London Guarantee Co. v. Fearnley*,[13] for example, a fidelity policy effected by an employer to protect himself against the risk of embezzlement by an employee had a condition which required the insured to prosecute the employee suspected when a claim had been made and which provided that he should give all information and assistance to the insurer to enable the latter to obtain reimbursement from the employee of any sums which the insurer was liable to pay. Clearly the second part of this condition could not be precedent to the insurer's liability since it could only operate when that liability was established. Despite that, the majority of the House of Lords, with some hesitation, held that the first part was a condition precedent since the policy contained a general declaration to that effect and the two parts were separate and independent.

In contrast is the decision in *Re Bradley and Essex & Suffolk Accident Indemnity Society*.[14] This concerned a condition in a workmen's compensation policy taken out by a farmer, condition 5. There was a similar general declaration to the effect that the conditions were precedent to the liability of the insurer. Condition 5 contained three sentences. The first provided that the premium was to be regulated by the amount of wages and salaries paid by the insured, the second required the keeping of a proper wages book and the third required the insured to supply information to the insurers regarding wages and salaries paid. The insured, who only had one employee, his son, failed to maintain a wages book and the insurer relied upon this to deny liability for a particular claim. By a majority, the Court of Appeal held that the insured was not guilty of a breach of a condition precedent. According to Cozens Hardy M.R., the first and third parts of condition 5 were incapable of being conditions precedent. While the second, the one in issue, could be, "I think the fifth condition is one and entire, and it is to my mind unreasonable to hold that one sentence in its middle is a condition precedent while the rest of the condition cannot be so considered. A policy of this nature, in case of ambiguity or doubt, ought to be construed against the office."[15] The judgment of Farwell L.J. is to the same effect, though his reasoning is much broader; he would have required that the insured be informed of and consent to conditions precedent to liability before the policy was effected before they could be binding. With respect, this is too wide, however laudable, to constitute the law, and it

[13] (1880) 5 App.Cas. 911.
[14] [1912] 1 K.B. 415.
[15] *ibid.* at 422.

conflicts with other authority.[16] Fletcher Moulton L.J., dissenting, followed the decision in *Fearnley* which he clearly regarded as conclusive.

Although one can applaud the Court of Appeal's determination to ensure that insurers frame their conditions precedent clearly and separately, it is difficult to distinguish the decision in the *Bradley* case from that in the earlier one. Perhaps all that can be said is that each decision turns on questions of construction and that other decisions are of small assistance unless the wording is identical.[17] It is probably fairly safe to suggest that a general declaration as to conditions precedent would normally be effective in so far as particular conditions or parts of them are clearly capable of being separated.

The onus of proof

In relation to an alleged breach of condition, "it is axiomatic in insurance law that, as it is always for an insurer to prove an exception, so it is for him to prove the breach of a condition which would relieve him from liability for a particular loss."[18] It is, however, possible for the wording of a policy to affect this, but it is clear that very clear words would be required to place the onus of proving that he complied with a condition on the insured.[19]

Practice in and Reform of the Law of Warranties and Conditions

As we have seen at various points in this chapter, many aspects of the law of warranties, in particular the basis of the contract clause, have attracted criticism from judges and others. The whole matter was examined by the Law Commission[20] along with their examination of the

---

[16] See the cases concerning offer and acceptance in the insurance context, discussed in Chap. 4 at p. 73–74.

[17] See MacKinnon L.J. in *Welch v. Royal Exchange Assurance* [1939] 1 K.B. 294 at 311.

[18] *Per* Lord Goddard C.J. in *Bond Air Services Ltd v. Hill* [1955] 2 Q.B. 417 at 427.

[19] *ibid.* at 428.

[20] Report No. 104, 1980 Cmnd. 8064. Warranties were considered because of their obvious links, when arising from the contents of a proposal form, with disclosure and because the proposed E.C. Directive on insurance contract law contained provisions modelled on the French law of *aggravation du risque* corresponding in some ways to the English law of warranties.

duty of disclosure. As explained earlier,[21] implementation of their report seems regrettably unlikely for the foreseeable future and detailed consideration of it will not be attempted here.[22] Briefly, the Commission wanted all warranties to have to be material and the abolition of the basis clause. They would have allowed an insurer to repudiate a claim on discovering a breach of warranty only if the breach was causally connected with the loss.[23]

Statements of insurance practice

This is in fact the position in practice when the Statements of Practice are relevant and are followed.[24] Paragraph 1(a) of the Statement of General Insurance Practice provides, "The declaration at the foot of the proposal form should be restricted to completion according to the proposer's knowledge and belief," thus abolishing the full effect of any basis clause, and paragraph 1(b) provides, "Neither the proposal form nor the policy shall contain any provision converting the statements as to past or present fact in the proposal form into warranties. But insurers may require specific warranties about matters which are material to the risk."[25]

---

[21] See pp. 119–120.

[22] For a little more detail, apart from the Report itself, see the first edition of this book, pp. 118–120 and Birds, "The reform of insurance law" [1982] J.B.L. 449. The recommendations on warranties were more widely accepted as fair than were those on the duty of disclosure.

[23] The insurer would still have been able to repudiate the policy for the future, although this aspect of the report will need careful re-examination in the light of *The Good Luck*, if it is ever thought fit for implementation; see pp. 129–132 above. Difficulties might have arisen in connection with the Commission's recommendations because they were limited to warranties in the strict sense and might have been easily evaded by insurers resorting to the use of conditions precedent to loss to cover obligations traditionally the subject-matter of warranties.

[24] For more detail on these, see the sources cited at p. 120, n.15, above. Remember that the Statements apply only to individual non-business insureds and that there is no guarantee that they will be followed by insurers who are not members of the Association of British Insurers or Lloyd's.

[25] See also para. 1(b) of the Statement of Long-Term Insurance Practice which is to generally similar effect. The second sentence is a little odd as no-one has ever denied insurers' rights to impose continuing obligations of a material nature. Insurers may still feel that they can make the contents of a proposal form into continuing warranties. *Quaere* whether this should in fact be allowed; there seems no reason why such terms should not be required to be contained in the body of the policy.

Paragraph 2(b)(iii) states that an insurer will not repudiate on grounds of a breach of warranty or condition where the circumstances of the loss are unconnected with the breach "unless fraud is involved," thus mitigating one of the harshest potential consequences of a breach of warranty.[26]

---

[26] As mentioned earlier (pp. 138 and 151), the law imposes a causal connection requirement for breaches of condition in any event. cf. para. 3(b) of the Long-Term Statement which is similar but further qualified. Para. 2(b) does not apply to marine or aviation policies, an exclusion which could work hardship on private aeroplane and boat owners. The exception for fraud is perhaps unfortunate; an insurer can always reject a fraudulent claim (see pp. 254–256, below); why should it not have to prove fraud instead of retaining the right to rely on an unconnected breach of warranty?

CHAPTER 8

PREMIUMS

The premium is the consideration given by the insured in return for the insurer's undertaking to cover the risks insured against in the policy of insurance.[1] It need not, although, of course, it usually will, take the form of a money payment; for example, it could be the liability to contribute to the funds of a mutual society insuring its members, imposed by membership of that society. Furthermore, if a policy is under seal, and hence does not require consideration to support it, strictly no premium is necessary, but needless to say, this is hardly likely to arise. The amount of premium is entirely a matter for the insurer and competition led to the end of agreed tariffs some years ago.[2] This can be contrasted with the position in some civil law countries where tariffs are standard, and with the position in some other countries where state approval of premium rates is required.[3]

Payment of premium

We have seen[4] that there is no general rule requiring the actual payment of the premium before the insurer is at risk, although this will frequently, particularly in life insurance, be required by a term of the policy. Prima facie, the proper mode of payment of premium is in cash, but of course it is just as common nowadays to find payment by cheque. The latter is only conditional on the cheque being honoured. Indeed, other modern forms of paying money are also, with the insurer's consent, frequently used. Predominant here are the systems of bank giro, standing

---

[1] *Lewis v. Norwich Union Fire Insurance Co.* [1916] A.C. 509 at 519.
[2] For a comprehensive criticism of the tariff system that used to exist in respect of fire insurance, see the Monopolies Commission Report on the Supply of Fire Insurance (H.M.S.O. 1972).
[3] See, *e.g.* Franson, "The prior-approval system of property and liability insurance rate regulations: a case study," (1969) 4 Wisconsin L.R. 1104.
[4] p. 73, above.

order and direct debit, their use depending upon the type of insurance concerned.[5] For example, a renewal notice for motor or property insurance will commonly contain a bank giro form for the insured's use if he chooses, while premiums on certain endowment policies, particularly those used in conjunction with a mortgage for house purchase, may well be paid by standing order or direct debit. There has been no case law on the use of such methods generally for payment for any goods or services, and no problems can arise unless the bank responsible is for some reason late in making payment. It seems likely that, if the insured has sufficient funds in his account, the insurer who permits the use of one of these methods of payment would be held to be bearing the risk of any default by the bank, despite the fact that the bank is acting as agent of the insured rather than of the insurer. If not, the bank would in any event be liable to the insured for any loss suffered.

Payment on credit

The effect of inflation on premiums, so that the renewal premium on, for example, a motor policy can amount to hundreds of pounds, has prompted insurers in this and some other classes of business to offer their insureds the chance to pay premiums by instalments. Provided that the insured is an individual or a partnership, rather than a company or some other corporate body,[6] it is clear that such an arrangement falls prima facie within the Consumer Credit Act 1974 where the amount of credit, that is, of the deferred payment of premium, does not exceed £15,000.[7] It would be a restricted use credit agreement within section 11(1)(a) of that Act and a debtor-creditor-supplier agreement within section 12(a). Therefore, *inter alia*, the licensing machinery of the Act and the provisions as to rate disclosure and advertising[8] would apply. However, one effect of section 16(5) of the Act and paragraph 3 of the Consumer Credit (Exempt Agreements) Order 1977[9] is to exempt from the operation of the Act agreements for the payment of premiums on credit where the number of payments to be made to the insured does not exceed four. It appears that,

---

[5] In addition, the major credit cards are often now able be used for the payment of premium.

[6] Consumer Credit Act 1974, s.189.

[7] *ibid.* ss.8 and 9, as amended.

[8] See generally, Goode, *The Consumer Credit Act, A Student's Guide*, Chaps. 11 and 13.

[9] S.I. 1977 No. 326.

in practice, insurers often take advantage of this exception by limiting the number of payments on credit to a maximum of four.[10]

Apart from these issues as to payment, the other major legal point concerning premiums is the situations when in law the insured is entitled to a return of premiums he has paid. It is to this that we shall devote the remainder of this chapter.

Return of Premium

An insured is basically entitled to a return of premium where there has been a total failure of consideration[11] and any action to recover it is in quasi-contract for money had and received. If the insurer has been at risk in any way or for any period, there is no entitlement at common law to a recovery of any part of the premium paid. In *Wolenberg v. Royal Co-operative Collecting Society*,[12] the insured had effected several policies of industrial assurance with different insurers to cover the cost of funeral expenses to be incurred on her mother's death. Having recovered that cost from one insurer, she sought to recover back the premiums paid on the policy effected with the defendant. It was held that as the insurer had been at risk there could be no return of premiums, even though, by reason of the principle of indemnity, the plaintiff had no claim on the policy. *Wolenberg* was thus a case of over-insurance. The same principle will apply to any situation where the insurer has been at risk at all, for example, where liability under the policy, though not the policy itself,[13] is avoided for breach of condition, where the policy is cancelled by either party after it has been in operation, and where the insurers' liability is discharged for breach of a continuing warranty.[14] In practice, the principle is expressly reversed in some of these cases, and usually, for example, the cancellation clause in a policy[15] will provide for a rateable return of premium following cancellation.

There are two broad heads of case where there will or may be a total failure of consideration entitling the insured to recover his premiums. The first is where the policy is never concluded, is cancelled *ab initio,* or is void

[10] Even if they do not, detailed consideration of the regime laid down by the 1974 Act is beyond the scope of this book.
[11] *Tyrie v. Fletcher* (1777) 2 Cowp. 666.
[12] (1915) 83 L.J.K.B. 1316.
[13] As to this distinction, see Chap. 5.
[14] See Chap. 7.
[15] See Chap. 4.

or voidable *ab initio*. The second, which is the less certain category, is where the policy is illegal.

Non-existent, cancelled and void or voidable policies

If an insured pays a premium in respect of a contract of insurance which is never concluded, he is obviously entitled to its return. The result is the same if a life policy is cancelled, or a proposal withdrawn, under the statutory procedures.[16] A policy may theoretically be void for mistake[17] or because it is *ultra vires* the insurer,[18] or it may be voidable at the insurer's option for non-disclosure or misrepresentation,[19] or at the insured's option for misrepresentation or non-disclosure on the part of the insurer.

Where a policy is avoided *ab initio* by the insurer, it seems, although there is no clear non-marine insurance authority, that the insured is entitled to recover premiums paid in all cases except where his non-disclosure or misrepresentation was fraudulent.[20] This would certainly be in accordance with principle. The same result will prima facie apply where the insurer is discharged from liability *ab initio* for breach of warranty since he was never at risk. However, it is not uncommon for an insurer to provide for forfeiture of premiums in the event of discharge for breach of warranty. Such a provision will be upheld,[21] even in a case where it appears quite clear that the insured did not act fraudulently,[22] because a breach of warranty does not destroy the entire contract.[23]

It must be a fairly rare occurrence where an insured is entitled, and wants, to avoid a policy for misrepresentation of fact by the insurer, but a

---

[16] See pp. 327–329, below.

[17] Although this is unlikely; see p. 93, above.

[18] Even though the *ultra vires* doctrine will not now have this effect where the insurer is a registered company (Companies Act 1985, s.35), it could still apply to insurers taking other corporate forms.

[19] See Chaps. 5 and 6.

[20] *Anderson v. Fitzgerald* (1853) 4 H.L. Cas. 484.

[21] *Duckett v. Williams* (1834) 2 Cromp. & M., 348; *Thomson v. Weems* (1884) 9 App. Cas. 671; *Sparenborg v. Edinburgh Life Assurance Co.* [1912] 1 K.B. 195.

[22] *Kumar v. Life Insurance Corp. of India* [1974] 1 Lloyd's Rep. 147 at 154; here the insurers undertook to return the premium *ex gratia*. *Quaere*, though, whether such a forfeiture might not be unenforceable as a penalty clause, as not being a genuine pre-estimate of the insurer's loss. Kerr J. in the *Kumar* case (at 154) clearly inclined to this view, but felt that he was constrained to uphold the clause by the weight of authority, particularly the cases cited in the previous note.

[23] See pp. 129–133, above.

notable instance is the case of *Kettlewell v. Refuge Assurance Co.*[24] Here the insured was minded to let lapse the life policy she had with the defendant insurers, but she was persuaded to continue with it by the false representation of an agent of the defendant that after four more years, she would obtain a free policy, that is, that the policy would remain in force but she would have no more premiums to pay. The Court of Appeal held that the insured had the right to avoid the policy and recover the premiums paid since the date of the misrepresentation as money had and received,[25] it being irrelevant that the defendant had been at risk during the period that the premiums were paid and the policy in effect, albeit voidable. Avoidance by the insured operated *ab initio*.

Illegal policies

Where a policy is void because of illegality, somewhat different considerations apply. It should be noted that here we are concerned with contracts that are themselves illegal, not those situations where recovery under a valid policy is illegal for reasons of public policy.[26] In the latter case, the premium is never recoverable.

While there are a number of circumstances which could, in theory, render an insurance contract illegal,[27] easily the most common, and that which has given rise to the problems in this area, is illegality due to lack of insurable interest required by statute.[28] The general rule with regard to illegal contracts, whether of insurance or otherwise, is that the court will not entertain any action in respect of them, except in three exceptional cases.[29] Thus, premiums paid under an illegal insurance contract are

---

[24] [1908] 1 K.B. 545; affirmed [1909] A.C. 243.

[25] Lord Alverstone C.J. considered that the money was also recoverable as damages in an action in deceit (p. 550). Buckley L.J. rested his decision on another ground entirely, considering that there had not been a total failure of consideration since the insured had had the right to enforce the contract until she avoided it. According to him, the money was recoverable as obtained by the insurers only by the fraud of their agent.

[26] For the distinction, see Chap. 5, and for avoidance on public policy grounds, see Chap. 12.

[27] See Chap. 5. Note the insured's statutory right, where the insurer is acting without authorisation, to recover the premiums: section 132(1) of the Financial Services Act 1986; see p. 26 above. The common law reaches the same result: *Re Cavalier Insurance Co. Ltd* [1989] 2 Lloyd's Rep. 430.

[28] *i.e.* the Life Assurance Act 1774; see Chap. 3.

[29] See further, Treitel, *Law of Contract*, Chap. 11.

irrecoverable unless one of the exceptions applies. These exceptions are (i) where the party bringing the action was less blameworthy than the defendant, or, as it is more traditionally put, where the parties were not *in pari delicto*; (ii) where he is one of the class protected by the statute which makes the contract illegal; and (iii) where he has repented in time, that is before the contract was executed. The second exception is inapplicable to insurable interest cases[30] and the third is unlikely to apply except in the rare case where the insured relents before the risk begins to run. The first exception thus raises the only notable issues.

Parties not in pari delicto

It must be said that in their consideration of this question, the cases are somewhat conflicting. Clearly, if there is no element of fraud or trickery on the part of the insurer or his agent, the parties will be *in pari delicto*, since it is a general principle that everyone is presumed to know the law, and there can be no recovery of premium. The problem concerns the degree of improper conduct on the part of the insurer or his agent which will suffice to negate this. In the badly reported case of *British Workmen's & General Assurance Co. v. Cunliffe*,[31] an agent of the insurers induced the insured to effect a policy on the life of his brother-in-law, in which he had no insurable interest. The Court of Appeal allowed the insured to recover the premiums he had paid. The headnote to the report states that the agent acted without any fraud but it does seem that the judges took the view that, even if he did not act fraudulently, his conduct was sufficiently improper as he knew what the law was and that the insured had no insurable interest, and despite this, assured the insured that the policy would be all right.[32]

This decision was distinguished in *Harse v. Pearl Life Assurance Co.*,[33] where the plaintiff insured the life of his mother in which he had no interest. Again, he had been persuaded to effect the insurance by an agent of the insurer, but the Court of Appeal held that the agent had acted quite innocently, the parties were *in pari delicto*, and there was no recovery of premiums. It was found that the agent had either forgotten or mistaken

---

[30] Though it would apply, at common law, to contracts with unauthorised insurers. Statute (see n.27) now makes express provision.
[31] (1902) 18 T.L.R. 502.
[32] *ibid.* at 503, per Vaughan Williams and Romer L.JJ.
[33] [1904] 1 K.B. 558; see further at p. 42, above.

the law, and it does appear that policies of the sort in question were being regularly sold at the time. The *Cunliffe* case was distinguished on the ground that it involved fraud. If these conclusions of fact were correct, then the decision in *Harse* is correct in principle, and distinguishable from that in *Cunliffe*, although it is somewhat difficult to accept, without demur, the dictum of Romer L.J.[34] that agents of insurance companies must not be treated as under any greater obligation to know the law than ordinary persons whom they approach with a view to persuading them to effect insurance.

In the last important case on this question, *Hughes v. Liverpool Victoria Legal Friendly Society*,[35] a differently constituted Court of Appeal was somewhat troubled by the decision in *Harse*. *Hughes*, though, was a clear case of an agent fraudulently persuading the plaintiff to take over existing policies on the life of someone in which he could not conceivably have had an insurable interest, there being no relationship at all between them. The plaintiff was held entitled to recover his premiums. All three judges were prepared to assume that there was no fraud or impropriety on the part of the agent in the *Harse* case, because until that case was decided, it was a genuinely open question whether or not a son had an insurable interest in the life of his mother, but Swinfen Eady L.J. commented: "[That decision] must not be regarded as deciding that where a person is induced to insure a life in which he has no interest, by an agent making a misrepresentation of fact, or of mixed fact and law, the parties are necessarily *in pari delicto*." It would seem safe to assume that, at least where the insured has acted quite innocently, the decision in *Harse* would be of little practical importance nowadays.[36]

---

[34] *ibid.* at 564.

[35] [1916] 2 K.B. 482.

[36] See, *e.g.*, the decisions of the Industrial Assurance Commissioner referred to in *MacGillivray*, (8th ed.) paras. 1015–1019. It is only in the context of industrial life assurance that the point appears ever to have been litigated, perhaps because of the particular sales techniques used there. Certainly, from the dearth of modern reported cases, it would seem that the area is rather academic nowadays.

CHAPTER 9

ASSIGNMENT

A number of very important questions in insurance law and practice arise under the general heading of Assignment. Essentially, though, there are three distinct, but closely related topics involved. The first concerns the effect of an assignment by the insured of the subject matter of his insurance policy. The second is the assignment of the benefit of a contract of insurance and the third concerns the assignment of a contract of insurance itself. Various points within these topics overlap, but the basic distinctions are crucial. We shall consider each one in turn. On the whole in this chapter we shall not be concerned with assignment in the context of life insurance. This is a suitably self-contained topic more aptly considered in the later chapter (Chapter 17) on life insurance.

Assignment of the Subject-Matter of Insurance

The point that arises here concerns insurance of property when that property is sold or otherwise disposed of by the insured. It has been most often considered in connection with the sale and purchase of land, and for this reason we shall concentrate initially on this area, but the principles established in the cases are equally applicable to dealings with personal property. The assignment of the subject-matter of an insurance policy cannot operate to assign the insurance.

Once contracts for the sale of land are exchanged, the purchaser obtains an equitable interest in the property, although the vendor retains the legal estate. At this stage, both parties clearly have an insurable interest in the property and, in practice, both may well be insured.[1] On completion of the purchase, or, where the title to the land is registered, upon registration of the purchaser as proprietor, the legal estate vests in the purchaser and obviously the vendor ceases to have an insurable interest.[2] If the property is then lost or damaged, he can recover nothing for this reason.

[1] See further below.
[2] *Ecclesiastical Commissioners v. Royal Exchange Assurance Corp.* (1895) 11 T.L.R. 476.

Claim by the purchaser

If, between contract and completion, the purchaser does not insure, the question arises as to whether, in the absence of an assignment of the benefit of the vendor's policy, which we shall consider shortly, he can claim the benefit of the vendor's policy. It is clear that the vendor can recover, as he still has an insurable interest to the extent of his unpaid interest in the property, but the suggestion in one of the cases that supports this[3] that he holds any money received for the benefit of the purchaser was soon dispelled by the decision in the leading case of *Rayner v. Preston.*[4]

Here fire destroyed the property which was the subject-matter of the insurance policy effected by P, after P had contracted to sell it to R. Despite this, the contract was completed in accordance with the general rule in conveyancing of real property[5] that the property is at the purchaser's risk from the date of contract, and P received the full agreed purchase price from R. P also received money from his insurers and the action was brought by R claiming that the assignment of the property to him operated also to assign the benefit of the insurance. R argued that, following the contract of sale, P held the land and the insurance contract on trust for him. By a majority, the Court of Appeal denied R's claim, holding that the insurance contract was merely collateral to the main contract and that the relationship between vendor and purchaser of land was not generally that of trustee and beneficiary. In the absence of an express assignment of the insurance policy or moneys, which was not in issue, there was no reason to say that P held the money for R.[6] As a result of this decision, P was of course in effect paid twice for the property, but his liability to repay the insurance moneys was subsequently established in *Castellain* v. *Preston,*[7] a decision which is examined further in Chapter 15.

Consequences of Rayner v. Preston

The effect of the decision in *Rayner v. Preston* may, as we shall see, be mitigated by an assignment of the benefit of the policy, but this may not

---

[3] *Collingridge v. Royal Exchange Assurance Corp.* (1877) 3 Q.B.D. 173.
[4] (1881) 18 Ch.D. 1.
[5] This rule may now be varied by contract; see below.
[6] Note though that R could perhaps have used the provisions of the Fires Prevention (Metropolis) Act 1774 to compel reinstatement; James L.J. (1881) 18 Ch.D. at 15. This point is discussed below in Chap. 14 at p. 282.
[7] (1883) 11 Q.B.D. 380.

be possible, for example, because the insurers refuse their required consent. If so, the decision hardly appears justifiable, because it requires that, if the risk lies with the purchaser, it is advisable that both vendor and purchaser insure, the former at least to the amount he is unpaid, and the latter at least to the amount of the full purchase price for which he will remain liable. This is surely wasteful, and it can hardly matter greatly from the insurer's point of view, if, the property insured is destroyed and the insured has an insurable interest, to whom the policy monies go.[8] This point is reinforced by the fact that fire policies do often contain a condition giving the purchaser the benefit of the insurance in this sort of case.[9] Insurers have thus recognised the harshness of *Rayner v. Preston*, and would presumably rely on it only rarely. Despite this, it must not be forgotten that vendor and purchaser do have different interests, and the vendor will generally be concerned to recover in total only the market value of the property, whereas the purchaser will probably want sufficient to rebuild. We shall take up this point again.

Considerations like those mentioned in the last paragraph led the Law Commission[10] to undertake a review of the law relating to the question of the risk under a contract for the sale of land. The consequences of their review are considered below.

Position of the vendor

We have already noted that after completion of the contract for the sale of land, or, indeed, upon receiving full payment,[11] the vendor can no longer recover because he no longer has any insurable interest, unless very exceptionally, he is allowed to and did insure for the purchaser.[12] Indeed his policy will lapse automatically once the subject-matter disappears.[13] This applies equally to the insurance of goods which are sold. In the case of a sale of specific goods, the contract itself may operate as a conveyance of

---

[8] Unless, of course, there is some material fact about the purchaser of which the insurers are entitled to be told.

[9] It is thought that such a provision would also have the effect of disallowing the insurer from exercising subrogation rights in the vendor's name against the purchaser; see p. 304 below.

[10] *Transfer of Land: Passing of Risk from Vendor to Purchaser*, W.P. No. 109, 1988; *Transfer of Land: Risk of Damage after Contract of Sale*, Report No. 191, 1990.

[11] *Ziel Nominees Pty Ltd v. V.A.C.C. Insurance Co. Ltd* (1976) 50 A.L.J.R. 106.

[12] See the discussion in Chap. 3 at pp. 69–71.

[13] *Rogerson v. Scottish Automobile & General Insurance Co. Ltd* (1931) 48 T.L.R. 17.

the property,[14] in which case the seller will be able to insure only if he retains actual possession, section 39 of the Sale of Goods Act 1979 giving him a lien for the price despite the transfer of ownership. However, once the seller surrenders possession, the policy will lapse. Thus in *Rogerson* v. *Scottish Automobile & General Insurance Co. Ltd*,[15] the insured had a motor policy covering a particular car. He exchanged that car for a new one of a similar type without informing his insurers. The House of Lords held that thereupon his policy lapsed.

It should be noted, though, that this applies only where the insurance policy has a defined subject-matter. Most policies do and must have, simply in order to satisfy the requirement of insurable interest, but it is perfectly possible for a liability policy to exist covering the insured against defined heads of liability to third parties without tying it to particular property. For example, a third party motor policy need not be referable to any particular vehicle; it could cover the insured when driving any vehicle. In *Boss* v. *Kingston*,[16] the insured held a policy insuring the third party liabilities in respect of his own described motor-cycle, and when he was driving a motor-cycle not belonging to him with the owner's consent. He sold his motor-cycle, but kept up his policy. One day he drove a friend's motor-cycle, and was charged with driving without insurance.[17] The magistrates convicted him on the ground that his policy had automatically lapsed when he sold his motor-cycle, following the *Rogerson* case, but the Divisional Court held that there was no such automatic lapse. The policy was merely a third party policy and it was not necessarily attached to any property. However, reluctantly they held that the insured had been rightly convicted. On the construction of the policy it had lapsed when the insured sold his motor-cycle, simply because it contained conditions precedent to the insurer's liability which could not be complied with if the motor-cycle was no longer owned by the insured.

The distinction from the *Rogerson* case is no doubt a valid one theoretically, but in practice it is unlikely to matter very much. The point is perhaps likely to arise only in the context of motor insurances and such third party policies are likely to contain conditions as in *Boss* v. *Kingston*, compelling the conclusion that, on the insured's selling the vehicle, the

---

[14] Sale of Goods Act 1979, s.18 r.1. It is open to the parties to agree to the contrary, which often happens in practice.

[15] (1931) 48 T.L.R. 17. See also *Tattersall v. Drysdale* [1935] 2 K.B. 174.

[16] [1963] 1 W.L.R. 99.

[17] Under the Road Traffic Act 1988, s.145; see Chap. 19.

policy lapses, even though strictly the vehicle might not be the subject-matter of the insurance.

In the case of the sale of goods insured where property does not pass at the time of the contract for sale, principally of unascertained goods, there should be no problems. Property[18] and risk[19] will usually remain with the vendor who can therefore recover if the goods are damaged or destroyed. The purchaser can have no interest in claiming the benefit of any insurance. Once property passes, and the price is paid, the insurance will lapse.

Assignment of the Benefit of an Insurance Policy

If the assignment of the subject-matter of an insurance policy does not of itself assign any benefit under the policy to the assignee, the question next arises as to whether or not that benefit might not itself be assigned. It must be stressed that we are not here considering the assignment of the policy or contract itself, but merely of the right to recover any benefits payable under it. There is no doubt that this benefit is a chose in action, one of those intangible pieces of property which can be assigned either at law, under section 136 of the Law of Property Act 1925, or in equity.[20] To bind the insurer, and make the latter directly liable to pay the assignee, notice will have to be given to it so that the assignment is legal. Otherwise the assignee can proceed only by suing the assignor to compel him to claim from the insurer. Such an assignment can take place before or after a loss[21] and the consent of the insurer is irrelevant.[22] What the insured is doing is simply saying that the proceeds from any claim he has or may have are to go to a third party.

However, the assignee will recover only what the assignor/insured is entitled to, that is the measure of the latter's insurable interest, and he will take subject to any rights the insurer may have, for example, to avoid the policy or liability for non-disclosure or breach of warranty. For these reasons, express assignment of the benefit may not avail the purchaser to the extent he would wish in the sort of case of which *Rayner v. Preston*[23] is an example.

---

[18] Sale of Goods Act 1979, s.18, r. 5.

[19] Sale of Goods Act 1979, s.20.

[20] For a fuller description of the assignment of choses in action, see Treitel, *Law of Contract*, Chap. 16.

[21] *cf. Tailby v. Official Receiver* (1888) 13 App. Cas. 523; *Peters v. General Accident Fire & Life Assurance Corp. Ltd* [1937] 4 All E.R. 628, *per* Goddard J.

[22] *Re Turcan* (1888) 40 Ch.D. 5.

[23] (1881) 18 Ch. D. 1; see above.

Statutory assignment

Section 47 of the Law of Property Act 1925 appears to have been introduced to remove the need for this sort of express assignment where the parties are the vendor and purchaser of property, whether land or goods. It was clearly intended to overrule the decision in *Rayner v. Preston* and provides, by subsection (1):

> "Where after the date of any contract for sale or exchange of property, money becomes payable under any policy of insurance maintained by the vendor in respect of any damage to or destruction of property included in the contract, the money shall, on completion of the contract, be held by or receivable by the vendor on behalf of the purchaser and paid by the vendor to the purchaser on completion of the sale or exchange, or as soon thereafter as the same shall be received by the vendor."

By subsection (2), the section has effect subject to (a) any stipulation to the contrary contained in the contract, which must refer to the contract of sale not the contract of insurance; (b) any requisite consents of the insurer; and (c) the payment by the purchaser of the proportionate part of the premium from the date of the contract.

The first point to note is that the section does not give the purchaser any direct rights against the insurer, as an express assignment under section 136 would. Secondly, and fundamentally, the question arises as to what section 47 purports to assign. Is it the contract of insurance itself or merely any benefits payable under it? In the absence of any judicial authority, it is suggested that there is no reason to regard the section as purporting to effect an assignment of the policy, as it refers merely to the money becoming payable under any contract of insurance. If this is so, the next question is as to the meaning of the second requirement (b above) in subsection (2). The ordinary understanding of "any requisite consents" would surely be "any consents as are actually required in the policy," but this is not the view that some of the leading works take.[24] It is often argued that the requirement specifies the need for express consent of the insurer. It is true that in practice this is usually impliedly given by the standard clause in fire policies on buildings to which we have already referred.[25] But it is submitted that, in fact, the consent of the insurer is

[24] See, *e.g. MacGillivray*, (8th ed.) para. 1849; Emmet, *Title*, pp. 42–43.
[25] See p. 165.

required only if it is expressly required. The section does not say that it operates "only with the consent of the insurer" and there is no reason to construe it other than with its literal meaning. As we have already argued, section 47 does not purport to assign the contract of insurance itself, in which case the consent of the insurer would be necessary.[26] It must not be forgotten though, that if the consent of the insurer is, in fact, required, it may well be very difficult for the purchaser to discover this.

It is thought, therefore, that section 47 overrules the decision in *Rayner v. Preston* in all but those cases where the insurers' consent is required and is not obtained. However, in the majority of cases, it would not be safe for a purchaser to rely upon the section. In the case of contracts for the sale or exchange of land, the purchaser is entitled to only what the vendor is entitled to, in the words of section 47(1), only money that "becomes payable" to the vendor is impressed with the trust. Thus the insurer may have a defence to the vendor's claim and, in any event, the amount of the vendor's insurable interest, the amount which he is entitled to claim, may, following the contract of sale, be less than the full value of the property or the cost of its reinstatement. If the risk has passed to the purchaser, the vendor's loss can only be the amount for which he has contracted to sell the property less the deposit he has already received from the purchaser.

The Law Commission review

The rule that the risk of loss, in the case of sales of land, lies on the purchaser from the time of contract, which underlies the decision in *Rayner v. Preston*,[27] and the uncertainties surrounding the true scope of section 47 led to the result in standard conveyancing practice that the purchaser effected his own insurance upon exchange of contracts.[28] Because the vendor would retain his own insurance to protect his own insurable interest, the result was the same property being insured twice against essentially the same risks. This seemed unnecessarily wasteful. It also potentially gave rise to double insurance problems.[29] Persuasive arguments were made that reform of the law was necessary.[30]

---

[26] See p. 171, below.

[27] (1881) 18 Ch. D. 1; see above.

[28] Often this would be done under a block policy held by the purchaser's solicitors.

[29] See Chap. 16.

[30] See *e.g.* Aldridge (1974) 124 N.L.J. 966; Adams and Aldridge, *Law Society's Gazette*, April 16, 1980.

The Law Commission took up the challenge and produced a working paper[31] arguing for a change in the law so that in effect the risk would remain with the vendor until completion.[32] They did not consider that there should be any change to insurance rules as such. Their view of the need for change was supported by the vast majority of respondents and their 1990 Report[33] upheld their provisional view.[34] However, by the time that Report was written, there had been a change in the standard contractual conditions applying to the vast majority of conveyancing transactions. The effect of these was the same as that of the Law Commission's recommendation and so the Commission concluded that, for the present at least, there was no need for a change in the law.

These contractual conditions are the relevant parts (clause 5) of the Standard Conditions of Sale.[35] These impose an obligation on the seller to transfer the property in the same physical state as it was at the date of contract,[36] "which means that the seller retains the risk until completion." The seller is under no obligation to the buyer to insure and section 47 of the Law of Property Act is expressly excluded. Most of this seems eminently sensible and should lead to a withering away of unnecessary double insurance. However, the view has been expressed that it is curious that the seller is not obliged to insure and, as a result, it seems that this part of the standard condition will not be followed in practice.[37]

---

[31] No. 109; see n.10, above.

[32] Their provisionally preferred solution was actually that by statute the vendor would be contractually obliged to convey the property in the physical condition in which it was as at the date of the contract, but for most purposes this has the same effect as altering the rule on the passing of risk.

[33] Law Com. No. 191.

[34] Subject always to the possibility of the parties being free to contract out of the new rule.

[35] These replaced the previous "rival" Law Society's General Conditions of Sale and the National Conditions of Sale.

[36] Except for fair wear and tear.

[37] See Silverman, *Law Society's Gazette*, October 23, 1991, p. 27. According to this article, some practitioners delete clause 5 altogether and reinstate the old position that the risk passes to the purchaser on contract, thus defeating the intentions of the Law Commission and giving rise to potential double insurance problems. If this happened to any significant degree, the Law Commission might press for a formal change in the law. For consideration of other insurance issues, see Harwood (1992) 136 S. J. 408.

Effect of section 47 on goods insurance

As far as contracts for sale or exchange of goods are concerned, there is no doubt that section 47 applies. However, in the case of specific goods where property may well pass at the time of the contract, it is irrelevant simply because the vendor will have no claim and will have no insurable interest to recover anything to which the purchaser can claim entitlement, unless, exceptionally, the risk remains with him. But in this event, the purchaser will not suffer any loss anyway. Where, however, property does not pass at the date of the contract, and a loss occurs before it does, there is no reason why the purchaser should not claim the benefits of any insurance maintained by the vendor, if he chooses to go ahead with the contract, subject to any consent expressly required by the insurer and to the other conditions in section 47(2).

Assignment of the Policy

Prima facie, any insurance policy is freely assignable, being itself a chose in action. This is statutorily confirmed in respect of life policies, which we shall consider separately,[38] and marine polices.[39] However, in respect of all other forms of insurance there are two conditions which must be satisfied before an assignment will be valid.

The first arises out of the personal nature of the insurance contract and requires the consent of the insurers.[40] The result is that, in effect, non-life and non-marine policies are not really assignable, since insurers would consent to an "assignment" to a new insured only in circumstances which would amount to the creation of a new contract or a novation. In *Peters v. General Accident Fire and Life Assurance Corporation Ltd*,[41] the vendor of a van handed over his insurance policy with the defendant insurers to the purchaser. The latter subsequently injured the plaintiff by the negligent driving of the van and the plaintiff sued the insurers under what is now section 151 of the Road Traffic Act 1988.[42] It was held that the insurers

---

[38] See Chap. 17 at pp. 329–332.

[39] Marine Insurance Act 1906, s.50.

[40] Note, though, that the personal nature of the insurance contract does not seemingly preclude an undisclosed principal from suing on a policy made by his agent: *Siu Yin Kwan v. Eastern Insurance Co. Ltd* [1994] 1 All E.R. 213; see p. 66, above.

[41] [1938] 2 All E.R. 267. See also *Bryant v. Primary Industries Insurance Co. Ltd* [1990] 2 N.Z.L.R. 142.

[42] See Chap. 19, at pp. 375–378.

were not liable to satisfy the judgment awarded against the purchaser, as the insured vendor could not simply assign his motor policy to the purchaser without the insurers' consent.[43] The policy would have lapsed upon the sale of the van for the reasons and under the authorities mentioned earlier.

The second necessary condition for a valid assignment of a policy is that it must be contemporaneous with the assignment of the subject-matter of the insurance. Obviously a non-life policy cannot be assigned in the absence of the assignment of its subject-matter otherwise the assignee would have no insurable interest. The requirement of strict contemporaneity is well-established in marine insurance[44] and there is no reason to doubt that it would apply equally to non-marine policies.

---

[43] It was also held that the clause in the policy extending the cover to a third party driving with the insured's consent was not applicable as the van was the purchaser's property and he was driving it therefore not with the insured's consent, but by virtue of his ownership.

[44] *North England Oil Cake Co. v. Archangel Marine Insurance Co.* (1875) L.R. 10 Q.B. 249.

CHAPTER 10

INTERMEDIARIES

The law concerning insurance intermediaries is of special importance since in effect all insurance business is conducted through the medium of agents of one sort or another. Most insurers are and have to be companies or, in exceptional cases, other corporate bodies or associations[1] and such bodies can of necessity act only through agents, ranging from directors and senior management down to junior employees. The only natural person who can be an insurer is a Lloyd's underwriter and by custom, enshrined in statute,[2] he can act only through the agency of a Lloyd's broker. Quite apart from the sorts of intermediary already mentioned, much insurance business is transacted through insurance brokers and other "independent" agencies.

This wide variety of types of agent raises important questions concerning their suitability and qualifications and has led to a number of different mechanisms for their regulation. These are briefly considered at the end of this chapter.[3] It may be helpful though for purposes of identification to attempt a rough classification of the different sorts of agent employed in insurance business.

The following is suggested[4]:

(i) Lloyd's Brokers; those brokers recognised by Lloyd's as the people through whom only can a Lloyd's policy be effected. An insured may act through another intermediary in approaching a Lloyd's broker.

(ii) All other Insurance Brokers; those brokers other than Lloyd's brokers who are registered under the Insurance Brokers (Registration Act) 1977,[5] and hence genuinely independent of any particular insurer or insurers.

---

[1] See p. 11, above.
[2] Lloyd's Act 1982, s.8(3).
[3] See pp. 189–193, below.
[4] See also O'Neill, "Insurance brokers and their commission" [1978] J.B.L. 339.
[5] See pp. 191–192, below.

(iii) Other "independent" agents, namely those agents not tied to particular insurers, but not registered under the 1977 Act, and hence not entitled to call themselves "insurance brokers." There is a measure of self regulation of such agents.[6]

(iv) Agents tied to particular insurers, who might be their employees or full-time agents such as the canvassing agent. In law the latter may or may not be technically "employees."

(v) Occasional "brokers," meaning people such as motor dealers, solicitors, building societies and estate agents, whose principal job is clearly not insurance, but who may sell insurance part-time or as an incidental part of their major work, often having pre-existing links with particular insurers.

Agent of Insurer or Insured

The first question to which we must turn is that of determining whose agent in law a particular intermediary is. This is not something about which it is easy to be dogmatic. As a general rule, only the agent under the direct employment or control of the insurer is the agent of the insurer, and even he may not at all times when dealing with an insured be regarded as the insurer's agent.[7] For most purposes, all other agents are in law the agents of the insured, and this is even so in respect of Lloyd's brokers.[8] However, there have been some cases where brokers have, for particular purposes, been regarded as agents of the insurer.[9] The position of the broker[10] and these cases merit further examination.

Position of the broker

The question of whose agent a broker is is of particular importance when the broker has notice of certain matters pertaining to the insurance

---

[6] See p. 189, below.

[7] See the line of authority of which *Newsholme Bros v. Road Transport & General Insurance Co.* [1929] 2 K.B. 356 is the leading case, discussed fully in Chap. 7 at pp. 145–150.

[8] *Rozanes v. Bowen* (1928) 32 Ll. L. Rep. 98; *Anglo-African Merchants v. Bayley* [1970] 1 Q.B. 311; *North & South Trust v. Berkeley* [1971] 1 W.L.R. 470; *McNealy v. Pennine Insurance Co. Ltd* [1978] 2 Lloyd's Rep. 18; *Roberts v. Plaisted* [1989] 2 Lloyd's Rep. 341.

[9] *Stockton v. Mason* [1978] 2 Lloyd's Rep. 430; *Woolcott v. Excess Insurance Co.* [1978] 1 Lloyd's Rep. 633 (original trial), [1979] 1 Lloyd's Rep. 231 (Court of Appeal), [1979] 2 Lloyd's Rep. 210 (retrial).

[10] For these purposes broker includes any independent intermediary.

contract, or purports to act on behalf of the insurer. As the broker is, as we have seen, the agent of the insured, the insurer should logically not be deemed to know or be bound by his actions. It is quite clear that a Lloyd's broker is always the agent of the insured,[11] although there is clearly some judicial unease about this.[12] A broker instructed to find insurance who goes first to reinsurers is the agent of the hitherto unidentified insurers/reinsured, not the agent of the insured.[13]

There are two relatively recent decisions which, however, have assumed that people who appear to have been independent, non-Lloyd's brokers were agents of the insurer. In *Stockton v. Mason*,[14] M's father, the insured, through his wife, instructed his brokers to transfer his existing motor policy from a Ford Anglia to an M.G. Midget. An employee of the brokers said that this would be all right for a temporary period, which the father naturally assumed meant that the previous policy, which covered the driving of the car by any authorised driver, was thereby transferred to the new car. Subsequently, the brokers wrote saying that cover on the M.G. was restricted to the insured only. M was driving the M.G. when he negligently injured the plaintiff. The issue was whether, under the Road Traffic Act 1972,[15] the plaintiff was entitled to sue M's father's insurers[16] and thus it depended on whether the latter were bound by the oral statement of the broker's employee purporting to authorise the M.G. to be substituted entirely for the Anglia. The Court of Appeal, consisting of three Lords of Appeal, held that the insurers were bound. "A broker in non-marine insurance has implied authority to issue on behalf of the insurer, or enter into as agent for the insurer, contracts of interim insurance . . . it seems to me to be quite unarguable that in saying 'Yes,

---

[11] *Roberts v. Plaisted* [1989] 2 Lloyd's Rep. 341.

[12] *ibid.* at 345, where it was commented by Purchas L.J. that to the person unacquainted with the insurance industry, it may seem a remarkable state of the law that someone who describes himself as a Lloyd's broker who is remunerated by the insurance industry and who presents proposal forms and suggested policies on their behalf should not be the recipient of full disclosure. The Court of Appeal, echoing the comments of Hodgson J. at first instance, thought that the matter should be referred to the Law Commission.

[13] *S.A.I.L. v. Farex Gie* [1995] L.R.L.R. 116; as a result knowledge obtained by the broker was not imputed to the insured. As to the imputation of knowledge, see pp. 180–182, below.

[14] [1978] 2 Lloyd's Rep. 430.

[15] s.149, now replaced by the Road Traffic Act 1988; see Chap. 19, at pp. 375–378.

[16] The brokers were also sued in the alternative.

that will be all right. We will see to that, Mrs. Mason,' the brokers were acting as agents for the insurance company and not merely acknowledging an order or request by Mrs. Mason to negotiate a contract with the insurance company on his behalf."[17]

In *Woolcott v. Excess Insurance Co. Ltd*,[18] a case which involved much dispute as to the facts, being referred back by the Court of Appeal to the trial judge on this issue, it was clearly assumed beyond argument by the Court of Appeal that the knowledge of a material fact by the broker in question was imputed to the insurers, and that the latter's defence of non-disclosure of that fact failed, even if the insured did not know that the insurer had the knowledge or was deemed to know.[19]

These two decisions were clearly to be welcomed as according with the reality of the situation, particularly as that is how it is no doubt perceived by insureds. Where appropriate, the extent of the broker's authority to bind the insurer will depend upon considerations which we shall discuss further, later. It does not seem, however, that the principles of these cases are generally applicable. In both of them there was a close relationship between the brokers and the insurers, the former being actually authorised to conclude at least interim contracts of insurance. More recently, in *Winter v. Irish Life Assurance plc*,[20] it was held that the knowledge of the broker, that both lives insured had cystic fibrosis, was not imputed to the insurers. As a general rule, therefore, it seems safe to say that where an insured negotiates through a broker with an insurer with whom the broker does not have a close relationship, or negotiates through one of the other sorts of agent other than a linked agent of the insurer, unless that broker or agent has actual authority from the insurer, the insured is not entitled to rely on principles of apparent authority.[21]

Broker's duties to the insured

In the cases where the broker is regarded as agent of the insurer, the question arises as to whether he remains the agent of the insured in any

[17] [1978] 2 Lloyd's Rep. 430 at 431–432, per Lord Diplock.
[18] See n.9, above.
[19] [1979] 1 Lloyd's Rep. 231 at 241–242 (per Megaw L.J.); see also [1979] 2 Lloyd's Rep. 210 at 211 (per Cantley J.)
[20] [1995] 2 Lloyd's Rep. 274.
[21] Unless, perhaps, the insurer has previously regarded itself as bound by representations of the broker or agent. For a brief description of apparent or ostensible authority, see below at pp. 178–180.

circumstances, so that, for example, he owes fiduciary duties and duties of care and skill to the insured? The answer must be in the affirmative in respect of the latter,[22] but there appears to be a potential conflict otherwise. The decisions in *Anglo-African Merchants* v. *Bayley*[23] and *North and South Trust v. Berkeley*[24] established, at least so far as Lloyd's brokers are concerned, that they cannot act for the insurer in investigating a claim without being potentially in breach of duty to their principal, the insured. The issue arose in both cases in relation to documents which, following a claim on the policies, the brokers had prepared for the insurers, which they refused to hand over to the insureds. This was regarded as a clear breach of duty on the ground that their true principals were the insureds and that they could not therefore act in accordance with the insurers' instructions without the consent of the insureds. This must continue to be the law, so that it appears that a broker, other than a Lloyd's broker,[25] may indeed be the agent of both insured and insurer. He may on appropriate facts be authorised to act for the latter in terms of granting cover or receiving knowledge of material facts, but otherwise he cannot act for the insurer in the context of investigating a claim without full disclosure of his position to the insured and the latter's consent.

Relevant Agency Principles

It is not possible, in the space available, to deal by any means comprehensively with all the principles of agency law which may be applicable to the insurance transaction.[26] We must therefore concentrate on those which appear to be of particular relevance, namely, the question of when a principal is bound by his agent's acts in favour of a third party; the question of when an agent's knowledge is imputed to his principal; and the relationship between principal and agent, especially when the principal is the insured.

Principal and third party

A principal is bound by any of the acts of his agent within the latter's actual, apparent (or ostensible) or usual authority and by an unauthorised

[22] See the cases which are discussed at pp. 182–188.
[23] [1970] 1 Q.B. 311.
[24] [1971] 1 W.L.R. 470.
[25] Who is clearly always the agent of the insured: *Roberts v. Plaisted*, above.
[26] See, generally, *Bowstead on Agency* (15th ed.) and Markesinis and Munday, *An Outline of the Law of Agency* (3rd ed.). There is some discussion of other agency principles in Chap. 3 at pp. 65–69, above.

act which he ratifies. The problems surrounding the concept of usual authority[27] do not appear to have been considered or indeed to be likely to arise in the insurance context, and need not detain us here.

Actual authority

Actual authority may be expressed or implied. What an agent is expressly authorised to do raises no problems. Implied actual authority arises where in the circumstances it must be the position that the agent had actual authority, but it was never conferred on him in so many words. If an insurer gives his agent blank cover-notes, he impliedly authorises him to effect binding temporary insurance contracts.[28] Similarly, the continuing adoption by the insurer of temporary oral contracts entered into by its agent will confer implied authority on that agent.[29] An example of the principle where the insured was principal is *Zurich General Accident and Liability Insurance Co. Ltd v. Rowberry*,[30] where the brokers were instructed to effect a policy in respect of the insured's forthcoming journey to France. The brokers mistakenly inserted in the proposal form that the insured's destination was Paris, whereas, in fact, he was going to Nice. The insured attempted to get out of the policy issued on the grounds of this mistake, but it was held that he was bound by the broker's actions, having given them authority to negotiate the proposal with no specific instructions as to his destination.

Ostensible authority

Ostensible or apparent authority arises where the principal, by words or by conduct, holds out his agent as having a particular authority.[31] It is really relevant only when the agent is exceeding his actual authority. The essence of ostensible authority is the representation made by the principal to the third party; it matters not what the agent says, nor whether he is acting fraudulently.[32] Thus, ostensible authority depends upon an estoppel,

---

[27] See, *e.g.* Markesinis and Munday, *An Outline of the Law of Agency, op. cit.*, pp. 24–29.

[28] *Mackie v. European Assurance Society* (1869) 21 L.T. 102; *Stockton v. Mason*, discussed above.

[29] *Murfitt v. Royal Insurance Co.* (1922) 38 T.L.R. 334.

[30] [1954] 2 Lloyd's Rep. 55.

[31] See generally, *e.g. Freeman & Lockyer v. Buckhurst Park Properties* [1964] 2 Q.B. 480.

[32] *Lloyd v. Grace, Smith & Co.* [1912] A.C. 716.

usually the representation being the conduct of the principal rather than anything expressly said.[33] Appointing an agent to a particular position confers on him ostensible authority to bind his principal in respect of the usual acts which someone in that position would have authority to do, and it is irrelevant, unless the third party is aware of this, in which case there can be no reliance on the representation,[34] that the agent is actually not authorised to do some of the usual acts.

Someone who holds the position of inspector in an insurance company will probably be regarded as having ostensible authority to vary the terms of a proposal form.[35] The payment of premiums to an agent will bind the insurer even if he is not authorised to accept them, if, nonetheless, he is held out as having authority to receive them.[36] The receiving of notice of loss by an agent, if he is the person with whom the insured has always dealt, should bind the insurer, unless there is an express indication to the contrary; the latter would negate any representation allegedly made by the insurer.[37] An agent held out as having authority to make alterations in a policy or to waive a breach of condition will bind the insurer.[38] Similarly, providing an agent with cover-notes gives that agent ostensible authority to conclude such temporary contracts, even if the insurer has expressly forbidden this so that implied actual authority is not available. On the other hand, an agent will never, unless actually authorised, have authority to bind the insurer by the issue of a formal policy,[39] nor will he have authority to fill in a proposal form on behalf of the insured at least if he is a mere canvassing agent,[40] although this rather curious rule has been criticised earlier.[41] An agent of the insurer has no authority to bind his principal as to the meaning or construction of a policy, though this is not

[33] An insurance example is *Eagle Star Insurance Co. v. Spratt* [1971] 2 Lloyd's Rep. 116.

[34] *Wilkinson v. General Accident Fire & Life Assurance Corp. Ltd* [1967] 2 Lloyd's Rep. 182.

[35] *Stone v. Reliance Mutual Insurance Society Ltd* [1972] 1 Lloyd's Rep. 469; see pp. 149–150, above.

[36] *Kelly v. London and Staffordshire Fire Insurance Co.* (1883) Cab. & E. 47.

[37] *Brook v. Trafalgar Insurance Co.* (1946) 79 Ll.L. Rep. 365.

[38] *Wing v. Harvey* (1854) 5 De G.M. & G. 265, see p. 181 below.

[39] *Stockton v. Mason* [1978] 2 Lloyd's Rep. 430; *British Bank of the Middle East v. Sun Life Assurance Co. of Canada (U.K.) Ltd* [1983] 2 Lloyd's Rep. 9. In practice only the directors or someone at least as senior as a branch manager might be actually authorised.

[40] *Newsholme Bros v. Road Transport & General Insurance Co.* [1929] 2 K.B. 356.

[41] See Chap. 7 at pp. 147–148.

so much a result of a lack of authority as of the rule that such a representation would be a representation of law, and in general these are not binding.[42]

Ratification

Even an unauthorised act not binding a principal by virtue of the principles of ostensible authority may, however, be ratified by the principal, provided that the agent was purporting to act as an agent[43] and that the principal was in existence and identifiable at the time of the agent's act. Ratification dates back to the time of the original act of the agent,[44] but it is unclear in non-marine insurance whether it is possible to ratify after a loss has taken place. In *Grover & Grover v. Mathews*,[45] where a broker effected without authority a renewal of the insured's policy, and the insured suffered a loss before he knew about the broker's actions, it was held that the insurer was not liable even though the insured ratified what the broker had done. It is, however, arguable that this case was wrongly decided and in *National Oilwell (U.K.) Ltd v. Davy Offshore Ltd*,[46] the judge would have refused to follow it.[47]

Imputing the agent's knowledge

Of particular importance in the context of insurance are the rules whereby, in certain cases, the knowledge of an agent is imputed to his principal so that the latter is deemed to know what the agent knows. These will be examined here only in the context of the agent being the agent of the insurer, that is where an insured is seeking to rely upon them, although the same principles will apply when the agent is the agent of the insured.

Most commonly, the issue will relate to material facts of which the insurer alleges non-disclosure by the insured, but which the latter claims

---

[42] *Re Hooley Rubber & Chemical Manufacturing Co.* [1920] 1 K.B. 257; compare, *e.g. Harr v. Allstate Insurance Co.* 54 N.J. 287 (1969).

[43] An undisclosed principal can sue and be bound only if the agent had actual authority: see generally, *Bowstead*, pp. 51–84. As to the possible use of an undisclosed agent to conclude an insurance contract, see pp. 66–68, above.

[44] *Bolton Partners v. Lambert* (1888) 41 Ch.D. 295.

[45] [1910] 2 K.B. 401.

[46] [1993] 2 Lloyd's Rep. 213.

[47] See pp. 68–69, above.

are deemed to be known by the insurer by virtue of its agent's knowledge. *Woolcott v. Excess Insurance Co.*,[48] which was described earlier,[49] is an example, and the matter was considered fully in the context of non-disclosure.[50] In general the agent's knowledge will be imputed to the insurer, because he will have been held out as having authority to receive it, but the position may well be different if an incorrect answer is given on a proposal form, even though the agent knows the truth,[51] and it is, it seems, essential that the information is received by a person who is able to appreciate its significance. In *Mahli v. Abbey Life Assurance Co.*,[52] the insurers had previously been told of material facts (alcoholism and malaria of the life insured) because they had declined an earlier proposal on this basis. However, the person responsible for considering the later application did not know of these facts. It was held by a majority of the Court of Appeal that the insurers had not waived their right to avoid the later policy.[53]

Another illustration would be where the agent knows of something which constitutes a breach of warranty or condition by the insured. His knowledge of the breach may be imputed to the insurer who may therefore, by subsequently accepting premiums, be deemed to have waived the breach. In *Wing v. Harvey*,[54] a life policy provided that it would become void if the assured travelled beyond the limits of Europe without the insurer's consent. An assignee of the policy subsequently informed an agent of the insurer that the life assured had taken up residence in Canada. For some time after this, before the life assured died, premiums were received by the insurer. It was held that the insurer had waived the breach of warranty; they were deemed to know what their agent knew and having accepted premiums subsequently, could not rely upon the breach.

---

[48] [1979] 1 Lloyd's Rep. 231.

[49] See p. 176.

[50] See pp. 105–106, above.

[51] *Newsholme Bros. v. Road Transport & General Insurance Co.*, above; Chap. 7 at pp. 145–150.

[52] [1994] C.L.C. 615.

[53] McCowan L.J., dissenting, thought that the situation was indistinguishable from the earlier Court of Appeal decision in *Evans v. Employers Mutual Insurance Association Ltd* [1936] K.B. 505 on the ground that there the only requirement for imputation of knowledge was that the agent in question was authorised to receive it. With respect, this seems more persuasive. See also the earlier case of *Stone v. Reliance Mutual Insurance Association* [1972] 1 Lloyd's Rep. 469, discussed earlier at p. 149, which seems to support the broader ground for imputation of knowledge.

[54] (1854) 5 De G.M. & G. 265.

What knowledge will be imputed depends upon the status of the agent receiving it, in other words, upon his actual or ostensible authority. In *Wing v. Harvey*, the agent was the local representative of the insurer at a branch office. A mere canvassing or soliciting agent would probably not be regarded as having such a wide authority, which is after all tantamount to varying the terms of the policy, but such an agent probably has authority to receive disclosures of material facts.[55] However, the knowledge of an agent is never imputed when the agent is acting in fraud of his principal.[56]

Relationship between principal and agent

If, for some reason, a principal cannot enforce a contract against a third party or he is liable to a third party because of the unauthorised acts of his agent, he may well have a remedy against the agent. Equally the relationship of principal and agent is a fiduciary one and duties arise as a result. For example, the insurer bound by a contract which he could have avoided for non-disclosure had his agent not known the non-disclosed facts and his knowledge been imputed to the insurer, can sue the agent for damages, being the amount of money which he has had to pay the insured.[57] Similarly, if an agent acts beyond his actual authority, but the insurer is liable by virtue of the principles of ostensible authority, the insurer will have a damages remedy against the agent.

It is more likely in practice, however, that it is the insured seeking a remedy against his agent, commonly, but not necessarily, his broker. Indeed brokers must now themselves be insured against this potential liability.[58] In this context, it is usual and convenient to split up the heads of liability into two; that arising by virtue of the fiduciary relationship between the insured and his agent, and the duties of care and skill required of an agent.

---

[55] *Ayrey v. British Legal & United Provident Assurance* [1918] 1 K.B. 136; *Blackley v. National Mutual Life Assurance of Australasia* [1972] N.Z.L.R. 1938; see Chap. 6 at p. 105.

[56] See a series of cases arising out of various problems at Lloyd's of London where it was held that the insureds were not deemed to know of their agents' fraud, applying the general principle of *Re Hampshire Land Co.* [1896] 2 Ch. 743: *P.C.W. Syndicates v. P.C.W. Reinsurers* [1996] 1 Lloyd's Rep. 241, *Group Josie Re v. Walbrook Insurance Co. Ltd* [1996] 1 Lloyd's Rep. 345, *Deutsche Ruckversicherung A.G. v. Walbrook Insurance Co. Ltd* [1996] 1 All E.R. 791.

[57] *Woolcott v. Excess Insurance Co.* [1979] 1 Lloyd's Rep. 231.

[58] See p. 192, below.

Fiduciary duties

A fiduciary relationship carries with it strict duties, in particular the overriding one that the fiduciary, the agent, must not put himself into a position where his own interests do or may conflict with his duties to his principal.[59] This means, *inter alia*, that he must not act for another in a matter relating to his principal without full disclosure to and the consent of his principal. It used to be standard practice for Lloyd's brokers to act for the underwriter in certain matters, despite the fact that, as was mentioned earlier, they are in law agents of the insured. This practice was condemned in *Anglo-African Merchants v. Bayley*[60] as clearly constituting a breach of fiduciary duty, unless the insured consented. Shortly afterwards the point arose again in *North and South Trust v. Berkeley*,[61] where a claim by the insured was investigated by assessors instructed by the brokers. Their report was handed to the brokers who showed it to the underwriters, but refused to let the insured have sight of it or know what it contained. They were thereupon sued by the insured who relied upon the earlier decision as establishing that the brokers had acted in breach of duty. Donaldson J. again condemned the practice of brokers acting for both parties and held that what had been done was a breach of duty, but, apart from admitting the possibility of a claim for damages by the insured, which was not, in fact, sought,[62] he refused to give the insured the remedy they did seek, namely, an order for delivery of the documents. This is rather curious,[63] but as it was expressly stated by the learned judge that a remedy would be available in future cases. The unsatisfactory nature of this decision need not detain us further.

Duties of care and skill

In respect of the duties of care and skill, an agent such as a broker owes a duty to his client, the insured, to take reasonable care and skill.[64] A comparatively high number of cases reported in recent years[65] reveals what

---

[59] *Boardman v. Phipps* [1967] 2 A.C. 46.

[60] [1970] 1 Q.B. 311.

[61] [1971] 1 W.L.R. 470.

[62] *Quaere* how valuable such a remedy might be in practice.

[63] See the trenchant criticism by Kay and Yates (1972) 35 M.L.R. 78.

[64] It may also be owed to a third party who the broker knows is to become an assignee of the policy: *Punjab National Bank v. De Boinville* [1992] 1 Lloyd's Rep. 7.

[65] Too many for them all to be considered in these pages. An excellent survey is contained in Jackson & Powell, *Professional Negligence* (2nd ed.), Chap. 7.

an important head of liability this potentially is. It should be noted that the insured's cause of action is in damages for breach of duty in contract or tort.[66] If what the insured is claiming is in effect the damages he has to pay to an injured third party, for example, this relates only to the measure of the broker's liability. The claim is not in respect of damages for personal injury, so that the relevant limitation period is six years, not three years.[67]

In advising his client with whom to insure, the broker must take due care. In *Osman v. J. Ralph Moss*,[68] the defendant brokers recommended to the plaintiff that he effect a motor policy with an insurer already well-known in insurance circles to be in a serious financial situation. The insurer was subsequently wound up, leaving the plaintiff uninsured. As a result, the plaintiff was convicted of driving without insurance and involved in an accident for which he was liable, with no insurer to foot the bill. The plaintiff was of Turkish origin and had difficulty in reading and understanding English. The only warning the defendants gave him was a letter asking him simply to insure elsewhere. It was held that the defendants were liable in damages for the amount he was fined and the damages he had to pay the third party. What is not completely clear is how much turned on the fact that the plaintiff was not really literate in English, so that the letter which the defendants sent could not possibly have been enough to satisfy the duty they owed him. The decision does not actually hold that a broker must always expressly warn his client of the impending insolvency of his insurer, if he is aware or ought to be aware of this, and there are passages in the judgments[69] referring to the particular position of the plaintiff. It is suggested that brokers ought to be under a duty at all times to all classes of insured to advise and warn about particular insurers, not just as to their financial stability but also as to the suitability of particular policies and their general record in treating their insureds, for example, as to their generosity in paying claims.[70] It seems clear that a

---

[66] *Henderson v. Merrett Syndicates Ltd* [1994] 3 All E.R. 506. See also *Osman v. J. Ralph Moss Ltd* [1970] 1 Lloyd's Rep. 313. It would require significant fault on the part of the insured before a negligent broker could successfully plead the defence of contributory negligence: *Mint Security Ltd v. Blair* [1982] 1 Lloyd's Rep. 188.

[67] *Ackbar v. Green* [1975] Q.B. 582.

[68] [1970] 1 Lloyd's Rep. 313. See also *Bates v. Robert Barrow Ltd* [1995] C.L.C. 207, where a broker was held liable for placing insurance with an unauthorised insurer.

[69] Sachs L.J. at 315; Phillimore L.J. at 319.

[70] There were many successful unreported claims on this basis in 1984 and 1985 against brokers who sold largely worthless life insurance polices issued by Signal Life, a Gibraltar-based concern not authorised to act in the U.K.

broker who fails to warn the insured of any special terms incorporated on renewal is negligent.[71] There is clearly a duty to obtain effective cover or to warn the insured about the insurer's particular terms.[72]

Another instance of negligent advice arose in *Cherry Ltd v. Allied Insurances Brokers Ltd.*[73] Here the defendants had been the plaintiff's brokers for some 50 years, but the plaintiffs became dissatisfied and proposed to put their business elsewhere. As a result, they wished to cancel all their policies held through the defendants well before their renewal date, and they instructed the defendants to seek to do so. The defendants cancelled most of the policies but advised the plaintiffs that the particular insurer concerned would not accept cancellation of the plaintiff's consequential loss policy. The plaintiffs having effected a new policy of this sort thereupon cancelled it to avoid being doubly insured. Subsequently, however, that first insurer did agree to a cancellation of the original policy, but the defendants failed to advise the plaintiffs of this. The latter then suffered a loss for which, because both policies had been cancelled, they were uninsured. It was held that the defendants were negligent in failing to advise the plaintiffs of the first insurer's cancellation, and were liable in damages for the amount which the plaintiffs would have recovered from their insurer had they been insured.

Duty regarding disclosure of material facts

Several cases have been concerned with the broker's position in respect of the duty of the insured to disclose material facts and not to make misrepresentations. This is obviously a crucial area as the insured who is dealing with a broker will not, in practice, have any direct communication with his insurer, and in general any knowledge the broker has will not be imputed to the insurer.[74] Thus the exact nature of the broker's duty with regard to advising his client about such matters is vital. If the broker fails to ask the insured questions about facts which he, the broker, knows are material, he will be liable in damages to the insured if the insurer subsequently avoids liability. In *McNealy v. Pennine Insurance Co.*,[75] the

---

[71] *Mint Security Ltd v. Blair* [1982] 1 Lloyd's Rep. 188.
[72] See *e.g. Harvest Trading Co. Ltd v. Davis Insurance Services* [1991] 2 Lloyd's Rep. 638.
[73] [1978] 1 Lloyd's Rep. 274.
[74] See p. 176, above.
[75] [1978] 2 Lloyd's Rep. 18.

plaintiff effected motor insurance through brokers. He was a part-time musician, a fact which, it was held, was material to the risk. The insurance company with which the brokers effected the insurance refused to cover musicians, among other groups, and was not told that the plaintiff was one. It was held that the brokers were liable in damages in respect of the plaintiff's liability to a third party, the insurer having avoided their policy. The brokers with their knowledge that the insurer refused to cover certain risks were under a duty to the insured to ask him whether or not he was affected by this.

It would seem to follow that the same result would apply if the broker actually knows of material facts which he fails to disclose to the insurer.[76] However, if the broker is unaware of material facts, and there are no special circumstances as in *McNealy* requiring him to make express enquiry of the insured, it appears unlikely that the court would hold that the broker was under a duty to warn the insured of his duty of disclosure. In *Warren v. Sutton*,[77] the plaintiff had an existing motor policy. He was going on holiday to France with a friend with whom he wished to share the driving. So he arranged for the friend to be covered under his policy. However, the latter had an appalling driving record with several convictions, none of which was disclosed to the insurer, so that the latter was able to avoid the policy and not pay in respect of an accident that occurred in France.[78] The plaintiff had arranged the policy and the extension through the defendant brokers whom he sued for damages. The facts of the case were somewhat complex and there was a crucial conflict of evidence, but it was found that the broker actually said to the insurer that there were "no accidents, convictions or disabilities" when the extension was being arranged. On this basis, the majority of the Court of Appeal held the broker liable. He had made a false representation to the insurance company in breach of his duty to the plaintiff. Lord Denning M.R. dissented strongly on the ground that the fault all lay with the plaintiff

---

[76] *Woolcott v. Excess Insurance Co.* [1979] 1 Lloyd's Rep. 231; *Ogden v. Reliance Fire Sprinkler Co.* [1975] 1 Lloyd's Rep. 52. Exceptionally, as we have seen (p. 176), the broker's knowledge may be imputed to the insurer; in this situation the insured will, of course, not need a remedy against the broker.

[77] [1976] 2 Lloyd's Rep. 276.

[78] The friend was driving at the time, though this was legally irrelevant. The insurer was liable in respect of the damages he had to pay for personal injuries, because of restrictions similar to those in the Road Traffic Act 1988 (see Chapter 19), but escaped liability in respect of third party property damage. The latter is now prohibited under the Road Traffic Act.

who never told the broker or insurer about his friend's record. However, the majority were clearly influenced by the trial judge's much more favourable assessment of the plaintiff as a witness as opposed to the attitude of the defendant broker. The broker's representation to the insurer was clearly false. He was under a duty to obtain cover for the friend and to make such enquiries as were necessary. Thus, not having made such enquiries, he was solely responsible for the representation he made, and it was this representation which was the cause of the insurer's repudiation. If, however, the broker had not made the representation, and the reason for the insurer's repudiation had simply been non-disclosure by the insured of which the broker was unaware, it appears that the result would have been the other way.[79] This supports the view that the court would not hold a broker under a duty to warn the insured of his duty of disclosure in the abstract.

Further support can perhaps be found in another Court of Appeal decision on a related point.[80] In *O'Connor v. Kirby*,[81] the plaintiff insured his car through the defendant broker. For some reason,[82] the latter incorrectly answered a question on the proposal form relating to the garaging of the car and the insurer subsequently avoided the policy for breach of warranty. The plaintiff sued the broker for failing to complete the form properly. It was held that he was not liable, as the plaintiff had signed the form containing the mistake and was solely responsible because it was his duty to see that the information therein was correct.[83] It is suggested that this reasoning is suspect in the light of the consideration that the insured dealing with a broker does place great reliance, and naturally so, on the latter. Far more satisfactory, it is submitted, is the reasoning of Megaw L.J. to the effect that a broker who completes a proposal form does owe a duty to the insured to take reasonable care that its contents are correct, but that in the circumstances the broker had fulfilled that duty since the mistake was at most due only to a slip or misunderstanding and the broker had given the form to the insured to check.[84] That this is the better ratio seems

---

[79] See Browne L.J. at 281.

[80] This was relied upon by Lord Denning M.R. in his dissenting judgment in *Warren v. Sutton*; it was not cited by the other members of the Court of Appeal in that case.

[81] [1972] 1 Q.B. 90.

[82] There was some evidence of collusion between the parties in order to get cheaper cover; this can hardly have disposed the court to look favourably on the plaintiff's claim.

[83] Following the *Newsholme* line of cases; see Chap. 7 at pp. 145–150.

[84] Compare *Reid v. Traders' General Insurance Co.* (1963) 41 D.L.R. (2d) 148.

to be supported by the more recent decision in *Dunbar v. A. & B. Painters Ltd.*[85] Here brokers who inserted incorrect answers on a proposal form were held liable in damages since it was shown that the answers required fell especially within the broker's knowledge. However, it seems likely that this last factor is crucial. If the broker is not in possession of the relevant information, primary responsibility in respect of both non-disclosure of material facts and the answering of questions seems to fall on the insured rather than the broker.

Measure of damages

If a broker is liable in damages to the insured, the measure of damages will, as has been seen, usually be that sum which the insured would have recovered from the insurer had the latter been liable. If the breach of duty by the broker is a failure to effect insurance at all, the question has arisen whether it is open to him to say that even if he had obtained the cover, the insurer would still not have been liable, and hence he should not be liable, because of some breach by the insured. The point arose neatly in *Fraser v. Furman*,[86] where the broker had failed in his duty to effect employer's liability cover for the plaintiff. The broker argued, however, that the insurer would not have been liable for the loss that subsequently occurred, because the plaintiff would have been in breach of a condition in the policy to take reasonable precautions to avoid loss. The Court of Appeal held that the broker was liable for the full amount of loss suffered by the plaintiff. Even if the defence would have been available to the insurer, which was doubted,[87] the fact was that in the circumstances the insurer in question would not have repudiated liability. Therefore, the question depends on the likely attitude of the insurer rather than the strict point as to whether the insurer would have been legally liable.[88]

---

[85] [1986] 2 Lloyd's Rep. 38, affirming [1985] 2 Lloyd's Rep. 616. *O'Connor v. Kirby* was not cited in this case.

[86] [1976] 1 W.L.R. 898. See also *Everett v. Hogg Robinson* [1973] 2 Lloyd's Rep. 217 and *Dunbar v. A.B. Painters Ltd* [1986] 2 Lloyd's Rep. 38.

[87] See further on this point, Chap. 18, at p. 353.

[88] But the position may be different if the insurance which the broker should have effected would have been void: *Thomas Cheshire & Co. v. Vaughan Bros. & Co.* [1920] 3 K.B. 240, and, where the insured is in fact virtually uninsurable, the damages payable by the broker are likely to be reduced: *O. & R. Jewellers v. Terry*, unreported, June 1993.

The Regulation of Intermediaries[89]

In an important study in 1970, the Consumer Council drew attention to the plethora of advice-giving intermediaries in the insurance industry and the consequently confusing picture facing the consumer. Anyone was entitled to set up in the business of selling insurance and call himself an insurance broker or give himself a similar fancy title, but this did not by any means necessarily imply competence or completely independent and impartial guidance. Also well documented is the potential conflict between the intermediary's duty to get the best deal for his client and his own interests in getting the best deal for himself. For example, where insurance is sold on a commission basis, the intermediary may well try to persuade the client to accept the policy that pays him the best rate of commission, rather than that which is best suited to the client's needs. There was an overwhelming case for the regulation of insurance intermediaries[90] and now the position has been remedied to some extent at least. Whether enough has yet been done will be considered later. The regulatory provisions in existence at present can be examined under two heads; first those applying generally to all intermediaries, and secondly the requirements surrounding the registration and regulation of insurance brokers. What are described here are the relevant statutory provisions concerning general insurance. Space precludes detailed examination of the provisions applying to the selling of most forms of life insurance[91] or of the self-regulatory control on non-broker intermediaries selling general insurance.[92]

---

[89] For a comprehensive account, see Hodgin, *Insurance Intermediaries: Law and Regulation* (1992).

[90] See the British Insurance Brokers' Association Consultative Document (1976); the White Paper, *Insurance Intermediaries*, 1977, Cmnd. 6715; see generally, Morgan (1978) L.M.C.L.Q. 39.

[91] These are governed by the Conduct of Business Rules made by the Securities and Investment Board under the Financial Services Act 1986. As to the forms of life insurance covered by this Act, see p. 325, below.

[92] See *General Insurance Business - Code of Practice for all Intermediaries (Including Employees of Insurance Companies) other than Registered Insurance Brokers*, promulgated by the Association of British Insurers in 1989, revising earlier versions. For a brief description see Birds, "Self-regulation and insurance contracts," *New Foundations for Insurance Law*, 1987, pp. 8–11. See also Hodgin, (1992) 2 Insurance L. & P. 22. The Code was referred to in the judgment in *Harvest Trading Co. Ltd v. P.B. Davis Services* [1991] 2 Lloyd's Rep. 638 (see p. 185, above) as providing useful guidance as to the standard of care expected of an unregistered intermediary.

General regulation

The provisions applying generally seek to ensure that intermediaries who are not genuinely independent of a particular insurer reveal that fact. Regulations 38 to 40 of the Insurance Companies Regulations,[93] made under section 74 of the Insurance Companies Act 1982, require any intermediary who is connected with the insurance company with which he is suggesting that a proposer for insurance, ordinarily resident in the United Kingdom, contracts,[94] to disclose in writing details of his connection, and require information of a similar sort where the insurer is not authorised or permitted under the 1982 Act, *i.e.* where it is an overseas (non-E.C.) insurer.[95] Failure to comply with either of these requirements is a criminal offence. "Connection" for these purposes is defined quite widely in regulation 38, and comprises the cases where the intermediary or any partner, director, controller or manager of the intermediary is a partner, director, controller or manager of the insurer or of any controller thereof; the converse case where the insurer etc. is a partner etc. of the intermediary; the case where the intermediary or controller thereof has a significant interest[96] in the shares of the insurer or any controller thereof and vice versa; and the case where the intermediary, under any contract or arrangement whether legally enforceable or not, other than a contract of employment, with an insurer or associated company, undertakes not to perform any services relating to any sort of insurance business for any other insurance company. Under the last case, the employee of an insurer is excluded but not, for example, an agent under a contract for services who is tied to a particular insurer.

Where the suggestion from the intermediary to insure is written, the information must be sent or delivered at the same time. Where the suggestion is oral, the information must be disclosed orally there and then, and confirmed in writing, either immediately where the person is present, or as soon as reasonably practicable by post where the person is not

---

[93] S.I. 1994 No. 1516, replacing regulations first made in 1976.

[94] The wide wording of reg. 38(1) of the Regulations is [invite] "to make an offer or proposal or to take any other steps with a view to entering into a contract of insurance with an insurance company."

[95] The Regulations do not apply to reinsurance contracts nor to industrial assurance or marine, aviation or transport insurance. Furthermore, there are a number of exceptions in reg. 40, particularly relating to certain renewals.

[96] Basically five per cent, or more; the Regulations apply certain provisions of the Companies Act 1985 for this purpose.

present, in other words, where the matter was discussed by telephone. An easy way of satisfying these requirements, sanctioned in regulation 39(4), where the suggestion to insure is on notepaper, is to include the relevant details on the notepaper. In the case of a Lloyd's broker, a simple statement of that fact suffices.

Regulation of brokers

The Consumer Council study mentioned above recommended the licensing of brokers as a safeguard against the dangers already outlined. At the suggestion of the Department of Trade, this was taken up in 1976 by the then main association representing brokers, the British Insurance Brokers' Association. Their Consultative Document was approved by the Government,[97] and formed the basis of a Private Member's Bill which had Government backing and became the Insurance Brokers (Registration) Act 1977. Widely hailed as an important advance in protecting the interests of consumers of insurance, which it undoubtedly is, albeit by itself it may be incomplete, the Act effects with statutory backing a self-regulatory machinery not dissimilar to that which exists with respect to solicitors.[98] In other words, the profession has statutory power to regulate itself, but Government approval is required of the Code of Conduct issued under the Act, and there are Government nominees on the Insurance Brokers Registration Council, the body charged with supervising the regulating machinery.[99]

Briefly, the Act requires that all brokers be registered with the Council. Acting as an insurance broker without registration is by section 22 a criminal offence, punishable on conviction on indictment by an unlimited fine. Rather curiously, however, the use of any other title, for example "insurance consultant" or "insurance advisor," and acting under such a title by an unregistered "broker," is not prohibited. This is arguably an unnecessary loophole. The average insurance consumer is unlikely to be

---

[97] Insurance Intermediaries (1977) Cmnd. 6715.
[98] It also formed the model for the self-regulatory system, backed by statute, established under the Financial Services Act 1986.
[99] See the Schedule to the 1977 Act. Note that the 1977 Act was amended in certain respects by the Financial Services Act 1986, s.138, primarily to ensure compatibility between the 1977 Act and the system of self-regulation in the financial services sector, including most forms of life insurance, established by the 1986 Act. The rules under the latter Act regulate the selling of most forms of life insurance by other than registered brokers or full-time employees of insurers.

aware of the provisions and effect of the 1977 Act, and may be equally as impressed by someone describing himself as "insurance consultant" as by the title "insurance broker."

The Council is under a duty to establish and maintain a register of insurance brokers.[1] To be registered, an applicant basically has to possess a recognised qualification[1] and have three years' experience in the profession, and the Council must be satisfied as to his character and suitability and compliance with solvency and independence from insurers. An unqualified applicant may apply for registration if he has five years' experience.[3] There is provision for appeal against a refusal to register.[4]

Under section 10, the Council has drawn up a Code of Conduct[5] and under sections 11 and 12, has made rules as to the conduct of insurance brokers' businesses.[6] Essentially, these rules require brokers[7] to have a minimum working capital of at least £1,000 and a margin of solvency of at least the same figure, to maintain independence from particular insurers, regarding which a questionnaire has to be completed every year, to keep insurance money in a separate bank account, to submit annual accounts to the Council, and to take out specified professional indemnity insurance. In addition, there is a scheme under section 12(2) of the Act whereby people who suffer loss from the bankruptcy, negligence or fraud of a registered broker are entitled to compensation.

Sections 13 to 20 of the Act provide for disciplinary proceedings,[8] the Council being empowered, *inter alia,* to investigate complaints from the public and, if necessary, to remove the name of a broker from the register.[9]

Future regulation

We have already noted the gap in the 1977 Act, and it is clear in general that it provides for only a partial regulation of insurance

---

[1] s.2.

[2] s.3, as amended by S.I. 1995 No. 2906.

[3] That the Council can insist on full-time experience during the five years was confirmed in *Pickles v. Insurance Brokers Registration Council* [1984] 1 All E.R. 1073.

[4] s. 4. See further as to the qualifications, etc., S.I. 1978 No. 1395, S.I. 1979 No. 490 and S.I. 1985 No. 1804.

[5] S.I. 1994 No. 2569, replacing S.I. 1978 No. 1394.

[6] S.I. 1979 No. 489, as amended by S.I. 1981 No. 1680, and S.I. 1987 No. 1496.

[7] Lloyd's brokers are exempted from some of the requirements.

[8] See also, S.I. 1978 Nos. 1456, 1457 and 1458.

[9] The court will be slow to interfere with the exercise of these powers: *James v. Insurance Brokers Registration Council, The Times,* February 16, 1984.

intermediaries. Bearing in mind the rough categorisation which we gave at the beginning of this chapter, it is clear that there are categories of intermediary who are still in a position to mislead the public, although of course this is not to suggest that all, or even most, of them would do so. A Government White Paper, *Insurance Intermediaries*,[10] promised to take the matter further. Among its tentative proposals[11] was the crucial one that insurance ought to be allowed to be sold only by registered brokers, insurers or their employees and agents of either of these, for whom their principals would be fully responsible. The clear intention was that part-time agents and unregistered "brokers" would disappear except in circumstances where insurers were prepared to take full responsibility for them. Since the White Paper, insurers have undertaken a measure of self-regulation in this respect.[12] It remains to be seen whether this will prove sufficient.[13]

---

[10] 1977, Cmnd. 6715.
[11] It also envisaged the reversal of the *Newsholme* rule; see Chap. 7 at p. 148.
[12] See n.99, above.
[13] For a valuable paper on the sales techniques adopted by insurance intermediaries, see the report of the Office of Fair Trading, *The Selling of Insurance Policies* (December 1986). See also the E.C. Recommendation of December 18, 1991 (92/48/EEC), which is likely in due course to be replaced by a Directive.

CHAPTER 11

CONSTRUCTION AND CAUSATION: RISKS COVERED AND RISKS EXCEPTED

Introduction

It may fairly be surmised that the average consumer, and quite possibly a fair number of business people, do not read and fully understand their insurance policies at the time they receive them.[1] No doubt, when the possibility of a claim arises, many people do make an attempt to discover whether or not they are covered for a particular loss, but even then it may be doubted whether they actually sit down and read through and fully comprehend their policy from cover to cover. As far as the other classic consumer-type or standard-form contracts are concerned, whether relating to sales of goods, for cash or on credit, or to the provision of services, for example, there is a broad range of statutory control of one form or another.[2] In contrast, in insurance, until recently, freedom of contract survived untramelled, and thus the only way to know whether or not a particular loss was within the ambit of a particular policy was to apply to the insurance contract the general principles of construction applicable to

---

[1] In a survey of motor insureds conducted on behalf of Sentry Insurance in 1977, 64 per cent claimed to have read their policies and 47 per cent to have had them explained to them, but high percentages were still mistaken in respect of important aspects of the cover provided.

[2] From, *e.g.* the Sale of Goods Act 1979 (as amended), the Consumer Credit Act 1974 and the Unfair Contract Terms Act 1977 controlling contract terms, to the Fair Trading Act 1973 vesting wide administrative powers in the Director General of Fair Trading. The Office of Fair Trading has shown more interest in insurance in recent years: see especially its reports on *Household Insurance* (September 1985), *The Selling of Insurance Policies* (December 1986), and a spate of reports in 1995 and 1996 on *Mortgage Repayment Methods, Extended Warranties, Travel Insurance* and *Health Insurance*.

all written contracts. It is to the description and illustration of such principles that this chapter is partly devoted. While these principles remain of crucial importance for all types of insurance, as far as individual consumers are concerned, there is now a measure of statutory protection afforded by the Unfair Terms in Consumer Contracts Regulations 1994.[3] The application of these to the questions considered in this chapter is considered shortly.

It should be noted that to refer to the rules of construction as affecting only risks covered and risks excepted is misleading, because these principles may well apply to the other contents of the insurance contract, for example, the meaning of questions and answers on a proposal form, or the warranties and conditions in a policy. It must also be pointed out that in certain respects, it is not strictly accurate to refer to the construction of words, rather the problem is one of describing their scope. For example, what "loss" means in the context of an insurance policy, a question which is considered later in this chapter, is not so much a question of construction, but of description or definition. The same can be said of the word "accident," another word commonly found in insurance policies, which we shall also consider later. The rules of construction do not help in finding out what these words mean, but some principles must be found to assist in explaining or defining them. This, it is suggested, justifies the consideration of those standard words in this chapter.

It is self-evident, given the great range of actual and potential sorts of insurance and the variety of insurers, that the actual number of words or phrases whose meanings may not be immediately apparent in all the insurance contracts which exist may be very large. Here, it is impossible to cover the whole ground, and the general points only can be illustrated. Some further guidance can be found in the later chapters dealing with specific types of insurance. In any event, it is felt that the approach adopted is justified on the ground that this is an attempt to elucidate the principles, not to give a totally comprehensive A-Z guide. Full citation of the authorities actually available on particular wordings can be found in the standard larger works on insurance law.

Although as a matter of construction, a loss may fall within the risks covered by a particular policy, it may still be necessary for the insured to show that the loss was caused by such a risk and not predominantly by an uninsured risk. Conveniently, this problem of causation is also considered in this chapter. In addition, there are some general considerations

[3] S.I. 1994 No. 3159.

regarding the nature of risks under an insurance contract which will be examined.

General

There are two points that can usefully be made at this stage before we examine the rules of construction in detail. To an extent these follow from comments already made in the introductory remarks, but, as we shall see, they will now be inapplicable to insurance contracts effected by an individual consumer insured. These points are that there is no requirement that an insurance policy be reasonably intelligible in terms of content, and there is no requirement that it be especially legible. Insurance policies are still often notoriously complex documents riddled with jargon, their layout is often muddled to the untrained eye, and the print, or some of it, may be very small. In one marine insurance case, *Koskas v. Standard Marine Insurance Co. Ltd*,[4] the judge at first instance refused to allow the insurer to rely upon a particular condition on the grounds that the print was so small that it was barely legible. The Court of Appeal,[5] however, overruled this bold attempt to interfere because the print was legible, albeit with difficulty. It is fair to say that even in commercial insurances, such an extreme example is unlikely to be found today and insurers often seek to write all their policies in "plain English". This can, though, still raise difficulties of interpretation and construction.[6]

Consumer Protection

Judges have on occasion railed against insurers for not producing their policies in a form intelligible to the ordinary consumer,[7] and consumer representatives and bodies, including the Director General of Fair Trading[8] and the Insurance Ombudsman, have frequently made the same point. The Law Commission clearly intended that conditions and exceptions in insurance contracts should be brought within the ambit of what became the Unfair Contract Terms Act 1977,[9] but pressure from the insurance

---

[4] (1926) 25 Ll.L.R. 363.
[5] (1927) 27 Ll.L.R. 61.
[6] See, *e.g.* the case of *Kausar v. Eagle Star Insurance Co. Ltd*, [1997] C.L.C. 129, considered at p. 118, above.
[7] See, *e.g.* Lord Wright in *Provincial Insurance Co. v. Morgan* [1932] A.C. 240 at 252.
[8] See the reports referred to in n.2 above.
[9] Second Report on Exemption Clauses (No. 69).

industry secured their exclusion from that Act[10] in return for their agreeing to promulgate the Statements of Insurance Practice.[11] However, many insurers did respond to criticism in particular by rewording their policies in "plain English". This is clearly to be welcomed, although this does not necessarily mean that the average consumer will still read and understand their insurance policies nor, as we have seen, does it necessarily mean that problems of interpretation will not arise.

More recently there have been further significant developments. The first arises from the existence and attitude of the Insurance Ombudsman. He has declared that he is prepared to find particular terms in insurance contracts unreasonable, arguing that the spirit, if not the letter, of the Unfair Contract Terms Act applies.[12] Among other things, he has refused to allow reliance on provisions producing an unexpected loss of cover secreted in a policy without warning and on exclusions of liability for loss of goods left unattended when those were not highlighted at the outset. He has also in effect rewritten the standard provision[13] which suspends cover in the event of a house being unoccupied for more than 30 days, holding that it applies only when the 30-day period has elapsed. While, with respect, the basis for his jurisdiction here was first open to dispute,[14] it was put on a sounder footing in 1992 when his terms of reference were amended to require him to reach a decision in each case which is "fair and reasonable in all the circumstances."[15] This development no doubt resulted in greater clarity of expression and layout in insurance policies.

More recently there has been an even more important development, more important because it is not dependent on a self-regulatory structure. This is the introduction of the Unfair Terms in Consumer Contracts Regulations to which reference has already been made. It needed E.C.

[10] Sched. 1, para.1(a).
[11] See p. 5, above.
[12] See in particular the Annual Report for 1990, paras. 2.4 and 3.9.
[13] See p. 118, above.
[14] The then Ombudsman stated in his Annual Report for 1990 that the industry agreed to be bound by the spirit of U.C.T.A. when they agreed to the Statements of Insurance Practice, but there is no evidence for this in the Parliamentary and A.B.I. statements made at the time of U.C.T.A., when the Statements were first issued and later, when the revised Statements were issued. All these show is a readiness to modify the application of the law in those areas specifically referred to in the Statements. As to these, see pp. 120–121 and pp. 154–155 above.
[15] See McGee (1992) 2 Insurance L. & P. 86.

legislation to produce this measure of consumer protection.[16] Some consideration has already been given to these Regulations.[17] In the context of this chapter, there are three points which need to be made. The first is the general requirement to use plain, intelligible language.[18] This reinforces the trend toward "plain English" already noted. The second is that the Director General of Fair Trading is under a statutory duty to monitor the use of unfair terms and can seek undertakings or court injunctions to prevent their use.[19] The third point is the most important one for present purposes and concerns the question of the application of the core part of the Regulations to the question of the cover provided by an insurance contract.[20]

This core part[21] strikes down any "unfair term" which contrary to the requirement of good faith causes a significant imbalance in the parties' rights and obligations under the contract to the detriment of the consumer.[22] However, it does not apply to any term which "defines the main subject matter of the contract."[23] It is thought that the provisions concerning the risks covered and excepted under an insurance contract must be within this exception,[24] as these do define the main subject matter of the contract. This, it is suggested, is also a sensible interpretation. In the result, it is thought that the impact of the Regulations on the matters under consideration here is limited to the requirement of plain and

---

[16] The Unfair Contract Terms Directive 93/13/E.C., agreed on April 5, 1993. It must be doubtful whether this would have happened otherwise.

[17] See Chap. 5, p. 91.

[18] reg. 6; note also the statutory confirmation therein of the *contra proferentem* rule (see pp. 206–208, below).

[19] reg. 8.

[20] Apart from the requirement of plainness and intelligibility of language which clearly applies.

[21] reg. 4.

[22] See further, p. 92, above.

[23] reg. 2(a).

[24] Although it is recognised that the Regulations can quite properly go beyond what the Directive required, the provisions of the Directive must surely nonetheless be an aid to construction. In the preamble to the Directive, it was stated that in insurance contracts, "the terms which clearly define or circum-stance the insured risk and the insurer's liability shall not be subject to [assessment of unfair character] since these restrictions are taken into account in calculating the premium paid by the consumer." Assuming that the preamble qualifies the text of the Directive (see Duffy [1993] J.B.L. 67 at 71–72), this is clearly effective to remove from its scope provisions defining the risk and exceptions to it.

intelligible language, supported by a statutory reinforcement of the *contra proferentem* rule.[25]

American approaches

In quite vivid contrast is the approach to construing insurance policies taken by the courts in many of the States in the United States of America.[26] Here doctrines described as "fulfilling the reasonable expectations of the insured" and "disallowing the insurer any unconscionable advantage" are well established,[27] following early recognition of the contract of insurance as a "contract of adhesion" *par excellence,*[28] in other words, as one of the classic cases in which there is absolutely no chance of the party which does not produce the standard form bargaining over the terms of the contract.

One particularly interesting example of this approach, of particular relevance because it has been reported in this country, is the decision of the Supreme Court of New Jersey in *Gerhardt v. Continental Insurance Companies.*[29] Here the plaintiff held a householder's comprehensive insurance policy issued by the defendant. A section of the policy provided for indemnity against any sums which the insured would become legally liable to pay to a third party for personal injury or property damage arising out of his occupation of his house, but set out on a separate page were certain exclusions to this section, one of which provided that the cover did not apply with respect to bodily injury to a resident employee arising out of and in the course of his employment by the insured. Such an employee was injured in the insured's house and sued the insured who called upon the insurers to conduct her defence. The latter relied on the exclusion mentioned, but it was held that they were not entitled to do so. Read by itself, the exclusion appears to have been clear and, on ordinary principles of construction, applicable. However, the court said that, on a simple reading of this policy, which was prepared unilaterally by the company and sold on a mass basis as affording broad coverage to homeowners, the

---

[25] See n.18, above.
[26] Perhaps the only real English judgment to similar effect is that of Farwell L.J. in *Re Bradley and Essex & Suffolk Accident Indemnity Society* [1912] 1 K.B. 415.
[27] See especially, Keeton, "Insurance law rights at variance with policy provisions," (1970) 83 Harv.L.R. 961 and 1281.
[28] See generally, Kessler, "Contracts of adhesion — some thoughts about freedom of contract" (1943) 43 Col.L.R. 629.
[29] [1967] 1 Lloyd's Rep. 380.

average insured, noting the section covering third party liability, would assume that an injury to a domestic employee was covered. The exclusion was not conspicuous, and as in earlier cases[30] the cover was described as comprehensive, and, while the insurer had the right to exclude particular types of liability, the doctrine of honouring the reasonable expectations of the insured required that it did so unequivocally.

It must be regarded as most unlikely that an English court would adopt such an approach.[31] While it has attractions, such as that it might cause insurers more often to clarify their policies, there are also other factors to be borne in mind. Decisions of this nature depend entirely upon cases coming before the courts for decision. A principle of this sort is so vague that it would be difficult, if not impossible, to predict the result on the facts of any particular case, and a system which depends on the courts' adjudicating every dispute may be undesirable. If further interference with policy terms is felt to be justified, it is submitted that it would be far better to have a regime of prior approval of policy forms within guidelines laid down by statute.

Risk

As has been pointed out already in this book,[32] the essence of insurance is that it provides protection against the risks of uncertain events befalling the insured, normally events which would be adverse to him. The concept of risk is fundamental, and there are a number of general points of universal application that must be made, as they may well apply, regardless of whether a loss appears to be covered as a matter of construction.

Intentional and negligent losses

First, as a general rule, the fact that a loss is occasioned by the negligence of the insured is irrelevant, but insurance does not cover losses

---

[30] e.g. *Bauman v. Royal Indemnity Co.* 36 N.J. 12 (1961).

[31] Unless, contrary to the view expressed, it was decided that the 1994 Regulations permitted such interference. No doubt in some instances the requirement of plain and intelligible language could lead to a measure of interference. Note, though, that Dr Clarke has made an interesting attempt to discover signs of such an approach in English cases; see "The reasonable expectations of the insured — in England?" [1989] J.B.L. 389.

[32] See especially the discussion of the definition of insurance at pp. 12–19, above.

deliberately caused by him. There are innumerable authorities confirming, for example, that the deliberate arson by the insured of property covered by a fire policy,[33] or the sane suicide of a life insured under a life policy, is not covered.[34] This point relates closely to principles of public policy applicable to insurance contracts, which we shall examine in a subsequent chapter, but leaving these aside for the moment, it is clear that express policy terms can, if appropriately worded, cover deliberate losses, so that the general rule is not an absolute one. In practice, however, this is likely to apply only in respect of suicide under a life policy. In addition, the general rule excludes only losses caused deliberately by the insured himself. The fact that his wife[35] or employee,[36] for example, intentionally destroys property he has insured does not prevent the insured who is not a party to the act from recovering.

That the insured who is negligent can recover is subject to the important qualification that a term of the policy may seek to exclude the insurer's liability in this respect, by imposing on the insured an obligation to take reasonable care.[37] This sort of term has been common for some years in liability insurance policies, where, sensibly, a requirement of reasonable care has been construed to be applicable only to reckless acts by an insured; otherwise such policies would not provide the very basic cover, against negligence liability, for which they are effected.[38] More recently, it seems, such a term has appeared in property and other first party insurances, requiring the insured, for example, to take reasonable care of insured property or to maintain it in a reasonable condition. Following some earlier doubts,[39] it now seems clear that such a term will be

---

[33] *Britton v. Royal Insurance Co.* (1866) 4 F. & F. 905.

[34] *Beresford v. Royal Insurance Co.* [1938] A.C. 586; see pp. 236–237, below.

[35] *Midland Insurance Co. v. Smith* (1881) 6 Q.B.D. 561.

[36] *Shaw v. Robberds* (1837) 6 Ad. & El. 75 at 84.

[37] This may be phrased as a warranty or condition (see Chap. 7) or as an exception to the risk. Whichever way it is done, the effect will be to relieve the insurer from liability.

[38] See, in particular, *Fraser v. Furman* [1967] 1 W.L.R. 898, discussed further at p. 353, below, and as to the effect of such a term in motor policies, see pp. 370–373, below.

[39] See the rather ambiguous dicta in *Stephen v. Scottish Boatowners Mutual Insurance Association* [1989] 1 Lloyd's Rep. 535 at 541, *Devco Holder v. Legal and General Assurance Society* [1993] 2 Lloyd's Rep. 567 (1988), and the approach of the first Insurance Ombudsman, who took a fairly strict view of the insured's duty particularly in household and travel insurance situations; see his Annual Reports for 1984, 1985 and 1986, pp. 5–6, 7–8 and 6–8, respectively.

construed in the same way as in liability policies, so that mere negligence by the insured will not preclude recovery.

In *Sofi v. Prudential Assurance Company Ltd*,[40] conditions requiring the insured to take "reasonable care to avoid loss" in a domestic all risks policy and a travel policy were interpreted in this way. Here, the plaintiff, who was travelling to France, arrived at the Dover ferry with time to spare. He left his car for 15 minutes in the unattended car park at Dover Castle with £50,000 worth of valuables locked in the glove compartment. During that time, the car was broken into and the valuables stolen. The Court of Appeal held that the plaintiff was entitled to recover, not on the facts having acted recklessly. In the light of this decision, insurers who wish to limit their liability without having to prove recklessness have to insert more specific terms in their policies, for example by excluding liability when goods are left unattended.[41]

Perils never insured

A number of perils are never covered by indemnity insurances. Primarily these are wear and tear and inherent vice, in other words, what occurs or happens naturally. Simply these are not fortuitous and are not therefore capable of being covered by an insurance contract, the essence of which is to cover uncertain risks. So, for example, decay in food or the rusting of a car or the natural wear of tiles on a roof cannot be insured against. The major exception here, of course, is in the field of contingency insurance, that is life and related contracts. A life contract obviously covers the natural process of dying; a health insurance contract obviously covers what may be inevitable illness.

Principles of Construction

Attention must now be turned to the detail of the rules of construction applicable to insurance policies. It should be noted that the question of

---

[40] [1993] 2 Lloyd's Rep. 559 (1990); see Birds (1991) 1 Ins. L. & P. 18. See also the New Zealand case of *Roberts v. State General Insurance Manager* [1974] 2 N.Z.L.R. 312 and *Port-Rose v. Phoenix Assurance Co. Ltd* (1986) 136 N.L.J. 333. The latter case concerned a situation where the insured under an all risks policy took her eyes off her handbag containing her jewellery at an airport for a brief moment, while she helped a fellow elderly passenger, during which time it was stolen. Hodgson J. disallowed the insurer's reliance on a reasonable care provision, although it is arguable that on the facts there was no negligence involved. The Insurance Ombudsman now follows the *Sofi* line; see his Annual Reports for 1989 and 1991 at paras. 2.4 and 2.12, respectively.

[41] As to such provisions, see p. 204, below.

construction is a question of law, and once a word or phrase has been judicially considered, that decision should be followed according to the usual rules of precedent.[42] A good fairly recent example of this principle is the decision in *Dino Services v. Prudential Assurance Co. Ltd*,[43] where the Court of Appeal followed long-established authorities[44] in construing cover provided against theft "by forcible and violent means", and denied recovery where the loss had been effected by thieves who used stolen keys to gain entry to the relevant premises without having to resort to "violence", such as breaking down a door or forcing open a window.[45]

It seems that up to 13 rules of construction can be found.[46] What may be regarded as the most important of these will be summarised in the following paragraph, before some examples are cited. Primarily it is the intention of the parties, as discovered objectively from the whole of the policy, that prevails. Written parts, if present, prevail over printed parts as more likely to express the agreement of the parties, and parol evidence is not in general admissible to vary or contradict the written document. The policy is construed according to its literal meaning; only if that is unclear can extraneous circumstances be examined. Words are normally understood in their ordinary meaning, but this is not the case where they have a technical legal meaning; here the latter prevails. Similarly, the context of a word may dictate a departure from its ordinary meaning. Words appearing in the one phrase are prima facie to be construed *eiusdem generis*. Finally, in the event that there is any ambiguity, the policy is construed *contra proferentem*, that is, against the person who drafted it and in favour of the other. This will normally, of course, be against the insurer and in favour of the insured.

It may be that different of these canons conflict in the sense that the application of different ones to the same facts may produce a different result. We shall see a good example of this later. In addition, it must be pointed out again that the primary rule, that the intention of the parties must prevail, is, in the majority of cases, founded on the often incorrect

---

[42] See, *e.g. W. J. Lane v. Spratt* [1970] 2 Q.B. 480 at 491–492, per Roskill J.

[43] [1989] 1 All E.R. 422. See [1989] J.B.L. 355.

[44] *Re George and Goldsmiths and General Burglary Insurance Ass. Ltd* [1899] 1 Q.B. 595, *Re Calf and Sun Insurance Office* [1920] 2 K.B. 366.

[45] The court did not like the result, though, and urged an *ex gratia* payment; *quaere* whether they were not a little hard on the insurers.

[46] See for a comprehensive list, Ivamy, *General Principles of Insurance Law*, (5th ed.), Chap. 35.

premise that the insurance contract is the result of bargaining between parties of equal strength, who having bargained, reduced their agreement to writing. Bearing such considerations in mind, we shall now examine just a small selection of the cases on some of the more important canons of construction.

Ordinary meaning

The words in a policy are prima facie to be understood in their ordinary meaning. For example, in *Thompson v. Equity Fire Insurance Co.*,[47] a fire policy taken out by a shopkeeper exempted the insurers from liability for loss or damage occurring "while gasoline is stored or kept in the building insured." The insured had a small quantity of gasoline for cooking purposes, but no other. It was held that the insurer was liable for a fire that occurred, as the words "stored or kept" in their ordinary meaning implied fairly considerable quantities, and imported the notion of warehousing or keeping in stock for trading. This was not the case and so the exception was inapplicable. In *Leo Rapp Ltd v. McClure*,[48] metal was insured against theft "whilst in warehouse." Some of the relevant metal was stolen from a lorry parked in a locked compound surrounded by a wall topped by barbed wire. It was held that the insurer was not liable, as the ordinary meaning of warehouse implied some sort of covered building, and not a yard, however secure.[49]

Technical meaning

In two respects, however, the ordinary meaning of words will not prevail. The first is where a word has a technical legal or other meaning. This will generally be the case in respect of words describing cover or exceptions to it which are also the names of criminal offences, such as theft, or have acquired a particular meaning.[50] The meaning in the latter

---

[47] [1910] A.C. 592.

[48] [1955] 1 Lloyd's Rep. 292.

[49] See also *Langford v. Legal and General Assurance Society Ltd* [1986] 2 Lloyd's Rep. 103, where it was held that a car was "attended" within the "sensible and practical meaning" of the word where it was left by the insured in her driveway for only a few seconds and was visible from her kitchen window. The fairly standard exception for property left unattended has given rise to a few cases in recent years; see also *e.g. O'Donoghue v. Harding* [1988] 2 Lloyd's Rep. 281.

[50] As to words which are the names of crimes, see Wasik [1986] J.B.L. 45. As to the meaning of "theft" in particular see n.51 and p. 222, below.

respect applies to the word in an insurance policy. The classic example is the decision of the House of Lords in *London & Lancashire Fire Insurance Co. v. Bolands*.[51] Here a policy on a baker's shop against loss by burglary, housebreaking and theft exempted the insurers from loss caused by, or happening through, or in consequence of, *inter alia*, "riot". Four armed men entered the shop one day, held up the employees with guns, and stole all the money they could find. There was no actual violence used, and no other disturbance nearby, yet it was held that the event constituted a riot, and thus the insured could not recover. The stated, and not unattractive,[52] reason for the decision was that "riot" is a technical term which in a criminal context requires only three people executing a disturbance such as might cause alarm to a reasonable person.[53] Applying this meaning to the insurance policy, there was clearly a riot on the facts of the case. However, it may not be entirely insignificant that the shop was in Dublin and the robbery took place at a time of great disturbances involving the I.R.A. and others. It is not impossible that such a body was behind the robbery, and to talk in terms of riot becomes a little more understandable.

It is instructive to compare the views of an American court[54] in holding that riot in an insurance policy meant what ordinary people would normally regard as a riot, distinguishing the decision in *Bolands* for these reasons. In the light of the well-established rules applying to technical words, the decision in *Bolands* is clearly correct. What may be questioned is whether it is a necessary or fair rule to apply to an insurance policy the meaning from another context when such a meaning may be totally different from the ordinary meaning. Fortunately, "riot" no longer commonly appears as an exception on the British side of the Irish Sea, though it does so on the other.[55]

Context

The second way in which the ordinary meaning of a word may not be adopted is where the context requires otherwise. Frequently, the list of

---

[51] [1924] A.C. 836. The rule as to technical meaning also seems to have been the basis of the recent House of Lords' decision in *Deutsche Genossenschaftsbank v. Burnhope* [1995] 4 All E.R. 717, where it was held that "theft" could not be committed by a company in the absence of the physical presence of someone senior enough to be regarded as the company's directing mind and will.

[52] But see Kemble (1976) 126 N.L.J. 1133.

[53] See, *e.g. Field v. Receiver of Metropolitan Police* [1907] 2 K.B. 853.

[54] *Pan Am v. Aetna Casualty* [1974] 1 Lloyd's Rep. 232; [1975] 1 Lloyd's Rep. 77.

[55] Where, however, state compensation is available.

perils covered by, for example, a fire policy does not list each peril individually but groups a few together. This is what happened in *Young v. Sun Alliance & London Insurance*.[56] Here, the plaintiff's household policy insured him against loss arising from a number of causes, one group of which was "storm,[57] tempest or flood." His house was built on a meadow. Several times water seeped in and caused damage to the ground floor lavatory. On one occasion, the water was three inches deep on the lavatory floor. The plaintiff claimed that this constituted a "flood" and that the insurers were therefore liable to indemnify him in respect of the damage. The Court of Appeal rejected his claim. At least two of their Lordships[58] appeared to accept that in the ordinary sense of the word there was a flood in the case, but they concluded in favour of a contextual approach. As "storm" and "tempest" both import notions of the abnormal, by analogy "flood," appearing in the same phrase, meant a much larger movement of water than natural seepage to a level of three inches. They were almost persuaded, in view of the two possible meanings of "flood," to apply the *contra proferentem* maxim and have been criticised for not doing so. *Young* is an illustration of the point made earlier that the application of different canons of construction to the same words can easily produce different results. It has therefore been suggested that the traditional rules be replaced by an enquiry as to what cover the parties really thought was being provided by the policy and as to the purposes behind the insurance in question.[59] This is perhaps an approach rather similar to the American rules of construction that were referred to earlier, and is, it is suggested, open to the same difficulties. As *Young* involved a consumer insurance policy, it is likely that the requirement of plainness and intelligibility[60] would now require a description of what the insurers understood by "flood", for example by the use of a glossary of terms used in the policy.[61]

Contra proferentem

The maxim that provides for ambiguities to be construed against the party responsible for drafting them[62] may be brought to the aid of the insured as two leading Court of Appeal decisions show.

[56] [1977] 1 W.L.R. 104.
[57] As to storm, see *Anderson v. Norwich Union* [1977] 1 Lloyd's Rep. 253.
[58] Shaw and Cairns L.JJ. Lawton L.J. regarding the problem as more straightforward, holding that flood ordinarily meant something violent and abnormal.
[59] Merkin (1977) 40 M.L.R. 486.
[60] And the statutory *contra proferentem* rule; see p. 199, above.
[61] This is in fact not uncommon.
[62] Now statutorily confirmed in respect of consumer insurances; see p. 197, above.

In *English v. Western*,[63] a motor policy effected by a 17 year-old youth
covered his liability for injury to all persons except, *inter alia*, in respect of
"death or injury to any member of the assured's household" travelling in
the car with the insured.[64] He negligently injured his sister when she was
his passenger. The insurers argued that they were not liable to indemnify
the insured against his liability to her by virtue of the above exception. It
was held that the expression "any member of the assured's household" was
equally capable of meaning "any member of a household of which the
assured was the head" as "any member of the same household of which the
assured was a member." It was therefore ambiguous and the meaning
more favourable to the insured, the former meaning, was adopted, so that
the insurers were liable.

Houghton v. Trafalgar Insurance Co. Ltd[65] also involved an exception in a
motor policy which excluded liability when the car was conveying "any
load in excess of that for which it was constructed." Here the insurer
argued that the carriage of six persons in a car designed for five was within
the exception. It was held that this was not a "load." While the carriage of
persons could be so considered, it equally, indeed more naturally, referred
to the carriage of goods.

The application of the *contra proferentem* maxim can hardly be said to be
free from doubt. It is clear that there must be a genuine ambiguity;
ambiguity must not be created simply to apply the maxim. However,
whether or not a word or phrase is ambiguous is not always apparent. It
could be said that there was ambiguity over the meaning of the word
"flood" in the *Young* case, and two of the judges admitted that counsel for
the insured had very nearly so persuaded them. A classic illustration of the
difficulties which gave rise to a difference of judicial opinion is *Alder v.
Moore*.[66] Here the dispute arose not from the wording of a policy itself, but
of an undertaking extracted from an insured following a payment under a
policy. The defendant had been a professional footballer and a member of
the relevant footballers' union when he suffered an injury to an eye which
it was thought would prevent him from playing professionally again. The
union had an accident policy under which its members who sustained
permanent total disablement would receive £500 from the plaintiff insurer.

[63] [1940] 2 K.B. 156.
[64] Such an exclusion is not now permitted under the Road Traffic Act 1988; see
p. 358, below.
[65] [1954] 1 Q.B. 247.
[66] [1961] 2 Q.B. 57.

The defendant received such a payment, in return for which he agreed that he would not take part "as a playing member" in any form of professional football. Subsequently he recovered sufficiently to take up occasional professional football, though at a much lower level than before. The plaintiff sued for return of the £500. It was argued for the defendant, *inter alia*,[67] that the undertaking was ambiguous, because "playing member" could mean either simply "player" or "player who is a member of the union." Moore was not, when he returned to football, a member of the union. The latter interpretation was reinforced by the argument that if the former were correct, the word "member" in the undertaking was superfluous and that in the original policy, "member" was expressly defined as a registered member of the union. Despite this, a majority of the Court of Appeal[68] held that the plaintiff should succeed and regarded the undertaking as perfectly clear. With respect, the dissenting judgment of Devlin L.J. is much more persuasive.[69] For the reasons outlined he held that the phrase was ambiguous, and, although he adopted what he termed a wider rule than *contra proferentem,* he was clearly of opinion that the phrase should be construed against the insurer. Whichever view is the better on the facts of the case, it does illustrate how even the judges cannot always agree as to whether or not sufficient ambiguity exists.[70]

Specific Descriptions and Specific Words

It is appropriate to turn now to consider how some of the specific descriptions sometimes applied to insurance policies and some of the standard wordings have been defined in the context of the cover afforded by an insurance policy. Looking first at descriptions, it is well known that insurers, no doubt at least partly for marketing reasons, sometimes attach descriptions like "Comprehensive," "Invincible," "Homeguard" or "Maxplan" to their appropriate policies. While judges have occasionally commented adversely on such descriptions because they give a somewhat misleading picture and may lead an insured to consider that his cover is complete and not subject to exceptions, which it usually will be, it is clear

---

[67] It was also argued that the forfeiture was a penalty clause and void for this reason, but the court held against this argument by a majority.

[68] On this point, Slade J. simply agreed with Sellers L.J.

[69] See Goff (1961) 24 M.L.R. 637.

[70] Even in *English v. Western*, above, which seems a pretty clear case of ambiguity, Goddard L.J. dissented on the grounds that it was not.

that descriptions of the sort mentioned above are not terms of art and do not carry any legal meanings.[71] The one exception to this is the description "All Risks." Frequently, for example, policies on valuables and contractors' policies are "all risks." The nature of an "all risks" policy was explained in the marine insurance case of *British and Foreign Marine Insurance Co. v. Gaunt.*[72] Basically, it covers all loss to the property insured as occurs through some accidental cause, but not "such damage as is inevitable from ordinary wear and tear and inevitable depreciation"[73] or from inherent vice. The other significant feature of "all risks" cover is that the insured has to show only that a loss is accidental; he need not show the exact nature of the accident or casualty which occasioned the loss.

However, even an "all risks" policy can be subject to exceptions which will be upheld on usual principles of construction if they are clearly stated. In the Australian case of *Queensland Government Railways and Electric Power Transmission Pty Ltd v. Manufacturers' Mutual Life Insurance Ltd,*[74] the plaintiffs held a contractors' all risks policy covering the construction of a bridge, but the policy excluded loss or damage arising from "faulty design." The bridge was being constructed to a design which, at the time, was the best available, but nevertheless, its piers were swept away by flood water after exceptionally heavy rains. It was held that the insurers could rely upon the exception. Even though the design was not negligent, because it was the best available, it was still "faulty" since otherwise the piers would never have collapsed.[75]

Fire

Insurance against loss or damage by fire is, of course, one of the standard and one of the oldest forms of cover, and the major part of any policy on real property. As fire does not have a technical meaning like, for example, theft or burglary, and because of its prominence, its meaning is

---

[71] Compare the attitude of some American cases; see, *e.g. Gerhardt v. Continental Insurance Companies* [1967] 1 Lloyd's Rep. 380; see p. 199, above, where the fact that the policy was described as a comprehensive one was one of the factors in the decision. Note also the strictures of the Insurance Ombudsman on the use of such titles; see his Annual Report for 1986, pp. 25–26.

[72] [1921] 2 A.C. 41.

[73] *ibid.* at 46, per Lord Birkenhead.

[74] (1968) 118 C.L.R. 314; [1969] 1 Lloyd's Rep. 214.

[75] This definition of faulty has been trenchantly criticised by Merkin (1977) 40 M.L.R. 486 at 489.

worth exploring. Apart from obvious losses by fire, the actual burning of property insured, the problems that have arisen have been whether it is necessary that there be actual ignition of the property insured and whether loss or damage occurring in or as a result of a "proper" fire is covered. Actual ignition is necessary and damage from excessive heat is not enough. In the old case of *Austin v. Drewe*,[76] the stock in a sugar refinery was insured against damage by fire. A flue passed up through all the floors of the refinery from a stove on the ground floor. At the top of the flue was a register which was closed at night to retain heat, but opened when a fresh fire was lit in the morning. One morning an employee of the insured forgot to open the register. The intense heat in the flue damaged sugar being refined on the top floor, but, although there was smoke and sparks, the fire itself was confined to the flue and the sugar did not ignite. It was held that there was no loss by fire.

On the other hand, if there has been actual ignition of some property, the fact that the insured property itself does not catch fire is irrelevant if it is damaged in such a way that the proximate cause of the loss was the fire.[77] We shall return to this point later.

There is no distinction in English law between a "friendly" fire and a "hostile" fire. In other words, the fact that the damage is caused by a fire in its proper place does not matter so long as the loss is accidental. In *Harris v. Poland*,[78] the plaintiff's personal property was insured against loss or damage caused by fire. One day, as a security measure, she concealed her jewellery in the grate under coal which was ready for lighting. Later she inadvertently lit the fire without removing the jewellery which, as a result, was damaged. It was held that there had been a loss by fire. "[The] risks against which the plaintiff is insured include the risk of insured property coming unintentionally in contact with fire and being thereby destroyed or damaged, and it matters not whether that fire comes to the insured property or the insured property comes to the fire."[79]

Damage caused merely by explosion or lightning is not damage by fire,[80] but explosion caused by fire, or fire following an explosion or lightning will be covered, subject to the rules about causation which will

---

[76] (1816) 6 Taunt. 436.
[77] *Symington v. Union Insurance Society of Canton* (1928) 97 L.J.K.B. 646.
[78] [1941] 1 K.B. 462.
[79] *ibid.* at 468, per Atkinson J.
[80] *Everett v. London Assurance Co.* (1865) 19 C.B. (n.s.) 126. As to "explosion," see *Commonwealth Smelting v. Guardian Royal Exchange* [1984] 2 Lloyd's Rep. 608.

be examined later, because here there has been actual ignition.[81] In practice, lightning damage at least is included in the cover provided by a standard fire policy.

Accident

Loss caused by or arising out of an accident or by accidental means or some similar phrase is a fairly common form of wording in insurance policies, and an essential one in particular types. The considerable problems involved in defining "accident" have occasioned the courts difficulties many times[82] and it is considered worthwhile, therefore, to devote space to this question. Particular policies where these problems arise are policies of personal accident insurance or policies such as motor policies which may well contain a personal accident component, and some policies of liability insurance.

As we have seen, insurance prima facie covers only unintentional acts anyway, so one problem is how the presence of the word "accident" qualifies this. Another is that even a deliberate act by someone may well be accidental from the point of view of the victim. Similarly, an insured may be engaged in a deliberate course of conduct when something happens which he did not intend. Is this an accident? It is suggested that the answers to these and other problems are best considered by a separate examination of first, those first party insurances where the description "accident" is to be found, and secondly, cases of third party or liability insurance where the liability of the insurer to indemnify exists only if the insured acted accidentally. It must be pointed out, however, that the cases do not necessarily adopt this distinction.

First party insurances

In the first sort of case policies of personal accident insurance predominate.[83] Leaving aside for the present the issue of causation which can be of importance in this field, it would appear that injury arising from accident

---

[81] *Stanley v. Western Insurance Co.* (1868) L.R. 3 Ex. 71.

[82] The classic illustration is perhaps the decision in *Trim Joint District School Board of Management v. Kelly* [1914] A.C. 667, a workmen's compensation case where the House of Lords split 4–3.

[83] Common also at one time were policies issued under the Workmen's Compensation Acts which gave birth to a considerable amount of litigation; see below.

can be defined as injury which arises from some unexpected or unintended event, which is not natural. So, for example, in *Hamlyn v. Crown Accidental Insurance Co. Ltd*,[84] the insured bent down to pick up a marble dropped by a child. In doing so, he wrenched his knee. As he had no history of knee trouble it was held that his injury was accidental. Although obviously he intended to bend down, he did not intend or expect to hurt his knee.[85] The fact that the insured is negligent is by itself irrelevant, so that being knocked down by a train when crossing a railway line without due care will be covered by a personal accident policy.[86] Death or injury from sunstroke or exposure would not normally be regarded as accidental, being the result of natural events.[87]

In *Marcel Beller Ltd v. Hayden*,[88] the plaintiff company insured their employees against death consequent upon "accidental bodily injury" being the sole cause. An employee having consumed alcoholic drink to the extent that he had much more than the permitted level of alcohol in his blood, was driving his car too fast when approaching a corner; he lost control, crashed and was killed. One of the points for decision was whether this was an accident. It was argued for the insurers that it was not, because the death was a reasonably foreseeable consequence of a deliberate act by the employee, that is, the consumption of a considerable quantity of alcohol. The judge rejected this argument and distinguished the difficult case of *Gray v. Barr*,[89] a decision on liability insurance which will be examined shortly. In his view, accident should be interpreted in its ordinary sense as an ordinary person would understand it. As, on the facts, an ordinary person would have said that the employee's death was an accident, because he did not intend to kill himself nor expose himself to deliberate risk, the death was prima facie covered by the policy.

If the insured does take a deliberate risk, an injury resulting may fairly be said not to be accidental. In one Canadian case,[90] cited in *Marcel Beller*

---

[84] [1893] 1 Q.B. 750. See also *Voison v. Royal Insurance Co. of Canada* (1989) 53 D.L.R. (4th) 299.

[85] It is not certain that the result in *Hamlyn* would be the same today, because the policy required "accidental means" (see below), but it is clearly still a good illustration of an "accident".

[86] *Cornish v. Accident Insurance Co.* (1889) 23 Q.B.D. 453.

[87] *Sinclair v. Maritime Passengers' Assurance* (1861) 3 E. & E. 478, followed recently in *De Souza v. Home and Overseas Insurance Co. Ltd* [1995] L.R.L.R. 453 (1990).

[88] [1978] Q.B. 694.

[89] [1971] 2 Q.B. 554.

[90] *Candler v. London & Lancashire Guarantee & Accident Co. of Canada* (1963) 40 D.L.R. (2d.) 408.

Ltd v. Hayden, the insured balanced himself on the coping of a hotel patio 13 floors above the street in order to demonstrate to a friend that he had not lost his nerve. Unfortunately he lost his balance and fell to his death. This was held not to be an accident. In the words of the learned judge in *Marcel Beller Ltd v. Hayden*, "It seems to me that a clear distinction can be drawn between cases where the predisposing cause is the deliberate taking of an appreciated risk and the cases such as the present where the predisposing cause, although it leads to the taking of risks, involves risk which was neither deliberately run nor actually appreciated."[91]

Sometimes, though probably rarely, cases are found where property damage is covered under a first party policy only if caused by or arising out of accident. In the Australian decision of *Lombard Australia Ltd v. N.R.M.A. Insurance Ltd*,[92] an approach similar to that of the personal injury cases was taken. There a car, the subject of a hire purchase agreement, was jointly insured against loss by accident by the hirer and the owner. The hirer deliberately committed suicide by driving it into a tree. It was held that the loss of the car was accidental so far as the owner was concerned and thus covered, as the latter certainly did not intend the loss.

Accidental means

One final, but very important, point to consider in this context is whether subtle changes in wording can affect the interpretation of words. For example, a personal accident policy may not simply cover death or injury "caused by accident," but one "caused by accidental means" or, in the fuller phrase often employed, "by violent, accidental, external and visible means."[93] Here it could be argued not just that the final event or injury must be accidental, but also the "means," in other words, the prior act of the insured or whoever is responsible for the act, so that if a deliberate act led to the final "accident," the insured is not covered. An argument along these lines seems to have been rejected in the *Hamlyn* case,

---

[91] [1978] 2 Q.B. at 705. Modern policies will probably contain an exception excluding liability if there is "wilful exposure to needless peril." This has the same effect. In *Morley v. United Friendly Insurance plc* [1993] 1 Lloyd's Rep. 490, it was held that this did not exclude the situation where the insured jumped on to the bumper of a car as a prank and fell off.

[92] [1969] 1 Lloyd's Rep. 575.

[93] The continuing use of this antiquated phrase is perhaps surprising, and it is thought that it could not now, in a consumer policy, survive the statutory requirement of plainness and intelligibility (p. 198, above).

which we have already examined, where the wording was of this sort and the bending over of the insured was clearly deliberate, but it has prevailed in the intervening years in decisions in some other jurisdictions, including a leading American case,[94] and was adopted by the Court of Appeal in the recent decision in *Dhak v. Insurance Company of North America (U.K.) Ltd*,[95] where recovery was denied in circumstances where the insured died from asphyxiation due to vomiting while under the influence of alcohol; she had drunk in order to control severe back pain. It is submitted that the earlier English approach is to be preferred. As that great American judge, Cardozo J., dissenting, said:[96] "The attempted distinction between accidental results and accidental means will plunge this branch of the law into a Serbian bog." It is to be hoped that in a future case, the Court of Appeal or House of Lords steers English law back away from this particular bog.[97]

Liability insurances

As far as the meaning of accident in a liability policy is concerned, it is convenient to examine separately cases on property damage and those on personal injury or death. Here a particular problem is that even an intended act by an insured will almost always be accidental from the point of view of the third party victim, but it is clear that this is irrelevant and indemnity will not be provided if what the insured did was not from his point of view an accident. However, in considering what is the degree of

---

[94] *Landress v. Phoenix Insurance Co.* 291 U.S. 491 (1933); see also, the Scottish case of *Clidero v. Scottish Accident Insurance Co.* (1892) 19 R. 355 supporting the distinction between means and results.

[95] [1996] 1 Lloyd's Rep. 632. See also the analysis of *Hamlyn* in *De Souza v. Home and Overseas Insurance Co. Ltd* [1995] L.R.L.R. 453 (1990).

[96] In *Landress v. Phoenix Insurance Co.*

[97] Other jurisdictions have generally done so: see, *e.g.* the Scottish Court of Session case of *Glenlight Shipping Ltd v. Excess Insurance Ltd* 1983 S.L.T. 241 (where the decision in *Clidero* (n.94, above) was ignored; see Davidson [1984] J.B.L. 391), the decision of the High Court of Australia in *Australian Casualty Co. Ltd v. Federico* (1986) 66 A.L.R. 99, the Canadian case of *Tracey-Gould v. Maritime Life Assurance Co.* (1992) 89 D.L.R. (4th) 726, and the decision of the New Zealand Court of Appeal in *Groves v. A.M.P. Fire & General Insurance Co. (N.Z.) Ltd* [1990] 1 N.Z.L.R. 122. The judgment of Hardie Boys J. in the last case, where recovery was given when the insured had died as a result of an unforeseeable consequence of the proper administration of anaesthetic prior to an operation, contains a very clear and relatively brief summary of the leading common law authorities on this question.

foresight necessary to prevent the insured from recovering, it appears that the courts have taken a stricter view in the case of injury to third parties than in the case of property damage.

Personal injury

The classic decision concerning personal injury is *Gray v. Barr*.[98] The insured's wife had been having an affair with the plaintiff's husband which the insured was led to believe had ended, which indeed may have been the case. However, on discovering one day that his wife was not at home, he suspected her to be with Gray and he set off for the latter's house with a loaded shotgun in order to frighten him. When he arrived there, he and Gray were involved in a struggle on the stairs as the result of which two shots were fired from the gun, the second one killing Gray. The insured was acquitted of murder and manslaughter, but was sued in tort by Mrs. Gray. He brought in his insurers as third parties, claiming that they were liable to indemnify him. The relevant liability aspect of his policy provided such an indemnity if the loss was "caused by accident." Tied up very much with the question of defining accident in the context were questions of causation and public policy which will be considered later, but it does appear that the majority of the Court of Appeal held that what happened was not an accident within the policy, on the ground that the death of Gray was a foreseeable consequence of Barr's intentional act of taking a loaded shotgun into the deceased's house.[99]

With great respect, it is submitted that the opinions of the trial judge[1] and Salmon L.J. to the contrary are to be preferred.[2] On the facts as found there was no intention to fire a shot nor to kill. Most people would surely regard what happened as an "accident" therefore, and to introduce questions as to prior acts is arguably to bring in that confusing distinction between means and results upon which we have already commented. It may still be the case that the result in *Gray v. Barr* was correct, but here we are only concerned with the meaning of the word "accident," not with the inevitable issues of causation and public policy which also arose in that case.

---

[98] [1971] 2 Q.B. 554.

[99] This was clearly the view of Phillimore L.J. Lord Denning M.R. seemed to base his decision more on the ground of causation, as to which see below, p. 232.

[1] [1970] 2 Q.B. 626; see also the comments in *Marcel Beller Ltd v. Hayden* [1978] Q.B. 694.

[2] Compare the Australian decision of *S. & Y. Investments (No. 2) Pty. Ltd v. Commercial Union Assurance Co. of Australia Ltd* (1986-87) 85 F.L.R. 285.

Property damage

So far as property damage is concerned, the Australian decision of *Robinson v. Evans*[3] is a good example of the use of what, it is suggested, is a sensible test, that the event must be unintended and unexpected from the point of view of the insured. Here the plaintiff sued the defendant company in tort for damages for the destruction of his crop of brussel sprouts. The plaintiff was a market gardener, the defendant owned a neighbouring brick works. The plaintiff's claim, which involved two separate incidents, was settled and the dispute concerned the defendant's claim to be indemnified by its public liability insurers, the terms of the policy providing such indemnity in respect of accidental damage only.[4] The court found that the damage to the plaintiff's crop was caused by the emission of fluoride. In respect of the first incident, the defendant's managing director knew about the danger. It was held that this claim was not for accidental damage. While it may have been unintended by the defendant, it could not be said to be wholly unexpected because of the managing director's knowledge. The test to be applied was whether an ordinary reasonable sensible man, in the position of the insured (or, in this case, its responsible officers), would or would not have expected the occurrence. The second incident in respect of which the plaintiff claimed arose after the defendant had built a much higher stack on its chimney which it was genuinely believed would cure the problem, but which did not. It was held that the defendant's insurers were liable to indemnify it in this respect. This damage was unintended and unexpected and hence accidental.

In contrast, the decision of the Canadian Supreme Court in *Canadian Indemnity Co. v. Walkem Machinery & Equipment Ltd*[5] is rather surprising.[6] W. Ltd was the agent and distributor for a company which manufactured a special type of crane. It negligently sold to a customer a crane which had been inadequately repaired and which was in a dangerous condition. This crane collapsed and W. Ltd was held liable to pay damages to a third party. Its comprehensive business liability policy, issued by the appellant insurer, indemnified it against liability to third parties arising from

---

[3] [1969] V.R. 885.

[4] The policy's actual wording was "damage caused by accidental means," but the court sensibly rejected the distinction between means and results.

[5] (1975) 52 D.L.R. (3d) 1.

[6] See Hasson (1976) 14 Osgoode Hall L.J. 669.

accident. It seems clear that W. Ltd took a calculated risk in selling the crane, so that the subsequent collapse could hardly be said to be quite unexpected, even if unintended, but the court held that the liability of W. Ltd arose from accident. It followed in particular some of the English workmen's compensation cases[7] in holding that accident means "any unlooked for mishap or occurrence," thus deciding that an unintended occurrence, however risky, was within the cover. The court laid great stress upon the fact that the policy was a comprehensive business liability policy and upon the fact that a narrower construction of accident would deny the insured recovery if an occurrence were the result of a calculated risk or of a dangerous operation. With great respect, this misses the point. Of course an insured can be covered against a calculated risk; a third party policy which indemnifies simply against legal liability to third parties, without any limitation by reference to accident, will cover all except deliberate risks. However, the inclusion of "caused by accident" must make a difference, especially it might be thought where the insured is a well advised businessman. It is suggested that this case would not and should not be followed here. It contrasts most strongly with the decision in *Gray v. Barr* which, it has already been suggested, goes to the other extreme.

Natural causes

An important point in this context concerns the relevance of natural causes to a third party policy insuring against liability caused by accident. As has been seen, in the context of personal accident policies, if the real cause of the loss is natural, it will not be covered, indeed it will usually be expressly excepted, and of course it is a general principle that insurance does not cover natural wear and tear. In *Mills v. Smith*,[8] a householder's liability policy indemnified the insured against liability for "damage to property caused by accident." The insured was held liable in damages to a neighbour for settlement damage to the neighbour's house caused by the root action of a tree in the insured's garden taking water from the soil on the neighbour's land. It was held that this was caused by accident. The learned judge was clearly disposed to give a wide meaning to these words in a householder's policy and the insured obviously did nothing which was intended or expected in any way. On the other hand, it could be argued

---

[7] *Fenton v. Thorley & Co. Ltd* [1903] A.C. 443 and *Clover, Clayton & Co. Ltd v. Hughes* [1910] A.C. 242.
[8] [1964] 1 Q.B. 30.

that the real cause of the insured's liability was entirely natural, namely the action of the tree roots, albeit there was an "accident" when the neighbour's foundations dropped. Paull J. regarded it as significant that the insurers had chosen to use the same words as used to appear in the Workmen's Compensation Acts and felt able to rely on leading decisions under those Acts with appropriate adjustments. That led him to the conclusion that there were two questions to be answered on the facts. The first was whether there had, at any moment in time, been some unexpected event leading to damage. Here the settlement was this event, being more than the natural movement of foundations. The second question involved determining the cause of this. His answer was that it was the action of the roots of the tree and that this meant that the insurers were liable.

With respect, this reasoning is difficult to follow. If the real cause of the loss was the action of the tree, that was surely natural and not "caused by accident." If the *causa proxima* rule means anything in this sort of case, a question to be discussed later in this chapter, the decision can hardly be supported on this ground. If it can be supported, it must be on the ground that the event must be looked at solely from the point of view of the insured, ignoring underlying "natural" factors. If, so far as he was concerned, the event was unexpected and unintended, then the loss was caused by accident. Perhaps underlying this is a rationale of providing broad support to the individual insured without too much regard to narrow principles of definition and causation.

Two further points can be made. The first is that changes in wording might make a difference to the result in a case like *Mills v. Smith*. If, for example, the policy had provided an indemnity in respect of damage "caused by an accident" or "caused by accidental means," it would have been more difficult to reach the same result.[9] Accident by itself is much more capable of a wide meaning than "an accident," and the use of "accidental means" according to the latest English authority requires that the entire causal history must be accidental.[10]

The second point concerns the relevance of workmen's compensation cases, which, as we have seen, have been relied on in some of the third

---

[9] See the judgment of Paull J. [1964] 1 Q.B. 30, 36.

[10] *Dhak v. Insurance Company of North America (U.K.) Ltd* [1996] 1 Lloyd's Rep. 632; see p. 214, above. On the other hand it has been argued above that the distinction between means and results should not be adopted and this was certainly the case in the property damage case of *Robinson v. Evans*, as we have seen.

party policy cases.[11] Clearly these cases may be useful when the wording of a policy is the same as that used in the Workmen's Compensation Acts, in other words "injury or damage caused by accident." But it is also true that workmen's compensation policies were construed more liberally than other insurance contracts because they were the system of first party insurance established for the benefit of employees before the days of state insurance under the social security system. For example, death or injury from natural phenomena has been held covered under a workmen's compensation policy, whereas it would not be so regarded under a personal accident policy. Workmen's compensation cases are therefore no more than useful and are certainly not binding in this context.[12]

Conclusions

The cases that have been reviewed here illustrate, if nothing else, that "accident" is a difficult concept to define accurately. The following tentative conclusions can perhaps be drawn. First, that the meaning of accident is wider in the context of personal accident cover than in third party cover. In the former, the event need be only either unexpected or unintended, provided that the insured does not expose himself to a deliberate risk. In the latter it should be both unexpected and unintended. However, the degree of foresight which is relevant to determining whether or not an event is unintended is not clearly established. *Gray v. Barr* suggests that not a great deal of foresight of an event is needed before it is so regarded as intended for these purposes, whereas *Robinson v. Evans* held that the insured as a reasonable man must have foreseen the event before he is denied indemnity. It may be that *Gray v. Barr* should be regarded as incorrect on this point and treated solely as an authority on causation and public policy. What is clear is that disputes over the meaning of accident will continue to be the subject of litigation.

Loss

The word "loss" appears frequently throughout this book and in policies of insurance, for obvious reasons. It is the risk of loss that is central to the

---

[11] Particularly *Mills v. Smith* [1964] 1 Q.B. 30 and in *Canadian Indemnity Co. v. Walkem Machinery & Equipment Ltd* (1975) 52 D.L.R. (3d) 1.

[12] See especially the comments in *De Souza v. Home and Overseas Insurance Co. Ltd* [1995] L.R.L.R. 453 (1990).

concept of insurance. In some contexts, "loss" appears merely as a part of a wider phrase, such as, for example, "loss by fire". In this sort of case, the meaning of loss itself is not important. Whether or not the insured can recover depends upon the meaning of fire and on whether his loss was caused by that insured peril. However, in other contexts, particularly perhaps in insurances of goods, "loss" is itself one of the forms of cover provided. A standard description is insurance against "loss, damage or destruction." The latter two words raise no problems of construction or definition, but the meaning of "loss" does, and it has exercised the courts on a number of occasions. A rather special case, which merits separate consideration, is loss by theft.

Constructive total loss

In marine insurance law, there is a doctrine of "constructive total loss" whereby, even if a ship or other property insured is not actually lost or cannot be proved to be so lost, the insured can by giving notice claim as for a total loss, the insurer thereafter becoming entitled to the ship or property if it should turn up.[13] This is because traditionally marine insurance has been regarded as insurance of the adventure as much as of the ship or other property insured. The same result can be achieved in non-marine insurance by agreement between insurer and insured, for example, an insurer might agree to pay in respect of a stolen car even if it cannot be shown to have been actually lost on the tests to be examined shortly, but it is well-established that there is no automatic doctrine of constructive total loss in non-marine insurance;[14] if necessary, the insured must prove an actual loss.

Missing goods

Obviously, if goods are actually destroyed, they are lost, but cover in this respect falls more naturally under the "destruction" part of the standard phrase quoted above. If goods are mislaid or are missing or have disappeared, then they become lost if after a reasonable time and a diligent but fruitless search, recovery of them is uncertain or unlikely. In *Holmes v. Payne*,[15] an insured necklace was mislaid and could not be found despite all

---

[13] See the Marine Insurance Act 1906, ss.60-63.
[14] *Moore v. Evans* [1918] A.C. 185.
[15] (1930) 37 Ll.L.R. 41.

the insured's efforts. The insurers agreed to replace it. Some months later the necklace was found in the insured's cloak, having probably fallen into the lining. It was held that it had been truly lost. The insurers were therefore bound by the replacement agreement, although, of course, the insured was not entitled to keep the necklace as well as the replacement jewellery. Indeed, she had, before the action brought by the insurers, offered it to them as salvage.

Irrecoverable goods

A rather different situation is where the insured knows where his property is, but he is unable to recover it. If it remains his property and is safely in the hands of parties who are bailees of it for him, then it is not lost even if physically he is temporarily deprived of possession. In *Moore v. Evans*,[16] just before the First World War, the insured jewellers sent a quantity of pearls to trade customers in Frankfurt and Brussels on sale or return. When war broke out, the Germans occupied Brussels. Thus for some four years, both sets of pearls were irrecoverable. However, the available evidence showed that they were being safely kept for the insured and had not been seized or interfered with by the German authorities. The House of Lords held that the goods were therefore not lost.

If, however, the insured property has been interfered with or taken by someone without authority, then it may well be lost even if in theory the insured might have a legal remedy which would entitle him to reclaim the property. The test would seem to be whether, after all reasonable steps have been taken, recovery is uncertain. In *London & Provincial Leather Processes Ltd v. Hudson*,[17] skins bought by the plaintiff company were as usual shipped from the seller directly to a German firm which was accustomed to process them for the plaintiff before sending them to the United Kingdom. The German firm entrusted some of the skins to a sub-agent who retained them in purported exercise of a lien for money owed to them by the firm. The firm then went bankrupt, whereupon the equivalent of its trustee in bankruptcy sold more of the skins for the benefit of the estate. It was held that the insurers of the skins were liable for both losses, even though in theory the plaintiffs might have had remedies in respect of them in the German courts. The policy here was an all risks policy, but that would appear to make no difference in principle.

---

[16] [1918] A.C. 185.
[17] [1939] 2 K.B. 724.

In *Webster v. General Accident Fire and Life Assurance Corporation Ltd*,[18] the plaintiff's car was stolen and passed through the hands of a number of people before it reached a purchaser who probably, but not necessarily, received good title to it under the provisions of the Factors Acts.[19] On discovering his loss, the plaintiff had taken all reasonable steps to recover the car by contacting the police and the motoring organisations. It was held that the car was lost within the meaning of the plaintiff's insurance policy.

Loss of proceeds

Finally, it must be the insured property itself that is lost and not, for example, a sum of money received for it. If, then, the insured voluntarily hands over his property to another, intending to part with ownership, he cannot claim to have suffered a loss of it if the cheque which he receives in return for it subsequently bounces. What has been lost is the proceeds of sale, not the property.[20] This contrasts neatly with the facts of the *Webster* case to which we have already referred. There, the circumstances were that the plaintiff entrusted his car to an auctioneer, when bidding for it had not reached the reserve price, upon the latter's saying that he had a private buyer. This statement was a lie, and the auctioneer intended at the time to deprive the plaintiff of the car. He subsequently sent several cheques which were dishonoured. Here there was a loss of the car because, apart from the point already mentioned, the plaintiff did not voluntarily part with property in the car. The auctioneer's dealings amounted to conversion and theft of the car.

Loss by theft

Rather than simply insuring goods against loss (as well as damage or destruction), it seems that modern policies on goods sometimes specify the risk more precisely, in particular by describing one of the particular relevant perils as "loss by theft". One issue here is whether there must

[18] [1953] 1 Q.B. 520.

[19] The point was not decided. It was held that the plaintiff did not have to sue to find out, having taken legal advice to the effect that he would probably not succeed, and thus having acted reasonably.

[20] *Eisinger v. General Accident Fire and Life Assurance Corp. Ltd* [1953] 2 All E.R. 897. Compare the decision in *Dobson v. General Accident Fire & Life Assurance Corp. plc* [1990] 1 Q.B. 274, discussed below.

therefore be a loss of the property in the sense just considered as well as a loss by theft, the latter clearly bearing its technical criminal law meaning in accordance with the principle described earlier.[21] The decision in *Dobson* v. *General Accident Fire & Life Assurance Corporation plc*[22] raised these points and gave what could be regarded as somewhat controversial answers. It was another case of an insured being induced to part with property by a rogue. The plaintiff had advertised a watch and diamond ring for sale and parted with them in return for what proved to be a worthless forged building society cheque. The Court of Appeal held that he could recover the value of the goods under his household insurance policy, their having been lost by theft.

It could be argued that there are difficulties with this decision. The reasoning of the Court of Appeal was concerned almost exclusively with whether there had been a theft in the criminal law sense, a matter which has caused some degree of difficulty since the enactment of the Theft Act 1968. In so deciding, the court followed the House of Lords' decision in *Lawrence*[23] rather than interpretations of the later decision of the same court in *Morris*,[24] and held that there had been a theft because the insured had merely consented to the rogue having his property, rather than giving an express authorisation by his parting with the property. While it is not within the province of this book to give an authoritative view of the criminal law distinction between theft and obtaining property by deception, it has been argued that the Court of Appeal's decision confuses or even obliterates this distinction in an unnecessary way.[25] However, the House of Lords has, in the criminal law case of *Gomez*,[26] approved the decision in *Dobson* and confirmed the decision in *Lawrence*. The matter must now therefore be regarded as settled in criminal law terms.

However, it seems difficult to reconcile *Dobson* with the earlier insurance cases just examined, at least if the presence of the word "loss" is meaningful. The facts are in reality indistinguishable from those in *Eisinger*.[27] Was there really a loss of the property, as opposed to a loss of the proceeds? It seems unlikely that the insurers intended the risk of being

---

[21] See p. 204.

[22] [1990] 1 Q.B. 274.

[23] [1972] A.C. 626.

[24] [1984] A.C. 320.

[25] See Smith and Hogan's *Criminal Law*, (7th ed.), especially at pp. 509–510; Clarkson (1992) 55 M.L.R. 265.

[26] [1993] 1 All E.R. 1.

[27] [1953] 2 All E.R. 897.

duped by a rogue to be covered by the wording they adopted. Perhaps the answer to this latter point is that the presence of the word "loss" here is of no significance and that the matter is to be determined solely by what is the proper meaning of theft; as we have seen, that is now abundantly clear. This suggestion is not, however, put forward with any degree of conviction, but if insurers do not wish to cover the risk of their insured being duped by a rogue, to be safe they will have to draft their policies accordingly.

Cover Provided — Consequential Points

Having considered the principal rules of construction applicable to determining the cover provided by an insurance policy, and examined some of the common wordings used, it is convenient to look now at three points which are nothing directly to do with these questions, but which follow neatly from them. The first point concerns the timing of the insured peril, the second the question of consequential losses, and the third the question of whether an insured peril must actually operate upon property insured and costs incurred in preventing an insured peril running.

Timing of the insured peril

We have seen earlier[28] that indemnity insurance policies are conventionally of a limited duration, typically for one year at a time.[29] It may often happen, particularly in the context of claims under insurances of land and buildings for loss arising from such matters as subsidence and heave, that the damage caused by a particular event may not evidence itself for some considerable time. It seems self-evident that, in the absence of express provision to the contrary, the insured cannot claim unless he can show that an insured peril occurred during the term of the policy — this was confirmed in *Kelly* v. *Norwich Union Fire Insurance Society Ltd*.[30] Here, leaks from water mains caused the clay under the plaintiff's property to expand and after a period this "heave" caused damage to the property. The

---

[28] See p. 86, above.
[29] In contrast life policies are usually entire and the problem dealt with here will not arise in connection therein.
[30] [1989] 2 Lloyd's Rep. 333; see [1990] J.B.L. 145.

crucial leak[31] occurred before the plaintiff effected the insurance with the defendant which provided that the latter would indemnify the insured "in respect of events occurring during the period of the insurance". The Court of Appeal held that the insurers were not liable. The most likely situation where in practice this principle will not apply is in the context of professional indemnity insurance, where the standard wording generally provides for retrospective cover.[32]

Consequential losses

Insurance of property prima facie covers that property only in respect of the loss attributable to its own value. How that value is measured will be considered in Chapter 13. In other words, consequential losses are not recoverable unless they are separately insured. So, for example, in *Maurice* v. *Goldsborough Mort*,[33] where consignees of wool insured it as trustees for the owners, so that they were liable to account to them for the insurance money received following a loss, they could not recover in respect of their loss of commission. Similarly, in the old case of *Re Wright and Pole*,[34] an insured inn was destroyed by fire, but the insured was unable to recover in respect of the loss of custom and the hire of other premises, and in *Theobald v. Railway Passengers Assurance Co.*,[35] loss of business profits were not recoverable under an accident policy.

It is possible to effect insurance against loss of profits arising as the result of loss of property, and such cover, now known commonly as Interruption Insurance, is popular with businesses.

Must the risk run? Prevention costs

The question that arises here is perhaps partly a matter of cover provided and partly a matter of causation. Traditionally, it is considered

---

[31] There was a subsequent leak which occurred after the plaintiff had taken out the insurance with the defendant, but he accepted that it was impossible to apportion blame between the two leaks and that, unless it was shown that the first leak was within the policy, he could not succeed in his claim. Perhaps there should be some mechanism for apportionment in such cases, as claims in respect of events like subsidence and heave are likely to involve events occurring over a substantial period of time.

[32] That is, in respect of claims made against the insured during the policy period, whether or not the negligence occurred earlier.

[33] [1939] A.C. 452.

[34] (1834) 1 A. & E. 621.

[35] (1854) 10 Exch. 45.

under the latter heading, but it is suggested that it is better examined on
its own.

The problem simply stated can be put in the following way. If property
is insured against a specific loss, can the insured recover if that loss does
not actually operate upon the insured property, but it is lost or damaged in
circumstances when the insured peril was imminent? Furthermore, if there
is no loss, but only because the insured incurs expenditure in preventing
what would have been a certain loss, can the insured recover this
expenditure? We shall deal with these questions separately.

Insured peril imminent

As regards the first, there is clear authority in marine insurance cases
that if the peril insured against has happened, and is so imminent that it is
about to operate upon the insured property, loss to the property caused by
measures necessarily taken to avert the risk happening to the insured
property is covered. It can be said that the proximate or real cause of the
loss is a peril insured against. In *Symington v. Union Insurance of Canton*,[36]
cork insured against loss by fire and stored on a jetty was jettisoned by
being thrown into the sea to prevent an existing fire from spreading. It
was held that the loss was covered, the real cause of it being the fire, an
insured peril. It was stated clearly that the peril must have happened and
be so imminent that the action was immediately necessary to avert the
danger. Although there appear to have been very few non-marine cases on
the point,[37] there is no reason to doubt that the same principle would
apply, so that if, for example, house contents are insured against fire and
are damaged by water to prevent an existing fire spreading, such damage
would be covered even if water damage was not covered or was an
excepted peril.

Costs of prevention

The answer to the second question is more problematical, there being a
clear distinction in that property insured is not actually damaged in any
way. Suppose, for example, the case of a house by a river insured against
damage by flood. Following heavy storms, the level of the river is rising
and it is as certain as it can be that unless measures are taken, the house

---

[36] (1928) 97 L.J.K.B. 646.
[37] One such is *Glen Falls Insurance v. Spencer* (1956) 3 D.L.R. (2d.) 745.

will be flooded. The insured incurs expenditure in buying equipment which successfully prevents such a flood. Can he recover such costs from his insurer? It might be regarded as a little strange if he could not, if he could prove that had he done nothing, the house would have been damaged by an insured peril and the insurer would have been liable. In marine insurance, a "sue and labour" clause would permit recovery,[38] and by analogy the same principle was applied to the case of a charter party involving marine risks: "sums paid to avert a peril may be recovered as upon a loss by that peril."[39] But in the absence of an express clause, it is not clear whether prevention costs are recoverable in marine insurance.

In *The Knight of St Michael*,[40] a cargo of coal from Newcastle, Australia, to Valparaiso was insured against loss by fire under a marine policy. Because of the overheating of part of the coal, some was discharged in Sydney. This was clearly necessary to prevent its spontaneous combustion. It was held that the consequent loss of freight was within the policy, and it was suggested that it was a "loss by fire," as there was an "actual existing state of peril of fire and not merely a fear of fire," although there was no actual fire. The problem with regarding this decision as clear authority is that there were also general words of cover in the policy covering "other losses" and the learned judge stated the opinion that if the loss was not by fire, it was within the other cover provided. In the United States of America there is clear authority that prevention costs can be recovered under a non-marine policy even in the absence of express coverage.[41] It is thought that this principle could usefully be followed here, and that such costs should be recoverable provided that there is an actual existing state of the peril insured, in other words that loss by a peril insured against is certain; mere danger of such loss would clearly not be sufficient.[42]

---

[38] See, generally, Ivamy, *Marine Insurance*, Chap. 39; *Integrated Container Service Inc. v. British Traders Insurance Co. Ltd* [1984] 1 Lloyd's Rep. 154.

[39] *Pyman Steamship Co. v. Admiralty Commissioners* [1919] 1 K.B. 49 at 53.

[40] [1898] P. 30.

[41] *Leebov v. United States Fidelity & Guaranty Co.* 401 Pa. 477 (1960) (Pennsylvania Supreme Court). A contractor caused a landslide, but, before it could do much damage, incurred expense in preventing it from causing certain further damage. It was held that his liability insurer was liable in respect of this expense. See further, Note (1971) 71 Col.L.R. 1309.

[42] *Becker, Gray & Co. v. London Assurance Corp.* [1918] A.C. 101.

However, in a recent liability insurance case,[43] the Court of Appeal refused to imply a term which would have permitted the insured to recover such prevention costs,[44] and it must be admitted that this approach seems likely to prevail in English law.

Causation

As has been noted several times in the course of this chapter, it is not sufficient in order that an insured should recover for a loss, that the loss falls within the cover provided as a matter of construction or definition. He must also show that the loss was proximately caused by an insured peril.[45] The proximate cause does not, however, mean the last cause, but the effective, dominant or real cause.[46] Working out what is the proximate cause in any situation is strictly a question of fact, so that decided cases cannot be binding but are merely illustrations. It should be noted that the doctrine can be excluded by appropriate wording.[47]

It has already been seen how the doctrine can operate to find an insurer liable where the insured peril is the real cause but not the actual instrument of the loss.[48] Otherwise it seems most relevant, and indeed it has been said to be relevant only really at all, in a case where, on the facts, there can genuinely be said to be competing causes of a loss, one of which is specifically covered by the policy and the other of which is expressly

---

[43] *Yorkshire Water Services Ltd v. Sun Alliance & London Insurance plc*, [1997] C.L.C. 213. See also *Corbin v. Payne, The Times*, October 11, 1990 and *Liverpool & London & Globe Insurance Ltd v. Canadian General Electric Co. Ltd* (1981) 123 D.L.R. (3d.) 513, where the Supreme Court of Canada refused to permit the recovery of prevention costs where the insured risk had not actually begun to operate. It should also be noted that, if prevention costs were claimed under a fire policy, and it was a loss by fire that had been prevented, there is the old authority of *Austin v. Drewe* (see p. 210, above), requiring that there must be actual ignition, which would have to be distinguished.

[44] One reason was that the policy contained a express term requiring the insured to take reasonable care and this made it clear that any prevention costs were to be at the insured's expense, but in addition the Court of Appeal seems to have ruled out the possibility of implying the equivalent of a sue and labour clause.

[45] For a useful review, see Clarke [1981] C.L.J. 284.

[46] The classical explanation of the doctrine of proximate cause is the judgment of Lord Sumner in *Becker, Gray & Co. v. London Assurance Corporation* [1918] A.C. 101.

[47] For an example in a household policy, see *Oei v. Foster* [1982] 2 Lloyd's Rep. 170; see [1982] J.B.L. 516.

[48] *Symington v. Union Insurance of Canton* (1928) 97 L.J.K.B. 646; see p. 226, above.

excepted.[49] Whether the doctrine can be at all relevant where there can be no question of an excepted peril is a matter to be considered later.

Determining the proximate cause

It has been said that determining the proximate cause of a loss is simply the application of common sense, and in many of the cases that would appear to be so. In *Marsden v. City & County Insurance*,[50] for example, a shopkeeper insured his plate-glass against loss or damage arising from any cause except fire. Fire broke out in a neighbour's property, as the result of which a mob gathered. The mob then rioted and broke the plate-glass. It was held that this riot, not the fire, was the cause of the loss and thus the insured recovered. In effect, the fire merely facilitated the subsequent loss rather than caused it. In *Winicofsky v. Army & Navy Insurance*,[51] goods were stolen from a building during an air raid. It was held that the theft not the air raid was the real cause of the loss; the latter merely facilitated it.

Two real causes

If it truly can be said that there are two real causes of a loss, discovering the cause which is the proximate cause is not always an easy matter. In a leading marine insurance case, *Leyland Shipping Co. v. Norwich Union Fire Insurance Society Ltd*,[52] a ship was insured against loss from perils of the sea, with an exception in respect of loss due to hostilities. The ship was torpedoed by an enemy boat during the First World War. It was towed to Le Havre and moored in the harbour where it was quite safe. Subsequently, the authorities there required that it be moved to just outside the harbour. There, because of the action of the sea, it sank. It was held that the loss was not covered, the real cause being the torpedoing and not the perils of the sea. Yet had the ship not been moved outside the harbour, it

---

[49] Lord Dunedin in *Leyland Shipping Co. v. Norwich Union Fire Insurance Society* [1918] A.C. 350 at 363. This point is supported by *J. J. Lloyd (Instruments) Ltd v. Northern Star Insurance Co. Ltd* [1987] 1 Lloyd's Rep. 32, where there were found to be two proximate causes of the damage suffered by a cruiser; adverse weather conditions and defective design. It was held that, as defective design was not an excepted peril and adverse weather was not required to be the sole cause, the insurers were liable.

[50] (1865) L.R. 1 C.P. 232.

[51] (1919) 88 L.J.K.B. 111.

[52] [1918] A.C. 350.

would have been all right. The point is that the original cause predominates and is regarded as the real cause of the loss unless it was merely facilitating a subsequent cause which totally changed matters.

This analysis, however, does not appear to fit very well with some of what have been called the accident cases. There has been a great number of cases on questions of causation in accident policies, two of which will suffice here for detailed illustration. In *Winspear v. Accident Insurance Association*,[53] the policy covered death or injury "caused by accidental, external and visible means" and excluded "any injury caused by or arising from natural disease . . ." While crossing a stream, the insured suffered a fit, fell in and was drowned. It was held that the cause of death was accidental, namely the drowning, and not the fit, even though had it not been for the latter the insured would not have died as the stream was very shallow. *Lawrence v. Accidental Insurance Co.*[54] is even stranger in that the policy, while including the same wording, also required that accidental injury be the "direct and sole cause" of death. There the insured suffered a fit while standing on a railway platform. This caused him to fall on to the track, whereupon he was run over by a train. It was held that the accident of being run over was the proximate cause of death.

Decisions like these can be interpreted in different ways. For example, it might be said that the natural cause, the fit, merely facilitated the real, accidental cause, but if that is so, surely it could be said of the *Leyland Shipping* case that the torpedoing merely facilitated the sinking by the perils of the sea. Alternatively, the judges[55] may have been interpreting "proximate" as meaning latest, which subsequent cases[56] revealed clearly to be wrong. A further possibility is that the cases can be justified on the ground that the accident superseded the prior, excluded, cause, to such an extent that it constituted a totally fresh cause,[57] but, with respect, this is difficult to understand on the facts. Perhaps the best explanation is the generosity of the English judges who decided these cases. Needless to say,

---

[53] (1880) 6 Q.B.D. 42.

[54] (1881) 7 Q.B.D. 216.

[55] See, especially, Watkin Williams J. in *Lawrence v. Accidental Insurance Co.*, above, at 221.

[56] Especially the leading House of Lords cases of *Becker, Grey & Co. v. London Assurance Corporation* [1918] A.C. 101 and *Leyland Shipping Co. v. Norwich Union Fire Insurance Society* [1918] A.C. 350. See also *Wayne Tank Co.* v. *Employer's Liability Assurance Corporation* [1974] 1 Q.B. 57 at 66 (Lord Denning M.R.) and 72 (Roskill L.J.).

[57] See the explanation in *Jason v. Batten* [1969] 1 Lloyd's Rep. 281 at 291.

insurers have been astute to draft changes in wordings so as to attempt to gain a more favourable result in this sort of case, and in what appears to be the latest reported accident case where the point arose for decision, they succeeded.

In *Jason v. Batten*,[58] the policy provided benefits to the insured if he sustained "in any accident bodily injury resulting in and being — independently of all other causes — the exclusive, direct and immediate cause of the injury or disablement." There was an exception in respect of "death, injury or disablement directly or indirectly caused by or arising or resulting from or traceable to . . . any physical defect or infirmity which existed prior to an accident." The insured suffered a coronary thrombosis after being involved in a motor accident, the clot blocking a coronary artery which had been narrowed by disease existing before the accident. It was held that the insurers were not liable. Stress associated with the accident had precipitated the thrombosis, but, assuming that the clot was an injury sustained in the accident, it was not "independently of all other causes" the exclusive cause of the insured's disablement. Equally efficient was the pre-existing disease. In addition, it was said, the loss fell clearly within the exception. It would appear therefore, that with the phrase "independently of all other causes" insurers should ensure that they are liable under their personal accident policies only when there is an accident and nothing else.[59] However, it is important to remember, as was stressed earlier, that each case ultimately turns on its own facts.

Two proximate causes

It may be that in a case without such a clause qualifying the *causa proxima* rule, the court cannot genuinely say that one cause is more effective than another, so that an excepted cause and a covered cause are equally strong. This was a possible view of the facts in *Wayne Tank and Pump Co. Ltd v. Employers' Liability Insurance Corporation Ltd.*[60] The plaintiff company was held liable to pay damages to Harbutt's "Plasticine" Ltd for breach of a contract under which they installed new equipment in

---

[58] [1969] 1 Lloyd's Rep. 281.
[59] For other attempts and a full discussion, see *MacGillivray*, Chap. 25.
[60] [1974] 1 Q.B. 57.

Harbutt's factory.[61] The equipment was defective and a resultant fire gutted the factory. Wayne Tank were insured by the defendants under a public liability policy which excluded indemnity for liability arising from damage caused by the nature or condition of any goods supplied by the insured. One cause of the plaintiff's liability was the defective nature of the equipment used, but another cause was the fact that one of its employees negligently and quite without authority turned on the equipment and left it on all night. Had this not happened, it was likely that the loss would not have occurred, as the equipment would have been tested under supervision and found to have been defective before any damage could be done.

However, the Court of Appeal was unanimous in holding that the real cause of the loss was the defective nature of the equipment, a conclusion clearly in accordance with authority such as the *Leyland Shipping* case, whereby the original cause predominates unless it merely facilitates the subsequent cause and the latter totally alters the situation. The Court commented *obiter*, though, on the result if it could not genuinely be said that one of the two causes was predominant, and held that the insurers would still be protected, on the ground that they had provided for exemption from liability for one of the causes and the only way to ensure this was to exempt them totally. It is perhaps unfortunate that they did not consider the possibility in such a case of apportionment of the loss.[62]

Cause not expressly exempted

One final point remains to be discussed. As was seen earlier, it was stated in one of the leading cases that the question of competition between causes becomes relevant only when there are two causes and one of them is expressly covered and the other is expressly exempted. In the case of *Gray v. Barr*,[63] however, to which we have already referred,[64] Lord Denning M.R. introduced the causation point where there was no express exclusion of a possible cause of the loss. In his view the proximate cause of the

---

[61] *Harbutt's "Plasticine" Ltd v. Wayne Tank and Pump Co. Ltd* [1970] 1 Q.B. 447. Had this case been decided correctly (see *Photo Production Ltd v. Securicor Transport Ltd* [1980] 2 W.L.R. 283), the subsequent insurance case would not have arisen. Harbutt's insurers rather than one of Wayne Tank's insurers would have borne the loss. It is clear that the insurance case was in substance a battle between two of the latter's insurers.

[62] See Ahmed (1974) 124 N.L.J. 592.

[63] [1971] 2 Q.B. 551.

[64] See p. 215.

liability of the defendant Barr was not the shooting of the gun, whether that was an accident or not, but his deliberate conduct in approaching and grappling with the deceased while holding a loaded shotgun. Although neither of the other judges mentioned the causation point, and thus it cannot form part of the ratio of the case, consideration of it is logical. It seems unlikely though, that it will matter in practice if it is considered.[65] In a case like *Gray v. Barr*, the same result can be, and indeed was, reached simply on the construction of "accident" and/or the application of principles of public policy. This would seem likely to be the position in most cases, that is, that the same result can be achieved by considering whether the loss came within the cover provided as a matter of construction or definition.

There is one type of case, though, where consideration of the causation rule, even though there is no question of an expressly excepted peril, might make a difference. This is where a possible cause of the loss is natural, whether from wear and tear or from the natural actions of living objects. An example, as pointed out earlier, is *Mills v. Smith*.[66] The learned judge in that case considered the matter as simply one of construction of the words "caused by accident," but if his attention had been directed towards the discovery of the proximate cause of the loss, the result might have been different.

[65] Compare the case of *J. J. Lloyd (Instruments) Ltd v. Northern Star Insurance Co. Ltd* [1987] 1 Lloyd's Rep. 32, described in n.49, above.
[66] [1964] 1 Q.B. 30; see p. 217.

CHAPTER 12

CLAIMS UNDER THE POLICY

Claiming for a loss under an insurance policy may be considered to involve not simply the formal requirements usually imposed upon the insured, but also the question of the possible application of the rules of public policy and the law regarding the making of fraudulent claims. It is convenient also to examine some of the issues which may arise when claims are settled.

Public Policy

In a famous dictum,[1] a judge once referred to public policy as an "unruly horse," and it is clear that in the insurance field as much as in any other, care is needed in assessing the relevance of public policy considerations.[2] There seem to be two relevant basic maxims which apply throughout the law, first, *ex turpi causa non oritur actio* (no action can arise from a wrongful cause) and secondly, a man may not profit from his own wrong or crime, the latter being probably merely a particular application of the former.[3] The very application of these maxims to claims on insurance policies may be questioned in some instances, but, even assuming that it is

---

[1] Burrough J. in *Richardson v. Mellish* (1824) 2 Bing. 229 at 252.
[2] In so far as the application of public policy in any of the insurance cases rests on the "public conscience", it may perhaps have to be reconsidered in the light of *Tinsley v. Milligan* [1994] 1 A.C. 340. However, it is thought that the views of the House of Lords in *Tinsley v. Milligan* should affect only cases where a contract is unlawful from its inception. What we are concerned with here is simply where performance of a contract may be denied on public policy grounds. See generally, Clarke, "Illegal insurance" [1987] L.M.C.L.Q. 201 and Clarke, "Insurance of wilful misconduct; the court as keeper of the public conscience" (1996) 7 Insurance Law Journal 173.
[3] For a useful brief summary in an insurance case, see the judgment of Kerr L.J. in *Euro-Diam Ltd v. Bathurst* [1988] 2 All E.R. 23 at 28–30. Although aspects of this judgments were commented on adversely in *Tinsley v. Milligan*, above, it is thought that this ignored the different situation in insurance cases; see n.2.

sensible to apply them, how they actually apply is not always clear. It is convenient to subdivide the insurance cases into two basic groups, namely first and third party insurance.

First party insurances

If an insured is claiming in respect of a loss suffered solely by him, then it is clear, as we have already seen,[4] that he cannot recover if the loss was caused by his deliberate act. This may be simply the true construction of an insurance contract,[5] or it may alternatively be regarded as the application of a principle of public policy.[6] In *W. H. Smith v. Clinton*,[7] an indemnity granted by a publisher against libel was held to be unenforceable, at least where the libel was intentional. In addition, there is a general principle flowing from the maxims mentioned, that an insured cannot recover in respect of a loss caused by his own criminal or tortious act. This was neatly applied in the case of *Geismar v. Sun Alliance and London Insurance*.[8] Here the plaintiff smuggled into this country certain items of jewellery without declaring them and paying the legally required excise duty on them. As a result, they were liable to be forfeited. They were among items subsequently insured by him with the defendant and later stolen. It was held that the plaintiff could not recover in respect of this jewellery, as to allow such recovery would enable him to profit from his deliberate criminal act, even though the profit was sought indirectly under the insurance policy. In contrast, the *ex turpi causa* rule did not prevent recovery in *Euro-Diam Ltd v. Bathurst*,[9] where diamonds sent by the insured on sale or return to a customer in Germany were stolen from the latter's warehouse. At the latter's request, the insured had supplied an invoice understating the price of the diamonds. This was to enable the customer to deceive the German tax authorities. Even though the insured probably knew this, they were not precluded from recovering on their policy since

---

[4] See p. 200, above.

[5] *Beresford v. Royal Insurance Co.* [1938] A.C. 586.

[6] Shand, "Unblinkering the unruly horse: public policy in the law of contract" (1972) 30 C.L.J. 144 at 161.

[7] (1908) 99 L.T. 840. See also Defamation Act 1952, s.11 confirming that indemnity or insurance against unintentional defamation is enforceable.

[8] [1977] 2 Lloyd's Rep. 62.

[9] [1988] 2 All E.R. 23.

they were not relying on any illegality and the only person who stood to benefit from it was the customer.[10]

Public policy will debar someone who has murdered a life insured from claiming the proceeds of the policy as beneficiary under the life insured's will,[11] on the latter's intestacy or as co-insured or nominee under the policy.[12]

It would seem that the commission of a crime or tort must be deliberate. It has often been recognised that insane suicide, when a crime, did not prevent recovery under a life policy.[13] So, for example, an insured might unintentionally commit a crime of strict liability in circumstances giving rise to a claim on his policy, but it is suggested that he would not be debarred from recovery. A nice question arises concerning the inter-relationship of the two principles mentioned. The rule that deliberate acts *per se* are not covered can, because it is not an overriding requirement of public policy, be expressly excluded. The usual example is the inclusion of suicide, sane or insane, in the cover provided by a life policy, although normally only after the policy has run for a period of one or two years. If the commission of such an act, however, is also criminal or tortious, the question arises whether the maxims of public policy debar recovery. The answer would appear to be in the affirmative, following the leading case of *Beresford v. Royal Insurance Co.*[14] Here the life insured deliberately took his own life at a time when suicide was still a crime. It was arguable, and indeed was held, that on the construction of the policy death by suicide was covered, but the House of Lords nevertheless denied the insured's

---

[10] As mentioned in n.3, above, some of the reasoning in this case attracted unfavourable comment in the House of Lords decision in *Tinsley v. Milligan* [1994] 1 A.C. 340. The latter decision would seem to suggest that if the insured stands to profit from his own illegal act that is an end to it; there is no question of then considering whether or not recovery would offend the "public cons-cience", as was reasoned in *Euro-Diam Ltd v. Bathurst*. It is suggested that the public conscience test is still useful in insurance cases, for the reason given in n.2. In any event, the decision in *Euro-Diam Ltd v. Bathurst* must still be good since, as indicated in the text, there was no question of the insured benefiting from their illegal act.

[11] *Cleaver v. Mutual Reserve Fund Life Association* [1892] 1 Q.B. 147.

[12] See, *e.g. Davitt v. Titcumb* [1989] 3 All E.R. 417, where the defendant, who had murdered his partner, had no claim to a share of the proceeds of the endowment policy effected by them jointly to cover their mortgage.

[13] *Beresford v. Royal Insurance Co.* [1938] A.C. 586.

[14] Above. For a more recent example, see *Husak v. Imperial Life Assurance. Co. of Canada* (1970) 9 D.L.R. (3d.) 602.

representative recovery. The principal ground for the decision was that recovery would permit a benefit to result to the insured from his criminal act,[15] although it was recognised that an assignee for value of the policy would have been entitled to recover, because then there could not be said to be such benefit. However, there must be a public policy in favour of enforcing contractual obligations which one party has freely undertaken. If the insurer had contracted to pay on the suicide of the life insured, why should they not have been held to that promise? This point was discussed by Lord MacMillan who concluded that the public policy considerations had to be weighed, finally concurring with the result in this way: "I feel the force of the view that to increase the estate which a criminal leaves behind him is to benefit him . . . And no criminal can be allowed to benefit in any way by his crime."[16] It may be thought that this is slightly unreal, a point to which we shall return when assessing the public policy question in general. There can be little doubt now that the actual result of the *Beresford* case would be different, not least because suicide is no longer a crime.[17]

Further, in respect of life assurance, account must now be taken of the provisions of the Forfeiture Act 1982.[18] Section 2 of this Act gives the court a wide discretion to allow a claim by someone who has unlawfully killed another to the benefits of, *inter alia*, a life insurance policy. It cannot apply where the claimant is guilty of murder[19] nor does it apply to cases of suicide,[20] but it would be apt to cover a case of manslaughter where there was no intention or recklessness.[21]

Third party insurances

Turning to consider the cases involving third party policies, the same general principles apply.[22] Thus, the intentional commission of a crime against the third party for which the insured is liable in damages in tort

[15] As will be seen, Lord Atkin referred also to other public policy principles.
[16] [1938] A.C. 586 at 605.
[17] Suicide Act 1961; see the comment of Salmon L.J. in *Gray v. Barr* [1971] 2 Q.B. 554 at 582.
[18] See generally, Kenny, (1983) 46 M.L.R. 66.
[19] s.5.
[20] Because it only applies where the beneficiary has killed "another" (s.1).
[21] See *Re S. (deceased)* [1996] 1 W.L.R. 235.
[22] The Forfeiture Act is of no relevance here because of the requirement in s.2(4) that the claimant has an "interest in property."

will not be covered by the insured's liability insurance. However, it is not clear what degree of deliberation is required, and it can be said again that there are competing public policy considerations involved.[23] In a sense, the idea of the insured benefiting from his own wrong in this sort of case is ridiculous, as any indemnity received goes to his third party victim. Furthermore, there is surely an important public policy consideration in attempting to ensure that the victims of tortfeasors receive any damages awarded to them, which in practice means in the majority of cases that the tortfeasor ought to be allowed to enforce his insurance policy.[24] This has at least been recognised in the context of compulsory motor vehicle insurance, and there are four important cases which support this line of argument. These cases will be examined first, before it is sought to be discovered whether there are any differences in any other contexts.

Motor insurance

Tinline v. White Cross Insurance Association[25] and *James v. British General Insurance Co.*[26] arose out of similar situations. The insured in both cases had third party cover in respect of injury or death arising out of the use of their cars, although this was not actually compulsory at the time. They were both involved in accidents resulting in the deaths of pedestrians in circumstances which led to their convictions for manslaughter. In *Tinline*, the insured was driving at an excessive speed; in *James*, he was drunk. Clearly both insureds were more than merely negligent, but on the other hand did not intend death or injury. In both cases it was held that their insurers were liable to indemnify them against the damages they were liable to pay in tort, despite the fact that, in the sense that the courts have used elsewhere, they would thereby profit from their own criminal actions.

If the insured acts deliberately, however, it appears that public policy is still against his recovering. This was made clear in the judgments in *Hardy v. Motor Insurers' Bureau*.[27] This case involved the deliberate injury of the plaintiff by an uninsured car thief. The plaintiff's claim against the

---

[23] See generally the excellent analysis by Shand in the article referred to in n.6.

[24] Public policy will not prevent a liability insured from being indemnified against liability to pay exemplary damages, at least where the insured did not act criminally: *Lancashire County Council v. Municipal Mutual Insurance Ltd* [1996] 3 All E.R. 545.

[25] [1921] 3 K.B. 327.

[26] [1927] 1 K.B. 311.

[27] [1964] 2 Q.B. 745.

defendant was resisted on public policy grounds. The Court of Appeal made it quite clear that, had the tortfeasor himself been seeking to enforce a motor policy, he would have been denied, but fortunately the Road Traffic Act 1988[28] permits a third party victim to sue the tortfeasor's insurer directly and, where the tortfeasor is uninsured, there is a right of action against the Motor Insurers' Bureau.[29] Thus, on the facts of the case, there was no question of the *ex turpi* maxim applying, and this will be the case in respect of all victims of car accidents. In what is perhaps the most lucid rationalisation by an English judge[30] of the place of public policy in the insurance context, Diplock L.J. referred to the importance of weighing up the different considerations:

> "I can see no reason in public policy for drawing a distinction between one kind of wrongful act, of which a third party is the innocent victim, and another kind of wrongful act; between wrongful acts which are crimes on the part of the perpetrator and wrongful acts which are not crimes; or between wrongful acts which are crimes of carelessness and wrongful acts which are intentional crimes. It seems to me to be slightly unrealistic to suggest that a person who is not deterred by the risks of a possible sentence of life imprisonment from using a vehicle with intent to commit grievous bodily harm would be deterred by the fear that his civil liability to his victim would not be discharged by his insurers."[31]

The decision in *Hardy* was approved and followed by the House of Lords in *Gardner v. Moore*,[32] where the facts were indistinguishable and it was held that the proper construction of the Road Traffic Act 1988 and the Motor Insurers' Bureau agreements, and the policy underlying them, required the M.I.B. to satisfy the motorist's liability to the innocent plaintiff.[33]

---

[28] s.151; see Chap. 19 at p. 375.
[29] See pp. 378–382.
[30] Followed in Australia in *Fire & All Risks Co. Ltd v. Powell* [1966] V.R. 513.
[31] [1964] 2 Q.B. at 769–770.
[32] [1984] A.C. 548.
[33] In the words of Lord Hailsham L.C., *ibid.* at 561–562, "To invoke, as [the M.I.B.] now do, the well-known doctrine of public policy that a man may not profit by the consequences of his own wrongdoing seems to me to stand the principle of public policy on its head."

Other compulsory insurances

The immediate question that arises is how far this sort of reasoning can be applied outside the motor insurance field. It is suggested that it will be applied wherever else third party insurance is compulsory in respect of personal injury or death, and particularly therefore to employers' liability insurance.[34] The fact that an employee is injured in circumstances involving a criminal offence, for example under the Factories Act, should not entitle his employer's insurer to invoke the defence of public policy, if the employer is liable in tort to the employee, however great the degree of negligence or recklessness. Considerations as to the insured's profiting from his wrong or not being deterred if insurance moneys are available, are outweighed by the consideration that Parliament deemed it of the utmost importance that injured employees should be compensated by making this insurance compulsory.

If, however, the crime or tort was intentionally committed by the employer or someone for whom he is responsible, then it is possible that the claim for insurance indemnity could be denied, because there is no machinery equivalent to the Road Traffic Act provisions for the injured employee to sue the insurer directly, and thus any litigation would necessitate the insured employer directly enforcing the policy to recover in respect of a deliberate wrong, something which even under *Hardy v. Motor Insurers' Bureau* and *Gardner v. Moore*, the courts would not permit.

Other third party insurances

Outside these areas where the countervailing public policy considerations can be invoked, it seems that the courts will, despite the more liberal tenor of the judgments in *Hardy*, adhere to the traditional approach. In *Haseldine v. Hosken*,[35] for example, a solicitor sought to enforce his professional indemnity policy in respect of a loss he had suffered by entering into a champertous agreement. Despite his claim that he had not known that he was committing a criminal offence, a claim that in any event it might be difficult to believe, the Court of Appeal held that he was unable to recover.[36] Scrutton L.J. commented: "It is clearly contrary to

---

[34] See Chap. 20.
[35] [1933] 1 K.B. 822.
[36] Another reason for the decision was that on its true construction the policy did not cover the loss in question.

public policy to insure against the commission of an act, knowing what act
is being committed, which is a crime, although the person committing it
may not at the time know it to be so." These are very wide words,
appearing to make no distinction between negligent and intentional
crimes.[37]

Whether such a distinction can be drawn must depend on the effect of
the decision in *Gray v. Barr*,[38] although it is not easy to formulate precisely
from the judgments here exactly what principles of public policy are to be
applied. This case was considered in Chapter 11.[39] It will be recalled that it
concerned the man who shot and killed his wife's lover. Although he was
acquitted of both murder and manslaughter by a jury in a criminal trial,
the Court of Appeal held in the civil action that he was in fact guilty of
manslaughter, a conclusion that cannot itself be faulted. It was also held
that, apart from any questions as to the construction of his insurance
policy, public policy required that he could not recover from his insurers
the damages he was liable to pay in tort to the deceased's widow. All three
judges regarded as of the utmost significance the fact that Barr carried a
loaded shotgun and threatened violence with it, thus engaging in a wilful
and culpable act. The public conscience would be shocked, it was said, if he
were allowed to enforce his insurance contract. Yet it may be noted that
the public conscience of the 12 of the public who sat as the jury in the
criminal trial can hardly have been shocked by Barr's actions as the
"wronged husband." Can it really be said that permitting him to recover
would have encouraged the greater use of violence and guns, which is
implicit in the court's reasoning? These more general questions will be
returned to shortly. *Gray v. Barr* did at least recognise that the motor
manslaughter cases were correctly decided, but the problem is whether
these are *sui generis*, or whether there are other distinguishing features. The
stress laid in the judgments on the intentional aspects of Barr's conduct,
that is the use of a loaded gun quite deliberately, does support the view,
perhaps, that genuinely negligent criminal acts by an insured will not
invoke the defence of public policy if committed in the course of perfectly
lawful behaviour. If, for example, a sportsman with an appropriate liability

---

[37] In fact the court doubted the correctness of the decisions in *Tinline* and *James*,
    doubts that were not finally removed until the decision in *Gray v. Barr* [1971] 2
    Q.B. 554.
[38] [1971] 2 Q.B. 554. See also, *Co-operative Fire & Casualty Co. v. Saindon* (1975) 56
    D.L.R. (3d) 556, justly criticised by Hasson in (1976) 14 Osgoode Hall L.J. 769
    and *Meah v. McCreamer (No.2)* [1986] 1 All E.R. 943 at 950–951.
[39] See p. 215, above.

policy negligently shoots someone mistaking them for a deer, it is suggested that he should be able to enforce the policy in respect of any damages he has to pay.

The present public policy rules can therefore probably be summarised in this way. In motor insurance on the personal injury side, and probably in employers' liability insurance, only deliberate criminal conduct could possibly prevent an insured from enforcing a claim on public policy grounds. In all other cases, mere negligence in the commission of a crime or tort would not matter, but public policy will be a good defence where the act causing the loss was deliberate or reckless and where the insured deliberately, or possibly recklessly, engaged in a criminal course of conduct, even if the final act causing the loss was accidental. It should be noted that there is also clear authority that insurance against the consequences of crime is strictly unenforceable for reasons of public policy.[40] Indeed, such insurance may itself be void, rather than merely a claim made under it. So, for example, insurance against parking fines would be against public policy. The same must apply to what used to be a common form of insurance, namely that offered to motorists against the consequences of being "breathalysed."[41] To drive with more than the permitted level of alcohol in the blood is a criminal offence. Policies offering chauffeur services, or an equivalent, for the period of the mandatory year's disqualification following such a conviction, must have fallen within this prohibition. In 1988, the Government threatened to outlaw such insurance by statute. It appears that insurers have voluntarily ceased to offer such insurance.

Some general comments

Running through these cases appear to be a number of justifications for these principles of public policy. Some of these we have already briefly examined and they have all been the subject of detailed scrutiny elsewhere,[42] but it is appropriate here to make some general comments. The principles appear to rest particularly upon three points. First, there is

---

[40] *Hardy v. M.I.B.* [1964] 2 Q.B. 745 at 760.

[41] This was the subject of the decision in *D.T.I. v. St Christopher's Motorists' Assurance Ltd* [1974] 1 All E.R. 395, discussed at p. 16, above.

[42] See, in particular, the articles by Clarke (n.2) and Shand (n.6) and the note by Fleming (1971) 34 M.L.R. 176 on the first instance decision in *Gray v. Barr* which, on public policy, was to the same effect as that of the Court of Appeal.

the idea that refusing to allow indemnity will deter others. Secondly, there is the theme that it is right to punish an insured in this way. Thirdly, there is what has been called the absolute rule, that simply the courts should not allow someone to profit from their wrong. With great respect, it is suggested that deterrence and punishment should have no place in the civil law. While Mr. Barr was no doubt punished as a result of the Court of Appeal's ruling, which was tantamount to the imposition of a fine on him, is this proper when at a criminal trial he had been acquitted? Can it really be said that someone in his position would be deterred from using a gun when the prospect of life imprisonment did not do so? Furthermore, as has already been argued, the idea that insurance being available means that the insured will profit from his wrong is curious, at least in cases of suicide and third party insurance. "In most cases of insurance . . . the people most likely to be harmed by withholding indemnity are the innocent victims of the fault insured against, who more likely than not will be left with an empty judgment against a man of straw."[43] As has already been noted, there were signs of a more rational approach in *Hardy v. Motor Insurers' Bureau*, but the effect of this, other than in the motor insurance field, appears to have been quite overlooked in *Gray v. Barr*. It is submitted that in all these cases, all the factors should be weighed, in other words, the particular gravity of the conduct of the insured against the likely real consequences of refusing to enforce the insurance.[44] However, the prospect of the courts' doing this without legislative intervention appears remote.[45]

The Claims Procedure

In the absence of any specific term in an insurance policy, it is unclear whether, upon suffering a loss, an insured is bound to claim for it within a reasonable time on pain of the claim being denied, or whether it is sufficient merely to claim before the statutory limitation period expires.[46] In practice, this is a purely academic question, as all policies contain conditions regarding such matters as when notice of a loss is required to be

---

[43] Shand, *p. cit.* at 160.

[44] Applying these sorts of considerations to the facts of *Gray v. Barr*, Shand (*op. cit.* at 164) suggests that the result would and should have been different.

[45] Furthermore, the notion of using a "public conscience" test to determine the issue, as suggested in *Euro-Diam Ltd v. Bathurst* [1988] 2 All E.R. 23 has been expressly disapproved in *Tinsley v. Milligan* [1994] 1 A.C. 340.

[46] Compare *MacGillivray and Parkington*, (7th ed.) para. 1584 with ibid., (8th ed.) para. 1704 and Ivamy, *General Principles*, p. 420.

given and what claims procedure and what proofs etc. are required. Invariably, nowadays, such conditions will be conditions precedent to the liability of the insurer, a breach of which will entitle the insurer to avoid liability for the particular loss, or, possibly, conditions precedent to the validity of the policy.[47]

In general, as with any other part of the insurance contract, an insurer is free to insert whatever conditions it chooses in this regard. However, the Statements of Insurance Practice[48] state that an insured will not be asked to report a claim and subsequent developments except "as soon as reasonably possible," and it is to be hoped that all relevant policies now have this wording rather than a strict time limit. In so far as they do, then obviously the relevant conditions will be legally binding, but it must be remembered that otherwise the Statements are not legally binding, so that there is no sanction if the wording of a particular policy has not been changed. However, any term regarding the claims procedure in a consumer insurance policy which is "unfair" will be struck down under the Unfair Terms in Consumer Contracts Regulations 1994.[49]

The matters which are usually contained in conditions governing the claims procedure can be examined under a number of heads.

Notice

The first basic obligation is to give notice of a loss. If the policy is a third party policy, the condition may well require that notice be given of any event that may give rise to a claim against the insured in addition to an actual claim. Oral notice is sufficient unless the policy provides otherwise.

Such conditions are strictly construed against the insurer. In *Verelst's Administratrix v. Motor Union Insurance Co.*,[50] a motor policy which covered the insured against death by accident required his representative to give notice in writing of a claim "as soon as possible" after it had come to his knowledge. This was construed subjectively so that the fact that notice was

---

[47] See pp. 150–153, above. A condition making the giving of notice a proviso, as in "provided that the insured shall give notice," has been held to be precedent to liability: *Millichap v. Pontrillas Timber and Builders Merchants Ltd*, unreported, November, 1992.

[48] As to these, see p. 5, above. They apply, of course, only to policies issued to individual insureds.

[49] See pp. 91–93, above.

[50] [1925] 2 K.B. 137.

given nearly one year after the accident was irrelevant, as the existence of the policy was unknown until just before notice was given and all the circumstances of the representative had to be taken into account. It is suggested that a similar interpretation should be given to conditions inserted as a result of the Statements of Insurance Practice, so that "as soon as reasonably possible" means as soon as the insured (or his representative) could be expected to give notice taking all the circumstances into account.

Time-limits

It is unlikely that, in those situations where they are not constrained by the Statements of Practice or the Unfair Terms in Consumer Contracts Regulations, insurers retain conditions as generous to the insured as that in *Verelst*. Far more likely are those requiring notice within a specific time limit. If such a condition is clear, and is precedent to the insurer's liability, a failure to comply, however inadvertent or excusable, will entitle the insurer to avoid liability. A relatively old example is *Cassel v. Lancashire & Yorkshire Accident Insurance Co.*,[51] where an accident policy required notice within 14 days. It was not until eight months after an accident that the insured became aware that he had been injured as a result of it, and he then gave notice, but it was held that the insurer was not liable. The term was clear and, simply, was not complied with. Similarly, in *Adamson v. Liverpool London & Globe Insurance Co.*,[52] a cash in transit policy had the following condition: "The insured shall, immediately upon the discovery of any loss, give notice thereof to the company . . . The company shall be under no liability hereunder in respect of any loss which has not been notified to the company within 15 days of its occurrence." Over a period of two years before the loss was discovered, an employee of the insured embezzled money entrusted to him for the purchase of National Insurance stamps. When the loss was discovered, the insured immediately notified his insurers. It was held that the latter were liable only in respect of the losses which occurred within the 14 days prior to notification, by reason of the last part of the condition. It does seem though that there was an element of ambiguity in the condition, the first part of which referred to the giving of notice immediately upon discovery. The insured had done this and indeed had done all that he could do in the circumstances. The decision can only be regarded as a little harsh.

---

[51] (1885) 1 T.L.R. 495.
[52] [1953] 2 Lloyd's Rep. 355.

The result of conditions such as these, if strictly relied upon, and it is not suggested that they always are, may be that an insured is treated harshly without real justification. There appears to be an unanswerable case for giving a court power by statute to relieve a breach of such a condition in favour of an innocent insured, or to prescribe that a breach can be relied upon only when the insurer can show that it has been prejudiced thereby, or alternatively that a breach can never be used to defeat a claim *per se*, but entitles the insurer to counterclaim for such loss as it can show that it has suffered as the result of the breach.[53]

Place of notice

In addition to stipulating time-limits, a condition as to notice may require that it is given to a particular place, for example, the insurer's head office. This will be upheld and a local agent will not have authority to waive the requirement,[54] but some power to relieve against technical reliance on a breach here seems desirable. In the absence of a specified destination, notice to any agent with usual authority to receive it will suffice. Notice need not be given by the insured himself, but by an agent of his authorised to do so. Whether or not a condition as to notice is satisfied if an unconnected third party informs the insurer of a loss depends on whether the decision in *Lickiss v. Milestone Motor Policies*[55] is followed. This will be discussed in the following section.

Particulars

The giving of notice of a loss is usually fairly informal, in the sense that it does not comprehend full details of a claim. These are normally separately required by a condition and frequently in practice consist of the filling in of a claim form sent by the insurer upon receipt of notice. In the absence of such a condition, the insured would simply have to prove his loss in the normal way if the matter were litigated.

The standard conditions imposing the legal obligation with respect to particulars appear to be of two types. One requires the insured to give full particulars of the loss, which has been defined as the best particulars he can

---

[53] Provisions such as these are common in other jurisdictions, for example, the U.S.A. and Australia.

[54] *Brook v. Trafalgar Insurance Co.* (1946) 79 Ll.L.R. 365.

[55] [1966] 2 All E.R. 972.

reasonably give which must be sufficient to enable the insurer to ascertain the nature, extent and character of the loss.[56]

The other standard condition requires the insured to give such proofs and information as may reasonably be required by the insurer.[57] What an insurer reasonably requires must be a question of fact, but it will be virtually impossible for an insured to resist anything of relevance to his claim, and, if he is a businessman, he may well have to submit matters of general relevance to his business. In *Welch v. Royal Exchange Assurance*,[58] the plaintiff insured his stock in trade against fire. Following a claim, the insurers denied liability and the dispute was referred to arbitration. The insurers, relying upon a condition of the sort mentioned, requested to see bank accounts which the insured used for the purpose of his business, but which were in his mother's name. The insured refused this until under cross examination in the arbitration proceedings. The arbitrator held that these details were reasonably required, and the Court of Appeal upheld that decision, the argument having centred on whether the condition was precedent to the insurers' liability. Having decided that it was,[59] the insured's claim was lost, as he had failed to comply before pursuing his claim to law, albeit, as it turned out, the bank accounts contained nothing of any relevance.

Personal compliance unnecessary?

An interesting point has arisen with regard to the insured's obligation to give full particulars, and a similar point could also arise with respect to the giving of notice. In *Lickiss v. Milestone Motor Policies*,[60] the insured motorcyclist was involved in an accident on May 17, in which he negligently damaged a taxi-cab. His policy covered him against such third party liability and required him to provide his insurers with full particulars of any accident as soon as possible and to forward immediately any summons, writ or similar matter relating to the accident. The insured never himself informed his insurers of the accident, but they learnt of it

---

[56] *Mason v. Harvey* (1853) 8 Ex. 819 at 820.

[57] "Proofs satisfactory to the insurer" will be interpreted in the same way; *Braunstein v. Accidental Death Insurance Co.* (1861) 1 B. & S. 782.

[58] [1939] 1 K.B. 294.

[59] The condition provided for no liability "unless" it was complied with; compare the construction of "until" in a similar context in *Weir v. Northern Counties Insurance* (1879) 4 L.R.Ir. 689.

[60] [1966] 2 All E.R. 972.

from the taxi driver. Neither did he forward a summons which he received, but the police on June 18 sent full details to the insurers. The main reason for the decision turned upon a point of waiver which will be examined later, but Lord Denning M.R., with whom Danckwerts L.J. agreed, held that the insured was not in breach of the condition mentioned on the ground that, although he himself did not comply, the insurers received all the necessary information, in particular from the police, within the necessary time.

This aspect of the decision is difficult to justify as a matter of strict law, as the condition did expressly provide that "*the insured shall give* full particulars . . .",[61] although it is impossible to deny its justice, as the insurers were in no way prejudiced by the insured's failure. Assuming that the decision is followed, and there has as yet been no subsequent relevant case, its logic must apply to any condition concerning the claims procedure, including the giving of notice, even if such a condition expressly appears to require personal compliance by the insured (or his duly authorised agent).

Further co-operation

In addition to the requirement of particulars, conditions in appropriate policies sometimes require further co-operation by the insured. Examples of this will be seen in the context of liability policies in Chapter 18, but a particular example is worth citing at this stage. In *London Guarantee Co. v. Fearnley*,[62] a fidelity policy taken out by an employer covered him against the risk of embezzlement by an employee. A condition precedent provided that, if a claim was made, the insured should prosecute the employee concerned if the insurer so required. Following a particular claim, the insured refused to comply with such a request and it was held that the insurer was thereby entitled to avoid liability.

Proof of loss

A condition may also require the insured to provide proof of his loss. This differs from particulars in that it means documentary proof of the loss, not merely a description of it. Sometimes the insured will be required to make a statutory declaration. Even though the proofs may show prima

---

[61] Emphasis added; see, on this point, the dissenting judgment of Salmon L.J.
[62] (1880) 5 App.Cas. 911.

facie that the loss is covered by the policy, the burden of proving this, should the matter be litigated, still rests upon the insured.[63]

Contesting insurer's denial of liability

Finally, a condition may require the insured, if the insurer disputes liability for a loss, to contest this denial by legal proceedings within a stated period, on pain of liability being totally avoided. Such a condition has been upheld in a case which involved a claim against third party liability.[64] The insured failed to contest the insurer's denial of liability within the year stated and his claim was thus totally defeated even though his actual liability to the third party was not established until long after the year after the insurers repudiated. The only course for an insured in this position will be to seek a declaration that his insurers are liable to indemnify him, if he should be adjudged liable to the third party.

Arbitration

Despite the undertaking which will be referred to shortly, it is still usual to find in insurance policies of most sorts a condition precedent to the insurer's liability to the effect that any disputed claim must go to arbitration before a court of law. Such arbitration clauses can refer to disputes over liability, but more likely now they will cover only disputes over the quantum of a loss.

While arbitration may be cheaper than litigation, it naturally does not attract the attention that court action does, so that insurers might thereby be able to rely upon "technical defences" without public opprobrium. Furthermore, legal aid is not available to a party to arbitration. Reporting in 1957, the Law Reform Committee[65] expressed concern and said that they had evidence that insurers had abused their position in certain cases against honest and careful insureds by insisting upon arbitration. However, they recommended no change in the law because at the time of their enquiry, the British Insurance Association and Lloyd's stated that their members had agreed not to enforce arbitration against the wishes of an insured in cases of disputes over liability. Excepted from this undertaking

---

[63] *Watts v. Simmons* (1924) 18 Ll.L.R. 177.

[64] *Walker v. Pennine Insurance Co.* [1980] 2 Lloyd's Rep. 156.

[65] Fifth Report on Conditions and Exceptions in Insurance Policies, Cmnd. 62, para. 13.

were reinsurance, marine insurance and certain aspects of aviation insurance where arbitration is specially negotiated and where the parties are perfectly capable of looking after themselves.[66] In many cases, therefore, the law surrounding the use of arbitration clauses is of practical importance only at all in respect of disputes over the amount of a loss.[67]

The leading case of *Scott v. Avery,*[68] which concerned an arbitration clause in an insurance policy, decided that such clauses in contracts generally are enforceable as conditions precedent provided that they do not purport ultimately to oust the jurisdiction of the court, and that they can cover disputes over liability as well as over quantum. If legal proceedings are brought by an insured in respect of a matter covered by an arbitration clause, the court has a discretion under section 4 of the Arbitration Act 1950 to stay the proceedings and thus enforce the clause. Obviously the onus is on the party seeking to keep the dispute out of arbitration. A number of insurance cases have considered the exercise of this discretion, and it seems that the legal proceedings will usually be stayed unless the dispute concerns difficult points of law or involves an allegation of fraud.[69]

Independent validity of arbitration clauses

The final question here concerns what has been termed the independent validity of arbitration clauses.[70] It is clear that if the insurer is seeking to deny the validity or very existence of the policy in question, it cannot rely on any of its terms to enforce arbitration,[71] unless the arbitration clause itself is worded widely enough to cover the reference of a dispute as to the validity of the contract.[72] There are, it seems, three clear instances in the insurance context where, for this reason, an arbitration clause cannot be

---

[66] In a consumer policy situation, an arbitration clause might well be regarded as unfair under the Unfair Terms in Consumer Contracts Regulations.

[67] Note, though, that if an insured is able to, and does, take advantage of the services offered by Personal Insurances Arbitration Service (see p. 5, above, at n.21), he is bound by the result. This is not so in respect of the Insurance Ombudsman.

[68] (1856) 5 H.L.C. 810.

[69] See *Clough v. County Livestock Insurance Assurance* (1916) 85 L.J.K.B. 1185 and *Smith v. Pearl Assurance Co.* [1939] 1 All E.R. 95, holding that the cost of arbitration for the insured and the unavailability of legal aid are not valid grounds for disallowing it.

[70] Powell, [1954] C.L.P. 75.

[71] *Heyman v. Darwins* [1942] A.C. 356.

[72] *ibid.*, at 385 (Lord Wright) and 392, 398 (Lord Porter).

relied upon. These are (i) where the existence of the contract is disputed[73]; (ii) where the insurer alleges that the contract is void or illegal, for example, for lack of insurable interest required by statute[74]; and (iii) where it is alleged that the policy has been avoided *ab initio* for non-disclosure or misrepresentation.[75] Where, however, an insurer is simply relying on the terms of the contract to deny liability, then the contract and hence the arbitration clause still stand. Thus, an allegation of breach of warranty or condition, or that a loss is not within the cover provided, does not affect the validity of an arbitration clause.[76]

One rather disputed situation is where the insurer avoids liability alleging a fraudulent claim. As will be seen, this has the effect of avoiding the policy rather than a particular claim, and it was suggested in *Jureidini v. National British & Irish Millers' Insurance Co.*[77] that the insurers could not therefore rely upon an arbitration clause. This dictum in a wider context has been subsequently disapproved of,[78] and it appears incorrect in principle. The avoidance of the policy is from the date of breach, and it still stands for the purpose of reliance upon its terms. In any event, under section 24 of the 1950 Act, it is likely that an allegation of fraud is a good reason for a court's refusing to enforce arbitration.

Waiver and estoppel

It is in connection with conditions regarding the claims procedure that the insured is most often likely to argue that the insurer is in some way precluded from relying upon a breach. Insurers may be so precluded by application of the doctrines of waiver and estoppel.[79] The use of the description "waiver" in this and similar contexts has been criticised, but it is well established and will be followed here.

While waiver and estoppel may have a common base, they are essentially different.[80] Waiver is a form of election. The insurer who has

---

[73] *Toller v. Law Accident Insurance Society* [1936] 2 All E.R. 952.

[74] But not where the insured merely fails to have the interest required by the contract: *Macaura v. Northern Assurance Co.* [1925] A.C. 619 (see p. 58, above).

[75] *Stebbing v. Liverpool & London & Globe Insurance Co.* [1917] 2 K.B. 433.

[76] As to the effect of a breach of warranty or condition, see pp. 95–97, above.

[77] [1915] A.C. 499 per Viscount Haldane; the other members of the House of Lords decided the case on other grounds.

[78] *Heyman v. Darwins*, above; see Powell, *op. cit.* But see *The Litsion Pride* [1985] 1 Lloyd's Rep. 437, discussed at p. 255, below.

[79] As to the application of those doctrines in respect of non-disclosure or breach of warranty, see pp. 106–107, above.

[80] See especially the judgment of Lord Goff in *Motor Oil Hellas (Corinth) Refineries S.A. v. Shipping Corporation of India, The Kanchenjunga* [1990] 1 Lloyd's Rep. 391.

the right to avoid liability may elect not to do so or may be deemed to have so elected, provided that it has knowledge of the breach and either expressly so elects or else acts in such a way as would induce a reasonable insured to believe that it is not going to insist upon its legal rights. Thus, waiver requires a conscious act by the insurer or its agent, but it does not require the insured to act in response in any way. Estoppel on the other hand requires a representation by words or conduct to the insured that the insurer will not rely upon a breach of condition which the insured relies upon and acts upon to his detriment. It does not depend upon the knowledge of the person estopped and is a doctrine of much wider significance. Waiver and estoppel may very well arise upon the same facts, but in certain cases the distinction may be crucial, as will be seen.

Evidence of waiver

It is clear that for waiver to operate, the insurer must know of the breach, but that knowledge may be the knowledge of an agent which is imputed to the insurer under general principles.[81] Apart from express affirmation, the conduct of the insurer that can amount to waiver may be constituted by the acceptance of a renewal premium, but perhaps the most likely form in this context will arise simply from its handling of the claim. If, with knowledge of the breach, the insurer does anything such as writing for further particulars or continuing to process the claim without denial of liability or without reserving its position, that will amount to waiver. The facts of *Lickiss v. Milestone Motor Policies*,[82] examined earlier,[83] provide a good illustration. The insured failed to forward any information to his insurers, but the police did so. Subsequently, the insurers wrote to the insured referring to the summons and indicating that they wished to arrange for his defence to it. It was held unanimously that this constituted waiver of their right to avoid liability. The insurers knew of the breach, yet had ignored it and written in terms indicating that they accepted liability.

On the other hand, a letter or an oral representation indicating that the insurers are still enquiring into the matter, without any indication that they regard themselves as bound, cannot amount to a waiver.[84]

The insurers may, knowing of a breach, continue to rely upon the policy to exercise a right given to them thereunder. If they do so without

---

[81] See Chap. 10 at pp. 180–182.
[82] [1966] 2 All E.R. 972.
[83] See p. 247.
[84] See, *e.g., Farrell v. Federated Employers' Insurance Ass.* [1970] 1 W.L.R. 1400.

reserving their position, they will have lost their right to complain. In *Craine v. Colonial Mutual Fire Insurance Co.*,[85] a fire policy required the insured to deliver particulars of loss within 15 days of the loss as a condition precedent to recovery. The insured failed to do so. In the meantime, however, under another condition in the policy, the insurer took possession of the premises and remained there for four months. It was held that by reason of this action, the insurer was precluded from relying upon the breach. Normally, of course, this would have been a clear case of waiver, but a condition in the policy, apparently accepted as valid, precluded the application of this doctrine unless confirmed in writing by the insurer. Thus, the judgment proceeded upon the basis of estoppel and is a useful illustration of the point made earlier as to the importance of the distinction between the two doctrines. By its conduct in taking possession of the premises, the insurer represented that it would not rely upon the breach. The insured relied upon this to his detriment by being deprived of possession of his premises for the period stated.

Waiver of future performance

Just as an insurer may waive an existing breach, it may also waive future performance of a condition. In *Burridge v. Haines*,[86] a policy on horses contained a condition providing that in the event of death by accident, the insured should obtain the certification of a qualified vet to the effect that death was caused by a peril insured against. Following the death of one horse, the insurer's own vet examined the animal and the insurer told the insured that this was acceptable and that it would accept evidence of the horse's death other than that prescribed in the policy. It was held that the insurer had waived its right to rely upon a breach of the condition, because by its conduct it had implied that it would not enforce it, and it had rendered it impossible for the insured to comply by appointing its own vet who dissected and destroyed the horse before a vet chosen by the insured had the chance to examine it.

Agent's authority

Just as insurers may be deemed to have knowledge of a breach through an agent, so also in appropriate circumstances an agent may have authority

---

[85] (1920) 28 C.L.R. 305 (High Court of Australia). The decision was affirmed by the Privy Council, *sub nom. Yorkshire Insurance Co. v. Craine* [1922] 2 A.C. 541, but rather on the construction of the condition in question.
[86] (1918) 87 L.J.K.B. 641.

actually to waive a breach. This will turn on the extent of the agent's
actual or ostensible authority. An agent who has authority to accept
premiums or settle claims will probably have at least ostensible authority
to waive a breach of condition.[87] A mere canvassing agent will not. In
Brook v. Trafalgar Insurance Co.,[88] the policy required notice of loss to be
given to the company's head office, and it was held that a mere local agent
had no authority by himself accepting notice to waive breach of that
condition.

Delay as waiver

Mere delay by the insurers in dealing with, for example, a late claim
does not amount to waiver. In *Allen* v. *Robles*,[89] a motor insured was
obliged to notify his insurer of a claim against him within five days of the
claim being made. Following an accident, he did not notify the insurers
that a claim was made against him until two months later. However, the
insurers did not deny liability to the insured for four months, although
they had informed the third party and had warned the insured one month
after the claim that they reserved their position. It was held that the
insurers had not lost their right to avoid liability merely by lapse of time.
In the words of Fenton Atkinson L.J.: "The lapse of time would only
operate against [the insurer] if thereby there was prejudice to the
defendant or if in some way rights of third parties intervened or if the
delay was so long that the court felt able to say that the delay in itself was
of such a length as to be evidence that they had in truth decided to accept
liability."[90]

Fraudulent Claims

The topic of fraudulent claims merits its own special treatment, as in
this respect the duty of the insured to act with the utmost good faith
survives to an extent beyond the effecting of the policy. Thus, it seems that
if the insured makes a fraudulent claim, the whole policy, and not just the

---

[87] See Chap. 10 at p. 179.
[88] (1946) 79 Ll.L.R. 365.
[89] [1969] 1 W.L.R. 1193.
[90] *ibid.* at 1196.

particular claim, is voidable.[91] It is not clear whether avoidance operates only from the date of the fraud or whether in addition the insurer may avoid the whole contract retrospectively so that the insured would be liable to forfeit any prior honest claims. It could be argued[92] that the latter is the legal position and this certainly seems to give the insurer sufficient protection. However, it was held in a marine insurance case, *Black King Shipping Corp. v. Massie (The "Litsion Pride")*,[93] that the insurer can avoid the whole contract *ab initio*. This was because the judge categorised a fraudulent claim as a breach of the general duty of utmost good faith imposed on an insured by section 17 of the Marine Insurance Act 1906 and construed the word "avoidance" in that section as meaning avoidance *ab initio*.[94] As the Marine Insurance Act is generally regarded as codifying the common law of insurance, this decision would be relevant to a non-marine case. In practice, a term giving the insurer the express right to repudiate for a fraudulent claim is invariably inserted in fire and similar policies. Clearly a breach of such a term only entitles repudiation from the date of breach, but this is an academic point if, in fact, the insurer can rely on a breach of the wider implied duty of utmost good faith.

However, the authority of *The Litsion Pride* has been somewhat shaken, even if it has not yet been overruled, by subsequent decisions. It now seems clear that there is no general continuing duty of utmost good faith,[95] and as far as claims are concerned, any duty is not broken by an innocent or negligent non-disclosure.[96] Further, it has been held that the requirement of utmost good faith adds nothing to the existing obligation not to

---

[91] *Britton v. Royal Insurance Co.* (1866) 4 F. & F. 905; *Orakpo v. Barclays Insurance Services Co. Ltd* [1994] C.L.C. 373. Note the not unattractive view of Staughton L.J., dissenting in the latter case (at 383), that an insured who knowingly exaggerated a claim should not as a matter of law be disqualified from any recovery under the policy, unless the contract expressly so provides; this is clearly, though, not the law.

[92] Relying especially on the disapproval of the dictum in *Jureidini v. National British & Irish Millers' Insurance Co.* [1915] A.C. 999 in *Heyman v. Darwins* [1942] A.C. 356; see p. 251, above.

[93] [1985] 1 Lloyd's Rep. 437, at 514–516.

[94] However, it was recognised that the insurers were not bound to avoid the whole contract; as s.17 merely provides that a policy may be avoided, they could choose simply to avoid the claim.

[95] See especially *New Hampshire Insurance Co. v. M.G.N. Ltd* [1996] C.L.C. 1692. See also p. 117, above.

[96] See, *e.g.* the comments in *Diggens v. Sun Alliance and London Insurance plc* [1994] C.L.C. 1146.

make a fraudulent claim.[97] It seems safer to assume therefore that there is simply such a general obligation, breach of which entitles the insurer to avoid the policy from that time.[98] This general obligation is often, as already noted, reinforced by an express term to similar effect.

Meaning of fraud

Clearly a claim is fraudulent if it can be shown that the insured intended to defraud the insurer, or put forward false evidence.[99] Otherwise, a fraudulent claim usually consists of an exaggeration by the insured of the amount of his loss. However, it is clear that mere exaggeration is not fraud. An insured may well claim higher than he knows he is entitled to as a bargaining device. Only, it seems, if he has a specific intent to recover more than he is entitled to is he fraudulent. In *Ewer v. National Employers' Mutual General Insurance Association*,[1] the insured under a fire policy claimed the current market price of goods destroyed, whereas he probably knew that all he was entitled to was their second-hand value. This was held not to be fraudulent. The figure claimed, which was "preposterously exaggerated," was merely a bargaining figure. On the other hand, in *Central Bank of India v. Guardian Assurance Co.*,[2] a claim figure of nearly one hundred times the actual value of the goods destroyed was, naturally, held to be fraudulent.

---

[97] *Manifest Shipping Co. v. Uni-Polaris Co., The Star Sea* [1995] 1 Lloyd's Rep. 651. Here it was held that any duty with regard to claims ceased once legal proceedings were commenced, so that exaggerated assessments of loss in the statement of claim were not a breach of duty; compare, however, *Transthene Packaging v. Royal Insurance Co.* [1996] L.R.L.R. 32. The decision in *The Star Sea* has been upheld by the Court of Appeal: *The Times,* January 23, 1997.

[98] Although it may be derived from the principle of utmost good faith, as was indeed stated in *Britton v. Royal Insurance Co.* (1866) 4 F. & F. 905, it is not a duty of disclosure akin to that existing before the contract is concluded (see Chap. 6) and a breach does not attract exactly the same legal consequences.

[99] The burden of proof in the insurers is a high one: *S. & M. Carpets (London) Ltd v. Cornhill Insurance Ltd* [1982] 1 Lloyd's Rep. 423, affirming [1981] 1 Lloyd's Rep. 677. See also *Diggens v. Sun Alliance and London Insurance plc* [1994] C.L.C. 1146.

[1] [1937] 2 All E.R. 193; compare *Norton v. Royal Life Assurance Co. The Times,* August 12, 1885 where the finding at first instance ((1885) 1 T.L.R. 460) that a claim for £274 in respect of a loss of £87 was not fraudulent was reversed.

[2] (1936) 54 Ll.L.R. 247. For a recent example, see *Orakpo v. Barclays Insurance Services Co. Ltd* [1994] C.L.C. 373 and see also the cases cited in Ivamy, *General Principles of Insurance Law,* (5th ed.), pp. 410–411 and Clarke, *The Law of Insurance Contracts,* Chap. 27.

Assignees and joint insureds

It appears that an assignee of the policy would not be defeated by the insured's fraudulent claim,[3] but that does not apply to the insured's trustee in bankruptcy,[4] nor to the case of a joint insurance where one insured's fraud will avoid the whole policy. However, joint insurance is only properly found where insurance is effected as regards property jointly owned by the insureds.[5] Insurance under one policy of composite interests, that is the different interests of the different insureds, for example, landlord and tenant or mortgagor and mortgagee, is not joint insurance, and fraud by one insured will not prevent the other who is innocent from recovering.[6]

Insurer's remedy

The insurer, who has paid out on what turns out to have been a fraudulent claim, may recover the money, but it is not entitled to recover as damages for breach of contract the costs incurred in investigating the claim.[7]

Settlement of Claims

Consideration of the precise legal rules governing the amount of compensation an insured is entitled to, following an insured loss, is deferred until the next chapter, but, at this point, it is convenient to consider some general points surrounding the settlement of claims other than the question of quantum. Frequently, of course, claims are settled following negotiations between insured and insurer, or parties acting on their behalf such as assessors and loss adjusters. The reported cases have been concerned with whether an insurer can reopen a settlement, but it is conceivable that an insured could do so on the ground of misrepresentation or undue influence by the insurer; this, though, would be difficult to show.[8]

---

[3] *Central Bank of India v. Guardian Assurance Co.*, above, at 260.

[4] *Re Carr and Sun Insurance* (1897) 13 T.L.R. 186.

[5] *Central Bank of India v. Guardian Assurance Co.*, above. Compare, though, the New Zealand view in *Maulder v. National Insurance Company of New Zealand* [1993] 2 N.Z.L.R. 351, holding that even insurance effected by joint owners may not be joint insurance.

[6] *General Accident Fire & Life Assurance Corp. v. Midland Bank* [1940] 2 K.B. 388.

[7] *London Assurance v. Clarke* (1937) 57 Ll.L.R. 254. An action in the tort of deceit, though, might lie; Goddard J. at 270.

[8] It is more likely when an insurer acting for its liability insured negotiates with the latter's victim as in *Horry v. Tate & Lyle Refineries Ltd* [1982] 2 Lloyd's Rep. 416; see Merkin (1983) 46 M.L.R. 99 and p. 355, below.

A simple promise by the insurer to pay is not binding unless the insurer is actually legally liable, but once an insurer has actually made a payment, that is irrecoverable unless the claim was fraudulent or the payment was made under a mistake of fact. Payments made under a mistake of law are not recoverable as a matter of general principle, so if, for example, an insurer pays upon what is later realised was an incorrect construction of the policy, it is bound by that payment.[9]

Mistake of fact

Payments made under a mistake of fact are recoverable by the action in quasi-contract for money had and received. This general principle was established in the insurance case of *Kelly v. Solari*.[10] Here a life policy provided for the quarterly payment of premiums, and in default the policy would lapse. The life insured died when one such payment had not been made, but the insurers paid the sum insured to his widow. It was held that, if the payment was made in ignorance or genuine forgetfulness of the facts, the insurers were entitled to recover it, and a new trial was order to ascertain this. "I think that the knowledge of the facts which disentitles the party from recovering must mean a knowledge existing in the mind at the time of payment."[11] The fact that the insurers may have been careless did not deprive them of their right to recovery.

Contracts of compromise

Somewhat different is the case where the insurer and insured enter into a contract of compromise. This might take the form of a replacement agreement, as in *Holmes v. Payne*,[12] where jewellery that was lost was replaced by the underwriters with jewellery of a similar value. Such a contract is binding unless one of the general grounds for rescission of a contract exists, such as misrepresentation or mistake. Fairly recently the

---

[9] The distinction between mistakes of fact and mistakes of law is easier to state than to apply, or even to justify; the distinction is apposite also in cases of misrepresentation. For discussion in an insurance context, see Clarke, *The Law of Insurance Contracts*, paras. 22–2B3 and 30–5.

[10] (1841) 9 M. & W. 54. For a consideration of recent Australian cases on this principle, the application of which is not as simple as it first appears, see Nicholson (1988) 1 Ins. L.J. (No.2) 67.

[11] *ibid*. at 58, per Lord Abinger C.B.

[12] [1930] 2 K.B. 301; see p. 220, above.

question has arisen as to what sort of mistake will render such a contract void or voidable. The traditional view was that a contract was void only for a fundamental common mistake affecting the subject matter of the contract.[13] A contract of compromise following an insurance claim could hardly ever be void on such grounds. The fact that an insurer entered into it under a mistaken impression that he was liable to the insured is a mistake as to the quality of the contract, the rights in respect of it. There is no mistake as to the nature of the contract. So, for example, the fact that an insurer need not have entered into it because he could avoid liability by reason of a right to avoid the policy for non-disclosure or misrepresentation or because the policy had lapsed would not render the contract of compromise void. Needless to say, the insurer could not possibly claim mistake if it compromised knowing of its right to avoid liability.

However, it now appears that whereas such a contract is not void for mistake, it is voidable in equity. In other words, the court has a discretion to set it aside. The leading case is *Magee v. Pennine Insurance Co.*,[14] where a motor policy was voidable for breach of warranty owing to misstatements by the insured on the proposal form. Following an accident, and unaware of this fact, the insurers agreed to a compromise. When the breach of warranty was subsequently discovered, they refused to pay the sum agreed. By a majority,[15] the Court of Appeal held that they were entitled to do so, Lord Denning M.R. following his earlier decision in *Solle v. Butcher*[16] to the effect that a contract can be set aside in equity if the parties were under a common misapprehension either as to the facts or as to their rights, provided that the misapprehension was fundamental and the party seeking to set the contract aside was not himself at fault. The other majority judge, Fenton Atkinson L.J., reasoned upon a different, and hardly supportable ground, but whatever the true *ratio* of the case, a question that has been fully discussed elsewhere, and whether or not it is strictly reconcilable with the House of Lords decision in *Bell v. Lever Bros*,[17] the result is obviously sensible. It may be thought, though, that the insured should have recovered at least some of the premiums paid. There does not appear to have been any fraud on his part. The proposal form that was incorrectly

---

[13] *Bell v. Lever Bros* [1932] A.C. 161. See generally, Treitel, *Law of Contract*, Chap. 8.

[14] [1969] 2 Q.B. 507.

[15] Winn L.J. dissented strongly on the ground that the case was indistinguishable from *Bell v. Lever Bros*, above.

[16] [1950] 1 K.B. 671.

[17] Above.

completed was filled in by the garage that sold him the car. The insurer
was therefore never truly at risk and under the equitable jurisdiction to
rescind, the court could have allowed this.[18]

Ex gratia payments

If an insurer consciously pays out on a claim for which, in fact, it is not
liable, then it is acting *ex gratia*. Such payments though are perfectly
proper and not *ultra vires* an insurance company,[19] but it is established that
they do not bind an insurer in the sense that the insurer who pays *ex gratia*
is not bound to pay in subsequent similar or even identical circumstances.[20]

---

[18] In *Solle v. Butcher*, above, a lease was held voidable in equity for mistake at the
landlord's suit, but only on terms that the tenant had the option to stay if he
paid more rent.

[19] *Taunton v. Royal Insurance Co.* (1864) 2 H. & M. 135.

[20] *London & Manchester Plate Glass Co. v. Heath* [1913] 3 K.B. 411. For a powerfully
argued case against the use in certain circumstances of *ex gratia* payments by life
insurance companies, see Selmer (1966) 33 U. Chicago Law Rev. 502.

CHAPTER 13

THE MEASUREMENT OF LOSS

This chapter is concerned with the legal principles surrounding the actual assessment of an insured loss. It is possible first of all to exclude certain categories of insurance, wholly or partly, from consideration here, in particular all contingency policies, in other words, those of life and accident and their variations which are not generally speaking contracts of indemnity, or contracts to pay the insured strictly only what he loses.[1] In these cases, there are no difficulties as the policies themselves will provide the fixed sums that are payable in the event of a loss. Equally, although third party liability policies are contracts of indemnity, the amount recoverable raises no real problems, since that is simply the amount of the insured's liability, subject to any maximum sum insured and to any excess clauses, as to which more will be said below.[2]

Essentially therefore, we are concerned with insurances on property of whatever sort, including both goods and land. The presumption is that such insurances are contracts of indemnity. This follows from the requirement of insurable interest at the time of the loss which is necessary in all such contracts unless it is waived.[3] Only in the case of valued policies is the principle of indemnity strictly irrelevant, and these will be examined separately. The modern "new for old" policies whereby insurers agree to pay the cost of replacing goods insured, are still indemnity policies, albeit of a different sort, despite the fact that there are not the same problems in calculating the measure of indemnity, as will be seen.

---

[1] See Chap. 3. An accident or sickness policy may be a contract of indemnity (see Chap. 15 at p. 284), but even where this is the case, the measure of the insured's loss will not give rise to any legal problems.
[2] This can include exemplary damages: *Lancashire County Council v. Municipal Mutual Insurance Ltd* [1996] 3 All E.R. 545.
[3] See Chap. 3.

Sum insured

One overriding point is that the insured can never recover more than the maximum expressly stated in the policy.[4] This is usually referred to as the "sum insured," and in property insurance, and to a lesser extent in liability insurance, the premium payable is calculated very largely according to that figure. The problems that can arise from that figure being inaccurate, in the sense of being below or above the actual value of the property insured, will be considered later. For the present it is assumed that there are no such problems of under or over insurance.

Claim for damages

A further general point is that the following detailed consideration concerns only the measurement of the insured's basic entitlement to an indemnity. A claim under an insurance contract is a claim for damages for breach of contract,[5] and it has been held that a wrongful refusal to pay by an insurer may render it liable in damages of more than this basic loss.[6] An example is the decision in *Grant v. Co-operative Insurance Society*,[7] where damages against an insurer who wrongfully repudiated liability were assessed on the normal contractual principles of remoteness and, in addition to recovering the costs of repair to the insured house, the insureds (husband and wife) recovered the costs of protecting the house while it was unoccupied and the cost of alternative accommodation. They were not entitled, however, to damages for discomfort nor for the mental anguish suffered by the wife against whom a wholly unfounded allegation of arson had been made.

There is New Zealand authority, *Stuart v. G.R.E. Assurance of New Zealand*,[8] to the same effect as *Grant*, but in a marine case, *The Italia*

---

[4] In some cases of liability insurance there is no such maximum. The most common is motor insurance, where statute prohibits a limit in respect of liability for personal injury; see Chap. 19.

[5] *Jabbour v. Custodian of Israeli Absentee Property* [1954] 1 W.L.R. 139 at 143, per Pearson J.; *Edmunds v. Lloyds Italico & L'Ancora Compagnia di Assicurzioni & Riassicurazione SpA* [1986] 1 Lloyd's Rep. 326 at 327 per Donaldson M.R.; *The Fanti* and *The Padre Island* [1991] 2 A.C. 1. In the *Jabbour* case, Pearson J. recognised that this was a somewhat odd classification, at least when the insurer admits liability to pay.

[6] If this is correct, the limit of the sum insured on the basic measure must be inapplicable. See, however, *Sprung v. Royal Insurance Co. (U.K.) Ltd* [1997] C.L.C. 70, below.

[7] (1984) 134 N.L.J. 81, available on LEXIS.

[8] (1988) 5 A.N.Z. Ins. Cases 75, 274.

Express (No 2),[9] the validity of these cases was doubted and it was held that the principle of recovery of damages beyond the basic indemnity was inapplicable to marine insurance.[10] Hirst J. felt that the nature of the contract of indemnity, in the light of the authorities, militated against the availability of such damages. He relied in particular on a dictum of Lord Goff in *The Fanti* and *The Padre Island*[11] that the promise of indemnity in an insurance contract is simply "a promise to hold the indemnified person harmless *against a specified loss or expense*."[12] The reasoning of the learned judge is persuasive and has recently been approved and applied by the Court of Appeal in a non-marine insurance case.[13] Despite the logic of this result, it could be regarded as unfortunate that, damages are not recoverable from an insurer who unjustifiably delays in paying.[14]

Total and partial loss

Property may be totally or partially lost, in other words it may be totally destroyed or lost, or it may only be damaged. The measure of recovery may well differ according to this distinction. Total loss need not necessarily mean, in this context, complete destruction, although it is obviously included. A total loss includes cases where "the subject matter is destroyed or so damaged as to cease to be a thing of the kind insured."[15] For example, a house may, after a fire, be left with walls and foundations standing, but if none of it is usable, it must be regarded as totally lost. The

---

[9] [1992] 2 Lloyd's Rep. 281.

[10] Because of the statutory rules as to recovery in the Marine Insurance Act 1906, in addition to Hirst J.'s conclusions (see below) as to the general nature of the contract of indemnity.

[11] [1991] 2 A.C. at 35. See also *Irving v. Manning* (1847) 1 H.L.C. 287, *President of India v. Lips Maritime Corporation* [1988] A.C. 395.

[12] Emphasis added.

[13] *Sprung v. Royal Insurance (U.K.) Ltd* [1997] C.L.C. 70.

[14] It is difficult, though, to see how this could be done. The obvious alternative is damages in tort, as the American courts regularly give; the principles are admirably summarised in Clarke, *The Law of Insurance Contracts*, para. 30–10. Unfortunately the very limited availability of a tortious remedy for pure economic loss and the rejection by the House of Lords in *Banque Financière de la Cité v. Westgate Insurance Co. Ltd* [1991] 2 A.C. 249 of the availability of damages for a breach by an insurer of his duty of utmost good faith (see pp. 123–127, above) make such a development extremely unlikely.

[15] *Halsbury's Laws of England* (4th ed.), Vol. 25, para. 298.

same will apply to the car that is a genuine "write off." It may be in practice that cars are written off because it is regarded as uneconomic to repair them, even though they may not be so damaged as to cease to be cars, because they could be repaired comparatively easily. Whether in law these would strictly be regarded as totally lost must be open to doubt, even though in practice they may be so treated. It is, of course, perfectly permissible for insurers to adopt this attitude, provided that the insured agrees. One or two problems that may flow from this sort of case will be discussed later.

Total Loss in the Case of Goods

It is convenient to deal separately with the two classes of relevant property, namely goods and land, assuming for the present a genuine total loss.[16] In respect of goods, the measure of what the insured has lost will prima facie be the market value of the property lost at the time[17] and place[18] of loss, in other words, its second-hand or resale value.[19] This is because it is that sum that it will cost him to obtain equivalent goods.

In *Richard Aubrey Film Productions Ltd v. Graham*,[20] a policy was effected by a film producer against loss of negatives and films. A film that was almost completed was stolen. The evidence showed that on completion it would have had a market value of about £20,000 but that finally to complete it would have cost between £4,000 and £5,000. The insured therefore recovered the difference between those sums. This measure ignores feelings of lost effort and concentrates purely on loss in material terms. Similarly, in an appropriate case, nothing is recoverable to compensate for what can be called sentimental value or hurt feelings. A family "heirloom," for example, will only attract its market value even

---

[16] We are only concerned here with the determination of the measure of indemnity in respect of the insured property itself. Many property insurances will also provide for the insured to be indemnified against additional costs, for example in the case of insurance of a motor vehicle, the cost of hiring a replacement, in the case of insurance of a house, the cost of alternative accommodation, surveyors' charges etc.

[17] *Re Wilson and Scottish Insurance Corp.* [1920] 2 Ch. 28; see below.

[18] *Rice v. Baxendale* (1861) 7 H. & N. 96.

[19] In assessing market value, latent defects in the goods can be ignored if the evidence shows that the appropriate reasonable buyer would not have detected the defects: *State Insurance Office v. Bettany* [1992] 2 N.Z.L.R. 275.

[20] [1960] 2 Lloyd's Rep. 101.

though its owners may have felt that it was worth much more than that to them.[21]

Value at time of loss

It is value at the date or time of loss that is recoverable, which, of course, may or may not correspond to the value at the date of commencement or renewal of the policy. In *Re Wilson and Scottish Insurance Corporation Ltd*,[22] a car was insured in November 1915 for £250, which was its purchase price at the time and which was stated by the insured to represent his estimate of present value. The policy was renewed in subsequent Novembers until the car was destroyed by fire in June 1919. It was then worth £400. The policy covered the car "up to full value." The arbitrator reserved for the court the question whether the insured was entitled to £250 or £400, and Astbury J. held that it depended upon when the increase in value took place. If it was even partly before the last renewal, the insured was entitled to only £250, but if it occurred totally since the renewal, he was entitled to £400.

There are a number of difficulties surrounding this decision. First, it is a little difficult to see how the insured could in any event be entitled to more than £250, as one would have thought that that figure, as it had never been changed, operated as the sum insured, the maximum recoverable. The answer to this must be that, on the construction of the policy, there was no such sum insured, as none was expressly stated and the policy undertook to pay "full value." Assuming this to be the case, there is an inconsistency in the reasoning. At one point in his judgment, Astbury J. suggested that on each renewal, "the insured must be deemed to have continued or repeated his 'estimate of present value' at £250," and he implied that if this was incorrect on the renewal in November 1918, the policy was voidable.[23] Whether this was because of a non-disclosure of a material fact, that is, the increase in value, or a breach of warranty of value, is not made clear. It is suggested that it can only be the former, there being no authority and no reason for holding that statements in a

---

[21] The strictness of the usual indemnity measure has no doubt astonished individual insureds from time to time; see the comments of MacKinnon J. in *Ewer v. National Employers' Mutual General Insurance Assurance Ltd* (1937) 157 L.T. 16 at 21.

[22] [1920] 2 Ch. 28.

[23] *ibid.* at 31, citing Creswell J. in *Pim v. Reid* (1834) 6 Man. & G. 1 at 25.

proposal form not referable to the future are automatically rewarranted upon renewal; indeed there is a clear dictum to the contrary.[24] If, then, the increase in value occurred before renewal and non-disclosure of it amounted to non-disclosure of a material fact, the policy was voidable and there was no basis for holding that the insured was entitled to anything as a matter of strict law. However, the insurers had agreed to pay £250 in any event, and must therefore be deemed to have waived any right to avoid the policy. If, as has been seen, there was no sum insured in this case, so that the figure of £250 in the proposal form was not to be taken as the maximum recoverable, the insured should have been entitled to the value of his car at the date of loss, namely £400, regardless of when the increase in value took place.

It is suggested therefore, that the decision itself in *Re Wilson* is open to question. However, the principle of value at the time of loss is clearly correct, and it would seem unlikely that the sort of facts there could recur, simply because estimates of value in a proposal form do usually correspond to the sum insured.[25]

Replacement value

As the basic principle of indemnity is only contractual, it can be contractually varied. Policies on goods can, and very often do, undertake to pay replacement value rather than market value, and indeed there may be cases where this is impliedly the measure, even if not actually spelt out.[26] Policies containing express undertakings to pay replacement value are increasingly common, and there can be no doubt that, subject to the sum insured, the insured is entitled to what it actually costs to replace the lost property by equivalent new property. These "new for old" policies are no doubt a major inroad into the traditional principle of indemnity, but it goes without saying that insurers demand higher premiums for such cover.

Total Loss in the Case of Land

Until fairly recently, there was very little real authority determining what the insured whose house or office or factory is totally destroyed is

---

[24] Winn L.J. in *Magee v. Pennine Insurance Co.* [1969] 2 Q.B. 507 at 517.
[25] It would also be most unusual now for a car to increase in value anyway.
[26] Particularly insurances of plant and equipment: *Roumeli Food Stores v. New India Assurance Co.* [1972] 1 N.S.W.L.R. 227 at 236–238.

entitled to claim, possibly because a total loss here is not that common. Logic might favour the market value approach as for goods, for the same reason that this measure should enable the insured to purchase an equivalent. In fact, an insured would not usually choose to do this; he would wish to be able to rebuild or reinstate. In some cases he may be compelled so to do.[27] For most of the time that insurance has been available, this probably did not matter, as the market value of property would cover the cost of rebuilding. Now it is notorious that this is less likely. Hence, whether or not an insured is entitled to the cost of reinstatement may be vital.

In most cases there will be such an entitlement as a result of the decision in *Leppard v. Excess Insurance Company*.[28] Here the Court of Appeal stressed that the insured is entitled to an indemnity against the amount of his loss and no more. There is no general principle dictating market value or cost of reinstatement. It is a question of fact, and all the relevant facts of the particular case must be examined in order to ascertain the actual value of the loss at the relevant date. In the case itself, the insured had purchased a cottage which was worth some £4,500, including the site value, when it was burnt, but which would cost some £8,000 to rebuild. On the evidence the insured never intended to live in the cottage. He had purchased it from his in-laws solely for resale. It was held therefore that his loss was the market value of the cottage, that is what he lost by not being able to sell it. The judgments indicate, however, that in the normal case of the insured who lives in or otherwise occupies his house, office or factory, the measure of indemnity will be the cost of rebuilding, because otherwise his actual loss will not be made good.

In *Leppard*, the insured had argued in the alternative that his policy contractually provided that he was entitled to the cost of reinstatement. He placed particular reliance upon facts which are probably fairly standard. These were, first, that in the proposal form he warranted that "the sums to be insured represent not less than the full value (the full value is the amount which it would cost to replace the property in its existing form should it be totally destroyed)," and secondly, that the policy contained a declaration by him that the sum insured represented and would at all times be maintained at not less than the full value of the buildings. The court held, no doubt correctly as a matter of law, that these could not affect the basic nature of the policy, which was otherwise in normal

---

[27] See Chap. 14.
[28] [1979] 1 W.L.R. 512. Noted in (1980) 43 M.L.R. 456 (Birds).

indemnity form. Such declarations were promissory warranties, on breach of which the insurer would have been discharged from liability.[29] The insured had, in fact, complied with them and had insured the cottage for, eventually, £14,000. More about the effect of such warranties will be said later. All that remains to be said here is that the insured may have felt somewhat aggrieved, and understandably so, at being required to pay a premium calculated on £14,000 worth of insurance on pain of the insurer being able to avoid all liability, when he was entitled to substantially less.[30]

Partial Loss under an Indemnity Policy

In respect of a partial loss, there can be no case for treating goods and land any differently. A measure based on market value is generally inappropriate, since the insured cannot go into the market and restore himself to his pre-loss position, and payment based on the difference in market value before and after loss may well not compensate him. Therefore, the basis for an indemnity ought to be the cost of repair,[31] less perhaps any amount by which the insured is better off than before the loss; the technical term for the latter is "betterment."[32]

Some potential difficulties

Before examining some of the cases, it must be pointed out that there may be difficulties arising from the adoption of the above measure. In the main, these stem from the problem in deciding whether or not a loss is to be regarded as partial or total. If a car is dented, however badly, or the roof of a house is damaged, these are clearly partial losses. But in practice a car may be so badly damaged that, although it is capable of repair and can be still properly termed a car, it is regarded as uneconomic to repair it; it

---

[29] See Chap. 7.
[30] *Quaere* whether he might have had a remedy against the broker who advised him.
[31] This is implied in *Scottish Amicable Heritable Securities Association v. Northern Assurance Co.* (1883) 11 R. (Ct. of Sess.) 287 at 295 and *Westminster Fire Office v. Glasgow Provident Society* (1888) 13 App. Cas. 699, although the actual decisions turned on other points. It has been held in Scotland that the insured is not entitled to interim payments in a situation where he is obliged to pay stage payments to the builder who is repairing the property: *Anderson v. Commercial Union Assurance Company plc*, Court of Session, May 23, 1996.
[32] In *Reynolds v. Phoenix Assurance Co.* [1978] 2 Lloyd's Rep. 440, (see below) Forbes J. held that the principle of betterment was well established.

may then be written off. Similarly, the top floor of a house might be damaged to such an extent that, although the bottom half is more or less intact and usable, in order to restore the house to its original condition, it is necessary to demolish the surviving part and start again. In the *Leppard* case, if Mr Leppard's cottage had been so damaged, would he have been entitled to the costs of repairing it, which may well have been more than the market value of the cottage? It must be likely that the law would follow what is presumably insurance practice and look at what the insured actually loses, so that Leppard would have recovered no more than he did get, the fact of his non-occupation being crucial. However, in the case of a car or similar consumer durable, or any goods which tend to depreciate in value, the problem may be more complex simply because such depreciation is usual.

A more complex illustration will demonstrate the point further. Imagine a modest family car some 10 years old but in very good condition for its age with low mileage and sound bodywork. Its market value will be reflected, however, primarily by its age, and, although it may attract the top price for a model of its kind of that age, this will hardly reflect its true worth to its owner. This top market price is £500. In an accident, the car is damaged on one side so that a wing and a door need replacement, there is some general tidying-up necessary, but the mechanics and the rest of the bodywork are sound. The work of restoring the car will cost £700 in total. Fairly clearly, the car is only partially lost, but is the insured entitled to £700, assuming this to be less than the sum insured, bearing in mind that this is more than the market value of the car, which is all he would get if the car had been totally lost? It is suggested that he is and that the courts would in such a case follow the principles adopted in respect of insurance of buildings in fairly recent cases, namely that a partial loss is assessed on the cost of repair or reinstatement save where the insured does not genuinely intend to reinstate.

Legal authorities

In *Reynolds v. Phoenix Assurance Co. Ltd*,[33] the plaintiffs in 1969 bought an old maltings which they insured for £18,000, which was a little more than they had paid for it. Subsequently, on the advice of their brokers and valuers, the sum insured was increased to cover the likely cost of

---

[33] [1978] 2 Lloyd's Rep. 440. See also *Pleasurama Ltd v. Sun Alliance & London Insurance Ltd* [1979] 1 Lloyd's Rep. 389.

reinstatement in the event of a total loss, and at the material time that sum insured was £628,000. The plaintiffs had a sound business reason for purchasing the maltings. A fire occurred which destroyed about 70 per cent of the buildings. This was clearly a partial loss. There was some dispute in subsequent discussions involving assessors employed by the plaintiffs and loss adjusters acting for the insurers as to the cost of reinstatement and as to the plaintiffs' intention in this respect. The insurers elected not to reinstate as they were entitled to under the policy,[34] but it was accepted that the plaintiffs intended to do so, although the insurers were unwilling to pay over a provisionally agreed settlement figure except in stages as the rebuilding progressed. The plaintiffs were unwilling to proceed on this basis, the settlement fell through, and the matter came to trial.

Forbes J. outlined three possible bases for indemnity. The first was market value, which would be difficult to assess, there being no ready market for buildings such as maltings, but which would probably be far less than the cost of reinstatement. The second was described as equivalent modern replacement value, namely the cost of building afresh a modern building for the purposes of the plaintiffs when commercially it would not be sensible to retain the original building. Again this would be considerably less than reinstatement cost. The third was the cost of reinstatement which worked out at something more than £200,000. The learned judge held that the policy was an ordinary indemnity policy, and, as in *Leppard v. Excess Insurance Company*,[35] this meant that the plaintiffs were not automatically entitled under the contract to the costs of reinstatement. However, the plaintiffs were entitled to a genuine indemnity and the basis of that indemnity was the cost of reinstatement where, as on the facts, the plaintiffs did have the genuine intention to reinstate. The test to be adopted on this latter point was taken from an Irish case on compensation under statute:[36] "Would [the owner], for any reason that would appeal to an ordinary man in his position, rebuild [the property] if he got replacement costs, or is his claim for these a mere pretence?" Forbes J. held, therefore, that the plaintiffs were entitled to the largest sum, less an allowance for betterment which, he held, was a principle too well established in insurance cases of this kind to be upset.

Frequently insurers will have an option under the policy to reinstate or repair rather than pay money. The different considerations that may arise if this option is exercised are considered in the next chapter.

---

[34] See Chap. 14.
[35] [1979] 1 W.L.R. 512; see p. 267, above.
[36] *Murphy v. Wexford C.C.* (1921) 2 Ir. R. 230.

The Insured with a Limited Interest

It has hitherto been assumed that the insured is the sole unencumbered owner of the property insured, but this may not be the case, and indeed the insured may not own the property at all but be, for example, tenant or mortgagee of real property or bailee, as under a hire-purchase contract, of goods. In certain exceptional cases, an insured may recover more than the value of his interest and hold the balance above his own loss for another. These circumstances were examined earlier in Chapter 3.[37] The measure of recovery here will be the value of the loss calculated in accordance with one or other of the ways already discussed.

Where someone with a limited interest insures or is entitled to recover in respect of only his own interest, problems may arise concerning the value of his interest and the amount of indemnity to which he is entitled. If a number of different interests in the same property are insured by the persons with those different interests, for example by different mortgagees, each insured is entitled to recover the value of his loss regardless of the position of the others and regardless of whether the total amount recovered by all the insureds exceeds the value of the property in question.[38]

In respect of certain insureds with limited interests, no problem will arise. For example, the indemnity claimable by a mortgagee will be the amount of his outstanding debt, and the same may be said of the hirer under a hire-purchase contract, unless the insured contracted for full value in order to cover his own and the owner's interests together. The case, though, of a tenant who insures the property which he has leased raises the problem quite neatly. If he has, in fact, covenanted to insure or to make good fire damage, he is only fully indemnified if he receives the full value of the property, which would normally, as has been seen, be the cost of reinstatement, regardless of the market value of his lease. Even if the tenant has not covenanted to insure or repair, it has been said that he is entitled to more than market value, since he will have been deprived of his home.[39] In *British Traders' Insurance Co. v. Monson*,[40] it was said that the market value of a lease coupled with an option to purchase of which the tenant had the benefit would prima facie determine the amount of the tenant's loss, though that would not be all he was entitled to. The actual calculation, apart from that, would be no doubt be somewhat speculative.

---

[37] See pp. 60–71, above.
[38] *Westminster Fire Office v. Glasgow Provident Society* (1888) 13 App. Cas. 699.
[39] *Castellain v. Preston* (1883) 11 Q.B.D. 380 at 400.
[40] (1964) 111 C.L.R. 86 at 92, 103–104 and 104–105. See further, p. 70, above.

Loss Under a Valued Policy

Although, as a general rule, a contract of property insurance is a contract of indemnity, the parties are free to contract out of this by agreeing conclusively that a certain sum is payable in the event of loss. If this occurs, the policy is a valued policy and, unless the value is hopelessly excessive, it is enforceable.[41] Valued policies are more commonly found in marine than non-marine insurance, but no doubt there are some non-marine policies.[42] A policy is a valued policy only if the parties expressly agree that the property is assumed to have the value attached to it. The mere existence of a sum insured does not mean that a policy is valued.

In the case of a total loss, the amount recoverable is obviously the agreed value, whether that is more or less than the insured's actual loss.[43] In the case of a partial loss, the formula worked out in *Elcock v. Thomson*[44] is applied, the insurer being liable for that proportion of the agreed value as is represented by the depreciation in the actual value of the property, that is the difference between market value before and after loss. A property insured for £100,000 which is worth £50,000 before loss and £30,000 afterwards, will attract a recovery of £40,000, that is, two fifths of the agreed value. It does not matter what it actually costs to repair the property, except that it was suggested in that case[45] that if, in fact, the insurers had exercised their option to repair, they would have been liable for those costs whether that sum was more or less than that produced by the formula.

Under-Insurance

Hitherto, it has been assumed that the sum insured is not less than the value of the property insured or the cost of its reinstatement. There will frequently be an obligation on the insured to keep to the latter, as is

---

[41] Excessive over-valuation might be non-disclosure of a material fact (see Chap. 6) or it might show that the policy was void as a gaming policy in contravention of the Gaming Act 1845 (see Chap. 3).

[42] A valued policy on a building would be difficult to justify if the Life Assurance Act 1774, especially s.3, applies, but as we have seen (pp. 49–52), the modern tendency is to disapply that Act to such cases.

[43] This is also treated as the loss for subrogation purposes: *Burnand v. Rodocanachi* (1882) 7 App. Cas. 333.

[44] [1949] 2 K.B. 755.

[45] *ibid.* at 764.

evident from the facts of *Leppard v. Excess Insurance Company*[46] as described earlier. Some nice questions arise if, in fact, the sum insured is less than either of these, that is, if there is under-insurance. Under-insurance is a problem that has concerned the insurance industry very much in recent times of high inflation.[47]

Insurer's right to avoid

The first point to note is that the insurers may well in such a case be entitled to avoid the policy or all liability under it, or else to use a right to avoid to compel the insured to settle for a sum less than his actual loss. This may arise by virtue of the duty of disclosure or by virtue of a breach of warranty. Failure upon renewal to disclose a change in the value of the property insured could be regarded as the non-disclosure of a material fact,[48] as most renewals amount to the making of a new contract.[49] Alternatively, the initial estimate of value by an insured may well be warranted and if incorrect entitle the insurer to be discharged from liability upon this basis, although, if that is the only warranty, and it is not of a continuing nature, there is, it is suggested, no basis for repudiation simply because upon subsequent renewals the sum insured has not been increased.[50] Perhaps more likely nowadays is an express continuing warranty of the sort that existed in the policy in *Leppard v. Excess Insurance Company*.[51] In such a case, there is a clear basis for repudiation of liability if the sum insured does not keep pace with the value or cost of replacement of the property.

Average

Quite apart from this, the insurer in a case of under-insurance may be able to rely upon the principle of average. This is irrelevant to a total loss,

---

[46] [1979] 1 W.L.R. 512.

[47] To such an extent that there has been a great deal of inertia selling of index-linked policies, and much publicity and exhortations to insureds to check their sums insured.

[48] This seems to be implied in *Re Wilson and Scottish Insurance Corporation* [1920] 2 Ch. 28, discussed above p. 265. In the case of buildings, where the problem of under-insurance has been especially acute, it might perhaps be possible to argue that the facts were common knowledge and hence, not required to be disclosed; see (1976) 126 N.L.J. 482.

[49] See p. 86, above.

[50] See p. 265, above.

[51] [1979] 1 W.L.R. 512; see p. 267, above.

because the sum insured is the maximum recoverable. But an insured may suffer a partial loss below the sum insured where the property is under-insured. If so, and the policy is subject to average, he will recover only that part of the loss which the sum insured bears to the value of the property; the insured is deemed to be his own insurer with respect to the balance. For example, if a house worth £60,000 is insured, subject to average, for £40,000, the insured will be entitled to only two thirds of any loss.

Commercial policies generally contain average clauses and it has been suggested that the principle of average would be implied, if not expressed, in commercial policies on goods.[52] However, average clauses are unusual, it seems, in household policies, except those issued by Lloyd's underwriters, and there is clear authority that the principle of average will not be implied in such a case.[53] Thus, in the absence of a breach of a relevant warranty, the insured in this case is entitled to recover fully up to the amount of the sum insured.

Excess and Franchise Clauses

It is convenient to mention here two devices often adopted which, if applicable, will limit the amount an insured recovers, although they raise few legal difficulties. Excess clauses or deductibles are common in motor, household and third party policies, among others. They provide that the insured is to bear the first amount of any loss, expressed either as an amount of money or as a stated percentage of any loss. The effect of an insured acting as a self-insurer in this way is considered later.[54]

Franchise clauses are perhaps less common in non-marine insurance. These take the form of relieving the insurer from liability completely in respect of losses below a certain figure or percentage, and at this level operate in the same way as excess clauses, whereas losses above the specified figure or percentage are fully covered.[55]

Payment of Interest

A question of some importance in some contexts is whether or not an insured is entitled to claim interest on the policy moneys payable to him.

---

[52] *Carreras Ltd v. Cunard Steamship Co.* [1918] 1 K.B. 118.
[53] *Sillem v. Thornton* (1854) 3 E. & B. 868.
[54] See Chap. 15, especially at pp. 290–292.
[55] *Paterson v. Harris* (1861) 1 B. & S. 336; a number of truly separate losses on separate occasions, each falling below the figure or percentage, cannot be added together so as to bring the loss above the figure or percentage: *Stewart v. Merchants' Marine Insurance Co.* (1885) 16 Q.B.D. 619.

This can only arise of course, if there has been some delay in payment. There is no rule that interest is payable as a matter of course from the date when the money becomes payable, but the court has a discretion under section 3(1) of the Law Reform (Miscellaneous Provisions) Act 1934 to award interest if it thinks fit.

Interest will be so awarded when the insurer has wrongfully detained money which ought to have been paid. In an ordinary indemnity policy, it appears that it will normally be awarded from the date when the loss has been quantified, in other words when the insured called upon the insurer to pay, to the date of judgment.[56] A similar principle applies to life policies.[57] Interest is not due from the date of loss because, for a period after that, it is reasonable for the parties to negotiate to find out exactly how much money was due in respect of a claim.[58] If the insured is a commercial undertaking which has been deprived of money of which it could make good use, the rate of interest is likely to bear some relation to commercial rates. In the case of an individual insured, a lower rate may be appropriate.

Somewhat different considerations may apply in the case of an insurer claiming interest when suing by virtue of subrogation rights. These will be examined in Chapter 15 in the general context of subrogation.

---

[56] *Burts & Harvey Ltd v. Vulcan Boiler & General Insurance Co.* [1966] 1 Lloyd's Rep. 354.
[57] *Webster v. British Empire Mutual Life* (1880) 15 Ch.D. 169; *Re Waterhouse's Policy* [1937] Ch. 415.
[58] *Burts & Harvey Ltd v. Vulcan Boiler & General Insurance Co.*, above.

CHAPTER 14

REINSTATEMENT

In certain circumstances an insurer may be entitled or bound to reinstate insured property which has been damaged or destroyed, rather than pay a sum of money to the insured. In so far as insurers may have a right to reinstate rather than pay money, this may arise under the terms of the policy or by statute. Reinstatement by contract will be permitted only if the policy expressly refers to it; if it does not, the insurers must pay money.[1] Insurers may become bound to reinstate by statutory provision. In this chapter, contractual and statutory reinstatement will be examined separately, together with one or two related matters. Of necessity, reinstatement is relevant only to property insurances.

Contractual Reinstatement

Clauses giving insurers the option to reinstate or repair have been common for a long time, particularly in insurances of real property,[2] but they are equally common nowadays in goods policies where they will often refer to replacement as well as to reinstatement or repair. Their purpose is to protect insurers against excessive demands and fraudulent claims.

The option depends upon the insurer's election to reinstate, repair or replace rather than pay money, and it is a general principle that if a party with the benefit of such an option wishes so to elect, he must give unequivocal notice to the other party, that is the insured in this context, within a reasonable time or within the time, if any, fixed by the policy. Once the election is made, the insurer is bound by it, so that it is important to know when it occurs. There are two rather conflicting Scottish decisions on the point. In the first, *Sutherland v. Sun Fire Office*,[3]

---

[1] Brett L.J. in *Rayner v. Preston* (1881) 18 Ch.D. 1 at 9–10.
[2] An early example appears from the facts of *Sadler's Co. v. Badcock* (1743) 2 Atk. 554.
[3] (1852) 14 D. (Ct. of Sess.) 775.

after investigation of a claim, the insurer offered a money payment, which the insured refused, and then offered to go to arbitration over the amount of the loss. This was also refused, whereupon the insurer elected to reinstate. It was held that this was a good election. By contrast, in *Scottish Amicable v. Northern Assurance*,[4] following the loss there were prolonged negotiations. The insureds claimed money or reinstatement; the insurers ignored the latter claim but disputed the amount of the loss and prepared for arbitration over it. Only when the insureds commenced proceedings 18 months after the fire did the insurers purport to elect to reinstate. It was held that this was too late. The distinction between the cases is, it seems, that in the latter the parties had agreed on a money payment, although the amount was disputed. Once this form of indemnity is agreed, it is too late for the insurer to elect to reinstate. In the former case, however, there had been agreement on nothing and therefore the election was still available.

Effect of election

At common law, once the insurer has made an effective election to reinstate, he is bound to restore the property to its original condition. In the old case of *Alchorne v. Favill*,[5] the premises when rebuilt were smaller than before the fire that caused the loss and, as a result, worth less. This was because of planning restrictions which prevented the insurer from rebuilding in the same manner. It was held, however, that having made their election, the insurers were bound by it and were liable to compensate the insured for the difference in value between the old and new buildings. It is likely nowadays that insurers protect themselves against the dangers of such planning restrictions by providing in the policy to the effect that reinstatement will be "as circumstances permit and in reasonably sufficient manner." Clearly they would still be liable in damages if the actual construction work were done badly, and the amount recoverable would be the cost of putting right the work and any foreseeable consequential losses, such as loss of rent or profit.

The effect of the election to reinstate is that the contract becomes a building or repair contract.[6] The correct legal analysis seems to be that the insured's claim is an offer which is accepted by the insurer's election to reinstate. The insurer is bound to complete the work regardless of cost,

[4] (1883) 11 R. (Ct. of Sess.) 287.
[5] (1825) 4 L.J. (O.S.) 47.
[6] *Brown v. Royal Insurance Co.* (1859) 1 El. & El. 853 at 858–859.

unless this contract is discharged by frustration. However, there is authority that the insured's only remedy against a defaulting insurer is in damages; specific performance will not lie.[7] Prima facie it does not matter that reinstatement costs more than was originally estimated, that it costs more than the sum insured in the policy, nor that the insured receives a better building as a result, unless there is a clause in the policy whereby the insured is bound to pay towards the costs in this sort of situation. Because the insurers who have elected to reinstate are in the position of building contractors, they must bear any loss or damage occurring while they are in possession for that purpose. In *Smith v. Colonial Mutual Fire Insurance Co. Ltd*,[8] the insurers elected to reinstate the insured house following a partial loss. While they were in possession, and when they had partly reinstated, a second fire occurred. The insurers claimed that they were entitled to deduct from the cost of reinstatement after the second fire the amount spent before that, but it was held that they could not do so. Having elected to reinstate, they had to complete the job properly, and were their own insurers while the work was in progress.

Impossibility

If it is impossible to reinstate before the insurers have made their election, for example, because planning permission will not be given, the insurers will be liable simply to pay the insured the amount of his loss.[9] If it becomes impossible after the election, there is authority that the insurers are nonetheless bound by their election and liable in damages for not reinstating despite the impossibility. Thus the insured might be entitled to compensation for the full value of the property, even if originally the loss was only a partial one. In *Brown v. Royal Insurance Co.*,[10] the only case directly in point, after the election to reinstate a partial loss, the Commissioners of Sewers under statutory authority ordered that the premises be totally demolished as being in a dangerous condition. It was held that the insured was entitled to the full value as damages for breach of the contract to reinstate. This case was decided, however, before the courts developed the doctrine of frustration,[11] under which a contract may

---

[7] *Home District Mutual Insurance Co. v. Thompson* (1847) 1 E. & A. 247.
[8] (1880) 6 Vict.L.R. 200.
[9] *Anderson v. Commercial Union Assurance Co.* (1885) 55 L.J.Q.B. 146.
[10] (1859) 1 El. & El. 853 at 858–859.
[11] The founding case was *Taylor v. Caldwell* (1863) 3 B. & S. 826.

be discharged where performance becomes impossible due to an unforeseen supervening event which is not the fault of either party. In circumstances such as the *Brown* case, or where, for example, the property is compulsorily purchased by the local authority following the election, a plea of frustration might well succeed. It would not necessarily be successful, however, if, for example, the insurers could have discovered what was going to happen.

If the contract to reinstate is frustrated, the insurers would not be liable in damages, but they would not be relieved of their original liability under the insurance contract to pay for the loss.[12] Thus the insured should still recover monetary compensation in full, even though the insurers may have incurred expenditure before the frustrating event.[13] It is arguable that the insurers might claim from the insured under section 1(1) of the Law Reform (Frustrated Contracts) Act 1943. Although that Act does not apply to contracts of insurance,[14] as we have seen, the contract here has become a contract to reinstate. Therefore the Act should apply. Section 1(3) provides that the party who has received a "valuable benefit" before the frustrating event may be ordered to pay such sum as the court considers just to the other party. However, it cannot really be said that the insured has received a valuable benefit if, in fact, he is deprived of his property by demolition or compulsory purchase.

Statutory Reinstatement

Section 83 of the Fires Prevention (Metropolis) Act 1774 is a potentially important, but perhaps relatively little used, provision. In essence it provides two things. Following a loss by fire, and only such a loss, it requires an insurance company, but not a Lloyd's underwriter,[15] to apply the policy moneys, so far as they will go, towards rebuilding or reinstating an insured building at the request of any person or persons interested in the building. Secondly, it authorises an insurance company so to act if they have grounds for suspecting that the insured was guilty of fraud or arson. The second point is obviously a useful protection to insurers, though it seems to add little to the usual contractual right they reserve which has

---

[12] *Anderson v. Commercial Union Assurance Co.* (1885) 55 L.J.Q.B. 146. See [1960] J.B.L. at 276–279.

[13] See further Clarke, *The Law of Insurance Contracts*, para. 29–2C.

[14] s.2(5)(b).

[15] *Portavon Cinema Co. v. Price* [1939] 4 All E.R. 601. *Quaere* whether it could apply to an E.C. insurer selling fire insurance directly from its country of establishment.

just been examined. Of more interest is the obligation arising under section 83.

It should be noted first that the section applies only to fire policies on buildings,[16] but that it is not limited to London. There is clear authority that it applies throughout England and Wales,[17] but it does not apply to Scotland or Ireland.[18] Under section 83, reinstatement need only be to the extent of the policy moneys available, which should be compared with the position under contractual reinstatement. However, this does mean the whole of the money potentially available under the policy, even if the "person interested" has, in fact, only a limited insurable interest in the building.[19]

Request to reinstate

The obligation on an insurer under section 83 arises only upon a clear and distinct request to reinstate by a "person interested" (see below) before the insurer settles with the insured. A mere request not to pay the insured, for example, is not enough. In *Simpson v. Scottish Union Insurance Co.,*[20] the tenant of premises insured them as he was obliged to do under his lease. Following a fire, the landlord wrote to the insurers asking them not to pay anything to the tenant and claiming that he was entitled to the benefit of the policy. Despite this, the insurers settled with the tenant. The landlord then proceeded to rebuild the premises and claimed that the insurers were liable to him. It was held that his claim was ill-founded. His request to the insurers was not sufficient to invoke the section; it was not a request to reinstate but rather a claim to the money, and he had no other right to the benefit of the policy. In any event, section 83 does not authorise a person to rebuild himself and then claim the cost.

Remedy against insurer

If an insurer fails to comply with a proper request under section 83, it is likely that the appropriate remedy is a mandatory injunction to compel

---

[16] See, *e.g. ex p. Gorely* (1864) 4 De G.J. & S., where s.83 was held inapplicable to a tenant's trade fixtures.

[17] *ibid.* It also applies to much of the Commonwealth.

[18] *Westminster Fire v. Glasgow Provident* (1888) 13 App. Cas. 699; *Andrews v. Patriotic Assurance Co.* (1886) 18 L.R.Ir. 355.

[19] *Simpson v. Scottish Union Insurance Co.* (1863) 1 H. & M. 618 at 628.

[20] (1863) 1 H. & M. 618.

them to do so. This was the opinion of Page-Wood V.-C. in the *Simpson* case, and although, in the later case of *Wimbledon Golf Club v. Imperial Insurance Co.*,[21] it was said that the only remedy is an injunction to restrain the insurers from paying the insured, it is submitted that the former opinion is the better one and certainly the one more in accord with the purpose of the section.

Person interested

The most interesting question is who is a "person interested" for the purposes of compelling the insurer to reinstate. As has been seen, it is not necessary that such a person has a full insurable interest in the property, nor is it necessary that he has any contractual relationship with the insurer. On the other hand, the insured must be entitled to enforce the policy. The insured, however, is not such a person interested, so that he cannot compel reinstatement,[22] but otherwise it appears that anyone with a legal or equitable interest in the property can. In *Sinnot v. Bowden*,[23] the mortgagee of the property, whose debt was considerably less than the amount of the loss, was held entitled to insist that the mortgagor's insurers reinstate, and there have been several cases where a landlord was held entitled to use section 83 against his tenant's insurer.[24]

Conversely, a tenant can compel his landlord's insurer to reinstate.[25] This provides a practical solution to some problems raised by the requirement of insurable interest. In *Lonsdale & Thompson Ltd v. Black Arrow Group plc*,[26] it was held that a tenant was entitled to use section 83 against the landlord's insurers even where the landlord had contracted to sell the freehold before the fire and thus no longer had any insurable interest. Although the benefit of the insurance did not pass to the purchasers of the freehold,[27] the policy was construed as enuring for the

---

[21] (1902) 18 T.L.R. 815.

[22] *Reynolds v. Phoenix Assurance Co.* [1978] 2 Lloyd's Rep. 440, especially at 462.

[23] [1912] 2 Ch. 414.

[24] *e.g. Vernon v. Smith* (1821) 5 B. & Ald. 1.

[25] *Wimbledon Golf Club v. Imperial Insurance Co.* (1902) 18 T.L.R. 815; *Lonsdale & Thompson Ltd v. Black Arrow Group plc* [1993] 3 All E.R. 648. As standard commercial leases provide for the landlord to insure, but also for the tenant's benefit (see pp. 303–304, below), this is the more likely scenario today.

[26] [1993] 3 All E.R. 648. See [1994] J.B.L. 188.

[27] See *Rayner v. Preston* (1881) 18 Ch. D. 1; see pp. 164–165, above.

benefit of the tenant,[28] whose entitlement clearly survived the sale of the freehold.[29]

It may also be the case that the purchaser of real property between contract and completion can invoke section 83 against his vendor's insurers. This was clearly stated, *obiter*, in *Rayner v. Preston*[30] and logically seems correct, provided that the insured vendor has not received the full purchase price and hence suffered no loss.[31] If so, some of the difficulties surrounding the insurance position in this situation and the true meaning of section 47 of the Law of Property Act 1925 can be circumvented if the new standard contract provision keeping the risk with the vendor is not adopted.[32]

The insured's duty to reinstate?

Finally, there arise a number of questions not concerned with the position as between insured and insurer, but with those cases where the insured has recovered money from his insurer which a third party claims should be spent by the insured on reinstatement.

By section 108(2) of the Law of Property Act 1925, the mortgagee of property has the right to compel the mortgagor, who has insured and received money, to use it on reinstatement. Trustees who have received

---

[28] The judge applied the analogy of the "bailee cases" (see pp. 60–62, above). This disposed of the arguments of the insurers, following *Castellain v. Preston* (1883) 11 Q.B.D. 380 (see p. 288, below), to the effect that allowing the tenant to benefit would result in the insured vendor profiting from his loss. In line with the modern trend (see pp. 49–52, above), the question of the possible applicability of the Life Assurance Act 1774 was ignored.

[29] The same would apply to the facts of a case like *British Traders' Insurance Co. v. Monson*, (1964) 111 C.L.R. 86 (see p. 70, above), where a tenant who has insured for full value is entitled only to the value of his interest and cannot claim the full value for the benefit of his landlord. If the landlord invokes section 83 in time, the result contended for by the tenant on the facts of that case would, practically speaking, be achieved.

[30] (1881) 18 Ch. D. 1 at 15; see pp. 164–165, above. See also *Royal Insurance Co. Ltd v. Mylius* (1926) 38 C.L.R. 477.

[31] See the decision of the High Court of Australia on an equivalent provision, *Kern Corporation Ltd v. Walter Reid Trading Pty Ltd* (1987) 61 A.L.J.R. 319 and the discussion in Derham, *Subrogation in Insurance Law*, pp. 61–64. The proviso mentioned is essential to overcome the decision in *Rayner v. Preston*, above, because it is unlikely that any insurance effected by a vendor could ordinarily be construed as effected also for the benefit of the purchaser.

[32] See pp. 169–170, above.

insurance money may reinstate trust property with it, but there is no obligation.[33]

Apart from these cases, it is likely that the insured and the third party are parties to a contract which, it is argued, expressly or impliedly, provides for reinstatement at the third party's option. A hire-purchase contract may, for example, contain such an express term for the benefit of the owner in respect of insurance he requires to be effected by the hirer. Another common example would be a covenant to reinstate in a lease. However, in the absence of an express covenant to reinstate, the court will not usually imply one even where the insured covenanted to insure.[34] It may be, however, that the circumstances including the imposition of a covenant to insure, show that the insurance was intended to be a joint one for the benefit of both parties, so that the third party may insist upon reinstatement.[35] In *Mumford Hotels Ltd v. Wheler*,[36] the tenant of property covenanted to pay what was called a "yearly insurance rent" equal to the premium necessary for a comprehensive policy on the premises. The landlord covenanted to effect such an insurance but did not covenant to reinstate. It was held that no such covenant could be implied, but the true inference from the circumstances was that the insurance was to be treated for the joint benefit of the landlord insured and the tenant, so that the latter had an interest in the policy moneys and could oblige the former to use them for reinstatement. On appropriate facts, this provides for an alternative route for such a tenant to achieve the same result as is available under section 83, as discussed, if, for example the section is no longer available because the insurer has settled with the landlord, or if section 83 does not apply at all.[37]

[33] Trustee Act 1925, s.20(4).

[34] *Lees v. Whitely* (1866) L.R. 2 Eq. 143.

[35] This question is discussed further in the next Chap. at pp. 303–309.

[36] [1964] Ch. 117.

[37] *e.g.* because the insurer is a Lloyd's underwriter; see above. See also the discussion on insurance of third parties' interests at pp. 69–71, above.

CHAPTER 15

SUBROGATION

This chapter is concerned with the fundamental correlative of the principle of indemnity, namely, the insurer's right of subrogation.[1] Although often in the insurance context referred to as a right, it is really more in the nature of a restitutionary remedy.[2] The "fundamental rule of insurance law" is "that the contract of insurance contained in a marine or fire policy is a contract of indemnity, and of indemnity only, and this contract means that the assured, in the case of a loss against which the policy has been made, shall be fully indemnified, but shall never be more than fully indemnified."[3] A number of points arise simply from that oft-cited dictum and the doctrine of subrogation has many ramifications which must be examined. It is convenient first, though, to consider some general points.

Application of subrogation

Subrogation applies to all insurance contracts which are contracts of indemnity, that is, particularly to contracts of fire, motor, property and liability insurance. It does not apply to life insurance[4] nor prima facie to accident insurance.[5] However, although payments under an accident policy are usually of a fixed stated sum or according to a fixed scale, it is possible to have such policies whereby payments are made on an indemnity basis, in other words are related to specific heads of loss suffered by the insured. This might well also be the case in, for example, a health insurance policy or a medical expenses section of a larger policy. There can be no real doubt

---

[1] An exhaustive and most useful monograph is Derham, *Subrogation in Insurance Law*, Law Book Company, 1985.
[2] See Goff and Jones, *The Law of Restitution* (3rd ed.), p. 523.
[3] Brett L.J. in *Castellain v. Preston* (1883) 11 Q.B.D. 380.
[4] *Solicitors & General Life Assurance Society v. Lamb* (1864) 2 De G. J. & S. 251.
[5] *Theobald v. Railway Passengers Assurance Co.* (1854) 10 Exch. 45.

that these policies are indemnity policies and therefore should attract the right of subrogation.[6] It has indeed been argued[7] that many forms of life insurance have indemnity intentions, a point discussed earlier and reinforced by the requirement of section 3 of the Life Assurance Act 1774.[8] Notable examples are "keyman" policies effected by employers on the lives of their employees, and policies by creditors on the lives of their debtors. The only real purpose of such insurance is to indemnify against the risk of a loss. However, whatever the attractions of such an argument, it seems safe to assume that the law would not regard any form of life insurance as attracting the right of subrogation.

Origins of subrogation

There has been some dispute as to the true origins of the doctrine of subrogation. Some claim to have found traces in Roman Law. It was probably first developed in this country in the Courts of Chancery and Admiralty,[9] and a number of authorities refer to it as a creature of equity.[10] On the other hand, some modern cases, particularly in judgments delivered by Lord Diplock, refer to it as a common law doctrine arising out of a term implied into every contract of indemnity insurance.[11]

The matter was considered by the House of Lords in *Napier v. Hunter.*[12] Here the question arose in an acute form. The insureds were members of a

---

[6] See various North American authorities: *Glyn v. Scottish Union & National Insurance Co.* (1963) 40 D.L.R. (2d) 929, where subrogation was held applicable to medical payments cover under a motor policy and *Gibson v. Sun Life Assurance Co. of Canada* (1985) 7 C.C.L.I. 65, where it was held applicable to a disability insurance policy; *Michigan Medical Services v. Sharpe* 339 Mich. 574, 54 N.W. (2d) 713 (1954), where there was an express term providing for subrogation; compare *Michigan Hospital Services v. Sharpe* 339 Mich. 375, 63 N.W. (2d) 638 (1954), a case which arose out of the same facts, where the absence of such a term was fatal. See generally, Kimball and Davis, "The extension of insurance subrogation" (1962) 60 Mich. L.R. 841, especially at 860–861.

[7] Kimball and Davis, *op. cit.*

[8] See Chap. 3, especially at pp. 41–45.

[9] Goff and Jones, *op cit.*, p. 523.

[10] See *e.g. Burnand v. Rodocanachi* (1882) 7 App. Cas. 333 at 339; *Morris v. Ford Motor Co. Ltd* [1973] 1 Q.B. 792 at 800-801.

[11] Especially, *Yorkshire Insurance Co. v. Nisbet Shipping Co.* [1962] 2 Q.B. 330 at 339; *Morris v. Ford Motor Co.*, above, at 809–812; *Hobbs v. Marlowe* [1977] 2 All E.R. 241 at 254–255.

[12] [1993] 2 W.L.R. 42. The views of Lord Diplock were treated with scant respect: see especially Lord Browne- Wilkinson at 65. Another important aspect of this decision is considered below at pp. 290–292.

Lloyd's syndicate who in effect reinsured the risks they had agreed to bear
by insuring with "stop loss" insurers. Claims on the insurance were made
and paid by the insurers and subsequently money was recovered from a
third party whose negligence had caused the loss to the insureds.[13] This
money was held by a firm of solicitors. There was no dispute as to the
entitlement of the insurers to at least some money back,[14] but the question
was whether the insurers had merely a personal claim pursued by means of
an action for money had and received, that is a common law right only, or
whether they had an equitable proprietary claim to part of the fund held
by the solicitors.[15]

Their Lordships were unanimous in holding that insurers have an
equitable interest in money received by the insured (or someone acting for
him). The opinions contain reviews of the history of the doctrine of
subrogation which indicate that at the very least it developed in equity as
well as at common law.[16] In the words of Lord Templeman:

> "The principles which dictated the decisions of our ancestors and
> inspired their references to the equitable obligations of an insured
> person towards an insurer entitled to subrogation are discernible and
> immutable. They establish that such an insurer has an enforceable
> equitable interest in the damages payable by the wrongdoer."[17]

[13] In fact, the third party was the syndicate's managing agent who had negligently
committed the insureds to the risks.

[14] By virtue of the first aspect of subrogation described below. The issue as to how
much is considered below at p. 290.

[15] Differing views were expressed on the question of whether insurers would have
an equitable claim to use the insured's name in litigation, the second aspect of
subrogation described below. Lord Templeman thought that they would have (at
52–53), but reserved the question (at 56) in the light of the views expressed by
Lord Goff (at 61). The latter was inclined to support the view expressed by Lord
Templeman, but referred to decisions indicating the contrary and preferred not
to reach a firm conclusion without full consideration of the authorities. This may
be important in the light of the decision in *Morris v. Ford Motor Co. Ltd* [1973] 1
Q.B. 792, where Lord Denning denied the use of this aspect of subrogation on
"equitable" grounds. See further, pp. 309–311, below.

[16] Particular reliance was placed on the decisions in *Randal v. Cockran* (1748) 1 Ves.
Sen. 98, *White v. Dobinson* (1844) 14 Sim. 273, *Commercial Union Assurance Co. v.
Lister* (1874) L.R. 9 Ch. App. 483 and *Re Miller Gibb & Co. Ltd* [1957] 1 W.L.R.
703, showing that equity enforced rights of subrogation against an insured as
well as intervening to enable the insurer to sue in the name of the insured. A
very persuasive argument to this effect is also made by Derham, *op cit.*, Chap. 1.

[17] [1993] 2 W.L.R. at 64.

The equitable interest of the insurers was to be satisfied by saying that they had a lien or charge over the money in question, rather than by saying that the money was impressed with a trust.[18] Thus, if the insured who has received the money goes bankrupt or, if a company, goes into insolvent liquidation, the insurers can recover the money without regard to the claims of other creditors.[19]

Although it has been clearly held that subrogation is a creature of equity, as well as of the common law, it is clear that its application can be modified, excluded or extended by contract. The extension of subrogation rights by express terms in insurance policies is commonplace, and examples of this appear throughout this chapter.

It should also be noted that the doctrine of subrogation applies more widely than simply to insurance.[20] However, it is probably safe to proceed upon the understanding that, although the essential nature of subrogation applies in all cases, each is self-contained, and in examining insurance subrogation, these other contexts may be ignored. Indeed it has been said in the House of Lords that it should not be assumed that principles which grew up in one area can be transplanted to another.[21]

The Two Aspects of Subrogation

The passage cited earlier from the leading case of *Castellain v. Preston*[22] by itself gives a picture of only one aspect of the doctrine of subrogation, namely that the insured cannot make a profit from his loss and that for any profit he does make he is accountable in equity to his insurer. Later passages, though, in the judgments in that case describe the second aspect of the doctrine. This is the right of the insurer who has indemnified his insured to step into the shoes of the insured — the literal meaning of "subrogation" — and in his name pursue any right of action available to the insured which may diminish the loss insured against. Typically, although not exclusively, the insured's right will be to sue a third party liable to pay damages in tort or for breach of contract, the third party's liability being in respect of the event for which the insured has recovered

---

[18] The imposition of a trust would, it was felt, impose too great a burden on the person actually holding the money.

[19] *Re Miller, Gibb & Co.* [1957] 1 W.L.R. 703, approved by the House of Lords in *Napier v. Hunter.*

[20] For a full description, see Goff and Jones, *op. cit.*, Chap. 27.

[21] *Orapko v. Manson Investments* [1977] 3 W.L.R. 229 at 234 (Lord Diplock).

[22] (1883) 11 Q.B.D. 380.

from his insurer. As already noted, the insured can, if necessary, be compelled to lend his name for the purposes of the action.[23]

Although the purposes of these two aspects of subrogation are the same, namely, the prevention of the unjust enrichment of the insured, they are essentially different and, to some extent, different principles are relevant and different qualifications surround each aspect. They will therefore be examined separately.

The Insured Cannot Make a Profit

The leading illustration here is still the case of *Castellain v. Preston*.[24] This was the sequel to the decision in *Rayner v. Preston*,[25] which was examined in Chapter 9.[26] It will be recalled that the insured vendor of a house which was burnt down between the contract and completion recovered money from his insurer for which he was held not accountable to his purchaser. The latter subsequently completed the purchase, as he was bound to do despite the fire, and paid the agreed price. It was held that the vendor was therefore bound to account to his insurer for the money the latter had paid. The Court of Appeal followed the slightly earlier decision in *Darrell v. Tibbits*,[27] where the owner of a house which was let to a tenant insured it against fire. The local authority caused an explosion which damaged the house, and paid compensation to the tenant. The insurers paid the insured, but then sought to recover this sum. It was held that they were entitled to succeed, as the insured had already been compensated by virtue of the tenant's receiving the compensation which had been used to repair the house. In both cases, to have allowed the insured to keep the insurance money would have meant that he would have been doubly indemnified, and would have profited from his loss. In *Darrell v. Tibbits*, the tenant had covenanted to repair the house in the event of losses such as occurred. It was made clear that the same result would in effect have happened had the insurers, upon payment to the landlord, used his name to sue the tenant under this covenant. This, of course, would have involved the other aspect of the doctrine of subrogation.

[23] *King v. Victoria Insurance Co. Ltd* [1896] A.C. 250 at 255–256; *Edwards v. Motor Union Insurance Co.* [1922] 2 K.B. 249 at 254.
[24] (1883) 11 Q.B.D. 380.
[25] (1881) 18 Ch.D. 1.
[26] See p. 164, above.
[27] (1880) 5 Q.B.D. 560.

The rule that the insured cannot profit from his loss is subject to three limitations. First, he is accountable only when he has been fully indemnified. Secondly, if he receives a gift following the loss, this may not necessarily be taken into account. Thirdly, if a surplus results after the insurer has recovered back its money, it seems that the insured is entitled to keep it. These three points must now be examined in detail.

Full indemnity

In *Scottish Union & National Insurance Co. v. Davis*,[28] the defendant insured's damaged car was handed to a garage for repair with the consent of the plaintiff insurers. After three attempts at repair by the garage, the insured was not satisfied with their work and took the car elsewhere. The garage nonetheless sent their bill to the insurers who paid it without getting a satisfaction note signed by the insured. The latter then recovered compensation from the party originally responsible for the damage and used this money to have his car properly repaired. The insurers claimed this latter sum, but the Court of Appeal had no difficulty in rejecting their claim. "You only have a right to subrogation in a case like this when you have indemnified the assured, and one thing that is quite plain is that the insurers have never done that."[29]

It was not clear from this decision whether the insured must merely be fully indemnified within the terms of the policy before the duty to account arises or whether he must be fully compensated. This is an issue which is likely to arise quite commonly in practice. Three simple illustrations can be given for the purposes of discussion. In the first, property insured for £100 may be worth £200 or cost £200 to replace; that is, it is under-insured.[30] If the property is destroyed, and the insured recovers £100 from his insurers and then subsequently receives £100 from the party responsible for the loss, must he account to his insurers for the latter sum, on the grounds that they have fully indemnified him under the terms of the insurance?[31]

For the second illustration, suppose the case of a motor insured whose car is damaged in an accident. His insurers pay the costs of repair, but

[28] [1970] 1 Lloyd's Rep. 1.
[29] Per Russell L.J., *ibid.* at 5.
[30] As to under-insurance generally, see p. 272, above.
[31] This assumes that the insured acted properly in accepting only £100 from the other party. If he did not, he will have failed to act in good faith and prejudiced his insurers' right of subrogation and be liable to the insurers accordingly; see p. 297, below. However, it may be that the insured was able to recover only £100 *e.g.* because of the third party's impecuniosity.

have no interest in pursuing their right to sue the person responsible for the accident. The insured recovers from the third party a sum which includes compensation for his uninsured consequential losses, for example the cost of hiring a substitute car while his was being repaired,[32] and, if the insured needs his car for business purposes, loss of profits while he was without his car. Can the insurers claim that he has profited because he was fully indemnified by them, even though he was not fully compensated?

A very common variant on this latter example is a third situation where the policy contains an excess, so that the insured bears the first part of any claim.[33] Can the insured keep the amount of this out of what he recovers from the third party?

Until recently, there were no clear answers to these questions in any decided English case.[34] In *Napier v. Hunter*,[35] the House of Lords gave an authoritative answer at least to the last one. The facts of this case have been briefly described earlier.[36] A relatively simple set of figures was used for the purposes of argument and decision. The loss suffered by the insured was £160,000. The limit of the insurers' liability, that is the sum insured, was £125,000, and there was an excess of £25,000. The sum recovered from the third party responsible for the loss was £130,000. The insurers paid the insured £100,000, that is the sum insured less the excess. The question was whether the insured was entitled to £60,000 of the sum recovered from the third party, so that he would recover the whole of his loss, and the insurer would therefore receive £70,000 back; or whether the insurer was entitled to a greater proportion of the £130,000, so that the insured would be under-compensated.

---

[32] See the facts of *Hobbs v. Marlowe* [1977] 2 All E.R. 241, discussed below at p. 308. It is now quite common for this sort of loss to be insured.

[33] See p. 274, above.

[34] A decision of the Canadian Supreme Court, *Ledingham v. Ontario Hospital Services Commission* (1974) 46 D.L.R. (3d) 699 seemed to support a general view that an insured had to be fully compensated before the insurers obtained rights of subrogation, and was cited and discussed in previous editions of this book as authority for that (see p. 241 of the 2nd ed.). There are other Commonwealth authorities to similar effect, admirably summarised in Derham, *op. cit.*, Chapter 12. However, except in respect of genuinely uninsured losses, this no longer seems supportable in the light of *Napier v. Hunter*, considered below.

[35] [1993] 2 W.L.R. 42. The lower courts' decisions are reported, sub nom. *Napier v. Kershaw Ltd*, at [1993] 1 Lloyd's Rep. 10. Saville J. at first instance held in favour of the insured, but the Court of Appeal's decision on this point was the same as that of the House of Lords.

[36] See p. 285.

It was held that the latter approach was the correct one. The effect of the excess was that the insured was deemed to be his own insurer for the amount of that excess, namely £25,000. Further, he must be assumed to have agreed to bear any loss over the sum insured, that is over £125,000. The result was that the insured was entitled to only £35,000 of the sum of £130,000 recovered from the third party, that is his uninsured loss of £60,000 less the amount of the excess, and the insurers were entitled to the balance of £95,000.

This aspect of the decision in *Napier v. Hunter* was considered in detail only by Lords Templeman and Jauncey. The former[37] rationalised the position by assuming that there were in fact three insurances, the first for the first £25,000 of any loss, the second for the next £100,000 and the third for any payment in excess of £125,000. On the loss of £160,000, the insured would recover £25,000, £100,000 and £35,000 from the respective insurers. On the recovery of £130,000, £35,000 would first go back to the third insurers and the remaining £95,000 would go back to the second insurers. The latter were, of course, the actual insurers in the case. The reasoning of Lord Jauncey is summed up in this dictum[38]:

> "When an insured loss is diminished by a recovery from a third party, whether before or after any indemnification has been made, the ultimate loss is simply the initial loss minus the recovery and it is that sum to which the provisions of the policy of assurance apply including any provision as to an excess."

Thus, on the assumed figures, the ultimate loss was £30,000, namely the initial loss of £160,000 less the recovery of £130,000, and the excess of £25,000 applied to the £30,000 so that the insured recovered from the insurers only £5,000. Although no previous authority pointed unequivocally to this result, dicta were cited[39] which, in the words of Lord Jauncey[40] were significant because of:

> "the emphasis they place upon the fact that in the context of recoveries subrogation is concerned only with the loss against which

---

[37] At 46–48.

[38] At 64.

[39] Especially from *Castellain v. Preston* (1883) 11 Q.B.D. 380 at 386, 393 and 395 and *Burnand v. Rodocanachi* (1882) 7 App. Cas. 333 at 339.

[40] [1993] 2 W.L.R. at 63.

the assured is insured rather than any general loss. If an assured has suffered an insured loss and an uninsured loss full indemnification of the former subrogates the insurers irrespective of the fact that the assured has not yet recovered the uninsured loss."

The logic of the reasoning here is difficult to fault, and it is hard to disagree with the result in a situation involving commercial insurance where it must perhaps be assumed that the parties are fully aware as to the significance of an excess. However, it may not be so easy in other contexts to rationalise the result by saying that the insured agreed to bear the amount of the excess. At least some insureds do not in reality so agree. In many classes of insurance, they have no choice as to whether or not there is to be an excess, although in some they may have a choice as to the amount of the excess.

Strictly *Napier v. Hunter* was concerned only with the effect of an excess on subrogation recoveries. However, the reasoning suggests a solution to the other two questions posed above, namely the cases of an under-insured insured and of the insured who recovers uninsured losses. In the case of under-insurance, Lord Templeman expressly stated[41] that the insured is deemed to be his own insurer of any loss above the sum insured. This suggests that, in the example given above, the insured would be bound to account to the insurer for the £100 received from the third party responsible for the loss. Again, this result might work harshly on some insureds.

However, the case of uninsured losses, the second illustration given above, seems quite different. They are simply not covered by the policy and it can hardly be said that the insured is deemed to be his own insurer in respect of them. Another way of putting it is to say that, as mentioned earlier, the purpose of subrogation is to prevent unjust enrichment, and an insured can hardly be said to be unjustly enriched until he receives full compensation for his loss, which includes for his uninsured losses.

Gifts

If the insured has been fully indemnified, but he also receives a gift from another to mitigate the effects of his loss, he will normally have to account to his insurers for the amount of the gift. In *Stearns v. Village Main Reef Gold Mining Co.*,[42] the defendant's insured gold was commandeered by the

---

[41] *ibid.* at 47.
[42] (1905) 10 Com. Cas. 89.

South African Government. The insurers paid the defendant for a total loss. The Government then returned a sum of money to the insured in return for the latter's agreeing to keep the mine open. It was held that the insurers were entitled to recover the equivalent of that money because it had been given in order to diminish the insured's loss. This decision can be compared with the earlier marine insurance case of *Burnand v. Rodocanachi*.[43] Here, during the American Civil War, the insured ship was destroyed by a Confederate cruiser. The insurers paid the agreed value. The insured subsequently received a gift from the United States Government. The House of Lords held that as, according to the construction of the relevant statute authorising the payment, this money was paid purely as a gift and intended to benefit the insured over and above any insurance money, the insurers were not entitled to claim it. It is clear that this case establishes the exception rather than the rule, and that the insured will be entitled to retain the gift only when it was intended as extra compensation for him.

A surplus

If, somewhat unusually perhaps, there happens to be a surplus after the insurers have recovered their money, the insured is entitled to keep it, in other words the insurers' subrogation rights extend only to the amount they actually paid to the insured. In *Yorkshire Insurance Co. v. Nisbet Shipping Co.*,[44] the point arose in a neat form. An insured ship was lost in 1945 as the result of a collision and the insurers paid its agreed value of £72,000. With the latter's consent, the insured started proceedings against the Canadian Government, owners of the other ship, and in 1955 the Government was eventually found liable. The damages awarded were some £75,000 which were properly converted into Canadian dollars at the rate of exchange prevalent at the time of the collision. That sum was paid to the insured in 1958, but when it was transmitted to this country and converted into sterling, it produced a sum of some £126,000, because the pound had been devalued in 1949. The insured could not of course deny the insurers' entitlement to £72,000, but disputed that they were entitled to the surplus of nearly £55,000. Diplock J. held that the subrogation rights of the insurers extended only to the sums they had paid out. Although he was construing the relevant section in the Marine Insurance

---

[43] (1882) 7 App. Cas. 333.
[44] [1962] 2 Q.B. 330.

Act 1906,[45] there can be no doubt that the decision is generally applicable. Although logically unimpeachable,[46] the result is somewhat unfair. After all, the insured had the benefit of prompt payment of the money in 1945. It was the insurers who were out of pocket for some 13 years or more. Had the insurer actually exercised their right to sue the Canadian Government in the insured's name, they would probably have been better off because they would have been entitled to claim interest on the money for their own benefit.[47]

The Insurer's Right to Take Action

The insurer's right to bring proceedings in the name of the insured is long established, being referred to as a commonplace occurrence as long ago as 1782 in *Mason v. Sainsbury*.[48] It is important to remember, however, that the action remains the insured's and that the defendant, if he is adjudged liable, gets a good discharge only if he pays the insured. If the insured should refuse to allow his name to be used, the insurer can, as an alternative to compelling it, bring proceedings against the wrongdoer and join the insured as second defendant.

A classic illustration of the insurer's right is the decision of the House of Lords in *Lister v. Romford Ice and Cold Storage Ltd.*[49] There an employee of the respondent negligently injured another employee; in fact, they were son and father respectively. The respondent was therefore vicariously liable to pay damages to the father, an award satisfied by the respondent's liability insurers, who then used the respondent's name to sue the negligent employee to recoup the loss. The claim was that the employee had failed to exercise the reasonable care and skill impliedly expected as part of an employee's duty to his employer, and, by a majority, the House of Lords held that the claim succeeded. The majority regarded the fact that

---

[45] s.79.
[46] But note the comments of Megaw L.J. in *Lucas v. E.C.G.D.* [1973] 1 W.L.R. 914 at 924, and the possible effects of express subrogation terms; see p. 302 below.
[47] *Cousins v. D. & C. Carriers* [1971] 2 Q.B. 230; see p. 300, below.
[48] (1782) 3 Doug. K.B. 61 at 64 (Lord Mansfield) — "Every day the insurer is put into the shoes of the assured." Note that if the insured is a company which has been wound up, the insurers have no rights since the insured's name no longer exists to be used: *M. H. Smith (Plant Hire) Ltd v. D. L. Mainwaring* [1986] B.C.L.C. 342.
[49] [1957] A.C. 555.

the action was in reality brought by the insurers as irrelevant. There was such an implied term in the employee's contract of employment and he had broken it. The main defence of the appellant was that, even if he should have acted with reasonable care and skill, if in fact his employer had insured against the consequences of a breach to a third party, there was equally to be implied in his contract of employment a term that he would be entitled to the benefit of that insurance. This persuasive reasoning was adopted by the dissenting judges, in particular by Lord Radcliffe, whose judgment is, it is suggested, much more realistic than those of the majority.[50] Although, as will be seen later, employers' liability insurers have as a result of this decision, agreed to forgo their subrogation rights in this sort of case,[51] the decision does illustrate the wasteful consequences of this aspect of the doctrine of subrogation.[52]

There are a number of very important limitations surrounding, and consequences, of, this aspect of the doctrine of subrogation. These will be examined under the following heads.

The insured must be indemnified

As with the first aspect of subrogation, the insured must be indemnified by the insurer before the latter's right arises, and this is in respect of all claims made by the insured in respect of the particular event. In *Page v. Scottish Insurance Corporation*,[53] P, while driving F's car, negligently collided with and damaged T's car, as well as damaging F's car. F's insurers instructed P to have F's car repaired, but refused to pay these costs and, before indemnifying P against the claim of T, claimed to have the right to sue P in the name of F for damages for negligently driving F's car, and to be able to set off against the repair costs the damages payable to T. The Court of Appeal held that the insurers' exercise of their subrogation rights in F's name was premature: "The underwriter [has] no right to subrogation unless and until he [has] fully indemnified the insured under the policy."[54]

---

[50] See also Parsons, "Individual responsibility versus enterprise liability" (1956) 29 A.L.J. 714, a comment on the Court of Appeal decision which was decided the same way but again only by a majority.

[51] See Gardiner (1959) 22 M.L.R. 652.

[52] See also p. 311, below, and compare *Morris v. Ford Motor Co.* [1973] Q.B. 792 discussed at pp. 309–311, below.

[53] (1929) 98 L.J.K.B. 308.

[54] *ibid.*, at 311, per Scrutton L.J.

The question again arises whether it is enough for the insurer fully to
have indemnified the insured under the policy, or whether the insured
must be fully compensated. Similar examples to those given earlier[55] can be
used to illustrate this point. Most apt, because of its likely occurrence, is
the case of the insured car driver fully indemnified for car damage but with
a claim for uninsured loss against the tortfeasor, which might be for
consequential loss and/or the sum not recovered from his insurer because of
an excess clause in his policy. In *Page*, Scrutton L.J. expressly reserved the
question whether full compensation is necessary.[56] There is some authority
that it is,[57] but it now seems certain that the courts would hold that full
indemnity only is necessary.[58] If, as the result of a subrogation action, the
insurer recovered more than it had paid the insured, the latter would be
entitled to the surplus in so far as it represented an uninsured loss. In any
event, as will be seen, if the insurer declines to sue, the insured can himself
bring proceedings.

In practice, this question may be a rather academic one. This aspect of
the doctrine of subrogation is frequently covered by an express clause in
the policy vesting subrogation rights in the insurer upon indemnification
under the policy or even, sometimes, before that.[59]

Who controls the proceedings?

It follows from the points just discussed that, until the insured is
indemnified and in the absence of anything to the contrary in the policy, as
a matter of general law he has the right to sue the wrongdoer and control
the proceedings. In *Commercial Union Assurance Co. v. Lister*,[60] the insured's
mill was damaged by an explosion for which, it was alleged, the local
authority was liable. He was insured for £33,000 but the damage was
estimated at £55,000. The insured wished to sue the authority, but the
insurers sought a declaration that they were entitled to the benefit of any

---

[55] See p. 289.

[56] (1929) 98 L.J.K.B. 308 at 312.

[57] *e.g.* the Canadian decision in *Globe & Rutgers Fire Insurance Co. v. Truedell* [1927] 2
D.L.R. 659.

[58] As a result of the decision in *Napier v. Hunter* [1993] 2 W.L.R. 42, discussed at
p. 290, above. Although the decision was not concerned with this aspect of
subrogation, the thrust of the reasoning dictates that there can be no distinction
on this point between the two aspects.

[59] See p. 302, below.

[60] (1874) L.R. 9 Ch. 483.

such action. It was held that as he would not be fully indemnified by his insurers, the insured was entitled to bring and control the action, provided he acted *bona fide* and sued for the whole loss.[61] In addition, before the insurers have the right to control, they must agree to indemnify the insured in respect of costs. It is also clear that even if the insured has been fully indemnified, he can if he wishes, sue the third party and control the proceedings if the insurer declines. The insurer has no right to stop the insured.[62]

In practice, though, many of these points may be redundant. Express subrogation clauses will often give the insurers the right to control the proceedings regardless of indemnification. One important question may then arise as to the position of the insurers who elect not to take control, in particular as to their liability for costs, as the standard term provides that if the insurers do take control, it is at their expense. Again the typical case may involve an under-insured insured who has been paid by his insurers and has a claim against a tortfeasor which he wishes to exercise to recover his uninsured loss. The insurers are not interested, save in the possibility of recovering anything if the insured is successful. The insured, as has been seen, must sue for his whole loss. Can he claim that the insurer must bear the costs of his action on the ground that, if he succeeds, it will be partly to the benefit of his insurers, and had they taken control, they would have been responsible for the costs? These facts arose in the New Zealand case of *Arthur Barnett Ltd v. National Insurance Co. of New Zealand*,[63] where the Court of Appeal held that the insurers were not responsible. This result is also implied by the course of events in *Hobbs v. Marlowe*,[64] a case on similar facts which will be examined later, but where the point was not actually in issue.

The insured must not do anything to prejudice the insurer

It has just been seen that the insured who takes proceedings against a wrongdoer must sue for his whole loss, even if he has been partly indemnified by his insurers who decline to exercise their subrogation rights. This is perhaps one aspect of the general principle that, once rights

---

[61] The requirement on the insured to act in good faith in the interests of the insurer was confirmed in *Napier* v. *Hunter*, above.

[62] *Morley v. Moore* [1936] 2 K.B. 359; *Hobbs v. Marlowe* [1977] 2 All E.R. 241.

[63] [1965] N.Z.L.R. 874.

[64] [1977] 2 All E.R. 241. See p. 308, below.

of subrogation exist or potentially exist for the benefit of the insurers, the insured must not do anything which might prejudice those rights on pain of his being liable to repay to the insurers as damages the amount which the insurers have paid or, where appropriate, of the insurers being able to avoid liability. If the insured does so act, he will have broken the duty of good faith imposed on him.[65]

Therefore, while a compromise entered into between the insured and the wrongdoer will normally bind the insurers, such a compromise, whether agreed before or after indemnification by the insurers, will amount to a breach of this duty of the insured. However, the insured must actually prejudice the insurers' position, so that if his claim against the third party is a doubtful one and he acts bona fide in the interests of the insurers as well as himself, he will not suffer. In *West of England Fire Insurance Co. v. Isaacs*,[66] the defendant was the sub-tenant of property which he insured with the plaintiff. Following a fire, he recovered money from them which he paid to the tenant of the property who had covenanted with both him and the head landlord to insure. He undertook also not to sue the tenant for breach of this covenant, it appearing that the latter had not adequately insured. It was held that the insured was liable to return the equivalent money to the insurers, having prejudiced their potential right to use his name to sue the tenant for breach of the insuring covenant. There are a number of other illustrations in the cases of the same point, involving insureds who compromised a statutory claim or a claim in tort against a wrongdoer.[67] The principle will obviously apply if the insured actually sues the wrongdoer and recovers only his uninsured loss.[68]

It can perhaps be commented that this principle could unjustifiably penalise an innocent insured not aware of the intricacies of subrogation and tort actions. For example, following a car accident, an insured who was the innocent party might well, because his insurance is comprehensive, agree quite reasonably with the other driver that he will not pursue any claim against him. If that were a binding agreement, it would prejudice the insurers' subrogation rights and yet it seems a harsh application of the principle. This is not to suggest, of course, that an insurer would

---

[65] As confirmed in *Napier v. Hunter* [1993] 2 W.L.R. 42.

[66] [1897] 1 Q.B. 226.

[67] *e.g. Phoenix Assurance Co. v. Spooner* [1905] 2 K.B. 753; *Re Law Fire Assurance Co.* (1888) 4 T.L.R. 309; *Horse, Carriage & General Insurance Co. v. Petch* (1916) 33 T.L.R. 131.

[68] That this is probably a fairly common occurrence is illustrated by the facts of a case like *Hayler v. Chapman* [1989] 1 Lloyd's Rep. 490.

necessarily take the point, but the question remains as to whether it should be there to be taken.

The wrongdoer's position vis-à-vis the insurer

It is self-evident that a wrongdoing defendant cannot claim in defence that in reality the plaintiff is an insurer and that the nominal plaintiff has already been fully compensated for the defendant's wrong.[69] Equally, it is no defence for him to claim that the insurer satisfied the plaintiff's claim when in law it was not bound to, for example, because the insurer had the right to avoid liability under the policy.[70] He can, however, rely on a prior agreement between himself and the insured that the latter would limit his rights. This would have been the result in *Lister v. Romford Ice and Cold Storage Ltd*,[71] if the reasoning of the minority had been accepted. There is County Court authority,[72] which appears correct in principle, that the defendant cannot rely upon a purported waiver by the insured after he knows of the insurer's payment to the insured and thus, that the insurer's subrogation rights have crystallised.

If, however, the insured, bringing proceedings by himself, has received judgment against the wrongdoer, the insurers will not normally be able subsequently to reopen the judgment on the grounds that the insured did not claim for his insured losses from the wrongdoer.[73] Further, if insurers exercising subrogation rights settle their insured's claim against the wrongdoer and sign a form of discharge of the claim which refers to all claims which might arise out of the relevant event, they will be bound by that discharge and unable to reopen the claim.[74]

Whether or not a defendant can rely upon what is commonly referred to as a "subrogation waiver clause" in the policy is also a question of some importance. Such a clause may provide, for example, that insurers will not exercise rights of subrogation against companies which are subsidiaries of

---

[69] The form of the insurer's indemnification does not matter; see, *e.g., Brown v. Albany Construction Co.* [1995] N.P.C. 100, where it took the form of the insurers purchasing the insureds' house from them at full market value.

[70] *King v. Victoria Insurance Co.* [1896] A.C. 250.

[71] [1957] A.C. 555; see p. 294.

[72] *Haigh v. Lawford* (1964) 114 L.J. 208 (Salisbury County Court).

[73] *Hayler v. Chapman* [1989] 1 Lloyd's Rep. 490. As indicated above, the insured who acts in this way without the sanction of his insurers will be in breach of his duty to act in good faith and not to prejudice the insurers' subrogation rights.

[74] *Kitchen Design and Advice Ltd v. Lea Valley Water Co.* [1989] 2 Lloyd's Rep. 333.

or associated with the insured or against someone who is a co-insured.[75] The better view would appear to be that the defendant cannot so rely, unless he is properly a party to the insurance contract; otherwise the defence would contradict the principle of privity of contract.[76] However, there are authorities which hold to the contrary,[77] and it is clearly a question which requires an authoritative ruling of the Court of Appeal or House of Lords.

Subrogation applies only when the insured has a right of action

If, quite apart from agreement or compromise, the insured has no right of action which he could pursue, the insurer can be in no better position. The leading illustration of this point is the decision in *Simpson v. Thomson*.[78] The insured owned two ships which collided due to the negligence of one of the masters. In respect of the ship which was negligently sailed, the insured paid money into court, as he was statutorily bound to do, in order to compensate the various parties involved. The insurers paid for the other ship and then claimed the right to use the insured's name as owner of this ship to claim against the fund. It was held that the insurers had no such right, as it would be tantamount to the insured suing himself, which, of course, is impossible. It would have been different had the ships been owned by different companies, albeit they were both owned or controlled by the same person.[79]

The insurer's claim for interest

The question may often arise whether insurers suing in their insured's name are entitled to claim interest for their own benefit. Nominally, that

---

[75] As to co-insurance, see p. 305, below.
[76] *National Oilwell (U.K.) Ltd v. Davy Offshore Ltd* [1993] 2 Lloyd's Rep. 582; see further p. 306.
[77] See the Canadian decision in *Clark & Sons v. Finnamore* (1973) 32 D.L.R. (3d) 236 and *Enimont Supply S.A.* v. *Chesapeake Shipping Inc., The Surf City* [1995] 2 Lloyd's Rep. 242. In the latter case, Clarke J. also relied on equity to defeat the insurers' claim; see further below, pp. 309–311.
[78] (1877) 3 App. Cas. at 279. See also *Buckland v. Palmer* [1984] 1 W.L.R. 1109, where the principle was applied when the insured had lost her right of action because of rules of court. See [1985] J.B.L. 54.
[79] (1877) 3 App. Cas. at 294 (Lord Blackburn).

award would go to the insured, the nominal plaintiff, but it is now clear that the insurers' subrogation rights include the right to appropriate interest under section 3(1) of the Law Reform (Miscellaneous Provisions) Act 1934.[80] In *H. Cousins & Co. Ltd v. D. & C. Carriers Ltd*,[81] it was argued in an action for damages for breach of a contract of carriage that the plaintiff was entitled to interest only in respect of the period that he really suffered, namely until he was indemnified by his insurers. It was held that there was no reason why the plaintiff should not be awarded interest to the date of judgment on the usual basis, because the appropriate part of it would rightly enure to the benefit of the insurers.[82]

Assignment as an alternative to subrogation

The essence of subrogation is, of course, that the insurers sue in the name of the insured. It is, however, possible for the insurers to seek to adopt an alternative, namely, to persuade the insured to assign his cause of action to them. A bare cause of action, that is the right to sue another, is not assignable, but one enforced by an insurer is legitimate because it is supported by the insurer's interest in recouping for himself the amount of the loss he has paid out as a result of the wrong of the defendant.[83] Provided that the assignment is complete, that is that notice is given to the defendant in accordance with section 136 of the Law of Property Act 1925, the insurer/assignee can sue in his own name.

Such assignments are probably rare. Insurers prefer to use the names of their insureds because of the consequent lack of publicity. However, assignment does have advantages over subrogation. In particular, there will be no requirement that the insured be fully indemnified before the insurer can sue, and it must be the position that the insurers can keep everything they recover from the action. The principle of *Yorkshire Insurance Co. v. Nisbet Shipping Co.*[84] will not apply simply because the cause of action is entirely the insurers' and the insured has forfeited all interest in it.

---

[80] See further p. 274, above.

[81] [1971] 2 Q.B. 230.

[82] The contrary views expressed in *Harbutt's "Plasticine" Ltd v. Wayne Tank & Pump Co.* [1971] 1 Q.B. 447 were clearly based on a misunderstanding. See (1970) 96 L.Q.R. 513.

[83] *Compania Columbiana de Seguros v. Pacific Steam Navigation Co.* [1965] 1 Q.B. 101.

[84] [1962] 2 Q.B. 330; see p. 293, above.

The effect of express terms[85]

It has already been seen in certain respects how express conditions in a policy may refer to subrogation rights. Such terms appear common and there is no doubt that they can exclude or modify some of the conditions surrounding the exercise of subrogation rights at common law. If a policy does contain such a term, the correct approach is to consider it first for a determination of the parties' rights and to refer to general subrogation principles only if there is ambiguity in the term or if it is not all-embracing. In *Lucas v. Exports Credit Guarantee Department*,[86] the courts were faced with a subrogation term in a policy issued by the Department.[87] The issue concerned a question very similar to that in *Yorkshire Insurance Co. v. Nisbet*,[88] and it was held that whether or not the insurer was entitled to an excess resulting after the wrongdoer had paid, and arising because of a variation in the Exchange Rate, depended entirely on the construction of the relevant term. Indeed, in the House of Lords, general principles of subrogation were not considered at all.

Express terms will commonly entitle the insurers to take proceedings before or after indemnifying the insured, and may well entitle them to control or take over proceedings taken by the insured in which they have hitherto taken no interest. It has been seen how, under the general law, even if the insured has been fully indemnified, he is perfectly entitled to proceed against the wrongdoer if the insurers choose not to. In practice express terms may well permit the insurers to take control and thus abandon such an action. It is suggested that this should only be permissible if the insurers act in good faith and with due regard to the interests of the insured, and that in practice insurers would not be so acting if the insured has suffered uninsured loss for which he seeks compensation.[89]

An express term may also purport to give subrogation rights in the name of a party who is not the insured.[90] In certain circumstances,[91] the insured may recover on a policy for the benefit of a third party. If that third party has a claim in respect of the loss against a wrongdoer, the

---

[85] See further, Birds, "Contractual subrogation in insurance" [1979] J.B.L. 124.
[86] [1974] 1 W.L.R. 909.
[87] Which at the time was a government department.
[88] [1962] 2 Q.B. 330; see p. 293, above.
[89] See further (1978) 41 M.L.R. 201 at 204 and [1979] J.B.L. 124 at 134–136.
[90] [1979] J.B.L. 124 at 129–130.
[91] See pp. 60–71, above.

insurer would probably not be subrogated to this right of action at common law simply because the third party has no direct right to sue the insurer. An express term of the sort mentioned is clearly an attempt to cure this problem, though it must be said that enforcement of it would necessitate the sanctioning of an exception to the doctrine of privity of contract.[92]

Two or more persons interested in the same property

Some nice subrogation questions may arise where two or more people have interests in the same property. This may happen, for example, in respect of landlord and tenant or mortgagor and mortgagee of real property, and it may well also involve questions of contribution to which we shall return in the next chapter. The parties may be separately insured, only one of them may be insured, or they may be jointly insured.

Where they are separately insured, the loss will fall on that party legally liable, and hence on that party's insurer. The other party's insurer alone can have subrogation rights if it indemnifies its insured first. If a bailor and bailee of goods are both insured and the goods are lost in circumstances whereby the bailee is responsible, his insurer bears the loss.[93] Similarly, if landlord and tenant are both insured, but the latter covenanted to insure or to repair in the event of a loss, the latter's insurer will bear the loss.[94] The converse will apply if the landlord covenanted appropriately.[95]

Even where only one of the parties is insured, it may be that the insurance enures to the benefit of the other so that the insurer can have no recourse against the latter. The point arose for the first time in this country in the important case of *Mark Rowlands Ltd v. Berni Inns Ltd*,[96] where property leased by the plaintiffs to the defendants was damaged by the negligence of the defendants.[97] Under the terms of the lease, the plaintiffs

---

[92] Whether the courts might "dispense" with privity in this sort of situation is considered at pp. 64–69, above.

[93] *North British & Mercantile Insurance Co. v. London, Liverpool & Globe Insurance Co.* (1877) 5 Ch. D. 569, discussed further at p. 316, below.

[94] *Darrell v. Tibbitts* (1880) 5 Q.B.D. 560; see p. 288, above.

[95] *e.g., United Motor Services v. Hutson* [1937] 1 D.L.R. 737.

[96] [1986] Q.B. 211; see p. 49, above for the insurable interest issues decided in this case and for a detailed note, Birds (1986) 6 Oxford J. Legal Stud. 304. The subrogation point was the primary issue.

[97] The defendants were insured but against third party liability, not under an insurance of the property itself, so that this was not the sort of case discussed above.

covenanted to insure and the defendants covenanted to pay a sum (an "insurance rent") of approximately one quarter of the premium. Further the defendants were relieved from their covenant to repair in respect of "damage by or in consequence of any of the insured risks." The Court of Appeal held that the plaintiffs' insurers could not exercise subrogation rights against the defendants[98]:

> "An essential feature of insurance by fire is that it covers fires caused
> by accident as well as by negligence. This was what the plaintiffs
> agreed to provide in consideration of, *inter alia*, the insurance rent
> paid by the defendants. The intention of the parties, sensibly
> construed, must therefore have been that in the event of damage by
> fire, whether due to accident or negligence, the landlord's loss was to
> be recouped from the insurance monies and that in that event they
> were to have no further claim against the tenants for damages in
> negligence."[99]

It was clearly crucial to the result of the *Mark Rowlands* case that the terms of the lease made it clear that the insurance was for the benefit of both parties. Not all leases will be so worded. It may be that the reasoning can be extended to other relationships between persons interested in the same property, for example vendor and purchaser of land where the vendor's policy expressly enures to the purchaser's benefit between contract and completion,[1] and owner and hirer of goods where the owner

---

[98] An odd feature of the case is the fact that it was openly admitted that the real plaintiff was the insurer. It could so easily have been fought as simply a landlord and tenant case, although it is not suggested that this would have made any difference to the result.

[99] *per* Kerr L.J. at 232. The learned judge relied on a number of Commonwealth and American decisions on the same point, especially three cases in the Canadian Supreme Court: *Agnew Surpass Shoe Stores Ltd v. Cummer-Yonge Investments Ltd* (1973) 55 D.L.R. (3d) 248; *Ross Southwood Tire Ltd v. Pyrotech Products Ltd* (1975) 57 D.L.R. (3d) 248; *T. Eaton Co. Ltd v. Smith* (1977) 92 D.L.R. (3d) 425. See Hasson (1976) 14 Osgoode Hall L.J. 769 at 779–782 and (1985) 5 Oxford J. Legal Stud. 416 at 430–433. See also *Marlborough Properties Ltd v. Marlborough Fibreglass Ltd* [1981] 1 N.Z.L.R. 464, commented on by Yates (1983) 3 Oxford J. Legal Stud. 431. Note that Canadian law does not excuse the actual negligent employee of the tenant; *Greenwood Shopping Plaza v. Beattie* (1980) 111 D.L.R. (3d) 257.

[1] *Cf. Rayner v. Preston* (1881) 18 Ch.D. 1 (p. 164, above) and *Castellain v. Preston* (1883) 11 Q.B.D. 380 (p. 288, above).

has insured pursuant to a term of the contract of hire.[2] It will not apply to the normal case where a mortgagee effects mortgage indemnity insurance against the risk of the mortgagor not repaying his debt, even if the mortgagor in effect pays the cost of the insurance.[3]

Co-insurance Cases

A different situation is where both parties are insured under the same policy, namely a situation of co-insurance.[4] This point arose in *Petrofina Ltd v. Magnaload Ltd*,[5] where it was held that the insurers under a contractors' all risks insurance policy could not use the name of the principal insureds, the owners of the property and main contractors working thereon, to sue the negligent subcontractors responsible for the loss. The latter were held to fall within the definition of "the insured" in the policy and to have an insurable interest in the whole of the contract works, with the result that the insurer's right was defeated by circuity of action.[6] Underlying this conclusion were reasons of "commercial convenience", which also featured strongly in the Canadian Supreme Court decision in *Commonwealth Construction Co. Ltd v. Imperial Oil Ltd*,[7] a decision upon which the judge relied heavily.

Petrofina Ltd v. Magnaload Ltd was followed in the slightly different circumstances of a shipbuilding contract in *Stone Vickers Ltd v. Appledore Ferguson Shipbuilders Ltd*.[8] Here subrogation was refused to the insurers of the head contractor who sought to use the latter's name to sue a sub-contractor who had supplied a defective propeller. On the assumption that the sub-contractor was a co-insured under the policy,[9] it was held that they

---

[2] See further Birds, *op. cit.*

[3] *Woolwich Building Society v. Brown* [1996] C.L.C. 625. Whether or not this is a fair result is another matter.

[4] Note that this is not joint insurance in the strict sense since this arises only where the parties' interests in the property insured are the same: see *e.g. Re King* [1963] Ch. 459, where a policy in the joint names of landlord and tenant was not a joint insurance.

[5] [1984] 1 Q.B. 127; see also p. 62, above and [1983] J.B.L. 497.

[6] See [1984] 1 Q.B. at 139–140 and the same judge's (Lloyd J.) earlier comment in *The Yasin* [1979] 2 Lloyd's Rep. at 54- 55.

[7] (1977) 69 D.L.R. (3d) 558.

[8] [1991] 2 Lloyd's Rep. 288. Although the decision was reversed by the Court of Appeal, [1992] 2 Lloyd's Rep. 578, this was on a point of construction and does not affect the reasoning of the judge at first instance on the point under consideration here.

[9] It was on this point that the Court of Appeal differed.

had an insurable interest, and were sufficiently interested, in the whole of the contract works to be able to resist the insurer's claim.[10] The legal basis for this result was, however, slightly different from that in *Petrofina*. In the judge's view, the exercise of subrogation rights would be so inconsistent with the insurer's obligation to a co-insured that there must be implied into the contract of insurance an exclusion of those rights.[11] A similar view was taken in the subsequent decision in *National Oilwell (U.K.) Ltd v. Davy Offshore Ltd*,[12] but here the supplier's claim to be a co-insured fell at the first hurdle.[13]

It is arguable, with respect, that the courts have reached what seem clearly the right results by unnecessarily straining the concept of insurable interest. This aspect of them has been considered earlier.[14] It has been suggested that there are three possible bases for denying subrogation in the context of co-insurance.[15] One is what has been described as the "fiction" of one assured. In essence it is that which was adopted in *Stone Vickers*, although dressed up in the language of implied terms.[16] The second basis is circuity of action, favoured in *Petrofina*. The third basis is a broader "equitable" approach which has been adopted in the United State of America. It is thought that there is merit in considering further such an equity based on commercial convenience and business efficacy, along the following lines.[17]

When in the circumstances, that is on a proper construction of the relationship between the parties (the contract between them if the

---

[10] On the insurable interest point, see p. 62, above.

[11] See [1991] 2 Lloyd's Rep. at 302.

[12] [1993] 2 Lloyd's Rep. 583, decided by Coleman J. who was also the judge at first instance in *Stone Vickers*.

[13] See further p. 68, above, where the important agency aspects of the case are considered.

[14] See p. 62, above and Birds, "Insurable Interests" in Palmer and McEndrick (eds) *Interests in Goods* (1993).

[15] See Derham, *Subrogation in Insurance Law*, Chap. 7. Compare, though, the learned treatment of this issue (and of *Petrofina* and other relevant authorities) by Brownie J. in (1991) 3 Ins L.J. 48. He concludes that there is no fundamental rule of law preventing one co-insured, *i.e.* the insurer exercising subrogation rights, suing another, but that the contract between them may be construed to have that effect.

[16] See also *National Oilwell*. This was the basis of the reasoning of the Canadian decision in *Commonwealth Construction*, above, heavily relied on by Anthony Coleman Q.C. in *Stone Vickers*.

[17] This may have motivated the court in the different context of the decision in *Mark Rowlands Ltd v. Berni Inns Ltd*, above. See also p. 310, below.

relationship is contractual) and the terms of the contract of insurance, it can fairly be assumed that one policy of insurance was effected to benefit more than one "insured", it must be inferred that there can be no liability between them in respect of losses insured by the policy, at least in the absence of deliberate causing of the loss by one, when the right to benefit is forfeited.[18] In this way, the same result is reached as that achieved in the *Petrofina* and *Stone Vickers* cases,[19] but without perhaps straining the concept of insurable interest. Whatever the exact legal basis for the denial of subrogation in these construction situations of co-insurance, it is suggested that the same principle would apply to other co-insurance situations, for example, an insurance by both hirer and owner of goods under a hire purchase contract.

Waiver of subrogation rights

Insurers may voluntarily agree not to exercise rights of subrogation in certain circumstances. This may arise in the context of an agreement between insured and insurer, for example, it could be a term of the policy[20] or of an agreement of settlement. Alternatively, insurers may simply undertake in general not to exercise their rights. The classic illustration of this is the undertaking by members of the British Insurance Association and Lloyd's that, as employer's liability insurers, they would not pursue claims in an employer's name against a negligent employee to recoup money paid out to indemnify the employer against a third party claim by a fellow employee based on the negligence of the employee.[21]

Insurers may also agree amongst themselves to waive their subrogation rights. The prime example was the "knock for knock" agreements between motor insurers, under which following an accident in which both damaged cars were insured against first party damage, that is, under the usual comprehensive motor policy, each insurer indemnified its own insured regardless of the strict legal position as to liability in tort. Although in practice "knock for knock" agreements have been abandoned, for the time

---

[18] *Samuel v. Dumas* [1924] A.C. 431 at 445–446; *Lombard Australia Ltd v. N.R.M.A. Insurance Ltd* (1968) 72 S.R. (N.S.W.) 45.

[19] And as would have been achieved in *National Oilwell*, had it been a case of co-insurance.

[20] See p. 299, above.

[21] See n.51, above This followed the decision in *Lister v. Romford Ice & Cold Storage Ltd* [1957] A.C. 555, discussed earlier at p. 294.

being at least, there is still merit in discussing the legal consequences of such agreements between insurers.[22]

The existence of such an agreement does not prevent the innocent insured from pursuing his tort claim, at least unless and until his insurer takes it over and abandons it, a question which was discussed earlier. In *Hobbs v. Marlowe*,[23] the innocent car owner did indeed pursue this course because he wished to recover his uninsured loss, namely, his uninsured excess and damages for having to hire a substitute car while his was being repaired. In this, he was supported by the Automobile Association. The House of Lords had no difficulty in rejecting the argument for the negligent driver, in reality the latter's insurer, that the existence of the "knock for knock" agreement between the two insurers concerned removed the victim's right of action. In practice the damages recovered by the plaintiff would largely have to be repaid to his insurer, which was then under the agreement bound to pay them to the defendant's insurer. It was held, however, that the plaintiff (or really the A.A.) was entitled to only those costs appropriate to an action to recover his uninsured loss and as these were below the limits of the County Court Arbitration Scheme, he was not entitled to his own solicitor's costs.[24] The plaintiff had sued for his whole loss, and the result is somewhat harsh in the light of the fact that, had he not done so, he could have been penalised by his insurer.[25] On the actual facts of *Hobbs v. Marlowe*, it appears that this was no real danger because of the attitude of the plaintiff's insurer, but in a future case, an insurer might not be so unconcerned. If an insurer did indeed insist upon the insured's suing for full damages, it is to be hoped that the court would exercise the discretion permitted to award full costs.[26]

---

[22] Although "knock for knock" had some advantages, in particular by eliminating costly and wasteful subrogation actions, there were disadvantages for the "innocent" driver, in particular the possible impact on any "no claims" bonus and the discouragement of actions to pursue uninsured losses; see further (1978) 41 M.L.R. 201.

[23] [1977] 2 All E.R. 241.

[24] County Court Rules Ord. 47, r. 5(4).

[25] Upon the principles discussed earlier at pp. 297–299.

[26] This point remains valid notwithstanding the general abandonment of the "knock for knock" agreements.

Denial of subrogation rights

It may be that the court has power to deny an insurer its subrogation rights in certain contexts. In *Morris v. Ford Motor Co.*,[27] Cameron Industrial Services Ltd (Cameron) contracted to clean at Ford's works. A term of this contract provided that Cameron would indemnify Ford in respect of any liability attaching to Ford for the negligence of the employees of either of them. Morris was injured by an employee of Ford for whom Ford was vicariously liable. Ford claimed an indemnity from Cameron under the term described and Cameron in return claimed upon indemnifying Ford to be subrogated to Ford's right to sue its employee for failing to take reasonable care and skill. Although Cameron was not an insurer as such, though no doubt it was backed by one, its position was analogous to that of an insurer and in particular to the position of the insurer in *Lister v. Romford Ice and Cold Storage Ltd.*[28] The undertaking given by insurers following the latter case, which has been referred to, was not relevant as that applies only when the injury in question is caused by one employee to another employee of the same employer. On the authority of the *Lister* case, Cameron should have succeeded in its claim. However, by a majority, the Court of Appeal held that subrogation would not be permitted. If the decision is correct, then its principles must apply to insurers directly and it cannot be written off simply as "not an insurance case."

One of the principal difficulties with *Morris v. Ford* is that the judges in the majority gave different reasons for their decisions, so that it is virtually impossible to say what the ratio is. Lord Denning M.R. claimed a broad jurisdiction to refuse to allow the enforcement of subrogation rights where it would not be "just and equitable." In his view, subrogation is an equitable remedy whose exercise is therefore subject to general equitable principles. That subrogation was, if not exclusively, recognised by equity is not in doubt[29]; but there are objections to this line of reasoning. First, there is no precedent for such a broad ground for dispensation, and secondly, even if there were, the "equity" ought strictly to refer to the position between insured and insurer, that is the merits of the insurer's

---

[27] [1973] Q.B. 793. See Powles (1974) 90 L.Q.R. 34. For another example, as well as the recent English cases mentioned below, where the wrongdoer was the son of the insured and subrogation was denied at least partly on moral grounds, see *Morawietz v. Morawietz* (1984) 5 C.C.L.I. 11; see the useful comment thereon by Baer, *ibid*.

[28] [1957] A.C. 555; see p. 294, above.

[29] See p. 286, above.

claim as between them. The "equity" or rather "inequity" here was much more general, being the potentially harmful effects of permitting subrogation on industrial relations at Ford's. In the alternative, Lord Denning said that if subrogation depended on an implied term, the circumstances showed that such a term should not be implied.

The reasoning of James L.J. is somewhat more convincing. In his view, subrogation, which would normally attach to such a contract of indemnity, was excluded by an implied term in the contract between Cameron and Ford, because that contract was made against the background of the decision in *Lister v. Romford Ice and Cold Storage Ltd* and the possible implications of that decision. This is not really the same reasoning as Lord Denning's alternative. The latter held that subrogation should not be implied in the first place to a contract of this sort. James L.J. held that it would normally be so implied, but the circumstances negated that implication. While the reasoning of James L.J., that it is possible to exclude a normal incident of a contract by implication, is no doubt legally sound, there is a difficulty in relating this to the facts of the case. As the dissenting judge, Stamp L.J., pointed out, to imply such a term in law the court must conclude that both parties would have said — "we did not bother to express it, it is too clear" — and there was no evidence to do so, the trial judge having found that Cameron did not know of the circumstances of the *Lister* case and the agreement resulting from it.

Despite this criticism, it is difficult not to sympathise with the result of the case. There are, it is suggested, sound reasons for not allowing risks of this sort to fall on individual employees when insurers have been paid to take them, a point of more general application which will be made again shortly. Further, there are increasing signs that the courts may follow this approach and deny subrogation on equitable grounds.[30] In *Woolwich Building Society v. Brown*,[31] it was said that the case "may be some support for asserting that equity will in certain circumstances not assist by compelling a party to use its name for the benefit of another so as to

[30] Note that *Morris v. Ford* was cited in *Commonwealth Construction v. Imperial Oil* (1976) 69 D.L.R. (3d) at 566, which influenced the recent English cases on co-insurance. As already explained, they have "denied" subrogation on more traditional grounds although it has been argued that these are somewhat tortuous on occasion, and a broad "equitable" approach might be sounder; see p. 306, above.

[31] [1996] C.L.C. 625.

enforce a subrogated claim,"[32] but it was pointed out that this would only apply in extreme cases.[33]

While there is no doubt that the decision in *Morris v. Ford* has effectively stymied the application of subrogation in the employer's liability field as a matter of practice, at least until a party is prepared to take the matter to the House of Lords, legally, the reasoning of James L.J. and the alternative reasoning of Lord Denning, cannot stand if an insurer inserts an express term conferring subrogation rights in its policy, although a solution might be found in a doctrine which requires the insurer to exercise its rights under the policy in good faith in the interests of itself and the insured.[34] Otherwise, we must await future cases for any further development.

The Future of Subrogation

It is appropriate to conclude this chapter with some general comments about the role of subrogation, although lack of space precludes any detail. There can be no doubt that to the extent that it prevents an insured from making a profit from a loss it is an eminently sound principle. However, in the context of subrogation actions, the doctrine has attracted criticism. First, it must be rare for an insurer to exercise subrogation rights except against a defendant who is also insured, simply because there is little point otherwise. If so, this can be said to be wasteful and expensive in resources; it unnecessarily promotes multiple insurance, requiring that the same risk be covered both by first party and third party policies. Secondly, if the defendant is not, in fact, insured, throwing liability on him relieves the insurer who has been paid to assume the risk in question and who is able to distribute the cost among the premium-paying public. In a sense, therefore, subrogation may work to curtail the very essence of insurance which is risk distribution. The arguments are, of course, political ones encompassing the whole question of individual responsibility for civil wrongs in the legal system. For reasons which have been merely outlined here, and have been much more cogently and more fully argued

---

[32] *per* Waller J. at 629.

[33] See also *Enimont Supply S.A. v. Chesapeake Shipping Inc., The Surf City* [1995] 2 Lloyd's Rep. 242. where it was common ground that subrogation would not be equitable in circumstances where the insurer had expressly agreed to "waiver of subrogation" (see p. 300, above).

[34] See further [1979] J.B.L. 124 at 134–136.

elsewhere,[35] it is suggested that no harm would be done, and a great deal of resources would be saved, if we followed the Scandinavian practice[36] of permitting insurers to exercise subrogation rights only against a wrongdoer who was guilty of real misconduct.

[35] See especially the forceful critique by Hasson, "Subrogation in insurance law — a critical evaluation" (1985) 5 Oxford J. Legal Stud. 416. See also Harper and James, *Tort*, para. 25–23; Fleming (1966) 54 Calif.L.R. 1478 at 1533–1542; Young, *Cases and Materials on Insurance*, p. 342. For a contrary view, see Horn, *Subrogation in Insurance Theory and Practice*.

[36] See Hellner, *Försäkringsgivarens regressätt (The Insurer's Right of Subrogation)* (1953) pp. 257 *et seq.* (English summary).

CHAPTER 16

CONTRIBUTION AND DOUBLE INSURANCE

Like subrogation, contribution is a principle designed to prevent unjust enrichment. It too applies only to those insurance contracts that are contracts of indemnity. Unlike subrogation, however, contribution applies not as between insured and insurer but as between insurers. There is nothing wrong in an insured effecting as many policies as he wishes on the same property or against the same risk, so that he may be doubly insured. If he suffers a loss, he is, of course, by virtue of the doctrine of subrogation, entitled to no more than a full indemnity, but he can at common law choose from which insurer to claim. The insurer which pays, unless it pays voluntarily,[1] is entitled to claim a contribution from the other insurer or insurers, as otherwise the latter would be unjustly enriched. The insurer claiming a contribution must sue in its own name.[2]

Rateable proportion clauses

In practice contribution is most unlikely to arise in quite this way because of a standard term in all indemnity insurances. This will provide that if there is any other insurance on the property or the risk covered by the policy, the insurer will not be liable to pay or contribute more than its rateable proportion of any loss or damage. Such a rateable proportion clause does not affect the basic legal principles of double insurance, but it simply prevents the insured from recovering all his loss from one insurer. He is compelled to claim the appropriate proportion from each and the insurers are relieved of the burden of having to claim contributions *inter se*.

It may be, though, that, notwithstanding a rateable proportion clause, one insurer does pay the whole of the insured's loss, perhaps because it is

---

[1] See below.
[2] *Austin v. Zurich General Accident & Liability Insurance Co.* [1945] K.B. 250 at 258 per MacKinnon L.J.; *Sydney Turf Club v. Crowley* (1972) 126 C.L.R. 420.

at the time unaware of the other insurance, and it subsequently claims a contribution from the other insurer. If the latter insurer would in fact have been entitled to reject a claim made upon it by the insured, the question arises as to whether this precludes the first insurer's claim. This question has produced conflicting authorities in recent years.

In *Legal and General Assurance Society Ltd v. Drake Insurance Co. Ltd*[3] the plaintiffs paid a motor insured's claim, discovering only some ten years later that the insured had also been covered by the defendants. Both insurance policies contained a standard rateable proportion clause and a condition precedent requiring the giving of immediate written notice of an event giving rise to a claim. The insured had obviously failed to comply with this provision as regards the second insurer. It was held first by the Court of Appeal[4] that the right to contribution, being dependent on a principle of equity, dictated that prima facie, when there was double insurance, the burden of any loss should be shared between the insurers. The breach of a notice provision did not modify or exclude the equitable right to contribution, because the unfairness to the defendant of being deprived of the defence and of being unable to investigate the claim itself had to be balanced against the unfairness in making the plaintiff liable for the whole loss when the insured might as easily have claimed and recovered against the defendant instead; the balance of equity was clearly in favour of enforcing the right to contribution.

However, because of the rateable proportion clause in its policy, the plaintiff had been legally liable to indemnify the insured as to only half of the third party's claim. The policy with the defendant was clearly "any other insurance". The plaintiff's payment of half of the loss therefore amounted to a voluntary payment and because contribution arose only where an insurer had been obliged under its policy to pay more than its rateable proportion, the claim for a contribution from the defendant failed.[5]

---

[3] [1991] 2 Lloyd's Rep. 36.
[4] Lloyd and Nourse L.JJ., Ralph Gibson L.J. dissenting on this point.
[5] This result was not affected by provisions of the Road Traffic Act. Although under that Act a motor insurer is liable to settle a third party's claim in full (s.151, see pp. 375–378, below), where there was double insurance and a rateable proportion clause in its policy, it could recover the proportion above its strict legal liability back from its insured, and so the excess payment remained a voluntary one.

The decision on the general point[6] was not entirely persuasive. What is the equity in making liable an insurer who, if a claim had been made against him, would have had a cast iron defence?[7] Considerations like this led the Privy Council to take a different view in *Eagle Star Insurance Co. Ltd v. Provincial Insurance plc.*[8] Here it was held that that the right to contribution was to be determined at the date of any judgment against the insurer which pays. Although, of course this decision could not technically overrule the decision in *Legal and General*, it seems safe to assume that it will be followed and that the insurer which has a cast iron defence to the insured's claim will be able to resist the other insurer's claim for a contribution.[9] However, the result of the decision in *Legal and General* on the voluntary payment point must be correct. Since invariably, as we have seen, policies contain a standard rateable proportion clause, the first insurer's claim for a contribution will be met by the argument that they paid more than they were legally liable to pay and that contribution does not apply to voluntary payments.

What is double insurance?

Whether the issue arises as a matter of general law or under such a rateable proportion clause, the same conditions must be fulfilled before it can be said that there is double insurance. Essentially these are that the same property or liability is covered against the same risk under policies which are both or all legally enforceable. A number of points require further elucidation.

Policies with different scopes

Whether the policies cover the same property or liability is fairly easily established. It is not required, though, that the scope of the policies as a

---

[6] Curiously the subject of only one previous reported case — *Monksfield v. Vehicle and General Insurance Co. Ltd* [1971] 1 Lloyd's Rep. 139 — which was to the opposite effect and was overruled.

[7] It is arguable that even the majority in *Legal and General* would have exempted the second insurer from liability if they had a good defence based on non-disclosure or breach of warranty; see the judgment of Nourse L.J., [1991] 2 Lloyd's Rep. at 42.

[8] [1993] 3 All E.R. 1.

[9] Thus reinstating the decision in *Monksfield v. Vehicle and General Insurance Co. Ltd*, above. On the facts of *Eagle Star*, both insurers were in fact held liable to pay, because of provisions in the Bahamian Road Traffic Act similar to those in the British statute (see p. 373, below).

whole be the same. There may be an overlap between a motor and an employer's liability policy that can give rise to double insurance.[10] Similarly, a household policy may cover certain property owned by the insured when it is taken outside the house. This would be regarded as a small part of the total cover. The insured under such a policy might take his watch, which is one of the items so covered, to be repaired, and while it is at the repairer's, it might be covered by a policy held by the latter. This would also be a small part of the repairer's cover. Prima facie, there would be double insurance, though it may well be that the position is affected by policy conditions.

Same risk

The requirement that the risk be the same means essentially that the same interest is covered by or on behalf of the same insured. In *North British & Mercantile Insurance Co. v. London, Liverpool & Globe Insurance Co.*,[11] grain which belonged to the bailor was in the possession of bailees who were wharfingers. The grain was lost in circumstances whereby in law the bailees were liable for the loss. Both parties had insured this grain, the owner under an ordinary property policy, the bailee under a floating policy. The bailees recovered from their insurers who then claimed a contribution from the bailor's insurers. The Court of Appeal held that there was no right to a contribution because the policies covered different interests. The loss in the circumstances fell on the bailees and hence their insurers; had the bailor's insurers paid their insured, they would have been subrogated to the latter's right to sue the bailees. Therefore, whenever in law the loss should be borne by only one of the insureds, there is no contribution.

It should be noted, however, that in practice this legal rule is often ignored. The most notable instance is by virtue of one of the rules of the

---

[10] *e.g.* the Australian case of *Albion Insurance Co. v. Government Insurance Office of New South Wales* (1969) 121 C.L.R. 342. This is much less likely to happen now in the U.K. because of changes to the compulsory insurance requirements; see p. 359, below.

[11] (1877) 5 Ch.D. 569. See also *Dawson v. Bankers' & Traders' Insurance Co.* [1957] V.R. 491, where it was held that there was no double insurance between a motor policy and an employer's liability policy where the former policy covered a negligent employee directly, *i.e.*, he was included as one of the insured, and the latter covered only his employer's vicarious liability; see also *Zurich Insurance Co. v. Shield Insurance Co. Ltd*, an unreported decision of the Irish High Court, July 29, 1985. Compare the *Albion* case (n.10), where only the employer's vicarious liability was covered under both policies and there was therefore double insurance.

Fire Offices' Committee whereby contribution is applied by agreement between insurers wherever real property[12] is, in fact, doubly insured by different people with different interests, regardless of questions of legal liability.[13]

Same insured?

The judgments in the *North British* case appear at times to imply not just that the same interest must be doubly insured, but that the insured actually be the same. It must be the law, though, that this is not required. Contribution must apply wherever an insured is entitled to recovery under another policy, even if he is not the insured under that policy and hence not legally entitled to sue upon it, if he recovers from that insurer. If, in what is likely to be the most common practical application, the bailor and bailee of goods both insure and a loss occurs in circumstances which attach no legal liability to either party, as in *Hepburn v. Tomlinson*,[14] and on the construction of the bailee's policy, he is entitled to claim for the benefit of the bailor, as also was the position in that case, there must be double insurance. Otherwise, the problem would be insoluble, neither party having rights against the other and thus neither party's insurer having rights to which they could succeed by virtue of subrogation to throw the loss on the other. If the bailee is entitled to recover only in respect of his own loss or only when he is legally liable to the bailor, then the position is quite different. The bailor has no claim against the bailee and hence against his insurer, and there is no double insurance.

As far as land is concerned,[15] double insurance might arise by virtue of one party having the right to call upon the other's insurer to reinstate the property under section 83 of the Fires Prevention (Metropolis) Act 1774.[16] In one case involving a landlord and tenant who were both insured,[17] it was argued by the tenant's insurer that, because the tenant had the right

---

[12] There is no agreement regarding goods, but in practice contribution may be applied *ad hoc*.

[13] For consideration of all the relevant insurers' agreements, including one which has the effect of making the *Albion* case (n.10) inapplicable in Britain, see Lewis (1985) 48 M.L.R. 275 at 286–289.

[14] [1966] A.C. 451; see p. 61, above.

[15] Assuming that the Life Assurance Act 1774 does not apply; see pp. 49–52, above.

[16] See pp. 279–283, above.

[17] *Portavon Cinema Co. v. Price* [1939] 4 All E.R. 601.

to require reinstatement under the Act by the landlord's insurer, the tenant was therefore doubly insured and the landlord's insurer was liable for a contribution. This argument was easily rejected. It was clear that the tenant had not exercised his statutory right and hence there could be no question on the facts of the case of his having a right under the two policies. The judgment implies that the result would have been the same even if he had made a demand for reinstatement but, with respect, this may be doubted. Following a proper demand, the landlord's insurer would have had to comply, thus indemnifying the tenant. As contribution is an equitable principle to prevent unjust enrichment, it must be flexible enough to allow that the tenant's insurer is liable for its share, otherwise the insurer with the primary liability might escape quite unjustifiably. The same would apply if the position of the parties was reversed or if their relationship was that of mortgagor and mortgagee or vendor and purchaser.

The Ratio of Contribution

Whether the question of contribution arises generally or as the result of a rateable proportion clause, it remains to be considered how the contributions of the different insurers are worked out. This can be a very complex question,[18] but for present purposes the basic principles only will be examined and it will be assumed that there are only two insurers involved. There has been a noticeable lack of case-law on this question, and the ratios to be applied may depend as much on the practices of insurers as much as on binding legal authority.

The real problems arise when the sums insured by each insurer are not the same or where the policies in question have different ranges so that it is difficult properly to compare the sums insured. It may be necessary here to distinguish between property and liability insurances, the reason being that in property insurance, the premium is calculated with particular reference to the sum insured, whereas there is not necessarily the same relationship in liability insurance. In property insurance where the cover provided under both policies is more or less the same, the contribution of each insurer can most fairly be assessed simply by reference to the sum insured. The proper result, therefore, should be that each insurer pays that proportion of a loss which his sum insured bears to the total of the sums insured. For example, if property is insured for £10,000 with insurer A and

---

[18] For more detail, see *MacGillivray*, (8th ed.), paras. 1850–1867.

for £20,000 with insurer B, A will bear one-third and B two-thirds of any loss.

This approach is termed the "maximum liability" approach, because it always takes account of the maximum of the two insurers' liabilities. The alternative standard approach is that based on "independent liability." Here, following a loss, it is asked what each insurer would independently have been liable for and the contributions are assessed according to the proportions that each such figure bears to the total of the figures. For example, X suffers a loss of £5,000. His policy with insurer A has a sum insured of £10,000; his policy with B a limit of £50,000. Each insurer would independently have been liable for the full amount of the loss. Their contribution is therefore equal because £5,000 plus £5,000 divided by £5,000/£10,000 is £5,000. If X's loss were £11,000, A would be liable independently for £10,000, B for £11,000. Therefore, A bears 10,000/10,000+11,000, that is 10/21, of the loss and B 11/21. On this basis, wherever the loss is smaller than the lesser of the sums insured, the insurers will bear it equally. A loss falling between the sums insured will attract a ratio whereby the insurer with the larger sum insured will gradually attract more liability. Only when the loss is the same as, or greater than, the total of the sums insured will the calculation be the same as under the maximum liability approach.

Liability insurances

It has been conclusively settled in *Commercial Union Assurance Co. v. Hayden*[19] that the independent liability approach is the legal basis in liability insurance. The principal reasons for this were first that liability insurance premiums are not calculated pro rata according to the sum insured; in the case itself the plaintiff had charged £6 for cover of £100,000, whereas the defendant had charged £5 for only £10,000 of identical cover. Secondly, the bulk of claims in liability insurance fall within a low limit.

> "Each limit of liability and each premium may be taken to be fixed without knowledge of the limit under any other policy . . . it is difficult to suppose that when a limit of £10,000 was fixed by the defendant, it could have been intended that if there happened to be another policy with a limit of £100,000, the defendant should be

[19] [1977] Q.B. 804.

liable for only one-eleventh of the claim, however small. The independent liability basis is much more realistic in its results. . . . The obvious purpose of having a limit of liability under an insurance policy[20] is to protect the insurer from the effect of exceptionally large claims: it seems to me artificial to use the limits under two policies to adjust liability in respect of claims which are within the limits of either policy."[21]

Finally, some stress was laid upon the fact that certain liability policies are unlimited; in these cases the maximum liability approach would simply be impossible to apply.

Policies with different ranges

There remains the question of which method of assessment applies where the policies have different ranges.[22] The example of the watch which was used earlier[23] can be used again here. Imagine that the owner's household policy has a sum insured of £10,000, but there is no specific sum for the watch which is worth £20. The repairer has a floating policy covering all goods in his possession from time to time, which is a goods policy and not a liability policy. His sum insured is £3,000. The watch is stolen, neither party being responsible, so that both insurers are prima facie liable. It could hardly be right here, albeit it is a case of property insurance, to apply the maximum liability ratio, so that the owner's insurer should bear 10/13 and the repairer's insurer 3/13 of £20. That would ignore the fact that both policies cover many other items and are essentially quite different. In this case the independent liability approach is the only realistic one so that each insurer is liable for half the loss up to the lesser of the sums insured. This was the method adopted in *American Surety Co. of New York v. Wrightson*[24] in relation to fidelity insurance effected by an employer against the dishonesty of his employees, where one of the policies also had a much wider scope, and it is submitted that it is the only workable approach.[25]

---

[20] This must mean in respect of liability policies only.
[21] Cairns L.J. [1977] Q.B. at 815–816.
[22] "Non-concurrent policies" is the usual jargon.
[23] p. 316.
[24] (1910) 103 L.T. 663.
[25] *MacGillivray*, (8th ed.), para. 1867, suggests that the independent liability basis might be adopted in all cases.

Conditions regarding double insurance

Apart from the rateable proportion clauses already discussed, most policies of indemnity also contain other conditions relevant to double insurance which are of importance. These fall into two categories. The first sort purports to oust the liability of the insurer if the liability is covered elsewhere. The second requires notification of double insurance.

Conditions ousting liability

Modern examples of this sort of condition are as follows:

> "There shall be no liability under this insurance in respect of any claim where the insured is entitled to indemnity under any other insurance except in respect of any excess beyond the amount which would have been covered under such other insurance had this insurance not been effected."

> "There shall be no liability hereunder in respect of any claim for which the assured are entitled to any indemnity under any other policy."

Problems will arise if one or both of the insurers covering the same risk have this sort of clause. If one insurer does have it, but the other does not, then the latter should be solely and wholly liable. The first insurer's liability is excluded and so far as the second is concerned, there is, therefore, no double insurance. If both insurers have such a clause, the position is more complex. It has arisen in a number of cases.

In *Gale v. Motor Union Insurance Co.*,[26] L was driving G's car when he caused an accident. Prima facie L was insured both by his own motor policy, because that had an extension covering the driving of cars other than his own with the owner's consent, and by G's policy on G's car, because that had a standard permitted driver extension.[27] However, both extensions had qualifications which in effect provided that they were not applicable if the person concerned was otherwise insured. Both policies also had rateable proportion conditions. Roche J. held that the conditions purporting to oust liability were not clear, and that the only way to read

---

[26] [1928] 1 K.B. 359.
[27] See pp. 365–368, below.

them was as referring to cases where the other cover gave complete and full indemnity. Here, because of the rateable proportion clauses, neither policy, when looked at from the point of view of the other one, gave complete cover. Therefore, neither clause applied and the insurers were both liable rateably. According to this reasoning, the presence of rateable proportion clauses in both policies was vital.

Weddell v. Road Transport & General Insurance Co.[28] involved similar facts in that a negligent driver was prima facie covered by both his own and the relevant car owner's policies. His own policy had a rateable proportion clause and a clause excluding liability if there was other insurance. The owner's policy was more subtly worded; under the extension, liability was excluded if there was other insurance. There was a rateable proportion clause but this had a proviso whereby it was declared not to impose on the insurer any liability from which, but for it, the insurer would have been excluded under the extension. In other words, the rateable proportion clause was not to apply to a situation of double insurance, and, as has been seen, the presence of a rateable proportion clause was crucial to the ratio in *Gale*. In fact, the driver's own insurer repudiated liability for breach of condition, so the question was whether the driver was entitled to half or all of his loss under the owner's policy. The owner's insurer did not seek to argue that it was not liable at all. Rowlatt J. went somewhat further than the judge in *Gale* had gone and held that it would be unreasonable to suppose that these extensions would cancel each other out. "The reasonable construction is to exclude from the category of co-existing cover any cover which is expressed to be itself cancelled by such co-existence, and to hold in such cases that both companies are liable, subject of course in both cases to any rateable proportion clause which there may be."[29] Thus, on the facts, the owner's insurers, because they had a rateable proportion clause, were liable for half the loss.

The judgment seems to admit that logically, if neither policy had a rateable proportion clause, neither insurer would be liable, and, further, that this ought to have been the result on the facts because of the proviso in the owner's policy whereby the rateable proportion clause should not have operated. There was "other insurance," namely, the driver's own, albeit this was not enforceable in respect of this loss, and therefore this should have excluded liability under the owner's policy. However, the insurer did not argue this and the ratio of the case appears wide enough to

[28] [1932] 2 K.B. 563.
[29] *ibid.* at 567.

exclude this sort of possibility. Indeed, this must be the legal position because *Weddell* has been approved by the Court of Appeal[30] where it was said:

> "The court should invoke the equitable principle of contribution between co-insurers to avoid the absurdity and injustice of holding that a person who has paid premiums for cover by two insurers should be left without insurance cover because each insurer has excluded liability for the risk against which the other has indemnified him."[31]

It is clear, therefore, that the courts have not taken kindly to these clauses and it is probably safe to assume that, whatever forms of wording are adopted, they will be construed in such a manner that, where there is genuine double insurance, they will cancel each other out.

Conditions requiring notification

Another standard condition, which may be found particularly in fire and other property policies, requires the insured to notify the insurer if he effects double insurance during the currency of the policy. Generally the sanction for non-disclosure will be forfeiture or repudiation of the policy. Obviously, such conditions may be inserted by insurers to protect themselves against the possibility of fraud but their use is much less common than was formerly the case.

A mere accidental overlap between policies does not bring such a condition into operation. In *Australian Agricultural Co. v. Saunders*,[32] the insured effected a fire policy on some wool while it was in storage, in transit by land to Sydney, Australia, or in storage in Sydney until shipped. The policy contained the relevant condition. Subsequently, some wool was carried by ship to Sydney and a marine policy was effected to cover this. When this wool was in store in Sydney, it was destroyed by fire. It was held that the fire insurer was liable. The court rejected the argument of the insurers that they should have been notified of the marine policy, as the

---

[30] *National Employers' Mutual v. Hayden* [1980] 2 Lloyd's Rep. 149; see also *Austin v. Zurich General Accident & Liability Insurance Co.* [1945] K.B. 250.

[31] *ibid.* at 152, per Stephenson L.J. See also Bridge L.J. at 154 and Templeman L.J. at 156.

[32] (1875) L.R. 10 C.P. 668.

risks covered were not the same and there was no double insurance. Even
if the policies had overlapped in their coverage for a brief period, it was
made clear that such accidental overlap would not have required notification, though presumably if the loss had taken place during the overlap,
there would have been double insurance.

An insured can only really be prejudiced by this sort of condition if it
appears in both of the policies. If it is in only one, that one will be
ineffective but the other will stand, unless, of course, the insurer can avoid
liability for some other reason. Even if it is in both policies, it will be only
rarely, it seems, that the insured will lose out completely. In *Equitable Fire
& Accident Insurance Co. v. Ching Wo Hong*,[33] a fire policy contained the
relevant condition. The insured effected a second policy, about which it did
not inform the first insurer, but this policy provided that it was not
effective until the first premium was paid. No premium was ever paid on
it. It was held by the Privy Council that the second policy never, therefore,
came into existence and the obligation to disclose it to the first insurer
never arose, so that the first insurer could not avoid its policy. The same
result must apply if the second policy is void, for example, for lack of
insurable interest.

However, the second policy may be valid but the insurer is entitled to
avoid liability under it for the particular loss by virtue of a breach of
condition, such as the failure to give notice in time. Here non-notification
of the second policy to the first insurer will entitle it to avoid its policy and
the second insurer will not be liable for the reason stated.[34] The same
would apply if the second insurer could avoid liability, but not avoid the
policy *ab initio*, that is for breach of a continuing warranty. In this case,
therefore, the insured will be prejudiced by a failure to comply with a
notification condition.

[33] [1907] A.C. 96; see also *Steadfast Insurance Co. v. F & B. Trading Co.* (1972) 46
A.J.L.R. 10.
[34] See Walsh J. in the *Steadfast* case, above, at 14.

CHAPTER 17

LIFE INSURANCE

Life insurance is chosen as the first area for consideration of principles peculiar to particular types of insurance rather than of general application. The modern forms of life policies are numerous, ranging from the traditional whole life policy, which simply pays an agreed sum of money on the death of the life insured, and the term policy, which pays on death within a stated time, through endowment policies to annuities and policies linked to investment in securities or property.[1] In addition being governed by the general scheme of regulation under the Insurance Companies Act 1982,[2] many life policies of the latter sort are in reality also investments and, as such, fall within the definition of "investments" in Schedule 1 to the Financial Services Act 1986.[3] They are thus subject to the scheme of investor protection provided for under that Act. Detailed consideration of the latter is outside the scope of this book,[4] but there is one aspect concerning insurance contract law, namely the cancellation provisions, which will be examined shortly.

There are a number of other respects in which life insurance has its own principles. Two such broad areas of principle, the assignment of life policies and the law relating to trusts of life policies, will be considered here because of their particular practical importance and because they have thrown up problems for life insurance, even though questions of assignment and trusts are, of course, of much more general application. Detail

---

[1] A contract which contains provision for life cover is still a contract of life insurance, especially for the purposes of the Life Assurance Act 1774 and the Insurance Companies Act 1982, where the amount of life cover is variable and no more than the amount for which the policy might be surrendered at any time: *Fuji Finance Ltd v. Aetna Life Insurance Co. Ltd* [1994] 4 All E.R. 608; see p. 38, above.

[2] See Chap. 2.

[3] See para. 10 to Part I of that Schedule.

[4] For an excellent description, see Page and Ferguson, *Investor Protection*, 1992.

on questions such as mortgages of life policies, the law of succession or the bankruptcy of the life insured is felt to be unnecessary here, as there are no principles peculiar to life insurance or problems raised by these in this area. Furthermore, there are certain technical questions, no doubt of great importance in practice, which are more than adequately dealt with elsewhere.[5] Examples of these would be the law relating to proof of death and proving title to a life policy.

Formalities — Disclosure

There are requirements for pre-contractual disclosure in life insurance introduced as a result of the E.C. Directives on freedom of services.[6] These apply to contracts entered into by a United Kingdom or E.C. company[7] or a member of Lloyd's which constitute the carrying on in the United Kingdom of long term business which is not reinsurance business or the provision in the United Kingdom of long term insurance,[8] but they do not apply to contracts regulated under the Financial Services Act 1986.[9] Before entering into such a contract the insurer must provide the prospective insured with the following information in writing:[10]

(a) a definition of each benefit and option;
(b) the term of the contract and the means by which it may be terminated;
(c) the method of paying premiums and the duration of the payments;
(d) the method of calculating bonuses and the distribution of bonuses;
(e) an indication of surrender and paid-up values and the extent to which these values are guaranteed;

---

[5] See especially, *MacGillivray*, Chap. 24.
[6] Insurance Companies Act 1982, Sched. 2E, para. 1. As to freedom of services, see generally Chap. 2 and, for the equivalent provisions regarding non-life insurance, pp. 77–78, above.
[7] As to these terms, see p. 27, above.
[8] They thus catch insurance sold from an establishment in the U.K. and insurance sold directly from another E.C. State.
[9] There are requirements imposed under that Act.
[10] There are also requirements to disclose details of the insurers' names and addresses etc. under Sched. 2E, para. 1(5) (for companies) and para. 1(6) (for members of Lloyd's). Where a contract involves two or more insureds, the information must be provided to each of them: para. 5(1).

(f) an indication of the premiums for each benefit;

(g) in respect of unit-linked policies, a definition of the units and an indication of the nature of the underlying assets;

(h) the arrangements with respect to the period within which the policy holder may cancel the contract;

(i) the tax arrangements applicable to the policy;

(j) the arrangements for handling complaints;

(k) any compensation or guarantee arrangements which will be available if the insurer is unable to meet its liabilities;

(l) whether the parties are entitled to choose the law applicable to the contract and, if so, the law which the insurer proposes to choose, or the law which will be applicable.

In addition to the disclosure of information before the contract is entered into, there are statutory requirements for disclosure of information by the insurer during the contract.[11] These apply to the same categories of insurers and primarily require the disclosure in writing of any changes to the information described in (a) to (g) above. In addition, if the policy provides for the payment of bonuses, information in writing as to the amount of bonuses which has become payable must be given once a year.

Cancellation Rights

Because the life insurance contract is a long-term contract, and because individuals may be persuaded by high pressure salesmanship to enter into contracts which may not be entirely appropriate for them, the law has for some years provided for a cooling off period, that is policy-holders are given a period within which they can change their minds and cancel an already legally binding contract without penalty.[12] There are two sets of requirements here, imposed either under the Insurance Companies Act 1982, ss. 75 to 77[13] or under the Financial Services (Cancellation) Rules

---

[11] Insurance Companies Act 1982, Sched. 2E, para. 2.

[12] These rules were introduced originally on the recommendation of the Scott Committee on Property Bonds and Equity Linked Life Assurance, 1973, Cmnd. 5281, and have their equivalent in the hire purchase and consumer credit legislation.

[13] And the regulations made thereunder, namely regs. 41 and 42 and Scheds. 7 and 8 of the Insurance Companies Regulations 1994, (S.I. 1994 No. 1516).

1977.[14] Failure to comply with the requirements does not affect the validity of any contract,[15] but a breach of the Cancellation Rules is actionable as a breach of a statutory duty.[16]

Since the implementation of the E.C. Life Directives, the scope of the provisions under the 1982 Act has been extended and a distinction drawn between an E.C. contract and a non-E.C. contract. An E.C. contract exists where the insurer is a United Kingdom, E.C. or EFTA company or a member of Lloyd's and the insured is habitually resident in the United Kingdom. A non-E.C. contract is basically one provided by an insurer carrying on life business in the United Kingdom to someone who is not habitually resident here.

The Rules apply to all life contracts which fall within the definition of "investment" in Schedule 1 to the 1986 Act.[17] This definition is likely to comprehend the vast majority of life insurance contacts in practice. The life contracts which are not investments are principally (i) those which are pure life insurance, that is where the benefits are payable only on death, (ii) those where the benefits on death (other than by accident) are payable within 10 years or before the life insured attains a specified age not exceeding 70, that is certain short-term policies, and (iii) those where the policy has no surrender value or where a single premium is payable and the surrender value does not exceed that premium. The provisions of the 1982 Act apply to most of these non-investment contracts.

Under both regimes, a notice of the right to cancel must be sent by post to the insured.[18] In addition, where, in the case of an E.C. contract within the 1982 Act, the statutory notice was sent before the contract was concluded, the insurer must also inform the insured in writing that it has done so within 14 days of the conclusion of the contract. The notice must

---

[14] Hereafter referred to as the Cancellation Rules. These are made, under s.51 of the Financial Services Act 1986, by the Securities and Investment Board as the designated agency under the Act. They are contained in Chap. V of *The Regulation of Investment Business*. By Sched. 10, para. 5(3) of the 1986 Act, the 1982 Act's provisions are superseded where relevant by the Cancellation Rules. It should be noted that the latter also apply to many unit trust schemes.

[15] Insurance Companies Act 1982, s.75(4); Financial Services Act 1986, s.62(4).

[16] Financial Services Act 1986, s.62(1).

[17] With some qualifications in respect of single premium policies. The distinction between what can be described as "investment insurance" and "non-investment insurance" under the 1986 Act is relevant in other contexts; see especially pp. 26 and 189.

[18] Except that in the case of an E.C. contract, it may be given by hand.

be in the prescribed form,[19] and contain the specified information relating to the salient features of the contract. Attached to the notice must be the prescribed form of notice of cancellation.[20] The right to cancel[21] an E.C. contract can be exercised before the end of the fourteenth day after that on which the insured has been informed that the contract is binding, and there is a similar 14 day period under the Cancellation Rules. In the case of a non-E.C. contract, the right can be exercised up to 10 days after the insured receives the notice of the right or when he knows that the agreement is concluded and makes his first or only payment of premium, whichever is the later.[22] Notice of cancellation operates to rescind any concluded contract or to withdraw any offer not yet accepted. Any money paid by the insured must be returned to him.[23]

Assignment of Life Policies

Life insurance policies are undoubtedly a valuable piece of property, normally attracting a surrender value after the payment of a number of premiums. They can be sold or otherwise disposed of or used as security, features which are assisted by the fact that the requirement of insurable interest exists only at the date the policy is effected.[24] Many dealings of this sort with life policies will in law be assignments, regarding which there are a number of special rules. The description "assignment" covers any case where the insured disposes entirely of his interest in the policy, whether by way of sale, gift or mortgage. If a policy is used as security, some of the statutory formalities as to assignment may be used even where the insured does not dispose entirely of his interest. The use of a life policy in such circumstances may very well attract some of the provisions of the Consumer Credit Act 1974, that is, if it is used in connection with a regulated consumer credit agreement.[25]

---

[19] Sched. 7 (non-Financial Services Act contracts) or sched. 8 (investment contracts) to the 1994 Regulations.

[20] Sched. 9 to the 1994 Regulations.

[21] Notice of which is deemed to be served when posted under both the 1982 Act and the Cancellation Rules.

[22] Under both regimes, if no notice of the right to cancel is sent, the right to cancel always exists.

[23] Subject to an allowance under the Cancellation Rules in respect of single premium policies.

[24] See pp. 38–41, above.

[25] For the detail see Part VIII of the 1974 Act and Hill-Smith, *Consumer Credit: Law and Practice*, Chap. 8.

Assignment as mortgage

If a dealing with a life policy appears to be an absolute assignment, but in reality is a mortgage as security for a debt, the mortgagee, the insured, is entitled to redeem the mortgage on repayment of the debt and recover his policy, notwithstanding any provision to the contrary. In deciding whether or not a dealing with a life policy is an outright assignment or a mortgage, the court will look at the surrounding circumstances and parol evidence is admissible. For example, in the Irish case of *Murphy v. Taylor*,[26] a policy for £999 was assigned for a consideration of £144. The evidence showed that the assignor in fact borrowed the latter sum from the assignee. The latter later recovered £600 from the insurer. It was held that the substance of the transaction was that of a mortgage to secure a debt. Therefore, after allowing for the debt of £144, the assignor was entitled to redeem the mortgage and recover from the assignee the remainder of the £600 that he had recovered from the insurer.

The rule allowing the insured to redeem what is in substance a mortgage of a life policy is part of the general law relating to mortgages whereby clogs or fetters on the equity of redemption or equitable right to redeem are void. Details on these should be sought elsewhere,[27] but one interesting example in the life insurance context is the decision in *Salt v. Marquess of Northampton*.[28] Here, X borrowed £10,000 from an insurer and secured this by a charge on his reversionary interest in certain property. In addition, he agreed to pay the premiums on a policy for £34,000 taken out by the insurers against the possibility of the interest not vesting. It was agreed that if X paid off the loan before the interest vested, the policy would be assigned to him, but if he died before repayment and vesting, the policy would belong to the insurers. The latter event occurred. It was held that, despite the agreement, the transaction was in substance a mortgage, and the personal representatives of X were entitled to redeem and recover the proceeds of the policy, after deducting the loan and interest.

Statutory assignment

Prior to the Policies of Assurance Act 1867, a life policy was not assignable at law. Although equity always permitted such assignments, the

---

[26] (1850) 1 Ir.Ch.R. 92.
[27] *e.g.* Megarry and Wade, *Law of Real Property* (5th ed.), pp. 964–971.
[28] [1892] A.C. 1.

assignee could only sue to enforce the policy if he joined the assignor in the action, and an insurer could not obtain a good discharge against payment from the assignee alone. The 1867 Act permits legal assignments so that the assignee of a life policy can, if the requirements of the Act are complied with, enforce it in his own name.[29] Furthermore, a life policy is a chose in action,[30] one of the forms of intangible personal property, so that an alternative procedure for assignment lies under section 136 of the Law of Property Act 1925. In addition, an assignment which is incomplete according to statutory requirements may well still be valid as an equitable assignment.

There is one essential difference between the two statutory procedures. Under the 1867 Act, an assignment is valid if it is of the assignor's whole interest in the policy or of merely a part of it, by way of mortgage. Under section 136, an assignment must be absolute, that is it must be of the assignor's whole interest. Therefore, a mortgage whereby the whole interest in a life policy is charged can be effected under section 136, but one whereby only part is charged has to be effected under the 1867 Act.

An assignment under the 1867 Act must be in the form prescribed in the Schedule to the Act or in words with a similar effect and it must be endorsed on the policy or contained in a separate instrument.[31] Written notice of the assignment must be given to the insurer at its principal place of business.[32] An assignment under section 136 must simply be in writing but again notice must be given to the debtor, that is the insurer. In neither case is the consent of the insurers necessary, but a condition in the policy making it non-assignable is effective to prevent a legal assignment, although it cannot prevent an effective equitable assignment.[33]

In most cases, therefore, the statutory procedures are alternative devices for achieving the same result, and which one is used must simply be a matter of preference. Even if one of the statutory procedures is not complied with, as we have seen, an assignment may be effective in equity. This may be because there was a failure to give notice to the insurer,[34] because there was merely an agreement to assign, or because the policy was simply delivered to the assignee, for example, as security. If there have

---

[29] s. 1.
[30] *Re Moore* (1878) 8 Ch.D. 519.
[31] s. 5.
[32] s. 3.
[33] *Re Turcan* (1888) 40 Ch.D. 5.
[34] *e.g. Williams v. Thorp* (1828) 2 Sim. 257.

been more than one purported assignments of the same policy, the well-established rules as to priority apply. Briefly,[35] a legal assignee has priority over anyone except an earlier equitable assignment of which he has notice or an earlier legal assignment. Equitable assignments generally rank in order of creation, except that the first such assignee to give notice to the insurers will take priority over any prior assignments of which he had no notice. If there is any doubt as to who is entitled to the policy moneys, in this or any other context, the insurer may pay them into court under the Life Assurance Companies (Payment into Court) Act 1896.[36]

Trusts of Life Policies

A life policy may often be held by the insured on trust for someone else. This will normally arise only on an own-life policy. If such a trust can be shown to exist, it has two distinct advantages. The first is that on the death of the life insured, the monies will belong to and go directly to the beneficiary, thus avoiding and not being counted as a part of the insured's estate. Secondly, if the insured becomes bankrupt, the beneficiary can claim the policy without its being subject to the claims of the insured's creditors, provided that the trust itself was not created in order to defraud creditors.[37]

Section 11 trusts

The easiest way to establish such a trust is under the provisions of section 11 of the Married Women's Property Act 1882, although this section is limited in its application. Under it, a policy effected on his or her own life by a married man or woman, and expressed to be for the benefit of his or her spouse and/or children,[38] creates a trust in favour of the spouse and/or children, and the money payable under the policy does not form part of the insured's estate. A joint life policy effected by a husband and wife may in reality create two separate policies, each within section 11.[39]

---

[35] *MacGillivray*, (8th ed.), paras. 1304–1315.

[36] *ibid.*, paras. 1466–1470.

[37] Insolvency Act 1986, ss.423-425; proviso to Married Women's Property Act 1882, s.11.

[38] "Children" includes adopted and illegitimate children; Adoption Act 1976, s.39; Family Law Reform Act 1969, s.19.

[39] *Re S. (deceased)* [1996] 1 W.L.R. 235.

It should be noted first that section 11 applies only to policies effected by a married man or woman on his or her own life. Thus, for example, a policy by a father on the life of his son, even if legal, which must be doubtful,[40] cannot fall within section 11.[41] If the section does apply, the insured is a trustee and must therefore act with respect to the policy in the best interests of the beneficiaries. For example, if he or she has an option to surrender the policy, that may properly be exercised only in the interests of the beneficiaries; it is not exerciseable in order to defeat the trust, and if the policy is surrendered, the money received will probably be held for the ultimate benefit of the beneficiaries.[42]

Section 11 applies to any policies securing benefits payable on the death of the life insured, including an accident policy covering only death by accident,[43] and an endowment policy which provides for payment if the insured dies before the expiry of the stated period.[44] If the policy names the beneficiary or beneficiaries, then the latter acquire an immediate vested interest in it. In *Cousins v. Sun Life Assurance Society*,[45] a wife was the named beneficiary of a policy effected by her husband whom she predeceased. It was held that the policy monies belonged to the wife's estate, even though the husband had remarried. It should be noted that divorce does not of itself change any rights under a section 11 policy, but that these can be varied as part of a general settlement of property rights under section 24 of the Matrimonial Causes Act 1973.

If the policy does not name the beneficiaries but is merely expressed to be for the benefit of the insured's wife and children, for example, the beneficiaries have only a contingent interest, and only those people who fit the description on the death of the life insured will be entitled to benefit.

Other trusts

If section 11 is inapplicable, then establishing a trust of a life policy necessitates proving an exception to the doctrine of privity of contract, whereby a third party to a contract cannot enforce it even if it was made

---

[40] See below p. 334 and Chap. 3 at p. 42.
[41] *Re Engelbach* [1924] 2 Ch. 348.
[42] *Re Fleetwood's Policy* [1926] Ch. 48.
[43] *Re Gladitz* [1937] Ch. 588.
[44] *Re Ioakimidis' Policy Trusts* [1925] Ch. 403.
[45] [1933] Ch. 126.

for his benefit.[46] In addition, it is a well-established principle of trusts law that a person will not be regarded as having declared himself a trustee of property in the absence of words showing a clear intention to do so.[47] Quite apart from these points, many of the cases dealing with trusts of life policies reveal other deficiencies in the law relating to life insurance. If A effects a policy on his own life for the benefit of B, there are no problems if a trust is created, the point to which we shall shortly return, and provided that B's name is inserted in the policy.[48] But often the point arises because it appears that A has effected a policy on B's life for the benefit of B.

The law is clear that A must therefore have an insurable interest in the life of B,[49] quite apart from whether or not there is a trust in B's favour. Many of the policies in the relevant cases took a form which it appears is quite common, whereby a parent insures the life of his child for the latter's benefit. It may well be an endowment policy perhaps effected for the purposes of paying school fees. Whether or not such a policy is lawful must be open to great doubt, as a parent does not usually have an insurable interest in the life of his child.[50] The question is rarely raised in this context, usually because the insurer will have already handed over the money, so that the sole question is whether A or B is entitled to it, and insurers who did raise it would attract unfavourable publicity. Nevertheless, the point should be recognised as a consequence of the narrowness of the law governing insurable interest, and perhaps also as a factor which should encourage the court to find a trust. If this is so, the position is not so much that A is insuring B's life for the benefit of B, as that A is acting for B in insuring B's life, perhaps because, as an minor, B is unable to do so himself.

The cases appear to reveal more willingness latterly to find that a trust has been created, but two things are clear.[51] First, the mere fact that A takes out a policy which is expressed to be for the benefit of B or on behalf of B does not constitute a trust for B. Secondly, the mere fact that the policy provides that the policy monies are to be payable to B does not

---

[46] *Beswick v. Beswick* [1968] A.C. 58. Note, though, that the Law Commission has recommended statutory modification of the privity doctrine which may apply to enable a third party to enforce a life policy effected for his or her benefit even if a trust cannot be shown: Law Com. No. 242.

[47] *e.g. Jones v. Lock* (1865) 1 Ch.App. 25.

[48] Life Assurance Act 1774, s.2; see Chap. 3, pp. 45–47.

[49] Life Assurance Act 1774, s.1; see Chap. 3, pp. 38–41.

[50] *Halford v. Kymer* (1830) 10 B. & C. 724.

[51] Plowman J. in *Re Foster* [1966] 1 W.L.R. 222 at 227.

create a trust in favour of B. For example, in *Re Engelbach*,[52] a father proposed "for his daughter" an endowment policy whereby she was to receive £3,000 if she should reach the age of 21. If she died before then, her father was entitled to recover the premiums paid. It was held that the father's estate, on his death, was entitled to the £3,000 when the daughter became 21. Simply, there was not sufficient evidence to create a trust. Similarly, in *Re Sinclair*,[53] the insured was godfather to a baby of six months. He effected an endowment policy wherein the baby was referred to as "the nominee" and the moneys were payable to the child at 21. Again no trust arose because there was insufficient evidence. In both these cases, and indeed in the other ones to the same effect,[54] the policies must strictly have been illegal for want of insurable interest.

It should be noted, though, that if on similar facts, the "beneficiary" is, in fact, paid the insurance money, he will normally be entitled to keep it, even if there was no trust in his favour. The only situation where this would not be the case is if the policy compels the conclusion that he was to receive it merely as nominee or agent for the insured.[55] A court is most unlikely to conclude this nowadays, unless the wording of the policy compels it, so that if the insurer pays the "beneficiary," the result is a useful way around the decisions just discussed.

Modern cases

Modern policy wordings and more modern cases evince in any event a greater willingness to find a trust. In *Re Webb*,[56] a father took out policies on the lives of his two children. He was described as "the grantee" and in the proposal form as wishing to effect insurance "on behalf of and for the benefit of the person . . . named as the life assured." Each policy provided (1) that on the child's death at or after the age of 21, the money would be paid to his representatives, and, on his 21st birthday, all the father's interest in the policy would cease; until then the father had power to surrender, assign and otherwise deal with the policy, and the father would

---

[52] [1924] 2 Ch. 348.

[53] [1938] Ch. 799.

[54] *e.g. Cleaver v. Mutual Reserve Fund Life Ass.* [1892] 1 Q.B. 147; *Re Foster* [1938] 3 All E.R. 357.

[55] *Re Schebsman* [1944] 1 Ch. 83, approved in *Beswick v. Beswick* [1968] A.C. 58, where the House of Lords disapproved of *Re Engelbach*, above, in so far as it held to the contrary.

[56] [1941] Ch. 225.

recover the premiums paid if the child died before the age of 21; (2) that if the father, having paid all the premiums due, died before the child reached 21, the policies would remain in force until the child's 21st birthday. The father did die before the children were 21, and the question was whether the policies which survived by reason of the term mentioned belonged to his estate or to the children. It was held that they belonged to the children, having been effected by the father on trust for them.

According to Farwell J., there was more than a mere taking out of a policy for the benefit of another as in the earlier cases. The terms of the policies were sufficient to establish a trust, especially that providing that the father's interest in them would cease completely when the children were 21 and that providing that the policy moneys themselves were never payable until the children reached the specified age, thus making it clear that the father had no interest in these. This is logically sound, since such provisions are inconsistent with the father or nominal insured having the whole beneficial interest in the policy. A beneficial interest must lie elsewhere, that is with the children, and hence there must be a trust.

Re Webb was followed in *Re Foster*,[57] where the policy was not quite in the same form. It provided that upon the child becoming 21, the rights vested in the father (the grantee) to surrender or charge the policy until the child reached that age were to be vested in the child. Plowman J. held that the fact that these rights were vested absolutely in the child at 21 was inconsistent with the father thereafter retaining any beneficial interest, so that although this latter point was not expressly spelt out, as in *Re Webb*, it was necessarily impliedly provided, and the same result followed.

As a result of these cases, it appears likely nowadays that the court will strive to find a trust where policies are taken out for children, not least because it avoids any insurable interest problems. In effect, therefore, the children in these cases were insuring their own lives through a trustee. At all times, the trustee must act in accordance with the responsibilities surrounding that position. For example, although he will probably until a stated age have the right to surrender or assign the policy, he can properly do so only if it is in the best interests of the child. When the latter reaches the specified age, he has full powers over the policy and, if the trust still exists, will be able to terminate it.[58] He will also, if necessary, be able to enforce it through the trustee, but he will be able to enforce it directly only if he becomes legal owner or if there is a new agreement arising by virtue

---

[57] [1966] 1 W.L.R. 222.
[58] *Saunders v. Vautier* (1841) Cr. & Ph. 240.

of his paying and the insurer accepting from him, the premiums due. It must be stressed, though, that all cases must turn on their particular facts and on the provisions in the policies, and it is by no means impossible that a case will occur when these are not sufficient to establish a trust. It has sensibly been suggested that section 11 of the Married Women's Property Act be extended to cover these child policies,[59] but the Law Commission has recently recommended that section 11 be left alone, noting that its recommendations to reform the doctrine of privity of contract should enable the third party beneficiary to sue on the contract.[60]

Group insurance

The trust question has hitherto been considered solely in the context of family arrangements. The other equally common area where the same problems can arise is that of group insurance policies, for example, taken out by an employer on the lives of his employees or a group of them for the benefit of the latter. The circumstances may make it clear that the employees are beneficiaries under a trust, as in *Bowskill v. Dawson (No. 2)*,[61] where the employer entered into a trust deed with the trustee company which effected the policy for the employees. There were clear references to the fact that, *inter alia*, any sums received by the trust company were to be held on trust for the employees and the court had no difficulty in holding that the latter were therefore beneficiaries under the trusts of the deed.

By contrast, there were no such references in *Green v. Russell*,[62] where an employer, called the insured, effected a group accident policy for the benefit of his employees named in a schedule to the policy. The policy expressly provided that the insurer was entitled to treat the insured as absolute owner and was not bound to recognise any equitable or other claim or interest in the policy. In the light of this, it was held that the employees had no legal or equitable claim to the policy, in spite of the fact that one of the employees covered, or rather his widow, had received a sum of money paid under the policy.[63] There was clearly no basis for implying a

---

[59] Law Revision Committee, 6th Interim Report, p. 32.
[60] Law Com. No. 242, especially at paras. 12.22 to 12.26.
[61] [1955] 1 Q.B. 13.
[62] [1959] 2 Q.B. 226.
[63] The case arose under the Fatal Accidents Acts, the question being whether the third party who caused the death of the employee in question could deduct the insurance money from the damages he was liable to pay to the widow.

trust on the authorities already mentioned. It must therefore be doubtful whether the policy was strictly legally enforceable, as the employer may not have had an insurable interest in the lives of his employees, or at least not to the extent of the amount each employee was insured for.[64] It seems in practice that group policies of this nature are not always effected with terms that would enable the court to find a trust, but if the Law Commission's recent recommendations[65] on reforming the doctrine of privity of contract are implemented, the beneficiaries of such policies may have a statutory right to benefit under them.

---

[64] See also the comments in Chap. 3, p. 45.
[65] Law Com. No. 242, 1996.

CHAPTER 18

LIABILITY INSURANCE

Insurance against the insured's potential legal liability to a third party, whether in contract or tort, is of course commonplace. In a number of instances, such insurance is required to be effected by statute, most notably in the fields of motor vehicle and employer's liability insurance. The additional requirements and restrictions imposed in these instances will be considered in chapters 19 and 20. This chapter will concentrate upon aspects common to all liability insurances, which range from those effected by householders to public liability and professional indemnity policies. Here we consider those matters which appear genuinely to be common to all such insurances, rather than points which arise as the result of detailed policy wordings concerning the risks covered and excepted.[1] For the latter, reference must be made elsewhere.[2]

There are four headings: first, the statutory protection given to a third party in the event of the insured's insolvency; secondly, the important questions that arise from standard conditions to be found in all liability insurance policies; thirdly, some questions which can arise concerning the

---

[1] Standard market practice has led to some standard words of basic cover and indeed basic exclusions. For example, a public liability policy will generally seek to cover tortious, but not contractual, liability. Although the opening words may refer to indemnity against sums which the insured is legally liable to pay, words which by themselves are wide enough to cover contractual liability, there will normally be an express exclusion of contractual liability. However, the use of the tautologous phrase "liable at law" in "all sums which the insured shall become liable at law to pay as damages" does not by itself exclude contractual liability: *M/S Aswan Engineering Establishment Ltd v. Iron Trades Mutual Insurance Co. Ltd* [1989] 1 Lloyd's Rep. 289. Professional indemnity policies often refer to cover against any "negligent act, error or omission", but the word "negligent" does not qualify the words "act" and "omission". *Wimpey Construction U.K. Ltd v. Poole* [1984] 2 Lloyd's Rep. 499.

[2] An excellent book, published in Australia, is Derrington and Ashton, *The Law of Liability Insurance*. See also, Enright, *Professional Indemnity Insurance*.

sums insured and costs; and fourthly, the insurers' duty to the victim of the insured.

Insolvency of the Insured

At common law, if an insured went bankrupt, or, if a company, went into liquidation, after a claim arose against him by a third party, any money paid by his insurers to indemnify the insured against the claim after the commencement of the bankruptcy or liquidation went towards the general assets of the bankrupt or insolvent company, and were not entitled to be claimed by the third party.[3] The latter had merely the right to prove in the bankruptcy or liquidation as an ordinary creditor along with all the other ordinary creditors of the insured, because he had no rights in respect of the contract between insured and insurer. This was clearly unjust and in 1930, the Third Parties (Rights Against Insurers) Act was passed to remedy the situation.[4] In essence, the Act statutorily subrogates the third party to the position of the insured, although, as we shall see, the protection afforded to the third party can prove somewhat illusory. Section 1(1) provides:

> "Where under any contract of insurance a person (hereinafter referred to as the insured) is insured against liabilities to third parties which he may incur then,
>
>   (a) in the event of the insured becoming bankrupt . . . or

---

[3] *Re Harrington Motor Co.* [1928] Ch. 105; *Hood's Trustees v. Southern Union General Insurance Co. of Australasia Ltd* [1928] Ch. 793.

[4] It was passed at the same time as compulsory motor insurance was introduced and the two cases referred to in n.3 both arose out of road accidents. It seems clear that at the time the Act was primarily envisaged as applying to such situations. It is not perhaps surprising that later developments, including the expansion of liability insurance, have led to situations where the Act does not seem to give sufficient protection to third parties. The Law Commission is currently examining the Act, having decided that it would be better to do so specifically rather than as part of its general recommendations on the doctrine of privity of contract (see Law Com. No. 242, paras. 12.18 to 12.21), and can be expected to recommend some reforms in the fairly near future.

(b) in the case of the insured being a company, [being wound up[5] or subject to receivership][6]

if, either before or after that event, any such liability as aforesaid is incurred by the insured, his rights against the insurer under the contract in respect of the liability shall, notwithstanding anything in any Act or rule of law to the contrary, be transferred to and vest in the third party to whom the liability was so incurred."

The same applies where the insured dies insolvent.[7] The other important provision in section 1 is subsection (3), relating to exclusions of the Act; this is considered separately below.

Section 2 casts upon the insured who becomes bankrupt the duty to inform the third party who has a claim of any relevant insurance,[8] and section 3 provides that settlements made between the insurer and the bankrupt or liquidated insured are of no effect as regards the third party. The latter provision, however, applies only to settlements made after bankruptcy or liquidation, and does not affect a prior settlement even in respect of a liability already incurred by the insured.[9]

The years since the passing of the Act have seen a number of reported decisions which, in varying degrees, tend to restrict its effectiveness so far as third parties are concerned. The effect of these decisions is considered in the following paragraphs. It is not, however, suggested that any of these decisions is wrong; they simply confirm that the 1930 Act has a fairly narrow impact and certainly cannot, as currently drafted, put the third party in a better position than the insured.[10] As already indicated,[11] it is

---

[5] Other than a voluntary winding up merely for the purposes of a reconstruction or amalgamation: s.1(6).

[6] By amendments made by the Insolvency Acts 1985 and 1986, this case is extended to the situations where a company is made the subject of an administration order or adopts a voluntary arrangement under the 1986 Act.

[7] s. 1(2).

[8] But this right exists only, as with s.1 (see below), when liability on the part of the insured has been established: *Nigel Upchurch Associates v. Aldridge Estates Investment Co. Ltd* [1993] 1 Lloyd's Rep. 535; *Woolwich Building Society v. Taylor* [1995] 1 B.C.L.C. 132.

[9] *Normid Housing Association Ltd v. Ralphs* [1989] 1 Lloyd's Rep. 265.

[10] See especially the recent House of Lords' decision in *Bradley v. Eagle Star Insurance Co. Ltd* [1989] A.C. 957 and *The Fanti* and *The Padre Island* [1991] 2 A.C. 1, both of which are considered in detail below.

[11] See n.4.

likely that the Law Commission will be recommending some reform of the Act.[12]

Liability must be incurred

It is clear first of all that the insured's rights are transferred to the third party only when a liability is incurred by the insured, and a liability is not incurred for these purposes[13] until the third party obtains judgment against or an admission of liability from the insured. In *Post Office v. Norwich Union Fire Insurance Co.*,[14] the insureds were contractors engaged in road works. In the course of their excavations they damaged a cable belonging to the Post Office. The latter claimed that this was the fault of the contractors, though this was denied, the contractors claiming that it was the fault of a Post Office engineer. The contractors having gone into liquidation, the Post Office sued their insurers under the 1930 Act before the insured's liability was established. It was held that the action was premature. The third party gets no better rights than the insured, and the latter's rights arise only when his liability to the third party has been determined or agreed.[15] The correct procedure in this sort of case is for the third party to obtain the leave of the court to bring proceedings against the insolvent insured. Only when these proceedings have been determined can the insurer be liable under the 1930 Act.

---

[12] These are hardly likely to be fundamental, as to effect changes which would put the third party in a better position than the insured would strike a severe blow at the current system of compensating the victims of torts, based on liability insurance. More likely are changes which provide the third party with a better right to information about the insurance (see n.8, above) and control settlements made before insolvency (see n.9). It is possible that there might be changes reversing the decision in *The Fanti* and *The Padre Island*, above (see p. 345, below). but the practical impact of this decision is likely to be confined to the very special situation of shipowners' mutual insurance clubs where, perhaps, the parties could be left to their own devices.

[13] For other purposes, *e.g.* regarding the limitation period for an action on a liability policy, the liability may be incurred when the event causing the loss takes place: *Chandris v. Argo Insurance* [1963] 2 Lloyd's Rep. 65. Contrast, however, *Green & Silley Weir Ltd v. British Railways Board* [1985] 1 All E.R. 237, especially at 242.

[14] [1967] 2 Q.B. 363.

[15] This was the *ratio* of.Lord Denning M.R. and the principal *ratio* of Salmon L.J. However, the latter also relied upon the fact that the third party takes subject to any conditions in the policy, one of which forbad the insured from admitting liability in any way without the insurer's consent (as to this, see below). Harman L.J. relied on this latter reason only.

The *Post Office* case was followed and approved by the House of Lords in *Bradley v. Eagle Star Insurance Co. Ltd.*[16] Here, the insured had been the company employing the plaintiff, Mrs. Bradley, against which the latter was assumed to have the right to claim damages as a result of her having contracted byssinosis while working in circumstances which involved the inhalation of cotton dust. The company had been dissolved in 1976 and so, there being no other possible defendant, Mrs. Bradley commenced proceedings directly against her employer's insurers. It was held that this action had to be struck out as disclosing no cause of action. No liability had been incurred by the insured employer to bring section 1 of the 1930 Act into operation.

While the decisions in the *Norwich Union* and *Bradley* cases cannot logically be faulted,[17] they are nonetheless somewhat artificial as almost inevitably in such cases the insurers will in practice be the real defendant and, once the insured's liability is established, will normally immediately satisfy it. However, insurers have their own good reasons for not wishing to appear as the defendants in civil actions, principally the fear that it would gain them bad publicity,[18] and these are clearly legitimate reasons within the context of the tort/liability insurance system.

Further, Parliament has enacted what in many cases, because the insolvent defendant would be a registered company, will in practice amount to a reversal of the decision in *Bradley*. Since 1989, an application to the court for a declaration that the dissolution of a company is void may be made at any time if it is for the purpose of bringing proceedings against the company for damages for personal injury or under the Fatal Accidents Act.[19] The likes of Mrs. Bradley can now use this procedure to find a defendant to sue, and then use the 1930 Act to claim against the latter's insurers.[20]

Third party's rights no better than insured's

One of the reasons for the decision in *Post Office v. Norwich Union* was that the plaintiff obtains his rights under the 1930 Act subject to the conditions

---

[16] [1989] A.C. 957.
[17] Notwithstanding Lord Templeman's vigorous dissent in *Bradley*.
[18] See Salmon L.J. in the *Norwich Union* case [1967] 2 Q.B. at 378.
[19] Companies Act 1985, s.651, as amended by the Companies Act 1989, s.141. Before this amendment, such an application could be made only within two years of a dissolution.
[20] This is still not foolproof, of course. For example, there will still have to be evidence that a particular insurer was the relevant insurer at the appropriate time.

of the policy.[21] There a condition forbad the insured from making any admission of liability without the insurer's consent[22]; the third party's statutory rights were subject also to this term. This point is of general application, so that, except in compulsory motor insurance and, to a lesser extent in employer's liability insurance, where insurers' rights are more circumscribed by statute,[23] any defence which the insurers have against the insured under the insurance contract is available against the third party. This might be the right to avoid the policy for non-disclosure or misrepresentation,[24] the right to avoid liability for breach of warranty or condition, or the right to insist upon arbitration.

In *Freshwater v. Western Australian Assurance Co.*[25] and *Smith v. Pearl Assurance Co.*,[26] the insurers' right in motor policies to insist upon arbitration as a condition precedent to liability was upheld against the injured third party. In fact these decisions have probably been overruled by statute so far as motor insurance is concerned,[27] but the principle holds good for other liability insurances.[28] In *Farrell v. Federated Employers' Insurance Association Ltd*,[29] a breach of condition by an employer who was insured against liability to his employees was held effective against an injured employee,[30] and in *Pioneer Concrete (U.K.) Ltd v. National Employers Mutual General Insurance Association Ltd*,[31] a breach of condition requiring immediate notification by the insured of legal proceedings instituted against it could be relied upon against the innocent third party.

Further, the third party will be bound by any limitations in the policy regarding the amount of indemnity provided,[32] and if the total insurance

[21] See n.15.
[22] As to such terms, see pp. 348–352, below.
[23] See Chaps. 19 and 20.
[24] *e.g. McCormick v. National Motor and Accident Insurance Union Ltd* (1934) 43 Ll.L.R. 361.
[25] [1933] 1 K.B. 515.
[26] [1939] 1 All E.R. 95.
[27] By s.148(5) of the Road Traffic Act 1988; see *Jones v. Birch Bros* [1933] 2 K.B. 597 and p. 375, below.
[28] See *Socony Mobil Oil Co. Inc. v. West of England Ship Owners Mutual Insurance Association (London) Ltd* [1984] 2 Lloyd's Rep. 408, noted [1985] J.B.L. 403.
[29] [1970] 1 W.L.R. 1400.
[30] The actual decision in the context of employers' liability insurance is over-ruled by the Employers' Liability (Compulsory Insurance) Regulations: see p. 392, below.
[31] [1985] 1 Lloyd's Rep. 274; see [1985] J.B.L. 333.
[32] *Averando (U.K.) Ltd v. National Transit Insurance Co. Ltd* [1984] 2 Lloyd's Rep. 613.

fund available is insufficient to pay all the claims made by third parties, the fund is distributed on a first come, first served basis.[33]

However, insurers cannot simply claim to set off against the amount due to the third party any premiums due but unpaid by the insured. In *Murray v. Legal & General Assurance Society*,[34] it was held that the rights and liabilities of the insured transferred to the third party are only those rights and liabilities in respect of the liability incurred by the insured to the third party. The right to claim premiums was a general right, not dependent on any term of the policy. It would appear that the effect of this decision would be reversed if there were an express term in a liability policy that it was a condition precedent to the liability of the insurer for any particular claim that all premiums owing under the policy before the claim arose were duly paid.

Exclusions of the Act

Section 1(3) provides that in so far as any insurance contract purports, whether directly or indirectly, to avoid the contract or to alter the rights of the parties in the event of the insured's insolvency, it shall be of no effect. The relatively limited effect of this provision, and the fact that in theory the application of the 1930 Act can be avoided quite easily, was demonstrated in the House of Lords' decision in two cases heard and decided together, *The Fanti* and *The Padre Island*.[35]

These concerned the standard provisions in the rules of shipowners' mutual insurance clubs which provide that the clubs, the insurers, do not pay an indemnity to their members, the insureds, until the latter have paid the third party making a claim against them; these are commonly referred to as "pay to be paid" clauses.

Both insureds in the cases had been wound up after their liability to third parties had been established but before the third parties' claims had been paid. It was held that the third parties did not have direct rights against the insurers under the 1930 Act. First it was held that section 1(3) was of no assistance to the third parties. The pay to be paid clause was a provision imposing a condition necessary to be fulfilled before any liability

[33] *Cox v. Bankside Members Agency Ltd* [1995] 2 Lloyd's Rep. 437.

[34] [1969] 3 All E.R. 794.

[35] [1991] 2 A.C. 1. Fully, the cases are, respectively, *Firma C. Trade S.A. v. Newcastle Protection and Indemnity Association* and *Socony Mobil Oil Co. Inc. v. West of England Ship Owners Mutual Insurance Association (London) Ltd*.

of the insurers could arise and was not a provision which applied on the happening of an insolvency. What were affected or altered by insolvency were not the rights of the insureds themselves but the ability of the insureds to exercise them. Thus, the provision applied equally before and after a winding up order and was not rendered ineffective by section 1(3). With this reasoning, it is submitted, there can be no quarrel. As worded, the subsection strikes down only provisions clearly aimed at affecting the rights of an insured in the event of its becoming insolvent in an attempt to contract out of the statutory assignment.

Two other arguments were, however, put forward by the third parties as to why the pay to be paid clauses should be regarded as ineffective. The first[36] was that there were transferred to the third parties rights to be indemnified by the insurers, subject to a condition that the third parties first paid to themselves the amounts of the liabilities to them which had been incurred by themselves. Such a condition precedent was impossible or futile for the third parties to perform and thus performance should be excused. This argument was easily rejected. What the 1930 Act transfers is the insured's right which, in the circumstances of the case, was a contingent right to indemnity, conditional on the insured having paid the third party's claim. If that condition was not satisfied, the insured had no present right to be indemnified. The statutory transfer could not put the third party in any better position than the insured.

The other argument was in effect that a principle of equity could override the "pay to be paid" provisions. It ran as follows. At common law the only remedy against an indemnifier under a contract of indemnity was an action of assumpsit by the person entitled to the indemnity, a condition of prior payment by him being implicit in the contract. Equity, however, intervened where reliance on that condition would defeat the indemnity altogether, by requiring the indemnifier to pay the third party directly or pay the indemnified person before he paid the third party, and the equitable remedy prevailed over the common law. While accepting that this principle was in substance as had been argued, the House of Lords rejected its application essentially on the ground that it could not be applicable in the face of the express "pay to be paid" provisions in the contracts of insurance.

The reasons given by the House of Lords cannot easily be faulted as a matter of strict law. The interpretation of the 1930 Act is logical and the

---

[36] In effect this was the basis of the decision of the Court of Appeal ([1989] 1 Lloyd's Rep. 239) which the House of Lords overruled.

rejection of the argument based on equity convincing. On the other hand, an instant reaction might well be to say that the result looks like yet another blow to an innocent third party who has lost out simply because he had the misfortune to have a sound claim against an insured who happened to go into liquidation. This looks like the sort of situation against which the 1930 Act was directed. This point was directly addressed by Lord Goff and it is thought that his arguments supporting the result are ultimately persuasive.[37] All that the 1930 Act was ever intended to do was to transfer to a third party such rights as the insured had under the contract of insurance. "[I]t is very difficult to see how it could be said that a condition of prior payment would drive a coach and horses through the Act, for the Act was not directed to giving the third party greater rights than the insured had." In sharp contrast, where liability insurance is compulsory, especially in respect of motor and employer's liability insurance, Parliament has expressly provided that provisions in contracts defeating the purpose of the insurance will be ineffective.[38] Further, Lord Goff recognised that the *Fanti* and *Padre Island* litigation was in substance fought between insurers. The third parties, the cargo owners, were no doubt insured as is customary, so in substance the plaintiffs were their insurers exercising subrogation rights. In the light of this, sympathy for an unfortunate third party is rapidly lost and it can be argued that there is little real merit in a first party insurer seeking to transfer the risk he has undertaken to a liability insurer.[39]

It also seems likely that provisions like the "pay to be paid" clauses are to be found only in contracts like those of mutual insurance clubs. The only weak and uninsured third parties likely to be at risk of being prejudiced by them are those injured or killed as the result of a shipping accident. The evidence was that in such cases the clubs do not rely on the condition of prior payment to defeat a claim. If they did, or indeed if other insurers sought to use the device to evade the 1930 Act, there can be little doubt that legislation restricting their freedom would follow.[40]

---

[37] See especially [1991] 2 A.C. at 38–39.
[38] See Chaps. 19 and 20.
[39] See also pp. 311–312, above.
[40] As already indicated, the Law Commission is currently examining the 1930 Act and some measure of reform is, it is thought, likely.

Contractual Provisions in Liability Policies

There are basically two common form conditions of relevance for present purposes. They concern first admissions of liability and the conduct of proceedings and secondly the obligation of the insured to take reasonable care.

Admissions of liability and the conduct of proceedings

The standard term reads something like the following[41]:

> "No admission of liability or offer or promise of payment, whether expressed or implied, shall be made without the written consent of the insurer, which shall be entitled at its own discretion to take over and conduct in the name of the insured the defence or settlement of any claim."

Professional indemnity policies may have in addition a clause providing that proceedings by the third party are not to be contested unless a Queen's Counsel so advises (the "Q.C. clause").[42]

Control of proceedings — duty of insurer

The clause cited contains two elements, that prohibiting unauthorised admissions of liability and that giving the insurer the right to control proceedings against the insured. In respect of the latter, it would seem from the standard wording that the insurer has an absolute discretion as to what is done, but it is clear that this discretion is controlled. The insurers have "the right to decide upon the proper tactics to pursue in the conduct of the action,[43] provided that they do so in what they *bona fide* consider to be the common interest of themselves and their assured."[44]

---

[41] This wording is unlikely to be used in liability policies sold to individual consumers and indeed should not be, as it is likely to fall foul of the plain and intelligibility requirements of the Unfair Terms in Consumer Contracts Regulations 1994; see pp. 197–198, above.

[42] As to this, see *West Wake Price & Co. v. Ching* [1957] 1 W.L.R. 45.

[43] Including the appointment of solicitors to represent the insured. However, the insurers cannot compel the insured to accept legal representation: *Barrett Bros v. Davies* [1966] 1 W.L.R. 1334.

[44] Lord Greene M.R. in *Groom v. Crocker* [1939] 1 K.B. 194 at 203.

A blatant ignoring of the interests of the insured occurred in *Groom v. Crocker*[45] where, quite without foundation and knowing of its inaccuracy, the solicitors acting for the insurers admitted to the third party claimant that the insured had been negligent. It was held that this was a clear breach of duty and the insured was entitled to damages for breach of contract and to damages in tort for libel. The contract damages, however, were only nominal, as the insurers had paid the third party the sum he claimed, and the court declined to award damages for the injury to reputation or feelings.[46] That *Groom v. Crocker* did not, however, establish a very strict limit on the insurer's discretion is evident from the later case of *Beacon Insurance Co. v. Langdale*.[47] Here the insurers did not admit that their motor insured was negligent, but without his knowledge they settled the third party's claim with a strict denial of liability. They then sued the insured for the £5 excess which the policy provided for and it was held that they were entitled to succeed. They had acted quite properly, had made an advantageous settlement and denied liability. With respect, the niceties of paying up but with a denial of liability may be lost on some insureds. The defendant in the case continued to deny that he was liable and would not therefore see why he should have to pay anything until the contrary were proved. Furthermore, such evidence as there is from the report suggests that the third party recovered sufficient to cover him only for his out of pocket expenses and not for the fairly severe injuries he recovered, implying that it was by no means certain that the insured was liable.

Despite any sympathy that might be felt for such an insured, it can safely be said that in law the insurer can settle with the third party so long as they do not unjustifiably admit liability, and, possibly, so long as they do not unjustifiably settle beyond the policy limits or refuse a settlement offer by the third party within these limits. There is no English authority on this latter point, but the question has been much litigated in the United States of America where there are decisions holding that if a liability insurer refuses an offer of settlement by the third party within the policy limits, and the latter subsequently recovers more than the sum insured in a civil action against the insured, the insurer is liable for the whole amount.[48]

[45] [1939] 1 K.B. 194.
[46] But see now, *e.g. Heywood v. Wellers* [1976] 1 All E.R. 300.
[47] [1939] 4 All E.R. 209.
[48] See especially, *Crisci v. Security Insurance Co.* 66 Cal. (2d) 425, 426, P. (2d) 173 (1967). The action was categorised as tortious. It has been followed on numerous occasions in the U.S.A.

It is suggested that such conduct on the part of an insurer here should also entail civil liability as a breach of the duty to act in good faith laid down by *Groom v. Crocker*. The American cases have often also awarded the insured punitive damages, but it is not suggested that the English courts would, or should, do so.

On the other hand, it is clear that the standard condition in English policies does not oblige the insurers to take over the insured's defence,[49] so that there can be no basis for any liability on the insurer if it chooses not to do so, other than to indemnify the insured within the limits of the policy if the latter is adjudged legally liable to the third party. In practice, a refusal by the insurer to conduct the defence is unlikely, since it would hardly wish to be without a say in negotiations.[50]

No estoppel

If an insurer does take control of proceedings under the standard condition, it is not necessarily thereby prevented from subsequently denying liability to indemnify the insured. This may arise because of a non-disclosure or breach of warranty or condition by the insured discovered only at a later date. If, however, the insurer does discover such a right to avoid liability, it will be deemed to have waived its right if it continues to act for the insured.[51]

Another situation where the insurer might seek to avoid liability is on the grounds that the event that occurred was not within the cover provided by the policy. Provided that the insurer does not clearly admit to liability, the question arises whether the mere fact that it conducted the defence is sufficient ground for holding that it cannot subsequently deny liability. The only conceivable legal basis for such a conclusion would be by application of the doctrine of estoppel. That such an estoppel could operate in this context has been denied by an English court in the case of *Soole v. Royal Insurance Co.*[52] The insured effected a policy to indemnify himself against the possible successful enforcement by his neighbours of a restrictive covenant on his property. His defence against the action by his

---

[49] As U.S. policies often do; see the discussion by Stephen J. in *Distillers Co. v. Ajax Insurance Co.* (1974) 48 A.L.J.R. 136, esp. at 147.

[50] But compare the attitude of the insurers in *Distillers v. Ajax*, above, discussed below.

[51] *Evans v. Employers' Mutual Insurance Association* [1936] 1 K.B. 505.

[52] [1971] 2 Lloyd's Rep. 332. Compare *Hansen v. Marco Engineering (Aust.) Pty Ltd* [1948] V.L.R. 198, where it was held that the insurer was estopped.

neighbours, which action was in fact successful, was conducted by the insurers, but they subsequently denied that they were liable to indemnify him. In fact they were held liable, but the court also held that, if they had not been, their conduct in defending the insured would not have estopped them from denying liability. That conduct did not amount to an unequivocal representation that they would indemnify the insured regardless, because no insurer when it takes over the defence of its insured can be sure that it will be liable in the long run. For example, the third party's claim might fail. The insurer's conduct of the defence is merely an indication that the proceedings may give rise to a liability to indemnify the insured.

Admissions of liability

The part of the standard condition which prohibits admissions of liability etc. without the insurer's consent is obviously very important, and is no doubt regarded by insurers as essential for the protection of their interests. There can be no doubt as to the validity of such a condition,[53] and it should not matter on principle whether or not the insurer has been prejudiced by an admission by its insured, for example if there can be no doubt whatsoever as to the latter's legal liability.[54] What is perhaps slightly disturbing about this standard condition is its width and the fact that an insurer could rely on a fairly casual "it's my fault" said or written to the third party by the insured to avoid liability, despite the lack of any real prejudice to their position. It must be admitted though that a case with no prejudice at all might not be so likely, as the insurer could always argue that it might well have persuaded the third party to accept a smaller settlement.

Insurer's refusal to defend

The question may arise whether an insurer is still entitled to rely upon this condition if it elects not to have anything to do with the insured's defence against the third party. The essence of the condition is that it prohibits the insured from settling without consent. If the insurer refuses to consent, the insured will be compelled to let the matter go to litigation, unless he can argue that by refusing to have anything to do with his

---

[53] See, e.g. Terry v. Trafalgar Insurance Co. [1970] 1 Lloyd's Rep. 524.
[54] ibid.

defence the insurer has forfeited its right to rely upon the condition. This question, which appears never to have been considered in the English courts, produced a difference of opinion in the High Court of Australia in *Distillers Co. Ltd v. Ajax Insurance Co. Ltd.*[55]

The dispute arose out of the manufacture of drugs containing thalidomide which the insured, a subsidiary of the United Kingdom company, had distributed in Australia. These drugs were taken by pregnant women and, allegedly owing to the negligence of Distillers, caused severe damage to their unborn foetuses. Distillers had public liability cover with Ajax, the policy containing the relevant condition. Upon being sued for negligence, Distillers wished to consider compromising with the third parties, but Ajax refused to consent to this, at the same time refusing to conduct Distillers' defence. By a majority, it was held that the insurers were entitled to refuse consent without incurring any liability. Gibbs J., dissenting, preferred to follow an Irish case[56] and held that the two aspects of the standard condition were linked, so that the right to rely upon no admissions without consent applied only where the insurer conducted the insured's defence.

The decision of the majority appears correct in principle, but Stephen J., one of the majority, in an important judgment which, it is suggested, should be followed, made it clear that the decision would not confer upon an insurer an arbitrary power to refuse consent. He referred in particular to the sort of case where a conflict between insured and insurer might arise, where the claim against the insured is above the sum insured under the policy and the insured is anxious to settle below that figure whereas the insurer would gain little from a settlement close to the limit and might prefer to fight the case. He said that in such a case, the insurer must exercise its powers under the policy with due regard to the interests of the insured, following *Groom v. Crocker*[57] on the analogous point already discussed. The position must depend on a reasonable estimate of the third party's claim. If that has every chance of succeeding, it would be improper for the insurer to refuse to consent to a settlement substantially within the policy limits. If, on the other hand, the third party's claim is doubtful, and the only or principal reason why the insured wishes to settle is to avoid the bad publicity attendant on being sued, the insurer would be justified in refusing its consent. The result is that if the insurer refuses its consent and

---

[55] (1974) 48 A.L.J.R. 136.
[56] *General Omnibus Co. Ltd v. London General Insurance Co. Ltd* [1936] I.R. 596.
[57] [1939] 1 K.B. 194; see p. 348, above.

leaves the insured to act alone, but the latter enters into a quite reasonable settlement, the insurer will be liable to indemnify him regardless of the breach of condition.

The obligation to take reasonable precautions

The second standard condition requires the insured to take reasonable precautions or care to avoid loss. This sort of condition has already been considered generally.[58] Such a clause construed literally would negate a large part of the cover intended to be effected, since one of the major purposes of a liability policy is to insure the insured against liability in negligence, and negligence is a failure to take reasonable care when a duty of care is owed. So the courts have adopted a common sense construction of this condition. In *Woolfall & Rimmer Ltd v. Moyle*,[59] an employer, the insured, was vicariously liable for the acts of a foreman who had failed to ensure that certain scaffolding was safe. The court rejected the insurer's argument that the insured had therefore failed to take reasonable precautions. The insured had complied with that condition by selecting a competent foreman and reasonably delegating to him certain tasks. The insured was not personally negligent, which was the circumstance when the condition might apply.

The Court of Appeal went further than this in the later case of *Fraser v. Furman*,[60] so that only recklessness or worse on the part of the insured will now amount to a breach of this condition. Reasonable care does not mean reasonable as between the insured and third party, but as between insured and insurer having regard to the commercial purpose of the contract which includes indemnity against the insured's own negligence. The insured's omission or act "must be at least reckless, that is to say, made with actual recognition by the insured himself that a danger exists, and not caring whether or not it is averted. The purpose of the condition is to ensure that the insured will not, because he is covered against loss by the policy, refrain from taking precautions which he knows ought to be taken."[61]

Sums Insured and Costs

It has already been noted how the sum insured in a liability policy may be of great importance in the context of an admission of liability condition.

---

[58] See p. 201, above.
[59] [1942] 1 K.B. 66.
[60] [1967] 1 W.L.R. 898.
[61] *ibid.* at 906, per Diplock L.J. See also *Aluminium Wire and Cable Co. Ltd v. Allstate Insurance Co. Ltd* [1985] 2 Lloyd's Rep. 280.

More generally, while the sum insured obviously puts the limit of the insurer's liability, and is commonplace except in relation to personal injury aspects of motor insurance where statute does not allow it, it may be expressed in different ways. For example, the policy may have a limit applying to any one contractual period, regardless of the number of claims made, or the limit may apply to each accident or each occurrence or each claim, with no global maximum. The first sort of limit causes no problems, and it has been held that where the limit is *per* accident, each separate claim by a third party arises out of a separate incident. For example, in *South Staffordshire Tramways Co. v. Sickness and Accident Assurance Association*,[62] a policy indemnifying the insured against liability for accidents caused by vehicles had a limit of "£250 in respect of any one accident." One of the insured's trams over-turned injuring forty passengers. It was held that each passenger had an accident and therefore the insurer was potentially liable for 40 x £250.

If, however, the limit is expressed to be *per* occurrence, then it seems that the number of occurrences is the number of times the insured is negligent. If there is only one negligent act, there is only one occurrence and the policy limit will apply regardless of how many individual claims may be made by third parties as a result. In *Forney v. Dominion Insurance Co. Ltd*,[63] a solicitor's professional indemnity policy had a limit of £3,000 *per* occurrence. His assistant was negligent in advising a client about a cause of action in tort. The matter involved a motor accident when a man driving negligently injured some of his family and caused the death of himself and his father in law. The survivors, including the driver's widow, were advised to sue the driver's estate, which was quite proper, but the assistant failed to issue the writs in time. In addition, she advised the widow to act as the driver's administratrix which was also negligent, because it meant that the widow would effectively lose her damages, not being able in her personal capacity to sue herself as representing the driver's estate. It was held that the two acts of negligence were two occurrences, and the insurer's maximum liability was therefore £6,000. It seems that the same construction applies where the limit applies *per* claim, that is, that claim means claim by the insured against the insurer rather than claim by each third party against the insured. This is certainly the

[62] [1891] 1 Q.B. 402.
[63] [1969] 1 W.L.R. 928.

construction adopted in a case where the relevant limit was contained in an excess clauses in a liability policy.[64]

Liability policies invariably include in their cover any costs incurred by the insured, in addition to the damages he is liable to pay. This would not usually include the costs of the insured in successfully defending a claim as the provision as to costs normally applies only where the insurer is liable to indemnify the insured,[65] but the insured will in general recover these from the plaintiff third party. Costs though will normally be limited; for example, by being included together with damages in the sum insured, or by being limited to the same proportion which the indemnity provided bears to the insured's loss where the latter exceeds the former because it is greater than the sum insured by the policy.

Insurer's Duty to the Victim

Frequently in practice liability insurers will negotiate directly on their insured's behalf with the latter's victim. For obvious reasons, but to the potential detriment of the victim, they will seek to keep their liability as low as possible and may well induce the victim to agree to a settlement for an amount below his legal entitlement. Where the victim so relies on the insurers, it is likely that a fiduciary relationship will arise and that the settlement will be voidable on the ground of undue influence unless the insurers either inform the victim of the desirability of seeking independent advice or make an offer which is realistic in respect of the victim's loss.[66]

---

[64] *Trollope & Colls Ltd v. Haydon* [1977] 1 Lloyd's Rep. 244. See also now the Privy Council decision in *Haydon v. Lo & Lo,* January 16, 1997. Although the actual words used may differ in different policies, for example they may refer to "cause" or "event", the same principle applies: see *e.g. Caudle v. Sharp* [1995] L.R.L.R. 80; *Cox v. Bankside Members Agency Ltd* [1995] 2 Lloyd's Rep. 437. In other contexts, especially in determining the cover under a policy, the word "claim" means claim by a third party against the insured: *Thomas v. New Hampshire Insurance Co.* [1988] 1 Lloyd's Rep. 7.

[65] *Cross v. British Oak Insurance Co.* [1938] 2 K.B. 167 at 174.

[66] *Horry v. Tate & Lyle Refineries Ltd* [1982] 2 Lloyd's Rep. 416, applying *Lloyds Bank Ltd v. Bundy* [1975] Q.B. 326; see Merkin (1983) 46 M.L.R. 91. The contract of settlement may also be voidable for misrepresentation: see *Saunders v. Ford Motor Co. Ltd* [1970] 1 Lloyd's Rep. 379.

CHAPTER 19

MOTOR INSURANCE

For many years, some form of motor vehicle insurance has been compulsory. What the law requires at present is that anyone who uses or causes or permits another to use a motor vehicle on a road must be insured against liability to pay damages for death or bodily injury or property damage caused by or arising out of the use of the vehicle.[1] The exact scope of this requirement will be considered shortly. The requirement in respect of property damage was introduced only at the end of 1988, pursuant to the Second E.C. Directive on Motor Insurance,[2] although in practice most motor policies have long covered third party property damage.

It has long been conventional to sell motor policies under particular labels, although these have no legal significance. Thus, a "comprehensive" policy will generally, in addition to what is compulsory, cover first party property damage, that is insurance of the vehicle as goods against loss, and first party injury, that is in effect a personal accident insurance under which the insured who is killed or injured when involved in an accident in his vehicle will receive a stated sum. It often also covers personal effects in the vehicle.[3] The other common form of motor policy which does not just cover third party liability is the third party, fire and theft policy; in addition to third party liability, this covers insurance of the vehicle itself but limited to those losses caused by fire or theft.

---

[1] Road Traffic Act 1988, ss.143 and 145.
[2] Directive 84/5, O.J. L8/17. This was implemented first by regulations and then consolidated in the Road Traffic Act 1988. Part VI of the latter contains the provisions regarding compulsory motor vehicle insurance.
[3] In addition, there are usually special provisions regarding windscreen damage whereby the insured may be able to have a broken windscreen replaced and only claim later, and without prejudice to his no claims bonus. Some policies now provide for the insured to be entitled to claim the cost of hiring an alternative vehicle while his is being repaired, and there are special policies available to people over particular ages.

In practice a motor policy may not just cover the insured or policy holder himself. The policy may extend either to named others or possibly to anyone driving the car with the insured's permission, and may also cover the insured driving other vehicles.[4] In addition, there are various categories of use, for example, "social, domestic and pleasure purposes" and "business purposes", adopted by insurers, which determine the uses to which the vehicle can be put while remaining covered.[5]

Other insurance practices are of special importance in the field of motor insurance, including excesses[6] and no claims and loyalty bonuses. No claims bonuses provide for specified reductions in premiums if no claim, or no·relevant claim, is made during the previous year.[7] "Knock for knock" agreement used to be common in the motor insurance industry, but have fallen out of favour in recent years.[8]

The Scope of Compulsory Cover

Part VI of the Road Traffic Act 1988,[9] which governs the compulsory aspect of motor insurance, as well as defining these obligations, also provides special protection to the injured third party from the strict contractual rights of the insurer as against the insured. The basic obligations will be examined at this stage and the latter aspect will be considered later.

Subject to the exceptions in section 144,[10] section 143 provides that "it is not lawful for a person to use, or to cause or permit to use, or to cause or

---

[4] For the double insurance problems that can arise as a result of these extensions, see pp. 321–323, above.

[5] See pp. 368–370, below.

[6] See p. 274, above.

[7] The practice of offering no claims bonuses has spread to other forms of insurance in recent years. Loyalty bonuses tend to allow for an unlimited number of claims over a longer period without their being lost. Technically, there may be difficulties in showing a legal entitlement to such bonuses since motor policies, like other indemnity policies, are of limited duration and each renewal is a separate contract. As to possible arguments around these difficulties, see p. 89, above.

[8] See p. 307, above. There are still other agreements which operate within the industry; see Lewis, (1985) 48 M.L.R. 275.

[9] This consolidated earlier legislation dating originally from 1930.

[10] Particularly, in respect of vehicles owned by public bodies and vehicles owned by a person who has deposited £500,000 in court. The latter sum was increased, from £15,000, by the Road Traffic Act 1991, s.20.

permit any other person to use, a motor vehicle on a road" unless there is
in force a policy which complies with the Act, in particular covering the
required third party risks or a security in relation to those risks.[11] The
requirements are stated in section 145. First, the policy must be issued by
an authorised insurer, which means for this purpose a person carrying on
motor insurance business in Great Britain and who is a member of the
Motor Insurer's Bureau.[12] The required risks are:

(1) insurance against liability in respect of death or bodily injury to
    any person[13] or damage to property caused by or arising out of,
    the use of the vehicle on a road in Great Britain;[14]

(2) insurance against any liability in the other E.C. member States
    which those States require; and

(3) insurance against liabilities in respect of emergency treatment.[15]

---

[11] Securities, which it seems are rarely used, are governed by section 146. This
requires first that they are given by either (1) an authorised insurer or (2) by
some body of persons which carries on in the U.K. the business of giving
securities of a like kind and has deposited and keeps deposited with the
Accountant General of the Supreme Court the sum of £500,000 in respect of
that business. Secondly, subject to the limits that the amount secured need not
exceed £5,000 or £25,000 in respect of an undertaking relating to the use of
public service vehicles, the security must consist of an undertaking by the giver
of it to make good, subject to any conditions specified in it, any failure by the
owner of the vehicle or such other persons or classes of persons as may be
specified in the security duly to discharge any liability which may be incurred by
him or them which is a liability required under s.145 to be covered by an
insurance policy.

[12] As to the Motor Insurers' Bureau, see p. 379, below. It is now perfectly lawful
for a motor policy to be issued by any E.C. insurer, subject only to the
requirement of M.I.B. membership. Note that cessation of M.I.B. membership
does not affect policies issued or obligations arising before such cessation:
s.145(6).

[13] But not the driver: *R. v. Secretary of State, ex p. National Insurance Guarantee
Corporation plc, The Times*, June 3, 1996.

[14] This does not mean that the user has to be insured against his potential liability
to the driver, *e.g.* because he has negligently let him drive an unsafe vehicle:
Cooper v. Motor Insurers' Bureau [1985] Q.B. 575. See also, *Limbrick v. French*
[1990] C.L.Y. 2709.

[15] This liability arises under s.158. Where medical or surgical treatment is
immediately required as a result of bodily injury (including fatal injury) to a
person caused by or arising out of the use of a motor vehicle on a road and such
emergency treatment is effected by a legally qualified medical practitioner, the

Where a vehicle is normally based in one E.C. Member State, and used in another, the compulsory insurance cover must be in accordance with the law requiring the greater cover.[16]

Heading (1) does not, however, require insurance in respect of the following:

    (a) the liability of an employer to an employee in respect of death or bodily injury arising out of and in the course of his employment, where there is effective cover under the Employers' Liability (Compulsory Insurance Act) 1969[17]; because employers' liability policies are no longer required to cover these risks,[18] in practice they are likely to be covered by a motor policy;

    (b) cover in respect of property damage of more than £250,000 "caused by, or arising out of, any one accident involving the vehicle"[19];

person who was using the vehicle at the time of the event out of which the injury arose must, on a claim being made under s.159, pay to the practitioner (1) a fee of £15 per person treated and (2) travelling expenses of 29 pence per mile (or part of a mile) for every mile over two miles that he had to travel. If the treatment is first effected in a hospital, the fee goes to the hospital. If the person using the vehicle was not the tortfeasor who caused the accident, he can recover the money paid from the tortfeasor. The claim under section 159 may be made orally at the time when the emergency treatment is effected; if not so made, it must be made by written request served on the user of the vehicle within seven days of the treatment. Note also the separate liability on insurers to pay for hospital treatment under s.157, although this is not part of the compulsory insurance provisions.

[16] Amendments made to s.145 by the Motor Vehicles (Compulsory Insurance) Regulations 1992 (S.I. 1992 No. 3036), implementing the Third E.C. Directive on Motor Insurance 90/232.

[17] The requirement of effective employers' liability cover, rather than a blanket exemption of employers' liability risks, was inserted by the 1992 Regulations; see n.16, above.

[18] 1992 S.I. No. 3172.

[19] s.161(3) provides that any reference to an accident includes a reference to two or more causally related accidents. The limit of £250,000 is much higher than that required by the Second Directive. Most policies on private vehicles do not have a limit though commercial policies often do. A limit was adopted in order to mitigate the effect on the Motor Insurers' Bureau (see below) in cases of uninsured drivers. Note that there is a broad construction of "accident" in this sort of context; see *South Staffordshire Tramways Co. v. Sickness and Accident Assurance Association* [1891] 1 Q.B. 402, described at p. 354, above.

    (c) liability in respect of damage to the vehicle;

    (d) liability in respect of damage to goods carried for hire or reward in or on the vehicle or in or on any trailer drawn by the vehicle[20];

    (e) liability of a person in respect of damage to property in his custody or under his control[21]; and

    (f) any contractual liability.[22]

The basic obligation arising from the words of section 143 cited above has been the subject of considerable case law. One problem has been the meaning of the word "road", defined[23] as "any highway and any other road to which the public has access." It is a question of fact whether any other road is a road for these purposes, so that, for example, a hotel forecourt habitually used by the public as a road has been held to be a road,[24] whereas a car park has been held not to be.[25] Insurance is required when part of a vehicle is on a public road after being driven from private property.[26]

Use of a vehicle

The major problem has been the meanings of the words "use" and to "cause" or "permit" use in section 143. "Use" includes the leaving of a car on a road, even though it is incapable at present of being mechanically propelled.[27] It has also been held to cover the case of someone who left their car because it had run out of fuel and caused an accident when they crossed the road for help.[28] On the other hand, the word is not so wide as

---

[20] This does not exclude liability in respect of goods carried gratuitously, although the next exception may do so.

[21] For example, the belongings of passengers. It is unclear how far this exception goes. It would probably apply to luggage in the boot of a car, although it can hardly apply to items of clothing or other things on the person of a passenger.

[22] s.145(4).

[23] s.192(1).

[24] *Bugge v. Taylor* [1941] 1 K.B. 198; compare *Thomas v. Dando* [1951] 2 K.B. 620.

[25] *Griffin v. Squire* [1958] 1 W.L.R. 1106. But see *Cutter v. Eagle Star Insurance Co. Ltd,* [1997] 2 All E.R. 311 and *Clarke v. Kato,* The Times, December 11, 1996.

[26] *Randall v. Motor Insurers' Bureau* [1968] 2 Lloyd's Rep. 553.

[27] *Elliott v. Grey* [1960] 1 Q.B. 367. It is otherwise if the vehicle is totally immovable: *Thomas v. Hooper* [1986] R.T.R. 1.

[28] *Dunthorne v. Bentley,* The Times, March 11, 1996.

to include, for example, the normal case of someone being a passenger in a motor vehicle[29] or asking another to transport some goods in his car, even though it could perhaps be said colloquially that that person was using the other's car. In the context of the Road Traffic Act, use implies an element of controlling, managing or operating the vehicle at the relevant time.[30] In *Brown v. Roberts*,[31] the passenger in a car was negligent in opening her door and thereby injured a pedestrian. It was held that she was not using the car in the statutory sense, because she had no control over the vehicle, so the driver was not therefore causing or permitting her to use it and thus not liable in damages for breach of statutory duty in not insuring her against her potential liability. There can, though, be more than one person using a vehicle at any given time within the statutory meaning, and in *Leathley v. Tatton*,[32] it was held that a passenger involved in a criminal adventure with others to steal and take away a car was using the car for the purposes of section 143.[33]

Causing or permitting use

Whether someone causes or permits another to use a vehicle is a question of fact. Clearly it is so if, for example, X allows Y to drive his car. The word "cause" involves an express or positive mandate to use a car in a particular way, whereas "permit" is looser, and merely denotes an express or implied licence to use a vehicle.[34] In *McLeod v. Buchanan*,[35] a man appointed his brother as manager of his farm and bought him a car which was insured for business and private use. The car having proved unsatisfactory, the man authorised his brother to buy a van instead; this was insured for business use only, but was in fact used for private purposes. It was held that the man had permitted his brother to use the van while uninsured. The van was given to him for the same purposes as the car, and the brother was not told not to use it for private purposes. In *Lyons v. May*,[36] a

---

[29] *B. (A Minor) v. Knight* [1981] R.T.R. 136; *Hatton v. Hall, The Times*, May 15, 1996.

[30] *Brown v. Roberts* [1965] 1 Q.B. 1 at 15, *per* Megaw J.

[31] [1965] 1 Q.B. 1.

[32] [1980] R.T.R. 21. See also *Cobb v. Williams* [1973] R.T.R. 113 and *Stinton v. Stinton* [1995] R.T.R. 167; compare *B. (A Minor) v. Knight* [1981] R.T.R. 136.

[33] This point is especially important in the context of the M.I.B. Agreements where the same words are construed in the same way; see p. 381, below.

[34] Lord Wright in *McLeod v. Buchanan* [1940] 2 All E.R. 179 at 187.

[35] [1940] 2 All E.R. 179.

[36] [1948] 2 All E.R. 1062.

garage owner was driving a car back from the garage after repair, at the request of the car's owner. It was held that the latter had caused or permitted the use of the car. In contrast, in *Watkins v. O'Shaughnessy*,[37] an auctioneer sold a car which the purchaser drove away immediately without, to the auctioneer's knowledge, being insured. It was held that the auctioneer had not caused or permitted the use of the car because, having sold it, he no longer had any control over it. In *Thompson v. Lodwick*,[38] a driving instructor was held not to have caused or permitted his pupil to use the vehicle when the latter owned it.

Policy required

Section 143 requires that there be in force a "policy" of insurance.[39] A policy exists for these purposes even though it is voidable,[40] and it has been held that avoidance does not amount to avoidance *ab initio* for criminal law purposes.[41] Policy includes a cover note.[42] However, it has been decided that the existence of a mere contract of insurance is not enough to satisfy the statute. In *Roberts v. Warne*,[43] the relevant policy did not cover the particular driver who was using the car, although a cover note had been arranged to effect this and when this expired, the insurers clearly regarded the driver as covered.[44] The driver was convicted for using the car without insurance and the owner for causing or permitting this. It was held that, even if the insurers were contractually bound to cover the driver, which may well have been the case, the policy did not cover him and hence there was no policy as section 143 requires. It is thought that this decision is wrong.[45] There seems no reason to read the word "policy" as meaning

---

[37] [1939] 1 All E.R. 384.

[38] [1983] R.T.R. 76.

[39] Unless there is a security; see above.

[40] For example for non-disclosure or misrepresentation: *Adams v. Dunne* [1978] R.T.R. 281.

[41] *Goodbarne v. Buck* [1940] 1 K.B. 771.

[42] s.161(1), although it must be contractually binding, see *Taylor v. Allon* [1966] 1 Q.B. 304, discussed at p. 82, above.

[43] [1973] R.T.R. 217.

[44] There were severe communication difficulties at the time because of a postal strike.

[45] See (1973) Crim. L.R. 244.

other than a legally enforceable contract of insurance. Even an enforceable oral contract should suffice.[46]

Certificate of insurance

In addition to the requirement under section 143 to have a policy, section 147 provides that the policy is of no effect unless and until the insurer delivers to the insured a certificate of insurance.[47] Notwithstanding this wording, it has been held[48] by the Privy Council that the substantially identical words in the equivalent Barbadian statute[49] did not operate to prevent the third party from suing the insurers under section 151[50] where a certificate was issued subsequently to the accident but expressed to be retrospective to a time before the accident and a cover note, which is ordinarily an effective insurance contract,[51] had been issued before the accident. Although this looks like a fairly generous interpretation of the equivalent of section 147, it nonetheless seems an entirely sensible decision. It is thought that it should also apply to the basic obligation under section 143,[52] so that someone with a fully effective contract of insurance should not be guilty of the offence thereunder notwithstanding that a certificate may not have been issued.

Certificates constitute the easily checkable evidence of compliance with the insurance obligation, in particular they must be produced in order to obtain a road fund licence for a vehicle.[53] While the certificate or parts of it may be incorporated into the contract of insurance or policy, for example,

---

[46] Compare *Scher v. Policyholders Protection Board* [1993] 3 All E.R. 384, where the Court of Appeal held that there was no magic in the word "policy" in the Policyholders Protection Act 1975; see especially at 396 per Lord Donaldson M.R.

[47] See s.147(2) for the certificate of security when the obligation is satisfied by a security rather than by insurance. Where a policy or security is cancelled, the insured must, within seven days, surrender the certificate or, if it is lost or destroyed, make a statutory declaration to that effect: s.147(4). The forms of certificates are prescribed by the Motor Vehicles (Third Party Risks) Regulations 1972 (S.I. 1972 No. 1217), as amended.

[48] *Motor and General Insurance Co. v. Cox* [1990] 1 W.L.R. 1443.

[49] Motor Vehicles Insurance Act, ss.4(7), 9(1).

[50] As to s.151, see pp. 375–378, below.

[51] See pp. 80–86, above.

[52] And also to the other relevant section of the Road Traffic Act, especially s.148, which is discussed below at pp. 373–375, where the same requirement is stated.

[53] s.156.

concerning the permitted user of the vehicle, if there is any conflict between the two, the policy prevails, and the certificate itself is not a contract of insurance.[54]

Sanctions for failure to insure

The consequences of a failure to comply with the obligation to insure under section 143 are potentially two-fold. First, it is a criminal offence of strict liability.[55] Secondly, commission of the offence is a breach of statutory duty and anyone who suffers loss as a result can sue in tort for damages. The importance of this is not against the negligent driver, who would be liable in negligence anyway, but against someone who used the car with him or caused or permitted him to use it. The meanings of these expressions, as already discussed, may therefore be of importance in this context as well as in the criminal context.

In *Monk v. Warbey*,[56] the defendant owner of a car lent it to a friend who permitted another to drive. Neither of the latter was insured. It was held that the plaintiff who had been injured by the negligence of the driver could sue the owner. It would appear that the owner's insurer, assuming that he has one, might be liable in such circumstances to indemnify him against this liability, as the standard policy wordings do not require the insured to be driving, but indemnify him against "legal liability . . . arising from an accident caused by, through or in connection with the insured car." Since 1946, the Motor Insurer's Bureau indemnifies such uninsured drivers,[57] but it has been held that this does not remove the action for breach of statutory duty. In the case in question, *Corfield v. Groves*,[58] judgment was awarded against the owner subject to the proviso that if the M.I.B. did satisfy the judgment, it could not be enforced against the owner. In practice, therefore, this action is really only relevant if for some reason the M.I.B. is not liable.

---

[54] *Biddle v. Johnston* [1965] 2 Lloyd's Rep. 121.
[55] Subject to the defences in s.143(2), which provide for no liability if a person proves (1) that the vehicle did not belong to him and was not in his possession under a contract of hire or loan, (2) that he was using the vehicle in the course of employment or (3) that he neither knew nor had reason to believe that there was no valid insurance or security.
[56] [1935] 1 K.B. 75.
[57] See pp. 378–382, below.
[58] [1950] 1 All E.R. 488.

Common Terms and Exceptions in Motor Policies

The standard terms and conditions that are found in motor vehicle policies are important to compulsory and non-compulsory insurance alike, because, even though, as will be seen, some of them may not be enforceable against a third party victim where insurance was compulsory, they may remain of effect between insurer and insured so that the insurer who has had to pay the third party may be entitled to recover this sum of money from the insured. The standard terms will be considered under three headings: standard extensions; limitations on use; and terms relating to the condition of the insured vehicle.

Standard extensions

It is common for motor policies to insure people other than the insured or policy-holder driving the car or vehicle in question. For example, cover may extend to the spouse of the insured, to particular named drivers or drivers identified by a class, or, most widely, to anyone driving the vehicle on the insured's order or with the insured's permission. Only the last sort of extension can give rise to legal problems, but before examining these, one important point of general interest relates to the status of the other driver in terms of the contract between insured and insurer.

At common law, the insured can enforce the contract in so far as it confers a benefit on a third party, there being in effect a waiver of any requirement of insurable interest.[59] The latter though cannot enforce the contract himself.[60] It is likely, however, that the common law is redundant in this context, for section 148(7) of the 1988 Act provides:

"Notwithstanding anything in any enactment, a person issuing a policy of insurance under section 145 of this Act shall be liable to indemnify the persons or classes of persons specified in the policy in respect of any liability which the policy purports to cover in the case of those persons or classes of persons."

---

[59] *Williams v. Baltic Insurance Association of London* [1924] 2 K.B. 282, see pp. 58–60, above. It would seem that the insured holds any money recovered on trust for the third party; see *ibid.*

[60] *Vandepitte v. Preferred Accident Insurance Corporation of New York* [1933] A.C. 70; see pp. 64–69, above. This is subject to the possible use of agency principles, as discussed *ibid.*

Thus, the third party can enforce the contract directly, subject, of course, to any right in the insurer to avoid liability,[61] and he is not dependent on the owner insuring as his trustee or agent.[62] In effect, he is by statute a party to the contract.[63]

Permitted drivers

The question of whether someone is driving with the insured's permission, other than in obvious cases, has occasioned some difficulty. It seems that the law would not sanction a permitted driver himself giving effective permission to another so that the other is covered, in the absence of the insured's direct consent. In the Canadian case of *Minister of Transport v. Canadian General Insurance*,[64] a son of the insured who was permitted to drive the car in question purported to give permission to a friend. It was held that the friend was not insured. It seems likely that an English court would reach the same conclusion.[65] In *Morgans v. Launchberry*,[66] the permitted driver, the husband of the insured, gave permission to another to drive the car. The latter was negligent and injured or killed the passengers in the car. Strictly the case involved only the point of tort law as to whether the insured as owner of the car was vicariously liable for the acts of the driver, and the House of Lords held that she was not. However, a passage in Lord Denning's judgment in the Court of Appeal[67] indicates that, if the insured was not liable, the insurers would not be liable to indemnify the driver because the latter did not have her permission. That is why the case was fought as one of vicarious liability.[68]

---

[61] *Guardian Assurance v. Sutherland* [1939] 2 All E.R. 246.

[62] *Tattersall v. Drysdale* [1935] 2 K.B. 174.

[63] It was undecided, before it was compulsory to insure against property damage liability, whether the statute covered only the compulsory aspects of a motor policy. For discussion of the point, see the second edition of this book at p. 299. It is now an academic point except where a policy provides more cover than s.145 requires, *e.g.* unlimited cover in respect of property damage cover rather than the £250,000 limit allowed. Even here, it is thought that where a policy satisfies s.145, it will be enforceable by a third party because of the reference in s.148(7) to "any liability which the policy purports to cover."

[64] (1971) 18 D.L.R. (3d) 617.

[65] See *Sands v. O'Connell* [1981] R.T.R. 42.

[66] [1973] A.C. 127.

[67] [1971] 2 Q.B. 245 at 253.

[68] At the time of the case, liability to passengers was not within the compulsory requirements, which is another reason why the case was argued as it was. Now, the injured parties would receive compensation from the M.I.B. in such a situation if all other claims failed.

That the insured can become the third party and recover as such if injured by the negligence of someone whom he permitted to drive the car is well established. In *Digby v. General Accident Fire and Life Assurance Corporation*,[69] the insured's policy covered anyone driving with her permission. She gave such permission to her chauffeur and was then, as a passenger, injured by his negligent driving. It was held that the insurers were liable to indemnify the chauffeur in respect of his liability to the insured. Permission may be expressly or impliedly limited to a particular class of use of the vehicle.[70] In *Singh v. Ratour*,[71] the driver had borrowed a van belonging to an association of which he was a member, the representative of the association believing that he had borrowed it for the purposes of the association. In fact he had borrowed it to attend a private social function. The driver sought an indemnity against the consequences of his negligence from his own insurers under a term in the policy which permitted him to drive vehicles belonging to another "provided he [had] the consent of the owner." The Court of Appeal held that he was not entitled to recover, as the consent was impliedly limited to use for the purposes of the association.

Permission once given can obviously be revoked. In the absence of such revocation, it appears that permission continues even when the insured dies. In *Kelly v. Cornhill Insurance Co.*,[72] the insured gave permission to his son to drive the insured car and soon afterwards died. Some eight months later the son was involved in an accident, the policy period not having expired. By a bare majority, the House of Lords held that the son was entitled to sue under the policy, the permission of his father not having been revoked by his death. It is noteworthy that there was little merit in the insurers' defence, as under the policy the father was expressly precluded from driving; it had been effected solely for the son's benefit. While there are obvious difficulties in saying that permission continues in such a case in the absence of its renewal by the insured's personal representatives, in whom the ownership of the car and policy will have vested, the result is sensible, since otherwise a permitted driver could automatically and without his knowledge become uninsured, even for example in the course of a particular journey. The decision implies that the insured's personal representatives in such a case would have the power to

---

[69] [1943] A.C. 212.
[70] As to limitations on use, see pp. 368–370, below.
[71] [1988] 2 All E.R. 16.
[72] [1964] 1 All E.R. 321.

revoke the permission. Otherwise it must continue only until the expiry of the policy. It would appear that revocation of permission is effective only when actually communicated to the permittee.

A purchaser of a car, however, cannot be claiming to drive with the former owner, the insured's, permission, unless the insurers expressly consent. Here the insured ceases to have any insurable interest in the car, his policy lapses and is not assignable.[73]

Limitations on use

As was mentioned earlier, insurers have well established categories of permitted user of an insured vehicle which are enforceable even against a third party.[74] These vary from, for example, use covering only social, domestic and pleasure purposes and use by the insured for travel to and from his place of business, to use by the insured in person or use by others in connection with the insured's or his employer's business. Few legal difficulties can arise over some of the distinctions adopted, but in one respect there is a body of case law.

If an insured is covered for social, domestic and pleasure purposes and not for business use, or at least only for travelling to and from work,[75] the distinctions become important and not always easy to apply. As Roskill L.J. pointed out,[76] there will be cases falling each side of the line when a phrase such as social, domestic and pleasure purposes is used, and it is impossible to state any firm principle under which it can be predicted on which side of the line a particular case will fall. It must depend on the facts of the particular case. In *Jones v. Welsh Insurance Corporation*,[77] the policy covered social etc. purposes and use in connection with the insured's business, which was stated in the schedule to be that of motor mechanic. In addition, the insured farmed a few sheep, really as a hobby but with the aim of making a small profit. He was carrying some sheep when the relevant accident occurred. It was held that the insurers were not liable.

---

[73] *Peters v. General Fire & Accident Insurance* [1938] 2 All E.R. 267; see p. 171, above. The insurer's consent would in law amount to the creation of a new contract.

[74] As seen below, many provisions in contracts of motor insurance cannot be relied upon against a third party.

[75] Travelling to work is not a social, domestic or pleasure purpose; it must be separately covered; see *Seddon v. Binions* [1978] 1 Lloyd's Rep. 381.

[76] *Seddon v. Binions*, above, at 384–385.

[77] [1937] 4 All E.R. 149.

The insured was carrying on the business of sheep farming; this was not stated in the schedule and thus the cover did not apply. In *Wood v. General Accident*,[78] a garage proprietor was being driven in his own car by one of his drivers to a firm with which he intended to negotiate a business contract when an accident happened. It was held that, though it was convenient and comfortable for him to make the journey like this, the car was not being used for social etc., purposes. In *Seddon v. Binnions*,[79] a father who helped his son occasionally on Sundays in the latter's business of carpet layer was driving home, in his son's car, his son's only employee who had toothache. Having delivered the latter, the father intended to go home for his lunch. The father's own policy covered his driving of other cars but only for social etc., purposes. The son's insurers had paid in respect of the accident that occurred and were claiming a contribution from the father's insurers. It was held that the latter were not liable, the essential purpose of the journey being a business one, namely the father transporting his son's employee back from work.

Use of driving for purposes connected with the motor trade may be excluded, as in *Browning v. Phoenix Assurance Co. Ltd*,[80] where a garage employee was authorised by the insured to drive his car in order to warm the engine oil before it was drained at the garage. It was held that the insurers were not liable in respect of an accident which occurred when the employee was driving the car for pleasure the day after the oil had been drained, although the principal ground for the decision was that the employee was not a permitted driver in this respect.[81] It was also clear that the car would not have been insured while the oil was being warmed. The exclusion, though, may be qualified so that cover is provided while the vehicle is merely in the custody or control of a motor trader for the

---

[78] (1948) 65 T.L.R. 53.

[79] [1978] 1 Lloyd's Rep. 381.

[80] [1960] 2 Lloyd's Rep. 360.

[81] This aspect of the decision was approved by the Court of Appeal in *Singh v. Ratour* [1988] 2 All E.R. 16, discussed at p. 367, above.

purposes of repair, that is so long as it is not being driven by someone other than the insured or a permitted driver.[82]

A case may arise when the purposes of a journey are mixed. For example, an insured covered for social etc., purposes but not for business purposes might be travelling to a business meeting followed by a social dinner. In *Seddon v. Binnions*,[83] the view of the trial judge was that there was a mixed purpose; the father was driving for social, etc., purposes in going home for lunch, not being an employee of his son and hence not strictly travelling from work, and for business purposes in taking his son's employee home. It was held, and the Court of Appeal confirmed this, that in this event the policy would not apply since the car was partly being used for an unauthorised purpose.

Conditions regarding the condition of the insured vehicle

Motor policies universally provide that the insurers are not to be liable when the insured vehicle is being driven in an unsafe or unroadworthy condition and/or if the insured fails to maintain the vehicle in an efficient or roadworthy condition.[84] Such provisions may be drafted as exceptions to the risk or found under the heading "conditions" and framed as conditions precedent or possibly promissory warranties. It is more common now for them to appear as conditions or warranties. If they are warranties rather than conditions, there is no requirement in law[85] that there be any causal connection between the breach and a loss.[86] In both cases, although the

[82] See the Court of Appeal's construction of somewhat difficult terms to this effect in *Samuelson v. National Insurance Guarantee Corp. Ltd* [1985] 2 Lloyd's Rep. 541. The actual decision was concerned with whether or not the insured vehicle was being driven by or in the charge of a person other than an authorised driver. It was made clear that once someone has completed his present journey, he is no longer in charge of the vehicle for insurance purposes. Thus, although the car had not been insured while being driven by a repairer on his way to collect spare parts, cover reattached once his journey was completed and the insured could recover for the theft of the car from where the repairer had parked it.

[83] [1978] 1 Lloyd's Rep. 381; see above.

[84] This is not interpreted in the same way as "reasonable care" provisions (see pp. 201 and 353, above). Negligence on the part of the insured will be a breach of such a provision: *Amey Properties Ltd v. Cornhill Insurance plc*, [1996] C.L.C. 401.

[85] Although there is such a requirement for non-commercial insurances under the *Statement of General Insurance Practice*; see p. 155, above.

[86] See generally, pp. 128–129, above.

insurers will not be able to rely upon a breach as against an injured third party, because of the provisions of the Road Traffic Act which will be examined shortly, they may well be able to recover from the insured as damages for breach of condition the money they have to pay to the third party.[87]

A marine analogy?

Application of the standard exception or condition has occasioned some difficulty. In *Barrett v. London General Insurance*,[88] Goddard J. held that, because of the verbal similarities, roadworthiness was to be interpreted in an analogous way to seaworthiness in a marine policy. In a marine policy, seaworthiness is required only at the commencement of a voyage. The learned judge applied the same reasoning to a car journey in deciding that a car whose foot brake failed at the time of the relevant accident was not unroadworthy in the absence of proof that it was not working when the insured set out on his journey. He may have been influenced by the fact that had the injured third party's claim arisen slightly later, the insurer would not have been able to take the point because of the imminent introduction of the statutory provisions which are now section 148 of the Road Traffic Act 1988.[89] This reasoning was expressly disapproved by the Privy Council in *Trickett v. Queensland Insurance Co.*,[90] though the exception in question there did not concern roadworthiness as such, but applied if the car was being driven in "a damaged or unsafe condition." The insured was involved in an accident at night at a time when the lights on his car were not working. It was held that this was sufficient to render the car damaged or unsafe. The knowledge of the insured was irrelevant, as was the question whether or not the lights were working at the beginning of the journey. The question was simply one of fact to be judged objectively.

More recently, it has been suggested that the marine analogy may be useful, but it appears unlikely that the decision in *Barrett* would be followed. The usual wording of this sort of an exception is "while the car is being driven," and this must include anything that happens during a journey and not just at the start of it.[91] In *Clarke v. National Insurance*

---

[87] Under s.148(4) of the Road Traffic Act or, it seems, at common law; see below.
[88] [1935] 1 K.B. 238.
[89] Goddard J. referred (above at 240) to the imminent introduction of the Road Traffic Act 1934.
[90] [1936] A.C. 159.
[91] *Clarke v. National Insurance Corporation* [1963] 2 All E.R. 375 at 377.

Corporation,[92] a four-seater car was driven with nine people in it. The Court of Appeal held that it was thereby rendered unroadworthy, although, with the normal number of people in it, it would have been quite safe. Unroadworthiness does not relate to just the mechanical condition of a vehicle, but can include any other relevant factors. In marine cases, overloading can render a ship unseaworthy, and the analogy was apt to this extent.

The term as a warranty or condition

In the cases just discussed, the term in question was an exception and phrased in such a way that, fairly clearly, it should be properly read in a continuing objective sense. As noted above, modern policies tend to have replaced this exception by a condition or warranty requiring the insured to maintain the vehicle in a roadworthy or efficient condition. It has been suggested that these alternatives mean the same,[93] but it would seem that a term is both narrower and wider if phrased as a condition or warranty. It is narrower because, as a condition or warranty, it cannot be read wholly objectively. If a car's lights or brakes, for example, fail quite unexpectedly in the course of a journey, it may not be possible to say that the insured has failed to maintain the car in a roadworthy or efficient condition, whereas it can be said that the car is being driven in an unroadworthy condition. An insured's failure to maintain imports the notion of his knowing or being in a position where he ought to know that something is wrong, which requires the insurer to show more than a simple fact. This view is supported by the decision in *Conn v. Westminster Motor Insurance Association Ltd,*[94] which is discussed below, where the insured should have known that his taxi's tyres were no good, as this was easily visible, but the same did not apply in relation to his braking system.

On the other hand, a warranty as to roadworthiness is wider than an exception because there need be no connection between the breach of warranty and an accident which subsequently occurs. In *Conn's* case, as mentioned above, the insured's tyres on his taxi were so badly worn that there was no tread on them and they were illegal. It was held that this

---

[92] [1963] 2 All E.R. 375.

[93] Sellers J. in *Brown v. Zurich General Accident and Liability Insurance Co.* [1954] 2 Lloyd's Rep. 243 at 246.

[94] [1966] 1 Lloyd's Rep. 407. See also *Lefevre v. White* [1990] 1 Lloyd's Rep. 569 and *Amey Properties Ltd v. Cornhill Insurance plc,* [1996] C.L.C. 401.

amounted to a breach of the obligation to maintain his vehicle in an efficient condition upon which the insurers could rely, even though the state of the tyres did not cause or contribute to the relevant accident.[95]

Insured's liability in damages

One question remains in this context. If a condition or warranty concerning the condition of the insured vehicle is broken, the insurers cannot rely upon the breach as against a third party, but, if they have to compensate such a person, they have a statutory right to recover this money from the insured.[96] It may be, however, that they also have a common law right, which would be important when the event was not required to be insured under section 145 of the 1988 Act.[97]

In *National Farmers' Union Mutual Insurance Society* v. *Dawson*,[98] the insured caused an accident when unfit to drive through drink. This was clearly a breach of a term of the policy requiring the insured to use all care and diligence to avoid accidents and prevent loss. Having paid the third party, the insurers sought to recover this sum from the insured. Their argument, based on what is now section 148(4) of the 1988 Act, failed, as it was held that they could in fact have avoided liability to pay the third party.[99] However, they succeeded in their claim to recover the money as damages for breach of contract. One may question whether this is a correct result where the insurers are not compelled by statute to pay the third party. What, then, is their loss? In addition, if, as is usual, the term is a warranty or condition precedent in the insurance sense,[1] it is arguable that it is not the same as a condition in other contracts. Its purpose is simply to relieve the insurers from liability, and it is thought that there is no merit or logic in allowing the insurers to recover from the insured.

---

[95] Note though that there are cases requiring a causal connection in respect of a mere "condition" (see p. 138, above and, for a recent example, see *Amey Properties Ltd v. Cornhill Insurance plc*, [1996] C.L.C. 401), and that in practice this is required where the *Statement of General Insurance Practice* applies (see p. 155, above). It is thought that in law the term in *Conn* was a warranty in the insurance sense; see p. 137, above.

[96] Road Traffic Act 1988, s.148(4), discussed at p. 374, below.

[97] Principally, in a case of property damage exceeding the £250,000 statutory minimum; see p. 359, above.

[98] [1941] 2 K.B. 424.

[99] See p. 374, below.

[1] See the discussion, pp. 129–133, above.

Third Parties' Rights Under the Road Traffic Act

As well as rendering much motor insurance compulsory, as we have already seen, the Road Traffic Act 1988 interferes with the contractual rights of insurers for the benefit of third parties to whom the insured is legally liable. Section 148(1) provides that, where a certificate of insurance has been delivered to the policyholder,[2] so much of the policy as purports to restrict the insurance of the persons insured by reference to any of a list of specified matters is of no effect as regards insurance required under section 145. This invalidates certain terms in policies regardless of their exact legal status, *i.e.* whether they are warranties, conditions or exceptions. Section 148(2) lists the matters as follows:

(a) the age or physical or mental condition of persons driving the vehicle;

(b) the condition of the vehicle;

(c) the number of persons that the vehicle carries;

(d) the weight or physical characteristics of the goods that the vehicle carries;

(e) the times at which or the areas within which the vehicle is used;

(f) the horsepower or cylinder capacity or value of the vehicle;

(g) the carrying on the vehicle of any particular apparatus;

(h) the carrying on the vehicle of any particular means of identification other than any means of identification required to be carried by or under the Vehicles (Excise) Act 1971.

In most respects the sorts of warranties, conditions or exceptions avoided by section 148(1) are clear. For example, conditions or exceptions relating to roadworthiness etc., will be of no effect; they fall within (b) above. A breach of warranty in a proposal form as to the value or size of engine of a vehicle will fall within (f). On the other hand, a condition requiring the insured to use all care and diligence to avoid accidents and prevent loss is not covered by the list,[3] and a limitation as to use is always effective as against third parties,[4] unless it relates to the use of a private vehicle under car-sharing arrangements.[5]

---

[2] This requirement of delivery of a certificate should perhaps be ignored in circumstances such as those in *Motor and General Insurance Co. v. Cox* [1990] 1 W.L.R. 1443, which is discussed above at p. 363.

[3] *National Farmers' Union Mutual v. Dawson* [1941] 2 K.B. 424. See above, p. 372.

[4] *Jones v. Welsh Insurance Corporation* [1937] 4 All E.R. 149.

[5] See s.150 of the 1988 Act.

Given that, if a term is enforceable, the third party will have recourse against the Motor Insurers' Bureau, as will be seen below, it is curious that the list in section 148(2) does not catch all provisions.[6] Why should an insurer be liable to a third party even if, say the insured has failed in the most deliberate and dangerous way to keep his vehicle roadworthy, whereas it could avoid liability for the slightest infringement of a limitation as to use? The logic of having an incomplete list as against a complete list or even no list at all is not easy to follow. As has already been noted, section 148(4) entitles the insurer compelled to pay the third party, but who would otherwise have avoided liability, to recoup this money from the insured.

Breaches of condition

Section 148(5) invalidates other breaches of condition by an insured so far as the third party is concerned. The conditions covered are those providing that no liability shall arise under the policy, or that any liability so arising shall cease, in the event of some specified thing being done or omitted to be done after the happening of the event giving rise to the claim. This clearly covers a breach by the insured of a condition regarding notice or particulars of loss, and it must also cover an admission of liability in breach of the standard conditions.[7] Whether an arbitration clause is caught by section 148(5) is an open question if it has the *Scott v. Avery* addition making it precedent to the insurer's liability.[8] The majority of the Court of Appeal in *Jones v. Birch Bros*[9] inclined to the view that such a clause would be caught, although it was held that one which did not provide that it was a condition precedent to liability was valid. In view of the unlikelihood of arbitration ever being used in motor vehicle disputes,[10] the question is probably totally academic now.

Section 148(6) allows insurers to insert in their policies provisions allowing them to recover back from the insured money which they have had to pay to a third party only by virtue of subsection (5). There is no automatic right given to insurers as there is under section 148(4), although

---

[6] The list has never been amended since its introduction in the Road Traffic Act 1934.

[7] See pp. 351–352, above.

[8] See p. 250, above.

[9] [1933] 2 K.B. 597.

[10] See p. 249, above.

it must be arguable that insurers would have that right in quasi-contract, as there is a general principle that a plaintiff compelled by law to make a payment discharging the defendant's liability to a third party can recover that sum from the defendant.[11]

Insurer's duty to satisfy judgments

The key provision so far as third parties are concerned is section 151.[12] In effect, provided that a certificate of insurance has been delivered to the insured and a third party has obtained a judgment against any person insured by the policy, the whole of the judgment, in respect of liability for death or bodily injury, and up to £250,000 of it in respect of liability for damage to property, must be satisfied by the insurer, notwithstanding that the insurer may be entitled to avoid or cancel, or may have avoided or cancelled, the policy.[13] Further, this obligation applies in respect of persons not insured by a policy, for example, persons not within the category of permitted drivers or even a thief of the vehicle,[14] except that in respect of liability for death or personal injury, it does not apply if the third party was allowing himself to be carried in or upon the vehicle knowing or having reason to believe that the vehicle had been stolen or unlawfully taken.[15] In all cases, any term in a policy which purports to restrict its operation by requiring a driver to hold a licence to drive is invalid.[16]

The insurer's obligation is qualified, however, by the provisions of section 152, in four respects:

---

[11] See Goff and Jones, *The Law of Restitution*, (3rd. ed.), Chap. 14.

[12] The equivalent provision formed the basis for denying the need for a certificate to be delivered for the purposes of s. 147 in *Motor and General Insurance Co. v. Cox* [1980] 1 W.L.R. 1443; see p. 363, above.

[13] s.151(1), (2), (5) and (6). The award that must be satisfied includes costs and interest awarded. Where a property damage judgment exceeds £250,000, s.151(6)(b) provides as to how the insurer's exact liability is to be assessed.

[14] In this situation the insurer can recover the amount paid to the third party from the driver or from the insured who caused or permitted the use of the vehicle: s.151(8).

[15] Unless he did not realise this until after the journey commenced and could not reasonably be expected to have alighted from the vehicle: s.151(4).

[16] s.151(3). The insurer can recover from the driver what he has paid out: s.151(7)(a).

(1) It arises only where the insurer was given notice, formally,[17] of the proceedings against the insured before or within seven days of their commencement[18];

(2) It is not execiseable where execution of a judgment has been stayed pending an appeal;

(3) It does not apply if the insured's policy was cancelled before the relevant accident, either by mutual consent or under a term in the policy, and the certificate of insurance was surrendered or the insured made a statutory declaration that it was lost or destroyed within 14 days of the cancellation, or within the same period the insurer commenced proceedings in respect of the failure to surrender the certificate;

(4) It does not apply if the policy was obtained by non-disclosure or misrepresentation of a material fact and the insurer, within three months of the commencement of the proceedings against the insured, obtains a declaration of the court to this effect, and the third party receives notice of the action for a declaration and the particulars of the non-disclosure or misrepresentation within seven days of its being commenced.[19]

The fourth qualification does not remove the insurer's right to avoid for non-disclosure or misrepresentation, but it limits the effectiveness of that right. However, it appears strictly not to include a discharge from liability for breach of warranty, for example by virtue of a misstatement on a proposal form warranted to be true. Section 152(2) refers expressly to the insurer's right to avoid apart from any provisions contained in the policy, meaning only the general right to avoid given by the common law or equity.[20] Warranties arise from express provisions.[21] Thus, an insurer can avoid liability for breach of warranty as against the injured third party,

---

[17] *Herbert v. Railway Passengers Assurance Co.* [1938] 1 All E.R. 650. A solicitor's letter to the insurers stating merely that the third party is being advised to issue proceedings is not sufficient to satisfy the requirement: *Harrington* v. *Link Motor Policies* [1989] 2 Lloyd's Rep. 310.

[18] This includes a counter claim by an injured defendant against an insured plaintiff, where appropriate: *Cross v. British Oak Insurance Co.* [1938] 2 K.B. 167.

[19] The third party has the right to be a party to this action.

[20] *Merchants' & Manufacturers' Insurance Co. v. Hunt* [1941] 1 K.B. 295.

[21] See, generally, Chaps. 5 and 7. In any event, it is not now strictly true to refer to a breach of warranty as giving rise to a right of avoidance of the policy; see p. 129, above.

without using the section 152 procedure, unless of course, the warranty relates to one of the matters in section 148(1), in which case the breach cannot be relied on at all. However, the cases have not always been too accurate in distinguishing non-disclosures, misrepresentation and warranties, and what appears strictly to be a breach of warranty has been treated as a misrepresentation or non-disclosure.[22]

Materiality is defined for the purposes of section 152 in the usual way,[23] namely, "of such a nature as to influence the judgment of a prudent insurer in determining whether he will take the risk and, if so, at what premium and on what conditions." [24] In addition, by statute it is not enough to show non-disclosure or misrepresentation of such a material fact. The insurer must also show that he himself was induced by the non-disclosure or misrepresentation to issue the policy as section 152(2) requires that the insurer show that the policy was obtained by non-disclosure or misrepresentation.[25] It was once thought that this made the Road Traffic Act position different from that at general law, but now there is a causal requirement at general law in any event.[26]

If insurers are liable under section 151 to satisfy a judgment awarded to a third party, but could have avoided liability as between themselves and the insured, but chose not to do so, they can recover from the insured the amount paid to the third party.[27]

By section 153, the fact that the insured goes bankrupt or dies insolvent or, if a company, goes into liquidation, administration or receivership, does not affect the liability of the insured in respect of compulsory insurance, notwithstanding anything in the Third Parties (Rights against Insurers) Act 1930.[28] In other words, the sections in the Road Traffic Act regarding the third parties' rights continue to apply, but otherwise section 153 incorporates the statutory assignment of the 1930 Act.

Information regarding insurance

Finally, under section 154, the driver against whom a claim is made in respect of damage compulsorily insurable is under a duty, enforceable by

[22] *Merchants' & Manufacturers' Insurance Co. v. Hunt*, above; compare *Zurich General Accident v. Morrison* [1942] 2 K.B. 53 which did concern a pure non-disclosure.
[23] See pp. 107–110, above.
[24] s.151(9)(b).
[25] *Zurich General Accident v. Morrison*, above.
[26] See pp. 109–110, above.
[27] s.151(7).
[28] As to the 1930 Act, see pp. 340–347, above.

criminal penalties, on the demand of the third party, to give him information as to whether or not he was insured and, if so, such details of his insurance as are specified in his certificate of insurance.

Third Parties' Rights Against the Motor Insurers' Bureau

The provisions just examined concerning third party rights under the Road Traffic Act have given rise to very few reported cases in recent years. This probably illustrates their relative unimportance since the M.I.B. was established. In 1937, the Cassel Committee[29] recommended that a central fund be established to protect the victims of road accidents who received no compensation despite the protection afforded by the Road Traffic Act. Obviously the Act could not cover the situation of the driver who did not have insurance cover, nor was it really relevant when an insurer went into liquidation. Furthermore, as has been seen, there are occasions when an insurer can rely on terms in the policy to avoid liability to the third party despite provisions in the Act. Finally, the victim of an untraced or "hit and run" driver can of necessity not be protected by the statute. In this last respect, the Cassel Committee did not consider it practicable to give such victims rights against the fund and this remained the position until 1969, although they did have a discretionary entitlement before then.

It was probably fears of possible nationalisation of motor insurance business that led the motor insurers to conclude, on December 31, 1945, the first agreement between their creation, the M.I.B., and the Minister of Transport. It is now a condition of authorisation to transact motor insurance business that the insurer is a member of M.I.B. Ltd.[30] There are now three agreements between the M.I.B. and the Secretary of State for the Environment. What will be hereafter referred to as the first one is now dated December 21, 1988, is in substance the original 1945 agreement with amendments, and is entitled "Compensation of Victims of Uninsured Drivers." The second agreement, dated November 22, 1972, but being an amended version of one first agreed in 1969, is entitled "Compensation of Victims of Untraced Drivers." The third agreement dates from 1977, bears the same title as the second and provides for an accelerated procedure for claims in respect of the victims of hit and run drivers.[31]

---

[29] Cmnd. 5528, paras. 151–168.
[30] s.145(5) of the Road Traffic Act 1988.
[31] All the agreements are published by the Stationery Office.

It should be noted that the M.I.B. agreements apply only if insurance was compulsorily required so that if, for example, the accident in question did not happen on a road, the M.I.B. can, and does, take the point in defence.[32]

The first M.I.B. agreement

This applies in respect of accidents occurring on or after December 31, 1988.[33] It provides in essence that if a person injured or killed in a road accident, or whose property is damaged therein, obtains a judgment in respect of any liability required to be insured against, and if that judgment is not satisfied in full within seven days, the M.I.B. will satisfy it.[34] Thus, the cases of the uninsured driver and the driver without effective insurance are covered.[35]

However, where a claim is made in respect of property damage, the M.I.B.'s liability is limited to £250,000.[36] In addition, an excess operates so that the M.I.B. is not liable for the first £175 of any unsatisfied judgment in respect of property damage,[37] and it may deduct from the sum it pays an amount equal to compensation received by the third party from any other source, e.g., the third party's own insurance policy.[38]

Different procedures operate depending upon whether or not the driver was insured, but his insurer was able to avoid liability.[39] If this is so, that insurer normally acts as agent for the M.I.B., although the latter pays the

---

[32] See, e.g. Buchanan v. M.I.B. [1955] 1 W.L.R. 488; Randall v. M.I.B. [1968] 1 W.L.R. 1900.

[33] Earlier accidents are covered by the earlier 1972 agreement.

[34] Clause 2(1). Nothing in the agreement prevents insurers from providing in their contracts of insurance that all sums paid by them or M.I.B. under the agreement are recoverable by them or the M.I.B. from the insured or from any other person: clause 4.

[35] The first M.I.B. agreement used also to cover the case of the driver whose insurer went into liquidation, but this is now covered by the Policyholders Protection Act 1975, under ss.6 and 7 of which the Policyholders Protection Board has a duty fully to satisfy the claims of the insured whose insurer becomes insolvent when the insurance was compulsory; see p. 33, above.

[36] Clause 2(2). This, of course, is the limit permitted by s.145 of the 1988 Act.

[37] Clause 2(4).

[38] Clause 2(3). This could apply in respect of damage to the third party's vehicle recovered under his own insurance and in respect of damage to other property separately insured.

[39] e.g. by reason of a breach of a limitation of use or a successful pleading of non-disclosure or misrepresentation.

claim. Only where there is no insurance or the insurer is not known is the claim made directly to the M.I.B.

There are a number of conditions precedent to the M.I.B.'s liability and a number of exceptions. The conditions[40] are:

(1) that notice is given before or within seven days of the commencement of the relevant proceedings to the M.I.B. or to the insurer concerned, depending on the procedure applicable[41];

(2) that the M.I.B. is supplied with any information it reasonably requires[42];

(3) that the claimant has obtained details of the driver's insurance[43];

(4) that if required, the applicant obtains judgment against all the tortfeasors involved; and

(5) that any judgment obtained is assigned to the M.I.B.

Exceptions

The exceptions[44] cover:

(1) vehicles owned by the Crown;

(2) cases where insurance was not compulsory by virtue of section 144 of the Road Traffic Act,[45] unless, in fact, there is insurance in such a case;

(3) claims made by insurers exercising subrogation rights;

(4) property damage claims where the claimant had failed to insure as required by the Road Traffic Act and either knew or ought to have known of this; and

(5) cases where the victim was a passenger and knew or ought to have known that the vehicle had been stolen or unlawfully taken or knew or ought to have known that there was no insurance in force as required by the Road Traffic Act.

The equivalent of this last exception was the subject of *Porter v. M.I.B.*[46] The plaintiff had brought a car into the country from Holland but was not

---

[40] Clause 5.

[41] Together with a copy of the writ, summons or other document initiating the proceedings.

[42] Including details of insurance covering any damage to property.

[43] *i.e.* the details specified in s.154 of the Road Traffic Act; see p. 378.

[44] Clause 6.

[45] The provision as to deposits; see p. 357, above.

[46] [1978] 2 Lloyd's Rep 463; see also *Stinton v. Stinton* [1995] R.T.R. 167.

insured to drive it. She asked an acquaintance to do so, knowing that he drove a car and assuming that he was insured. In fact, he was not. He negligently caused an accident and injured the plaintiff. The M.I.B.'s argument that they were not bound to satisfy the judgment awarded against the friend by virtue of the exception failed. The exception was to be construed from the point of view of the victim. She assumed that the acquaintance was insured and there was nothing which should have caused her to have reason to believe otherwise.[47]

The first agreement covered hit and run victims only on an *ex gratia* basis, a most unsatisfactory state of affairs highlighted by the decision in *Adams v. Andrews*[48] and its sequel.[49] This was remedied in 1969.

The second M.I.B. agreement

This agreement is necessarily much more complex than the first, because there will of course be no judgment against a tortfeasor for the M.I.B. to satisfy. A number of conditions must be satisfied by an applicant for an award:

(1) The applicant must be unable to trace the person responsible for the death or injury or a person partly so responsible.

(2) The death or injury must have been caused in circumstances such that on the balance of probabilities the untraced person would have been liable to the applicant in damages.

(3) That liability must have been one required to be insured against under the 1988 Act; this is assumed in the absence of evidence to the contrary.

(4) The death or injury must not have been caused deliberately, because such a victim would have a statutory claim from the Criminal Injuries Compensation Board.

(5) The application must be made in writing within three years of the accident.

---

[47] Note, however, that the decision was concerned to construe the earlier (1972) agreement, which in respect of this exception was worded differently and probably more generously to the victim. It could be argued that it is easier to show that someone "ought to know" (the 1988 wording) that a driver is uninsured than that it was to show that the victim had "no reason to believe" (the 1972 wording construed in *Porter*) that.

[48] [1964] 2 Lloyd's Rep. 349.

[49] A full account is given in Williams, *The Motor Insurers' Bureau*.

Clause 1(2) contains exceptions which are much the same as the exceptions to the first agreement already mentioned. The amount of compensation awarded to the applicant is assessed on the same basis as a court would assess damages in a tort action,[50] except that the M.I.B. does not award damages for pain and suffering or loss of expectation of life or loss of earnings in so far as they have been paid by the applicant's employer.[51]

Clause 5 contains the special provisions dealing with the cases where an untraced driver was only partly to blame for the accident. Here the applicant may be required to obtain judgment against the known driver or the known principal of an unidentified driver, or the applicant may have obtained such judgment without being required to do so. If this judgment is not satisfied at all within three months, the M.I.B. awards an amount equal to the untraced person's contribution to a full award, namely, that proportion which a court would have awarded if proceedings had been taken against all the tortfeasors. If this judgment is only partly satisfied within three months, the M.I.B. awards an amount equal to either the unsatisfied part of the judgment or the untraced person's contribution, whichever is the greater. If the applicant has not obtained, and is not required by the M.I.B. to obtain, judgment against the known driver, and has not received any payment as compensation from any such person, the amount the M.I.B. awards is an amount equal to the untraced person's contribution to a full award.

Conditions precedent

Clause 6 specifies three conditions precedent to the liability of the M.I.B., namely, (1) the applicant must give all such assistance as the M.I.B. reasonably requires to enable any necessary investigation to be carried out; (2) if required, the applicant must take all reasonable steps to obtain judgment against any person or persons in respect of their liability to the applicant; this is subject to his being indemnified against costs by the M.I.B.; (3) if required, the applicant must assign to the M.I.B., or their nominee, any judgment obtained by him; if this produces a surplus over what the M.I.B. paid the applicant, the M.I.B. is accountable for this after deducting the reasonable expenses of the recovery of the sum for which the judgment was given.

---

[50] Clause 3.
[51] Clause 4.

By virtue of clause 8, if required to do so, the applicant must furnish a statutory declaration concerning the facts and circumstances upon which his claim is based.

Investigation and report

The M.I.B. must, by clause 7, investigate any claim made to them. They may decide that the case is not one covered by the agreement and thus reject it giving these reasons.[52] Otherwise they must cause a report to be made on the basis of which they must decide whether to make an award and the amount of the award. A number of issues arising out of clause 7 and other clauses arose in *Persson v. London Country Buses*.[53] P, a bus conductor employed by the first defendants, was injured when the bus he was on stopped suddenly. The first defendants rejected his claim against them on the ground that the accident was caused not by the bus driver but by another motorist. This motorist was untraced, and so P made a claim against the M.I.B. who rejected it on the ground that they were not satisfied that in the circumstances the untraced driver would have been liable. P then sought to sue the M.I.B. without pursuing his rights of appeal under the agreement. This point is considered below, but in the course of the case the court considered the basic nature of the M.I.B.'s obligation under clauses 3 and 7. Clause 3 states that the M.I.B. "shall award" such damages as a court would which, P argued, put them under an obligation to do so. It was held, however, that clause 3 was expressly subject to the later provisions in the agreement, including clause 7. Under clause 7, the M.I.B. has a duty to make a decision in respect of an award, but not actually to make an award if they consider that the facts do not warrant it.

Decision and appeals

Clause 9 provides that, when the M.I.B. has decided whether or not to make a payment, they must notify the applicant of their decision, setting out the circumstances and evidence of the death or injury, and, if they refuse to make an award, the reasons for that refusal. Clauses 11 onwards deal with appeals. The applicant may appeal against any decision unfavourable to him, including on the quantum of the award, within six

[52] Clause 9(1).
[53] [1974] 1 All E.R. 1251.

weeks, to an arbitrator.[54] He may also or alternatively make comments to the M.I.B. which may result in further consideration. If there is further communication from the M.I.B. following such comments, the applicant has six weeks from the date of this communication to consider his appeal. Clause 12 provides that when appealing, the applicant must undertake to abide by the decision of the arbitrator.

Where the appeal is only on quantum, the M.I.B. may ask the arbitrator to consider also the issue of liability.[55] The M.I.B. sends all the relevant documents to the arbitrator, who can ask for further investigation.[56] The applicant must be allowed to comment on such further investigation.[57] If the arbitrator considers the appeal to be unreasonable, he may award that the applicant pay his fees. Otherwise, these are born by the M.I.B. and each party to the appeal bears its own costs.[58]

The result of the provisions regarding appeals, in particular the undertaking required under clause 12, is that on questions of fact, the applicant has no recourse to the courts. *Persson v. London Country Buses*[59] decided that the applicant's action against the M.I.B. disclosed no clause of action, since P had not complied with the provisions for appeal in the agreement, in accordance with the general principle that, where the parties to a contract have agreed in language which clearly shows who is to decide certain facts, then no right of action in the courts is vested in the parties until the facts have been decided according to the contract.[60] The arbitrator's decision will thus be final unless he or the M.I.B. have misapplied the law. Legal problems for decision by the court may arise on, for example, the construction of the agreement itself, on whether or not a case is within the Road Traffic Act requirements, or if the arbitrator has placed the burden of proof on the wrong person.[61]

The third M.I.B. agreement

As seen earlier, the third agreement dating from 1977 also deals with the victims of untraced drivers. It provides for a quicker procedure for

---

[54] The latter must be a Queen's Counsel selected by the Secretary of State from a panel.
[55] Clause 14.
[56] Clause 15.
[57] Clause 17.
[58] Clauses 21 and 22.
[59] [1974] 1 All E.R. 1251.
[60] *Cipriani v. Barnett* [1933] A.C. 83.
[61] See, *e.g. Elizabeth v. M.I.B.* [1981] R.T.R. 405.

settling such claims where no known motorist was involved. After a
preliminary investigation, the M.I.B. may instead of making a report
simply offer a sum in compensation to the applicant, assessed as under the
second agreement. If that offer is accepted, in the form specified in the
schedule to the agreement, that concludes the matter and there is no right
of appeal to an arbitrator. If the offer is not accepted, the matter will be
determined in accordance with the procedure under the principal
agreement.

Procedural questions

A number of procedural questions have arisen in the context of the
M.I.B. agreements. The first relates to their enforcement. It is clear that, if
necessary, the Secretary of State could sue the M.I.B. as a party to the
agreements which in law are binding contracts as given under seal. On the
other hand, strictly speaking, an injured person has no right to enforce any
of the agreements, not being a party to them, though it may be that he
could enforce them indirectly by joining the Secretary of State as a party to
an action brought against the M.I.B.,[62] and he could enforce a judgment
awarded against the M.I.B. in favour of the Secretary of State.[63] In practice
this is all rather academic. The M.I.B. has been sued on a number of
occasions by injured third parties and has said that it will never take the
point of privity.[64] Should it ever be so minded, there can be little doubt
that legislation would follow.[65]

Joinder of the M.I.B.

Another point concerns the right of the M.I.B. to be joined as a
defendant in an action brought by an injured third party. There can be no
doubt now that the court will allow M.I.B. to be joined as a defendant

---

[62] See Lord Denning M.R. in *Gurtner v. Circuit* [1968] 1 All E.R. 327.
[63] *ibid*.
[64] See, *e.g. Albert v. M.I.B.* [1972] AC 301; *Coward v. M.I.B.* [1963] 1 Q.B. 259 at
265.
[65] No doubt the same would result if the M.I.B. terminated the agreements as,
strictly, it is entitled to do on giving twelve months' notice.

when liability may arise on them under the first agreement.[66] The second and third agreements raise different issues. In the normal event, of course, there will be no action, the defendant being untraced. But, as has been seen, under the second agreement, the M.I.B. can require the applicant to take action against identified persons who may have been partly responsible. In this sort of case, it has been held[67] that the M.I.B. could not claim to be joined as it was not necessary to do so. Under the terms of the second agreement, the M.I.B. will in practice be "behind" the plaintiff because of the considerable powers of control the agreement gives them.

Substituted service

A final question concerns the right of an injured plaintiff to obtain an order for substituted service of his writ claiming damages on the M.I.B.,[68] when it is not possible to serve the writ on the tortfeasor. It is clear that this can be done only if the plaintiff's cause of action is truly against an uninsured driver. In respect of an untraced driver, there is no right to sue the M.I.B. unless and until they have refused to consider an application.[69]

---

[66] Ord. 15, r. 6(2)(b) of the Rules of the Supreme Court now authorises the joinder as a party of "any person between whom and any party to the cause or matter there may exist a question or issue arising out of or relating to or connected with any relief or remedy claimed in the cause or matter which in the opinion of the court it would be just and convenient to determine as between him and that party as well as between the parties to the cause or matter." Even before the wider wording of this rule was introduced, it was held that M.I.B. could be joined in an action against an uninsured driver: *Gurtner v. Circuit*, above.

[67] *White v. London Transport Executive* [1971] 3 All E.R. 1.

[68] Under R.S.C. Ord. 65, r. 4.

[69] *Clarke v. Vedel* [1979] R.T.R. 26.

CHAPTER 20

EMPLOYERS' LIABILITY AND OTHER COMPULSORY INSURANCES

This chapter is concerned with those liability insurances other than motor insurance which are compulsory. Foremost among these is employers' liability insurance.

Employers' Liability Insurance

An employee injured at work has, broadly speaking, the right to claim compensation from the State, regardless of questions of fault, under the social security legislation.[1] This replaced workmen's compensation insurance which was an important class of insurance business for many years. The employee who can show that his employer, or someone for whom the latter is responsible, was at fault in some way will also have the right to claim damages in tort from him. This may be in negligence or it may be for breach of statutory duty. Statistically, work accidents rank with road accidents as the most common source of tort actions. Against an employer who is not insured or not effectively insured this tort action may be worthless. Some notorious instances of employers being without cover led to the enactment of the Employers' Liability (Compulsory Insurance) Act 1969.

Section 1(1) provides that, subject to some exceptions which will be considered later, every employer carrying on any business in Great Britain shall insure and maintain insurance under one or more approved policies with an authorised insurer against liability for bodily injury or disease sustained by his employees, and arising out of and in the course of their employment in Great Britain in that business, but except in so far as

---

[1] Strictly this legislation covers "employed earners" which is wider than "employees." See generally Ogus and Barendt, *Law of Social Security* (3rd ed.), Chap. 7.

regulations otherwise provide, not including injury or disease suffered or contracted outside Great Britain.[2] However, such an employers' liability policy is no longer[3] required to cover risks which must be insured under the Road Traffic Act.[4] Thus, in practice, although an employers' liability policy could cover such risks, this is not now likely.

As is also the case in respect of motor insurance, a policy effected by an employer can be wider than the statute prescribes. For example, it might not be limited to liability "arising out of and in the course of employment." In practice, though, this phrase does appear as the standard limit in employers' liability policies. Its meaning is thus important both for this reason and because it defines the scope of the statutory requirement. The phrase also appears in the Road Traffic Act 1988,[5] and it was the classic formula used in the workmen's compensation legislation to determine eligibility.[6] It is clear that it has the same meaning in any of these contexts where it survives unchanged, but the fact that its meaning has been enlarged in the social security context[7] must be ignored.[8] On the other hand, the formula is still the basic one for industrial injury benefit purposes, and it must be the case that decisions on its interpretation in the statutory context, which are not concerned with the statutory extensions, are of relevance to its meaning in an employers' liability policy and section 1 of the 1969 Act. There is a very large number of decisions on its meaning in social security legislation, but this is not the place where those decisions can be considered in any detail.[9] One or two will, however, be referred to.

Out of and in the course of employment

Broadly, the formula covers two different principles. "In the course of employment" means that "the accident must arise when the employee is

---

[2] The Act was brought into force on January 1, 1972 by the Employers' Liability (Compulsory Insurance) Regulations (S.I. 1971 No. 117), hereafter referred to as the "Regulations."

[3] Since July 1, 1994.

[4] Employers' Liability (Compulsory Insurance) Exemption (Amendment) Regulations 1992 S.I. 1992 No. 3172.

[5] s. 145; see p. 359, above.

[6] That legislation also required an "accident"; see pp. 211–219, above.

[7] See, e.g. Social Security Contributions and Benefits Act 1992, s.99.

[8] *Vandyke v. Fender* [1970] 2 Q.B. 292.

[9] See, e.g. Ogus and Barendt, *op. cit.*, pp. 261–278.

doing what a man so employed might reasonably do during a time during which he was employed and at a place where he may reasonably be during that time to do that thing."[10] Therefore, employees travelling to and from work are not in the course of their employment, even if travelling in vehicles provided by their employers, unless their terms of employment oblige them so to travel.[11] In *Vandyke v. Fender*,[12] V and F were employees of R Ltd. They worked some distance from home and R Ltd agreed to provide a car in which F would drive himself and V to work. R Ltd also paid an amount towards petrol costs. While they were driving to work one day, V was injured owing to F's negligence. One of the questions for decision was whether R Ltd's employer's liability insurers were liable to pick up the bill or whether the relevant motor insurer[13] was liable. It was held that the employer's liability insurer was not liable as the accident did not arise in the course of employment, V not being obliged to travel in the car.

In contrast, in *Paterson v. Costain & Press (Overseas) Ltd*,[14] the plaintiff employee was injured due to the negligence of his employer's driver while being taken from the office to the construction site where the plaintiff had been told that he was required. It was the defendant employer's practice to transport their employees to the site. It was held that the accident did arise in the course of the plaintiff's employment as he was in the vehicle under an obligation to go to the site in obedience to what he had been told. The defendant's employers' liability insurers were therefore liable to indemnify them against their liability to the plaintiff.[15]

Even an accident at work is not necessarily in the course of employment. A policeman playing football for his force in a match against another force

---

[10] Lord Loreburn in *Moore v. Manchester Liners Ltd* [1910] A.C. 498 at 500–501.

[11] Note, however, that in an industrial injury benefit case, the test of obligation to travel has been held inapplicable: *Nancollas v. Insurance Officer* [1985] 1 All E.R. 833. Doubt was raised by Donaldson M.R. on the interpretation of old workmen's compensation cases put forward in *Vandyke v. Fender* (see below). It may be therefore that when the opportunity arises in a dispute on an employers' liability policy, the courts will adopt the view of the *Nancollas* case that there is no overriding principle concerning whether or not travel is in the course of employment.

[12] [1970] 2 Q.B. 292.

[13] In fact, it was the M.I.B., as the motor insurer had gone into insolvent liquidation.

[14] [1979] 2 Lloyd's Rep. 204.

[15] As an employers' liability policy is no longer required to cover motor risks (see above), it is unlikely that cases with facts like those of *Vandyke v. Fender* and *Paterson v. Costain & Press (Overseas) Ltd* will arise in the future.

at the force sports ground was held not to be covered for state compensation when he was injured during the match even though participation was expected of him.[16] The Court of Appeal rejected the argument that "in the course of employment" includes matters reasonably incidental to employment, except where the accident occurs at the place of work during an interruption, for example, for a tea break.

If an employee is injured outside his strict hours of work, this will not necessarily not be in the course of employment. A reasonable period at the beginning and end of work will usually be included.[17]

The other limb of the formula, namely, "out of employment," is somewhat looser. Essentially it requires a causal connection between the employment and the accident. It seems unlikely that it can give rise to any problems in the employers' liability insurance field. If an employer has been adjudged or has agreed to be legally liable in tort to an employee, a necessary precondition of the insurers' liability, it must follow that the liability of the employer arose out of the employee's employment.

Employees covered

Section 2 of the 1969 Act defines "employee" for the purposes of the obligation to insure under section 1. It means anyone who works under a contract of service or apprenticeship, express or implied, written or oral, thus excluding any obligation to insure against liability to the self-employed, those who work under a contract for services. The distinction between a contract of service and a contract for services can be a fine one. It has caused problems in many areas of the law and reference should be made elsewhere for details.[18] Section 2(2) also excludes the obligation to insure in respect of employees who are close relatives within the list specified and employees not ordinarily resident in Great Britain, except in so far as regulations provide otherwise.[19]

Prohibited conditions

There is one further and very important point arising under section 1(1) of the Act. This requires that insurance be by "approved policies," defined

---

[16] R. v. National Insurance Commissioner, ex p. Michael [1977] 1 W.L.R. 109.
[17] See, e.g. R. v. National Insurance Commissioner, ex p. East [1976] I.C.R. 206.
[18] See, e.g. Smith & Wood, Industrial Law (4th ed.), Chap. 1.
[19] Note Reg. 4.

as policies of insurance "not subject to any conditions or exceptions prohibited for these purposes by regulations".[20] The regulations which brought the Act into effect duly list four prohibited conditions "in whatever terms" which will be examined shortly. It is clear that the prohibited conditions may not be conditions in the strict sense; they may be warranties. However, they are only prohibited if they are conditions precedent to liability under the policy, either generally (*i.e.* as warranties) or in respect of a particular claim (*i.e.* as conditions precedent).[21] Thus it is perfectly permissible to have conditions which are not precedent to liability, but merely give the insurer the right to claim damages for breach. This is confirmed by regulation 2(2), whereby a policy can expressly provide for the insured to pay the insurer any sums which the insurer is liable to pay and which have been paid to employees.

The conditions prohibited are those "providing that no liability shall arise or liability shall cease":

    (a) "in the event of some specified thing being done or omitted to be done after the happening of the event giving rise to a claim under the policy."

This is analogous to section 148(5) of the Road Traffic Act 1988,[22] and covers such matters as failure to give notice or particulars of loss in time and unauthorised admissions of liability. Thus, it reverses *Farrell v. Federated Employers Insurance Co.*,[23] although it is doubtful whether it prohibits a condition making the prior payment of due premiums by the insured precedent to liability, as it only covers things "after the happening of the event . . ."[24]

    (b) "unless the policyholder takes reasonable care to protect his employees against the risk of bodily injury or disease in the course of employment."

As has been seen earlier,[25] the courts have interpreted conditions in liability policies generally which require the insured to take reasonable care

---

[20] s. 1(3).
[21] See generally Chaps. 5 and 7.
[22] See p. 375, above.
[23] [1970] 1 W.L.R. 1400; see p. 344, above.
[24] See *Murray v. Legal & General Assurance Co.* [1969] 3 All E.R. 794, discussed at p. 345, above.
[25] Chapter 18, p. 353.

as broken only if the insured is more than merely negligent, so in this sense the prohibition changes nothing. Even recklessness would not entitle an insurer to avoid liability, it is suggested, if it relies merely upon a condition to take reasonable care, for such a condition is prohibited.[26] However, a condition expressly providing that recklessness debars liability would arguably be enforceable.

> (c) "unless the policy-holder complies with the requirements of any enactment for the protection of employees against the risk of bodily injury or disease in the course of their employment."

The meaning of this is evident.

> (d) "unless the policy-holder keeps specified records or provides the insurer with or makes available to him information therefrom."

It is not uncommon for premiums for employers' liability policies to be adjusted by reference to wages and salaries actually paid by the employer, and for the policy to provide for the keeping of records for this purpose. Failure to comply cannot now defeat an employee's claim.[27]

Sums insured

Employers are not required to maintain policies with no limit on the maximum liability of the insurer, but policies must have a sum insured of £2 million in respect of claims relating to any one or more of their employees arising out of any one occurrence.[28]

Exceptions

Section 3 of the 1969 Act exempts certain employers altogether from the requirement to insure. Basically these are certain local government

---

[26] Contra Hasson, "The Employers' Liability (Compulsory Insurance) Act — A broken reed" [1974] I.L.J. 79 at 84, esp. n.32.

[27] With respect, Hasson, *op. cit.* at 85, is wrong to suggest that this "merely restates the common law rule." Although such a condition was held not to be precedent to liability in *Re Bradley and Essex & Suffolk Accident Indemnity Society* [1912] 1 K.B. 415 (see p. 152, above), this was as a matter of the construction of the policy in question, not as a general rule.

[28] s.1(2) and reg. 3. As to "occurrence," see p. 354, above.

councils, nationalised industries and any employer specifically exempted by regulations. The latter[29] list a number of other public bodies which are exempt.

Enforcement

Enforcement of the 1969 Act is effected first by ensuring the display of certificates of insurance, secondly by permitting inspections of certificates and policies, and thirdly by criminal penalties.[30]

Section 4(1) requires insurers to issue certificates in the form prescribed in the Regulations, and regulation 6 requires these to be displayed at any place of business where an employer employs any person whose claims may be the subject of indemnity under the insurance. Employers must produce their certificates, or copies, to an officer of the Health and Safety Executive on being served with notice to do so.[31] In addition, any inspector authorised by the Secretary of State can demand to inspect any policy of employer's liability insurance on reasonable notice.[32]

Comment[33]

When compared with the Road Traffic Act provisions relating to third party motor insurance, the 1969 Act and the regulations made thereunder appear paltry and inadequate. There is no mechanism whereby the injured employee can recover directly from the insurer, save where his employer becomes insolvent so that he can use the provisions of the Third Parties (Rights against Insurers) Act 1930.[34] There are no restrictions on the right of the insurer to avoid the policy for non-disclosure, misrepresentation or breach of warranty, and it is conceivable, though perhaps unlikely in practice, that policies could contain quite wide-ranging exceptions which do not fall foul of the prohibitions in regulation 2. Further, it has been held by the Court of Appeal that the directors of a company which has failed to insure as required by the 1969 Act are not personally liable in tort for breach of statutory duty.[35] Perhaps most importantly, if an employer is

---

[29] S.I. 1971 No. 1933, S.I. 1974 No. 208 and S.I. 1981 No. 1489.
[30] As to the penalty, see s.5.
[31] s.4(2) and reg. 7 (as substituted by S.I. 1975 No. 194).
[32] s.4(2) and reg. 8.
[33] See also Hasson, *op. cit.* and Simpson (1972) 35 M.L.R. 63.
[34] See Chap. 18.
[35] *Richardson v. Pitt-Stanley Ltd* [1995] 1 All E.R. 460.

not insured or not effectively insured, there is no equivalent of the Motor Insurers' Bureau. These deficiencies seem all the stranger when it is considered that the event which gave the final impetus to the enactment of the Act was a fire in Glasgow when the employer's insurers successfully avoided liability for non-disclosure and injured employees were uncompensated. It can hardly be denied that the compulsory insurance scheme for employers is a half-hearted system. Some changes may result from a review currently being undertaken by government.[36]

Other Compulsory Insurances

There are a number of other instances where third party insurance is in effect compulsory although in none of these are there any provisions affecting the contractual position between insurer and insured. The most important of these are the following. Professional indemnity insurance may be required, not by statute, but by the rules of the profession. If, as for example is the case with the Law Society, one has to be a member of the body concerned in order to practice, insurance is effectively compulsory. In this particular instance, the Law Society now operates a self-insurance scheme to which all solicitors must subscribe. Insurance is required by statute or by rules made under statutory authority in an increasing number of similar cases.[37]

Riding establishments are required to insure against their liability to those who hire and use their horses and against the liability of the latter for injury to third parties.[38] The operator of a nuclear establishment is required to effect insurance under the Nuclear Installations Act 1965-1969, though this is done in a rather special way with a committee of insurers. Although statute does not in terms require it, aircraft operators are in practice required to insure against third party liabilities because an applicant for an air service licence must state what provision he has or proposes to have in respect of such insurance,[39] and an applicant providing an unsatisfactory answer is hardly likely to be granted a licence.

---

[36] Any changes seem likely to be confined to increasing the minimum required sum insured, perhaps to £10m (which in practice is the usual sum anyway), to clarifying the meaning of "occurrence", to exempting "one person" companies and to providing for a better enforcement mechanism. It seems most unlikely that an "Employers' Liability Insurance Bureau" will be created.

[37] For example, under the Insurance Brokers Registration Act 1977, the Estate Agents Act 1979 and rules made under the auspices of the Financial Services Act 1986.

[38] Riding Establishments Act 1964, s.1.

[39] Civil Aviation (Licensing) Regulations 1964 (S.I. 1964 No. 1116) made under Civil Aviation (Licensing) Act 1960, s.2.

INDEX